WITHDRAWN

Public Services Ma

Public Services Management

Public Services Management

Edited by

Aidan Rose and Alan Lawton

An imprint of **PEARSON EDUCATION**

Harlow, England · London · New York · Reading, Massachusetts · San Francisco · Toronto · Don Mills, Ontario · Sydney
Tokyo · Singapore · Hong Kong · Seoul · Taipei · Cape Town · Madrid · Mexico City · Amsterdam · Munich · Paris · Milan

PEARSON EDUCATION LIMITED
Edinburgh Gate
Harlow
Essex CM20 2JE
England

and Associated Companies around the world

First published in Great Britain in 1999

© Pearson Education Limited 1999

The right of Aidan Rose and Alan Lawton to be identified as
Authors of this Work has been asserted by them in accordance
with the Copyright, Designs and Patents Act 1988.

ISBN 0 273 62524 1

British Library Cataloguing in Publication Data
A CIP catalogue record for this book can be obtained from the British Library.

10 9 8 7 6 5 4 3 2 1

Typeset by M Rules
Printed and bound in Great Britain by Redwood Books Ltd, Trowbridge

The Publishers' policy is to use paper manufactured from sustainable forests.

Contents

Part 3
THE PUBLIC SERVICES ASSESSED

Preface

Public Services Management as a title for a textbook would not have been conceivable twenty years ago. Then courses were entitled 'public administration' and focused on a range of issues including the structure of public service organisations and how they had been subjected to political reform. Twenty years later, political reforms remain a theme but the pace is much greater and the direction different. The world is more open, organisations – considerably different ones today – face a more dynamic environment and are facing new agendas. The use of the term 'management' reflects international recognition of the changing nature of these services, with greater emphasis on the management of the resources – human, financial, informational and otherwise. It also reflects the need for organisations to address the changing environment and the social, economic and technological pressures that have a key role to play in determining the agenda for management of those services. These concerns are not confined to the United Kingdom.

This book addresses these themes. It is written both for students studying public management for the first time and for practitioners who wish to examine the key debates in the subject area. Analysis is not confined to specific academic disciplines. Indeed, the study of management is multidisciplinary in its approach, drawing on politics, philosophy, economics, psychology, sociology and the management sciences. Instead, the analysis draws on the full range of academic disciplines and combines these with illustrative examples of practice in the public services. The book does not take a single perspective on public service reform, but encourages the reader to consider various positions and arguments in order to reach a point of view.

In pursuit of this agenda, the book aims to provide the reader with:

- an introduction to public services management, contrasted with earlier ways of looking at public services;
- an examination of the changing context of public service management;
- an exploration of the specific components of the public service management task;
- the opportunity to reflect on the changes that have taken place in the public services;
- an exploration of the international dimensions of public services management and the tools with which to examine them.

The book is divided into three parts. Each chapter encourages the reader to engage with the issues raised. Chapters have clear aims and introductions setting out the key issues. The main text is supported by examples and articles from the *Financial Times*. These extracts are the copyright of the *Financial Times*, which has kindly given permission to reproduce them. The FT articles chosen provide examples from public services management to stimulate the reader to consider, or students to debate in class, the issues raised in the text. References and lists of further reading at the end of each chapter encourage readers to seek out more detailed material on the subjects discussed. Many of these sources are widely available in academic libraries. Others may be less accessible, but are included because the points the authors make are particularly salient to the debate.

- Part 1 of the book examines the **context** of public services. It includes a detailed discussion of the environmental factors that impinge on public services. This discussion of political, economic, social and technological trends is combined with an analysis of the distinctiveness of public services and their accountabilities. Part 1 concludes with an analysis of changing organisational forms.
- Part 2 examines specific **management tasks** and skills. It begins with a chapter providing an overview of strategic management. This is followed by chapters examining specific components of the management task.
- Part 3 **assesses** the changing nature of public services. Key themes of culture and ethics are discussed and there is an examination of the extent to which public services are responsive. The chapter on comparative management enables the reader to analyse public services beyond the shores of the United Kingdom.

A team of authors from diverse disciplinary and professional backgrounds was commissioned to prepare chapters for this book. We believe that their diversity of experience adds an important dimension to the book. As editors, we hope that we have ensured a consistency of approach without curtailing the essence of their contributions.

We would like to thank the contributors for the considerable time and effort they have devoted to this text, in addition to their other commitments, and for the richness and diversity of thought and practice that they have added to the work as a whole.

The editors are grateful to a number of people who provided valuable assistance in the preparation of this book. In particular, Gillian Fawcett reviewed a number of chapters and made perceptive comments. Yurii Polianskiy provided essential bibliographic information.

At our publishers Penelope Woolf and Sadie McClelland encouraged us to follow on from the two editions of our previous book, *Organisation and Management in the Public Sector*, with a more comprehensive treatment of public services. Without their insistence and persistence this book would not exist. Beth Barber and Liz Tarrant provided invaluable support towards the conclusion of the project.

A *Lecturer's Guide* with OHP masters is available from the publishers free of charge to lecturers adopting the book.

Aidan Rose
Alan Lawton

Contributors

Dr David Chapman
Senior Lecturer in Marketing, Sheffield Business School, Sheffield Hallam University and Chair of Chartered Institute of Marketing.

Michael Dempsey
Senior Trade Union Manager and Visiting Fellow, Centre for Strategic Trade Union Management, Cranfield School of Management, Cranfield University.

Charles Edwards
Lecturer in Public Sector Management, The Open University Business School.

Dr Ken Harrop
Head of Division of Government and Politics, Faculty of Social Sciences, University of Northumbria at Newcastle.

Dr Jacky Holloway
Lecturer in Public Sector Management, The Open University Business School.

Jennifer Law
Senior Lecturer in Public Sector Management, University of Glamorgan Business School.

Dr Alan Lawton
Senior Lecturer in Public Sector Management, The Open University Business School.

Dr Sandra Nutley
Senior Lecturer in Public Sector Management, Department of Management, University of St Andrews.

Dr Aidan Rose
Reader in Public Administration and Public Management, School of Law, Governance and Information Management, Faculty of Environmental and Social Studies, University of North London.

Professor J A Taylor
Professor of Management and Dean of Faculty of Business, The Business School, Glasgow Caledonian University.

Dr Ian Worthington
Principal Lecturer in the Department of Corporate Strategy, School of Business, De Montfort University, Leicester.

Plan of the book

PART 1 · THE CONTEXT OF PUBLIC SERVICES MANAGEMENT		
Chapter 1 Political context	Chapter 2 Social and economic context	Chapter 3 New technologies
Chapter 4 Distinctiveness	Chapter 5 Accountabilities	Chapter 6 Bureaucracy and markets

PART 2 · THE MANAGER'S TASK			
Chapter 7 Strategic management	Chapter 8 Managing human resources	Chapter 9 Financial management	Chapter 10 Marketing public services
Chapter 11 Managing networks	Chapter 12 Managing performance		Chapter 13 Managing change

PART 3 · THE PUBLIC SERVICES ASSESSED				
Chapter 14 Culture	Chapter 15 Ethics	Chapter 16 Responsiveness	Chapter 17 Comparative approach	Chapter 18 Conclusions

PART 1

The context of public services management

'Management is management is management . . .' proclaim those for whom management is a generic rather than a particular activity. Whether the context be manufacturing industry, financial services, the arts, civil engineering or government, the challenge of management, and its methods and methodology, are essentially common. The manager's skills are transferable and will travel across sectors and organisations. So runs the argument.

The organisation and delivery of public services in the UK and beyond have, of course, been undeniably transformed in the 1980s and 1990s, even to the extent that the traditional concept of 'public' and 'private' sectors has diminished in descriptive accuracy and explanatory power. The outright privatisation or selling off of public assets, accumulated resource constraint, the introduction of so-called business styles of management, the increase in the numbers of non-elected bodies and the development of an intensely competitive performance culture have all served to challenge the notion of a public sector as traditionally conceived. Public administration has, for the moment, seemed to give way to the new public management. The ethic of selfless public service has been replaced by the language of business. In local government, social workers have become care managers and in the health service, nursing sisters or charge nurses are 'ward managers'. The 'welfare state' has become the 'enterprise state' (Cochrane, 1991). The public space is being redrawn, government reinvented (Osborne and Gaebler, 1992). Traditional distinctions between public and private are no longer valid. 'Public' services paradoxically may be delivered privately.

Public–private partnerships and multi-agency provision transcend traditional boundaries. Moreover, the privatisation of government has been paralleled by the governmentalisation of the private (Moe, 1990). Global firms, for example, may describe themselves as corporate citizens and publish policy papers on issues such as sustainable development or environmental responsibilities. Deregulation of the public sector has been accompanied by self-regulation of the private. In this confusing post-modern whirl, the business of government and the government of business are blurred.

Chapter 1 analyses this political context, taking the reader from the so-called post-war consensus to the present day. This picture is illustrated with examples from key actors in the process and gives the reader a grounding from which subsequent chapters can be interpreted.

In Chapter 2 we examine the social and economic context. Changing social trends and the performance of the UK economy have provided a key backdrop for policy discussions about the nature and role of public services. The resolution of these, often conflicting, demands is discussed here.

The rapidly changing technological environment is discussed in Chapter 3. The present government places a high degree of emphasis on the role of technology in linking government to the citizen. This is not, however, without its problems and issues of accessibility and accountability are key to the discussion.

This enables us to return to the issue of the distinctiveness of public services which was raised in Chapter 1. Much has been made of the need for public services to emulate private services. Again, this is a contested issue and Chapter 4 examines these issues in detail.

One of the key issues in this debate is accountability. Chapter 5 discusses the various dimensions of accountability and analyses public service reforms which have raised questions of accountability.

Chapter 6 provides the link with Part 2 of this book by discussing the changing organisational forms of public services. Chapter 1 raised the concept of the uniform 'one size fits all' public service. The bureaucratic model which provided this is contrasted with new models of public service organisation.

REFERENCES

Cochrane, A (1991) 'The changing state of local government: restructuring for the 1990s', *Public Administration*, 69, pp 281–302.

Osborne, D and Gaebler, T (1992) *Reinventing Government: How the Entrepreneurial Spirit is Transforming the Public Sector*. Reading, MA: Addison-Wesley.

Moe, R (1990) 'Public and private sectors: allies or adversaries?', paper presented at George Washington University, February.

1 The political context of public services management

Ken Harrop

AIMS

This chapter will:

- provide an understanding of the so-called post-war consensus, and its significance for the growth and nature of the public services in Britain after 1945;

- discuss why the consensus was first strained under Labour in the 1970s and then broken by the Conservatives in the 1980s;

- explore the consequences of its demise for public service organisations;

- explain the massive changes in the organisation and culture of public service delivery over the past twenty years by reference to these broad political themes; and

- develop a sense of how broader political and societal values may be given institutional expression in the structure and organisation of public service delivery.

INTRODUCTION

The professional service culture – of the old local government, for example, or the health service – and the hegemony of the administrative class elsewhere have been rudely challenged by the rise of a new, hands-on, can-do management class, vigorously committed to its own sometimes imperfect performance culture. Pompous 'fat controllers' have been derailed by the 'lean schemers'. Business and commercial metaphors stalk the corridors of hospitals, town halls, and schools throughout the land. Councillors in local government have been encouraged to see themselves as company directors rather than politicians. A formal commitment to performance measurement is virtually universal and the language of the quality movement on every ambitious manager's agenda, the utterings of its gurus chanted as mantras. So widespread is the emphasis on private sector management values that it has been deemed to constitute one of the seven 'doctrinal components' of the new public management (Hood, 1991).

Despite all of this however, a strong case can still be made, not for the uniqueness, but for the distinctiveness of public service management. Just as John Harvey Jones has identified his personal passion for the manufacturing process as a significant ingredient in the success of his own career in industry and business management with ICI, so a deep understanding and grasp of the nature of public service is probably a *sine qua non* of effective management in that sector.

For Stewart and Ranson, defining public sector management in negative (that is, 'non-market' or 'not-for-profit') terms is an inappropriate starting point (Stewart and Ranson, 1988; Ranson and Stewart, 1989):

> There are dangers if, consciously or unconsciously, management in the public domain adopts models drawn from outside organisations. That is not to say that management in the public domain cannot learn from management in the private sector, or vice versa. Specific management ideas can be transferable. What is not transferable is the model of management – its purposes, conditions and tasks (Stewart and Ranson, 1988, p 13).

The distinctive 'purposes' of public management concern the processes of debating political priorities and arranging collective choice out of the plurality of competing individual and group preferences. Thus, public service management is about 'making democracy work' (Rutter, 1980; Stewart and Ranson, 1988). The 'conditions' refer to the framework within which political discourse and the implementation of collective action will take place. The right to speak and to be heard are essential conditions for public management, conditions not constraints. The 'tasks' of public service management are also broader than in the private sector, including for example the need to maintain a balance between freedom and order. This combination of distinctive purposes, conditions and tasks together make public service management an arguably more complex activity than management often is in business. It is the complexity of the multivalued choice which can make life difficult. As Ranson and Stewart point out, an organisation which has to deal with citizens is qualitatively different from one which knows only customers (Ranson and Stewart, 1989; Stewart and Ranson, 1988). Equity is a bigger issue for the public service manager than merely having in place an equal opportunities personnel policy.

Others have addressed this question of distinctiveness in different ways. Thus Allison (1979) reviews the respective contexts and pressures on 'public' and 'private' managers in terms of environment, dominant coalition and technical core, an analysis developed by Willcocks and Harrow (1992). Among the 11 major differences between the management of public services and management in the private sector, identified by the latter, are 'statutory and parliamentary regulation', 'the relative openness of government and decision-making' and 'responsiveness to political masters' (Willcocks and Harrow, 1992, p xxi). Starling (1993) takes a different tack, identifying three 'core functions' of management common to both public and business administration. They are 'program management' (e.g. human resource management or leadership), 'political management' (e.g. politics, ethics or interagency relationships) and 'resource management' (e.g. human resource management or budgeting). The relative importance of these activities varies, political management occupying a much greater wedge of a public service manager's time than in that of a counterpart in business (Starling, 1993). Further distinctiveness is described in terms of 'different structures' involving more blurred patterns of responsibility in public administration (cf. Willcocks and Harrow's 'more formal constraints'), 'different incentives' including the need to satisfy a plurality of stakeholders (cf. Willcocks and Harrow's greater diversity and intensity of external influences), 'different settings' – greater public expectations of probity, accountability and scrutiny contributing to 'public administration . . . as business administration in a fishbowl' – and 'different purposes' including vaguer and less tangible objectives (cf. Willcocks and Harrow's 'more ill-defined policy directives; complexity of policy implementation').

Acknowledging therefore the importance of the political environment to a public service manager, the aim of this chapter is to provide an overview of political developments in the public service environment in post-war Britain. The account adopts a chronological framework in tracing the development and decline of what has now come to be called the post-war consensus, now replaced perhaps by an altogether different neo-liberal orthodoxy. The material, following Seldon (1994) and others, is organised into a series of phases:

- 1945–76   Delivering the post-war dream
- 1976–9   Straining the consensus
- 1979–90   Smashing the consensus
- 1990–7   Fighting for the centre ground
- 1997–8   'New Labour, New Britain'

1945–76: DELIVERING THE POST-WAR DREAM

These years, covering the period from the end of the Second World War right through to Jim Callaghan's government of the late 1970s, are typically characterised – even caricatured perhaps – as an age of stability in British politics. It was a time when the major political parties, Conservative and Labour in those heydays of two-party competition, displayed an unusually high measure of agreement on political fundamentals – on the role of the state, for instance – as well as on policy instruments in, for example, sectors such as education, health or housing. Sometimes evoked as a golden age, this was the epoch of the so-called post-war settlement or consensus, a concept, argues Seldon, 'vital to understanding policies and politics in the 1990s' (Seldon, 1994). For those seeking to understand the contemporary environment of public service organisations as well as for public service managers seeking to come to terms with enormous cultural change and working practices within the compass of a single professional generation, an understanding of the concept of the post-war settlement is essential.

Hennessy, in the first volume of his history of post-war Britain, has set the tone:

> I've called the first volume *Never Again* as, for me, the phrase captures the motivating impulse of the first half-dozen years after the war – never again would there be war, never again would the British people be housed in slums, living off a meagre diet thanks to low wages or no wages at all; never again would mass unemployment blight the lives of millions; never again would natural abilities remain dormant in the absence of educational stimulus; . . . Virtually every serious politician, certainly every senior one, acted and calculated within the boundaries of what became known as the 'post-war settlement' built around an understanding that Britain would remain a great power abroad while operating a mixed economy and building a welfare state at home, a presupposition that a change of government from Labour to Conservative in 1951 did little to alter (Hennessy, 1993, pp 2–3).

The slogan 'Never Again', employed by Labour in its 1945 General Election campaign, captured the country's mood neither to return to pre-war levels of economic and social distress nor to fail its returning war heroes, as a previous generation had been failed after the so-called Great War. On that occasion, as the character of Grandad in the television series *Only Fools and Horses* wistfully observed, instead of the promised homes fit for heroes there were only heroes fit for homes. This time there would be no such betrayal.

The dimensions to that consensus are well enough known (Kavanagh, 1996; Kavanagh and Morris, 1994 and Seldon, 1994). They included:

- a shared framework of understanding and a broad social democratic agreement across the political divide. Variously termed 'welfare capitalism' or 'pink Toryism', the bi-partisan concord would become most famously nicknamed 'Butskellism' after R A ('Rab') Butler, Conservative architect of the 1944 Education Act as well as of other influential policy papers, and Hugh Gaitskell, leader of the Labour Party between 1955 and 1963;
- a shared commitment to full employment (in practice seeking to hold unemployment at no more than 2–3 per cent);
- a shared commitment to building a Beveridgean welfare state, funded from progressive taxation, as well as by post-war Marshall Aid from the United States;
- an underpinning economic orthodoxy – Keynesianism – which recognised not only the right but also the responsibility, the duty of governments to intervene in the market mechanism;
- despite continuing hardship and austerity, in spite of shortage and rationing, a 'vision thing', a dream, a popular mood of optimism in the country and a belief in the capacity of government to deliver on the promise. Six years of total war and total government had helped to unify the country. Having won the war, they could also win the peace. Many a post-war politician drew not only on the 'campfire conversations' of wartime but also on the practical experience of active service. Denis Healey, for one, would later reflect: 'I found my army staff training invaluable . . . Indeed post-war politics in both parties was largely shaped by men who had learned a new way of looking at problems as the result of their practical experience in the services during the war. That is why 'Rab' Butler was able to convert the Conservative Party to economic planning and the welfare state' (Healey, 1990, p 73). Thatcherism, argued Healey, would only be possible once that generation had passed from centre stage.

   'Six years of war', argues Seldon, 'united the country against a common enemy while the privations of war instilled a widespread desire for a new and better beginning' (Seldon, 1994, p 43).
- a consensual style of planning and policy making – again partly the result of the wartime experience of coalition government – which recognised and respected the mutual interdependence of central government and other public bodies as partners. Local government, for example, had an undisputed place in building the welfare state and the trades unions were formally involved in policy making.

Of course the degree of consensus can be exaggerated and overemphasised (Finer, 1980; Kavanagh and Pimlott, 1989). Conservative Prime Minister Edward Heath, for example, in the early 1970s appeared determined 'to reject the Macmillan inheritance', promising his party 'a change so radical, a revolution so quiet and yet so total, that it will go beyond the programme for a parliament' (Sampson, 1983, pp 39–40), and his Chancellor of the Exchequer, Anthony Barber, argued: 'There never *was* a consensus in the sense of a deliberate effort of will. The parties never came together in their policies. Even the idea of "Butskellism" was sloppy and inaccurate' (Sampson, 1983, p 40). Sked and Cook, in their political history of post-war Britain, characterise the years of Heath's government as 'the politics of confrontation' (Sked and Cook, 1993). Mr Heath was, however, for u-turning.

   A decade later the former Labour minister and founder member of the SDP, Bill Rodgers, would also argue that the so-called post-war settlement was somewhat illusory:

Has this 'social democratic consensus' ever really existed? Is it true that British economic and industrial policy ran, if not in one straight line, then in one broad general direction from 1945 to

1979? That was certainly not how it seemed at the time to each party in opposition as it put forward a radical prospectus for change, and so successive Governments staggered from crisis to U-turn. There were certainly elements of continuity, most strikingly between the politics of the late Macmillan and early Wilson Governments. But generally the picture was one of sharp political conflict with frequent changes in emphasis, policies and institutions (Rodgers, 1982, p 71).

Rodgers, of course, as a member of the breakaway 'Gang of Four' had a vested political interest in declaring that consensus had not existed because the SDP case depended heavily on offering a new alternative to the endless bickering of Conservative and Labour, a middle way. Revisionist contributions to the debate were therefore inevitable but even so Rodgers' argument tends to be supported by Pimlott's that the post-war consensus made more sense from the 1980s than it did at the time.

As Hennessy puts it:

By the late 1970s the legacy of this consensus, the accumulated inheritance of the 1940s, was the very stuff of political dispute. The understanding had broken down and with it came a revived partnership whose stridency spilled over into retrospective writings about the period (Hennessy, 1993, p 3).

Even Hennessy himself though, such a graphic depictor of the post-war settlement, lends support to the Rodgers' line:

Like any consensus, the legendary post-war one was very much a top brass affair. Politically, too, it never permeated that far into the rank-and-file of the Labour or Conservative parties. If the rhetoric of party conference or ward party is anything to go by, prejudice, nasty and simple, has persistently ruled at that level (Hennessy, 1993, p 439).

Despite such necessary qualifications, however, the idea of the post-war consensus is a critical concept in understanding the public service environment in post-war Britain. It captures the unusual unity of purpose which, between 1945 and 1951 alone, found expression in:

- a modern welfare state, free at the point of delivery and consumption;
- a National Health Service;
- education for all on the back of the 1944 Education Act;
- a comprehensive town and country planning system, at the centre of which was the 1947 Town and Country Planning Act, the corner-stone of physical reconstruction and renewal;
- the nationalisation of key sectors of the economy including banking and finance, civil aviation, coal, steel, railways and waterways, electricity and gas.

Nor were the effects of the political consensus restricted to domestic social and economic policies. They were also evident in defence and foreign policies at a time when vigorous state building at home was paralleled on the international scene by the birth of institutions of global order. The Bretton Woods monetary conference of July 1944 created the International Monetary Fund and the World Bank and would significantly contribute to post-war prosperity:

More, perhaps, than any other single gathering, it helped to shape the post-war world . . . it set the framework for monetary order, based on freedom of trade and currency movements, and so underwrote the greatest half-century of economic expansion that the world has ever known (McRae, H (1994) *The Independent*, 21 July).

7

Other elements of international order would include the General Agreement on Tariffs and Trade (GATT), the North Atlantic Treaty Organisation (NATO) and the Organisation for Economic Co-operation and Development (OECD). In Western Europe, the cockpit of two global wars within a generation, a mood of post-war 'reconstruction, reconciliation and integration' (Dinan, 1994) led in 1957 to the Treaty of Rome which founded the Common Market. Throughout Europe the Cold War lent a measure of stability to the relationship between freedom and order. Versions of Britain's post-war settlement were evident elsewhere on the Continent. Butskellism at home was paralleled by, for example, the 'Grand Coalition' of Christian and Social Democrats in West Germany after 1966 while in Italy the Christian Democrats under Aldo Moro 'opened to the left' in the 1963 coalition with the Socialists (Young, 1991). Although cautioning that 'the idea of a stable post-war settlement in the 1950s and early 1960s should not be exaggerated', Young nevertheless observes that 'By about 1960 even ideological differences between the Socialist and Conservative parties appeared to lose their significance' (Young, 1991, pp xv, xvi).

At home, stable political assumptions and expectations were reflected in stable public service organisations recognisably organised according to the bureaucratic principles articulated by Max Weber (1864–1920). The ideas of Weber, increasingly as represented and codified by classical organisation theorists such as Fayol, Taylor or Urwick, were abundantly evident in institutions committed to, for example, formal hierarchy, formal lines of command, control and communication, and to written rules and roles (Garrett, 1972). Such Weberian bureaucracies, strong on departments and committees, were not flexible, responsive or innovative – but their very inflexibility, unresponsiveness and conservatism spoke volumes about their priorities. Strict observance of routine administrative procedures and rigid conformance to the rules dominated the thinking of bureaucratic administrators who would, without obvious irony, bask in the description of public servants.

As a result, 'bureaucratic' would become a perjorative term, acquiring negative connotations of red tape and obstructive officialdom, rather than the enlightened rational discharge of modern legal authority intended by Weber himself. Administrative convenience, not political problem solving or customer satisfaction, would guide the thinking of many a petty bureaucrat or 'jobsworth'.

In local government, the traditional local authority could be seen as an exemplar of the classic bureaucracy. For each service or function there would be a 'permanent' department of specialist officers led by a chief officer reporting to a similarly named supervising committee of elected members. Hence, the education service would be administered by an education department led by a chief education officer reporting to an education committee; and so on for other services and within individual services. Such 'skyscraper' organisations (Benington, 1995) displayed vertical rather than lateral integration and were caricatured as a series of separate empires without a corporate heart. For the town clerk, a figure of recognisably Dickensian lineage, the key question would be 'Is it legal?' (Benington, 1995). 'Professional service administration' perhaps describes the style better than 'management'. Similarly, the academic study of public administration both reflected and reinforced organisational characteristics. Thus the study of local government could still in the mid-1970s be criticised for its excessively legalistic, historical and institutional preoccupations (Stanyer, 1976). In a sense, Jackson's definitive post-war account of local government in England and Wales (Jackson, 1945) had perhaps declared the dominant paradigm for a generation of scholars.

1976–9: STRAINING THE CONSENSUS

Nothing lasts forever. It never does. It never can. By the mid-1970s it was clear that the days of the post-war settlement were numbered if not already over.

These years, 1976–9, saw Labour in government nationally, first and briefly under Harold Wilson's premiership and for the remainder of the period under James Callaghan whose government the BBC's former political editor described as 'the last flowering of consensus politics' (Cole, 1995). 'It was', writes John Cole, 'the last fling of the old post-war consensus, before the Thatcher revolution began a new era in British politics' (Cole, 1995, p 158).

The forces which strained the consensus were essentially economic in nature; the global political economy might in the 1990s be the framework for describing events but twenty-five years ago it was the evil of international capital, that *bête noire* of old Labour and the bugbear of international socialism. Despite North Sea oil at home, successive increases in the price of oil worldwide highlighted the UK's economic vulnerability. International economics blasted the domestic heath. Economics, apparently the mother of politics, prompted political turmoil for the Labour Party.

When precisely one should date this straining of the consensus is a matter for debate. Seldon (1994), for example, refers to the 'consensus under stress' between 1970 and 1979, being overturned only after the election of Mrs Thatcher in 1979. Richard Crossman as early as December 1970 had said: 'There is a cracking sound in the political atmosphere: the sound of the consensus breaking-up' (quoted in Sampson, 1983, p 79).

Although the early 1970s were prosperous years, nevertheless the end of economic growth by the middle of the decade and the inability to fund expanded welfare out of progressive taxation prompted political soul-searching among senior Labour politicians. Roy Jenkins, for example, would publicly reflect on the limits to the growth of the state, Jim Callaghan declare the metaphorical death of Keynes and Anthony Crosland bring down the curtain on local government's party.

Perhaps 1976 was the watershed year. 'A dangerous year,' as the pop group Pogue's Shane McGowan would call it twenty years later. The year 1976 saw Harold Wilson – maybe coincidentally – suddenly resign as Labour Prime Minister and make way for an older man, James Callaghan. The change of personnel and leadership was not of course in itself responsible for some of the dramatic events which would follow, although one might usefully reflect on how things might have worked out had Wilson not enigmatically resigned. Tony Benn, in his diaries and tapes, has vividly described some of the political events of 1976: the public expenditure cuts early in the year at the behest of the world banking community; the sterling crisis in September which prompted Chancellor of the Exchequer Denis Healey to turn round at the airport, cancel at the last minute his planned attendance at a Commonwealth Finance Ministers' Conference in Hong Kong and instead fly up to the Labour Party Conference at Blackpool where he delivered a typically Healey cocktail of intellect, intelligence, charm, wit, straight-talking and browbeating in an impromptu speech which divided the Labour Party; and the conditions of the International Monetary Fund loan and the further public expenditure cuts in December.

A dangerous year and one of great significance in post-war British politics. Whatever their birth certificates may state, Tony Blair and Gordon Brown politically were born in 1976.

Had Treasury forecasts been accurate, much of this might have been avoided.

Nevertheless, despite the Callaghan government's continuing ideological attachment to the welfare state, despite therefore implementing public expenditure cuts reluctantly and despite continuing to operate within the framework of existing legislation, Labour in its last two years in office presided over a more effective programme of public spending cuts than Mrs Thatcher was able to do in her first two years (Loughlin, 1982). Anathema to the wider Labour movement, however, the government's reluctant but effective monetarism led to politically grave consequences. Its 'social contract' with the trade unions – one of the factors in Labour's election win in October 1974 – was irreparably ruptured. In due course industrial action by public service workers would feature significantly in the so-called winter of discontent of 1978–9. With its emotive media images of uncollected refuse and of the dead lying unburied, this public service discontent would in its turn contribute to electoral defeat at the hands of the ideologically radical Mrs Thatcher in May 1979. For 18 years, Labour would be out of national office and for the public sector things would never be the same again.

By 1979, monetarism might not yet have become the new orthodoxy but it had certainly supplanted Keynesianism in Cabinet rooms. It was not Mrs Thatcher – armed with the writings of Hayek and Friedman, the policy advice of the free-market think-tanks such as the Institute of Economic Affairs, the Centre for Policy Studies or the Adam Smith Institute and the political insight of trusted politicians such as Sir Keith Joseph – it was not she who introduced monetarism into the British political arena. She certainly embraced it and elevated it to a new status during the 1980s but the introduction had been made under Labour. For some thirty years, Conservative and Labour governments alike had built up public services – increasingly in the welfare fields – and munificently connived in camouflaging the true costs. The 1970s however marked the end of that growth and the culture and expectations built upon it. The endless, infinite, expansion of resources which led to a manager's worth being measured in terms of input measures such as the size of departmental budgets or number of staff rather than outputs let alone outcomes was at an end. Attention turned to how managers might contribute to the task of what then was called cutback management. Over the next decade the hoary old interview question, 'How would you spend an extra £1 million on your budget?' would become, 'How would you cut £1.5 million'.

The realisation that resources for continued public service growth might no longer be available upon reasonable demand shattered the assumptions of those who might have grown complacent during years of sustained plenty. Now, much greater attention would have to be given to setting of priorities, to performance review and to the evaluation of policies. In other words, scarce resources prompted more systematic policy making. This did not of course happen only after 1976. Already for a decade or so, government had shown an interest in initiatives designed to introduce more purposive, learning-based approaches into its affairs. From the late 1950s onwards, for instance, central government had sought to break the connection between policy making and budgeting on the one hand, and the parliamentary or calendar year on the other, by introducing a public expenditure survey process (Hambleton, 1978). Following from the original Committee on the Control of Public Expenditure chaired by Lord Plowden in 1959, annual surveys had been produced since 1961. Introduced by the Conservatives, the process was strengthened under Labour after devaluation in 1968. The result was the Public Survey Expenditure Committee or PESC. In 1970, the Conservatives – back in government under Edward Heath – created the Central Policy Review Staff (or 'think-tank'), intended to evaluate government policy in the generality as well as the specific. Also set up in 1970 was Programme Analysis and Review (or PAR) which assessed central government departments in terms of objectives and achievements (Hambleton, 1978). In local government, the corporate authority became the norm (Greenwood and Stewart, 1974; Hambleton, 1978; Rhodes, 1979), especially after the publication of the Bains Report in 1972. Propelling local government from a 'traditional' to a 'governmental' conception of its role (Rhodes, 1979), the wholesale adoption of corporate management introduced the language of rational policy making, learning, cybernetics and systems theory into town halls and civic centres. Resource-conscious managers and notions of general rather than specialist management, both rare in the traditional authority, came to the fore in the form of, for example, policy and resources committees and chief executive officers (rather than town clerks) for whom the defining question would be how to achieve corporate priorities within available resources. Ironically, the very corporate structures introduced to provide more effective means of managing finite resources themselves sometimes became early victims of 'cutback management'. The academic study of local government both reflected and promoted the new approaches, the legal and historical predilections of the previous generation being replaced by an attention to public policy making and analysis (based on the work of Dror, 1968, for example, or Wildavsky, 1974), organisational developments (Greenwood and Stewart, 1974; Greenwood *et al.*, 1976) and management development.

1979–90: SMASHING THE CONSENSUS

In British politics, as in its football perhaps, success has tended to come through the middle rather than down the wings. Mrs Thatcher, contrary as ever, did it differently.

Her stall was set out in her foreword to the 1979 Conservative Manifesto:

> No one who has lived in this country during the last five years can fail to be aware of how the balance of our society has been increasingly tilted in favour of the State at the expense of individual freedom. This election may be the last chance we have to reverse that process, to restore the balance of power in favour of the people. It is therefore the most crucial election since the war (Conservative Party, 1979).

From the right wing, Mrs Thatcher set out to break the mould of post-war British politics, deliberately setting out to roll back the frontiers of the state and to lift the dead hand of oppressive government from the British people. The nanny state would be replaced by, well, the nanny Mrs Thatcher, fussily and bossily organising the photo-call line-up for international summits, domineering her Cabinet and pushing the nation in its metaphorical pram while simultaneously preaching the virtues of personal responsibility, individual initiative and enterprise. Whereas the Labour government of the late 1970s had adopted monetarist, expenditure-cutting strategies with apparent regret, Mrs Thatcher's first two administrations at least – either ideologically or pragmatically convinced of her historic mission – set about the task with zeal and ardour.

Her self-righteous, slightly puritanical, lower-middle class financial prudence with its weekly household budget approach to financial matters seemed to view public expenditure not as an expression of beneficent public service but of waste, if not actually evil. Ironically, her 1980s would produce materialist excesses unparalleled in post-war Britain.

Some have sought to argue that Mrs Thatcher actually changed very little. While referring to 'Thatcherism's enduring legacy', for example, Wilding (1992) nevertheless notes dissenting views, especially if Thatcherism were meant to be about capturing the hearts and minds of the British people. He notes the words of Crewe, for example, who described Thatcherism as 'a crusade that failed' and of Skidelsky, who claimed that she was unable 'to create a larger constituency of understanding. She failed as an educator' (Skidelsky, 1990). For Wilding, however, her enduring impact lies in ten lasting legacies:

- the challenge to collectivism
- the promotion of private provision
- the 'cuts'
- the new managerialism
- greater social division
- the attack on local government
- the mixed economy of welfare
- the rights of citizenship
- the regulatory state
- the impact on the Labour Party (Wilding, 1992).

Seldon (1994) similarly identifies four respects in which Mrs Thatcher subjected the post-war consensus to 'absolute transformation'. First, unlike her predecessors, she never committed herself to full employment nor shrank from the political and social consequences of not so doing; second, she reduced the industrial power of the trade unions and marginalised them politically; third, the balance of the mixed economy shifted away from public towards private provision; and fourth, she made no claim for the role of government in promoting equality, instead viewing inequality as a creative force in stimulating enterprise and economic activity (Seldon, 1994, pp 53–4).

However, it was only really in Thatcher's second term, between 1983 and 1987, that she set about these pillars of the post-war consensus. Part of the reason for that lies in her progressive purging of the so-called wets she had inherited in her first term:

> The return of Thatcher, with a large parliamentary majority, marked the emphatic end of the old assumptions of consensus, whether in the country or in the Tory party. The second Thatcher government, after the disappearance of most of the 'wets', had only Lord Hailsham as a link with the Macmillan government of twenty years earlier (when Macmillan himself watched the election results in June 1983 he was heard to say that he could hardly recognise his old party). The old orthodoxy of the consensus – of maintaining full employment, consulting with the trade unions, co-operating with industry and the unions to promote planning and industrial harmony – had been replaced in only a few years by the new orthodoxy: of confronting the unions and beating down inflation by strictly controlling the money supply and keeping unemployment high (Sampson, 1983, pp 480–1).

In the face of the political challenge, Labour had disengaged from credible alternative, opposition politics, preferring instead to comfort itself with the ideological totems of an earlier age. Thus the Labour Party, under Michael Foot's leadership, had gone into the 1983 General Election committed to more nationalisation, unilateral nuclear disarmament and leaving Europe, perhaps symbolising the bipolar high-water mark of post-war ideological divergence between Conservative and Labour. The latter party seemed an electoral liability, the former seemed the natural party of government.

In the public sector, the Thatcher governments wrought a revolution. Successive programmes of privatisation, especially from 1983 onwards, swept public assets in, for example, telecommunications, gas, electricity, water and public transport into private ownership – thereby generating an income stream to sustain tax-cutting strategies even in economic recession. Those services and functions remaining under public control, as well as the organisations and personnel charged with their delivery, would be shaken from their complacent, self-serving, bureaucratic excesses and instead exposed to the rigours of a competitive performance culture. The Audit Commission (created in 1982), the Rayner scrutinies of government departments, the Financial Management Initiative and its successor the Next Steps (or Ibbs) Report would all pursue the goals of economy and efficiency – with perhaps rather less emphasis initially on effectiveness – in all areas of government, including the National Health Service where the Griffiths reviews would contribute to a wholly transformed culture.

The extent to which all the changes constituted a new paradigm for public service delivery or just how different the so-called new public management was from the old public administration are legitimate topics of debate (Hood, 1991; Hood and Dunleavy, 1994; Midwinter, 1990). What is unmistakable and undeniable is that the changes were real. Public sector neo-Marxists were routed by neo-markets. Representative accountability lost ground to economic accountability. A situation of more jobs than work gave way to one of more work than jobs. The 'iron rice bowl', as the Chinese refer to a job for life, was dashed from the hands of public sector workers and managers – with no financial compensation.

In local government, troublesome democratically elected authorities (the Greater London Council and the metropolitan county councils) were summarily abolished in 1986. The fictional South Riding County Council (Holtby, 1936) as a model of local government would give way to the flagship London Borough of Westminster, and Alderman Mrs Beddowes to Lady Porter.

By the late 1980s, six key themes could be traced in the government's local government programme (Stewart and Stoker, 1989, pp 2–3). They were:

1 *Fragmentation and plurality*. Local authorities as large, free-standing monoliths were a thing of the past. No longer were they all-purpose providers from cradle to grave. Instead they would be expected to provide services in a network of partnerships and multi-agency teams with other agencies in the public sector as well as with the private and voluntary sectors. Moreover, the increasing importance of the bodies of the non-elected state eroded the significance of local government.

2 *Competition*. At first in response to government legislation to improve service quality in housing maintenance and connected fields, the introduction of Compulsory Competitive Tendering (CCT) statutorily exposed local authorities to the stimulus, if not always the reality, of competition. Progressively expanded into other defined service activities and sometimes adopted as a matter of local purposive choice, management by contract ousted management by committee as 'hierarchy' gave way to 'contract' (Harrison, 1993).

3 *Enabling*. A somewhat elastic concept stretching from the minimalist interpretation of Nicholas Ridley to a much broader community development brief, enabling nevertheless captured the shift from direct service provision to the setting of strategic direction, the specification of levels and quality of service, and performance evaluation. Local education authorities, for example, losing responsibilities upwards (to national

curriculum, assessment and inspection bodies), downwards (to the governing bodies of individual schools and colleges following the 1988 Education Reform Act) and sideways (to opted-out schools, City Technology Colleges or Training and Enterprise Councils) would need to reformulate and redefine their role (Audit Commission, 1989).

4 *Paying for and receiving services*. A much more explicit connection between the cost of producing and paying for services was an essential consideration behind the rationale for Mrs Thatcher's fateful, flagship Community Charge which would see virtually everybody contribute to the local taxation base, albeit at the discounted rate of 20 per cent.

5 *Customer choice*. The hegemony of producer interests, the excesses of 'bureaucratic paternalism' (Hoggett and Hambleton, 1987) and deformed 'disabling professionalism' (Elcock, 1983) – so characteristic of the health service as well as of central and local government – were eroded in their entrenched dominion by the opening up of consumer choice, if not consumer sovereignty. The 'public' or clients were redefined as customers free to make rational choices. The Public Service Orientation, and later the Citizen's Charter, would serve to redress the imbalance between producer and consumer interests.

6 *'Business-like' management*. Despite resource constraints, hands-on managers would occupy a discretionary space, and be free to manage (Hood, 1991). Strategic management, business planning, performance measurement, cost centres and the disaggregation of large units of production in favour of management responsibilities devolved closer to the point of service delivery all became widespread (after Stewart and Stoker, 1989).

Organisational structures and management processes do not exist in a political vacuum. They reflect and contest dominant political values. Thus, if the 1970s was the decade of the corporate local authority, the 1980s would become the decade of the contracting authority, the 'commercial contractual model' or 'hypermarket' as Benington called it in his four-fold taxonomy (Benington, 1995). With the task of introducing quasi-market relationships and commercial principles into a local authority's business, the organisation necessarily separated out the client and contractor functions (Mallabar, 1991), just as purchasers and providers would need to be disentangled in the NHS. Created are: 'Stand alone business units and devolved cost centres, which compete for business within both internal and external markets. The organogram can therefore be pictured as a hypermarket, with a number of separate shopping malls and stores trading and competing with each other, but sheltered under one certified dome' (Benington, 1995, p 3).

Compared with the corporate local authority, power and control are, according to Benington, much more dispersed and information may reside within the smaller purchaser and provider units as much as in the central corporate capability. This is reflected in the information technology architecture where personal computers have supplemented the corporate mainframe. In such an authority, the former chief executive may have been redesignated a managing director and will be concerned to make services 'more commercial and more financially competitive'. Price is its currency (Benington, 1995).

1990–7: FIGHTING FOR THE CENTRE GROUND

In November 1990, John Major was elected leader of the Conservative Party and succeeded Margaret Thatcher as Prime Minister, in part precisely for the very reason that he was not the intractable Mrs Thatcher obstinately sticking to her guns on Europe and the

Community Charge. Although some sought to regard Major, her anointed heir, as the very culmination of Thatcherism, he nevertheless immediately struck a more conciliatory, less confrontational chord. To local government for example, he offered a corporate involvement more reminiscent of the 1970s than the antagonism of the 1980s. Three consultative papers – on the structure of local government, taxation and internal management – were swiftly published, the second proposing a Council Tax in place of the unpopular Community Charge. In another field, the criminal justice system would be referred to a Royal Commission, none of which Mrs Thatcher had created in all her years in office. Her preference had been for the advice of independent right-wing 'think-tanks'. Elsewhere, on Europe for example, Mr Major's position would sometimes not have been to his predecessor's liking. Not always with the unanimous support of an increasingly divided Conservative Party, he often seemed to be seeking to return his party from the doctrinaire right to the centre ground of British politics.

The Labour Party meanwhile was busy reprofiling and reinventing itself. Under Neil Kinnock's leadership until 1992, John Smith's between 1992 and 1994, and Tony Blair's from 1994, Labour had worked to dissolve the electorate's fear of itself, seeking to lose its public image as the tax and spend party, to loosen its ties with the trade unions and to represent itself to the country as a modern, democratic and credible party of government.

The year 1994, just as 1976 had been, turned out to be a fascinating one in British politics. It was the premature death of John Smith which acted as the catalyst to events, causing as it did a contest to elect his successor. On 21 July 1994 that successor emerged as Tony Blair, Labour's seventh and youngest ever leader. Securing impressive wins in each of the three sections of the electoral college, Blair was elected without the rancour and bitter political infighting which had characterised internal Labour Party politics over the previous twenty years. His method of election to the leadership as well as the man himself symbolically differentiated Blair from many Labour traditions.

For the country he variously offered 'a crusade for change', 'a mission of national renewal', 'a mission of hope, change and opportunity' and 'a new politics to take us into a new millennium'. However his project of modernising Britain could not be accomplished without first modernising the Labour Party itself. Rejecting the 'one more push' approach to delivering a Labour victory, in his acceptance speech Tony Blair promised to 'wage war in our party against complacency wherever it exists'. The fact that the Conservatives had lost the nation's trust did not mean that Labour would automatically gain it. Thus he set out to prepare the Labour Party for government, waging war against disabling, old-style Labourism, grubbing out restrictive practices and discarding anachronistic totems and talismans – most famously the so-called Clause 4. That section of the Labour Party constitution, drawn up originally by Sidney and Beatrice Webb in 1918, promised 'to secure for the workers . . . the full fruits of their industry . . . based on the common ownership of the means of production, distribution and exchange'. For many in the Labour Party, it was an article of faith, a statement of historic commitment, a defiant declaration of Marxist socialism which must never be sacrificed by ambitious and opportunist modernisers who would trade the party's birthright in their hunger for office and power. For Tony Blair, however, it was out of date and of dubious relevance to the party he intended to lead into office. It was a millstone, a straitjacket, a distraction which substituted means for aims. Its revision was crucial. Blair prevailed. Additionally, he further loosened links with the trade unions, offering no special privileges in his modern pluralist party. Thus, the abuse of his Shadow Education Secretary, David Blunkett, at National

Union of Teachers conferences provided New Labour with the opportunity to show the public that it stood for 'education, education, education', not for the organised interests of teachers. It served to identify the party with the quality of public service rather than the interests of producer groups and public service unions. More generally, his flexible ethical socialism displaced the rigid class rhetoric of Marxist socialism.

In his first 12 months as Labour leader, Tony Blair succeeded in strategically repositioning Labour in the centre ground of British politics, specifically targeting middle-class, middle-income, middle England without alienating core Labour support in the less prosperous, more peripheral reaches of the United Kingdom. The shift in ideological and policy direction may not have received unanimous endorsement in all Labour quarters but he nevertheless seemed able to manage the tensions between old Labour Club and cappuccino-chic socialism. The personal popularity of the Islington moderniser in his Labour heartland constituency of Sedgefield seemed symbolic of a greater achievement.

All of this was deeply troubling for the Conservatives. Labour had committed to the family, to welfare and benefit reform and by September 1994 claimed to be the party best suited to run a market economy. As Hugo Young put it at the time, 'Tony Blair has already done something rare in the history of British opposition parties. He has taken possession of the centre ground' (Young, 1994). For the Tories, it presented a strategic dilemma. Should they seek to put some 'clear, blue water' between themselves and New Labour which would involve a shift to the right towards the Portillo wing of the party and vacate the centre ground for the Opposition to occupy? Should they pursue the so-called Coke option which acknowledged the similarity of the products on offer but claim that theirs was 'the real thing'? Or should they work on the electorate's suspicions about the Labour Party, claiming that Tony Blair was only the acceptable public relations image of a party fundamentally unchanged and still committed to its old ways, that in government it would revert to type?

As the summer of 1994 proceeded it was clear that the Labour and Conservative parties were converging in their strategic jockeying for position. One political cartoon showed Tony Blair sawing a limb from the third letter of his name to reveal the word Tory; another showed a naked John Major bemoaning to colleagues the fact that an equally naked Tony Blair had stolen all his political clothes. The Prime Minister said that Labour was talking Tory language and his Chancellor, Kenneth Clarke, more colourfully referred to New Labour as political cross-dressers and transvestites. Of great significance in the autumn was John Major's leader's speech to the Conservative Party conference in Bournemouth. The Prime Minister was apparently resisting any further move to the right and appeared to break with the Thatcher inheritance. 'Major breaks links with Thatcher', proclaimed the headlines as he appeared to be bringing to an end the years of upheaval in the public services. He personally pledged himself to the future of the National Health Service and, in education, promised no more changes to the National Curriculum for five years. The continuous revolution of his predecessor appeared to be slowing down. The following month, in November, the proposed privatisation of the Post Office was shelved – the first time such a thing had happened since the Conservatives came to power in 1979.

Thus, 1994 saw two youngish political leaders edge their respective parties back towards the middle ground of English, if not, British politics. John Major returned the Conservatives from the far right whereas Tony Blair shifted Labour towards the centre, seeking to edge Major further to the right without following him too far and alienating support. Such convergence was at odds with the ideological divergence of the Thatcher years. Both appeared to have chosen the same battleground – middle England and the working middle class – the key target group identified by Bill Clinton in the 1992 American presidential contest. In moving towards the centre, each party had overturned previous policy positions, loosened commitments to historic ideals and, in so doing, strained support from sections of their own party. Together, they wrong-footed the Liberal Democrats.

It could be argued that the election of Major and Blair as leaders of their parties served to drive political ideology from the arena. Jacques (1994), for example, argued, 'There is no great political project, no totalising ideology'. Even so, despite continuing policy differences on, for example, the Social Chapter or the minimum wage, the elements of a new post-Thatcherism consensus were emerging. Its elements were:

- a shared commitment to a mixed economy;
- low taxation, low inflation rather than full employment;
- continuing resource constraint;
- welfare reform, crucially involving the ending of automatic universal entitlement, in effect the end of the post-war welfare state;
- a renewed concern for community.

This, of course, was a very different consensus from the shared understanding of the post-war settlement. For public service managers, the prospect of a Labour victory in the coming General Election could in no sense be understood as a prospective return to the good old days.

CASE STUDY 1.1

The role of the State continues to change as governments seem unwilling to finance public expectations concerning welfare. Policy debates revolve around the issue of who is to fund the gap.

PARTIES WARNED WELFARE STATE FACES DEATH BY A THOUSAND CUTS

By Nicholas Timmins

Conservative and Labour spending plans do not look credible without cuts in public services, the Institute for Fiscal Studies warned yesterday. It said the UK could be heading for a new-style minimal welfare state.

The government's plans for the next three years envisaged lower sustained growth in public spending than had been achieved at any time in the past three decades, the institute said. Labour had signed up to those plans for the first two years – aside from the windfall levy to fund its welfare-to-work programme.

Overall, spending was set to rise by an average of 0.4 per cent a year against 1.9 per cent on average over the past 18 years: a difference that would put public spending in the last year of the next parliament about £24 billion lower than if the previous trend was maintained.

Spending on the National Health Service in particular was 'strikingly tight', the IFS said – in spite of both parties' commitment to real-term year-on-year increases. There was cash to allow for a real rise this year but zero increases for the following two years.

Either the plans were not feasible and would be broken, or there were likely to be 'serious implications' for the NHS as a universal provider of free health care, the institute said.

Ms Alissa Goodman, a senior economist at the institute, said that, averaged over three years, health spending would rise by 0.6 per cent a year, a fifth of the level of the past 18 years, certainly the lowest sustained level for 30 years, and quite possibly the lowest since the NHS was founded.

The institute pointed out that health overspent almost every year but that this time the contingency reserve, an unallocated pot of money traditionally used to allow higher spending, was unusually small. That meant there was less flexibility 'without breaking the overall spending limit'.

'None of the major parties seems to have any satisfactory response to the very large gap likely to arise between spending plans and public expectations,' the IFS added.

'It is almost certain that over the next five years, either public spending, and therefore tax and/or borrowing, will be higher than planned, or substantial radical reform of public sector provision will occur, either explicitly or by default.'

Both parties' plans also meant that the state would only provide a minimal pension, Mr Paul Johnson, an IFS economist said. And on present longer-term plans it was possible that other aspects of the welfare state would go that way, including health and other parts of social security.

'The state will provide a minimum service and people will be encouraged to buy more provision for themselves on top,' said Mr Johnson. 'We think that is the way the welfare state will change more generally.'

Already, permanent health insurance was growing because disability benefits had been cut. The nursery voucher provided £1,000 but invited parents to top it up, help to the jobless with mortgages now started only after nine months, and the government's long-term care plans also implied more help for those who help themselves.

The institute pointed out that spending on private health had doubled from 5 per cent to 10 per cent of public health spending since 1979, with private education spending up from 8 per cent to 15 per cent. 'This change in the balance between public and private provision can only continue if the share of public spending in the overall economy is to continue to fall over the longer term,' it added.

That was the Conservatives explicit aim. But 'Cutting back the size of government must imply serious choices about the public sector's role in the provision of pensions, education and health,' the institute said.

'If we are really talking about not raising taxes and not raising spending, or getting it lower then we need to debate that,' said Mr Johnson. 'If we don't talk about it, nobody will be able to plan or do what they need to do to achieve that.'

Source: Financial Times, 10 April 1997. Reprinted with permission.

Questions on the case study

1 What evidence exists that there has been radical public sector reform since this article was written?

2 Are we moving to a system where the State will provide a minimum service?

1997–8: 'NEW LABOUR, NEW BRITAIN'

If the political vocabulary of the 1980s was harshly economic in nature, that of the 1990s appeared to take a more ethical turn (Jacques, 1994). Tony Blair's vision, for example, of a 'new and young country . . . One Britain . . . where your child in distress is my child, your parent ill and in pain is my parent, your friend unemployed and helpless is my friend, your neighbour my neighbour' struck a different note from Mrs Thatcher's pronouncements on society and community, or even from John Major's vision of Britain as 'the enterprise centre of Europe'. Nevertheless, when Mr Blair led Labour out of the political wilderness on 1 May 1997 with an overall parliamentary majority of 179 it was not into a Utopian land of idealistic public service that they were headed. In the second year of his government, the deceased resident of an old people's home could be regarded by a local authority in Northumberland as 'business waste'. Not much could be more brutally economic than that description.

In general terms, the Blair government would describe its thinking in terms neither of Thatcherism nor of Butskellism but by reference to the 'Third Way'. Phrased in terms of 'a new contract', 'a new deal' and 'a new partnership', New Labour's Third Way is meant to address, among other issues, the balance between rights and responsibilities – concern for the former, through the articulation of political and sexual rights in the 1960s and 1970s and economic rights in the 1980s, being perceived as having outgrown the latter.

Defining it on its unveiling, Foreign Secretary Robin Cook referred to the Third Way as: 'a political project as distinct from the individualist politics of neo-liberalism as it is distinct from the corporate ethos of old-fashioned social democracy' (Robin Cook at the Royal Society of Arts, 22 April 1998). In other words, it was neither Mrs Thatcher's way ('the individualist politics of neo-liberalism') nor the way of Jim Callaghan or Harold Wilson ('the corporate ethos of old-fashioned social democracy'). Critics of the new government both within and outside the Labour Party, would however point to a greater resemblance to Mrs Thatcher's approach than to earlier Labour governments. Blair, like Thatcher, showed himself to be a conviction politician who wielded power to dominate first his party and then his country's politics. His agenda, even in government, could still be referred to as the Blair, rather than Labour's, agenda. He could, like Mrs Thatcher, show an authoritarianism and be accused of a presidential style and of cronyism. In matters of style as well as substance, critics drew the parallels. For example, one disillusioned Labour MEP described Mr Blair as being 'closer to a Thatcherite than a social democrat . . . I think Mr Blair is not even a right-wing social democrat these days but is much more a conservative with a small "c", who really wants to run a government of national unity as far as I can see' (Hugh Kerr, MEP, *The Daily Telegraph*, 29 December 1997).

Mr Kerr could easily be dismissed by the Labour hierarchy as a 'known troublemaker'. Perhaps more telling is Peter Mandelson's own observation that New Labour's strategy was to move forward from where Margaret Thatcher left off, with no intention of dismantling everything she did.

Mrs Thatcher would have approved of the way in which Mr Blair used political power to get things done. Unlike John Major perhaps, he is in power as well as in office. His government hit the ground printing as well as running and within its first year could point to considerable success in Northern Ireland, on constitutional reform, on welfare to work and in education spending.

Not only in the exercise of power but also in terms of substantive policy were there points of contact between the Blair government and the Thatcher years. In pursuit of a stable economy for example, control of inflation and low taxation were given higher priority than full employment, even when in 1998 increasing numbers of job losses were announced by inward investors in the high-technology sector, such as Siemens in North Tyneside and Fujitsu at Aycliffe (neighbouring the Prime Minister's own constituency), as well as elsewhere. Eddie George, Governor of the Bank of England to whom responsibility for setting interest rates had been delegated, made the politically unfortunate but otherwise no doubt true revelation that job losses in the North were regarded as a price worth paying to avoid overheating in the South. The Prime Minister told lobbying workers that he could not save their jobs. Like Mrs Thatcher, he did not shrink from the consequences of his policies.

Tight control of public expenditure would also continue as a matter of policy, although in his July 1998 Comprehensive Spending Review, the Chancellor of the Exchequer announced extra expenditure over the next three years for education (£19 billion), health

(£20 billion), public transport (£1.7 billion) and urban regeneration and housing (£4.4 billion). This investment was explicitly linked to continued public service reform, including the development of cross-departmental budgets, a new Invest to Save budget, new quality standards and efficiency targets, better procurement to secure cost savings, investment in call centre technology and the 'best value' performance framework for local government. In other words, new investment was tied to further advances in the competitive performance culture of modern public service delivery.

As for privatisation, much of the British public sector had already been sold off by the time that Tony Blair entered Downing Street. However, far from pledging renationalisation, his government offered no ideological opposition to privatisation. Indeed, in October 1998, it published plans for the privatisation of the air traffic control function in a private-public partnership arrangement.

Privatisation of the London Underground remains a possibility. The marketisation of public services will also continue. Although the purchaser/provider split in the NHS is to be abolished and Compulsory Competitive Tendering in local government replaced by a more comprehensive regime of Best Value, the message to the private sector has been clear. New Labour is not its enemy. Ironically its close links with business, rather than with the trade unions, have sometimes embarrassed the government in its first year. The exemption of Formula One motor racing from a ban on tobacco advertising, for example, led to suggestions that Labour had become a political party in which Philip Morris had more influence than William Morris.

Another point of continuity with the 1980s is the apparent continuing commitment to small government and the hollowing out of the state. Old Labour's predisposition to statism has given way to the minimalist state. Indeed, given Cool Britannia, the Millennium Dome and parties for rock stars, satirists have suggested that under Tony Blair a concern for 'state' has perhaps been squeezed by its anagram 'taste'. As the satirist Ben Elton put it, paradigm has become parody. As a final example, reducing the dependency culture through the Welfare to Work programme has a Thatcherite resonance to it.

The Blair agenda also, of course, pursues themes which Mrs Thatcher would have heartily detested. One such is the programme of constitutional reform and devolution which has found expression in the provisions for a Scottish Parliament, a Welsh Assembly, the Greater London Assembly and an elected mayor for London, as well as proposals for Regional Development Agencies and perhaps in due course elected assemblies for the English Regions. Another is electoral reform – evident in the intended method of election to the new institutions already mentioned and certain to be given further impetus by the publication of the report of the Jenkins Commission (1998). Other new departures since 1997 include the renewed concern for community and its strategies for inclusion and sustainability as well as the government's overarching social policy agenda.

The point for public service managers, however, is that despite the rhetoric of change and modernisation, there are nevertheless strong links of continuity connecting the New Labour government to the Thatcher years. Change and continuity are, of course, two key themes in the study of politics (Kavanagh, 1996) and after any General Election both are more or less evident. No incoming administration starts with a *tabula rasa*. Even if it so wished, the Blair government would have real practical problems in rooting out the neo-liberal values which had penetrated public service organisations during almost twenty years of Conservative rule; even if it so wished . . .

As for practical arrangements the message for public service managers is clear. Joined-up problems need joined-up solutions which demand joined-up government, or joined-up governance more accurately perhaps. Key themes are the integration of policies, partnership and joint working. 'Coherent' and 'strategic' help to define better government. Working together to solve problems. No one is ruled in. No one is ruled out. Neither Sinn Fein nor Gerry Adams. None is excluded in the drive to solve problems, provided there is a willingness to make a constructive contribution. Thus, the message to the Trades Union Congress at its annual conference in 1997 was 'modernise or die'. In similar tones, David Blunkett said to the annual conference of the National Union of Teachers at Blackpool in April 1998, 'Our job is to work with you in partnership . . . slogans won't do it.'

The message to all public service organisations has been the same. To local government, for example, the gauntlet has been dropped by the Prime Minister:

> I want the message to local government to be loud and clear.
>
> A changing role is part of your heritage. The people's needs require you to change again so that you can play your part in helping to modernise Britain and, in partnership with others, deliver the policies on which government was elected.
>
> If you accept this challenge, you will not find us wanting. You can look forward to an enhanced role and new powers. Your contribution will be recognised. Your status enhanced.
>
> If you are unwilling or unable to work to the modern agenda then the government will have to look to other partners to take on your role.
>
> The choice for local government is clear. I hope that councils all over the land will choose to work with a modern government for a modern Britain.

(Blair, 1998)

The challenge is abrasively stark. Local government continues to exist only on conditional approval. If it renews itself and regenerates its culture, it will be a valued partner. If not, however, one can probably assume that it will cease to exist in any meaningful sense.

The organisational implications are equally clear. Again, let us take local government as an example. If the 1960s saw the 'traditional' authority in action, the 1970s the 'corporate' authority and the 1980s the 'contract' authority, the 1990s have seen the emergence of the 'networked' authority (Benington, 1995). Variously drawing upon ideas from the world of business, especially in relation to strategic management, quality assurance and organisational form, Benington (1995) describes the authority being:

> based upon four interacting centres of power and initiative:
> ● a strong political leadership often concentrated in a small cabinet-style political executive;
> ● a small group of strategic managers with corporate responsibility for translating political values and strategy into action throughout the organisation;
> ● a group of operational managers responsible for the management and delivery of policies and programmes;
> ● frontline services with a high degree of devolved responsibilities for budgets and staffing and decentralised action, in response to, and in conjunction with users of services and community organisations (Benington, 1995, p 3).

Responsibilities for strategic and operational management may often be separated out, intermediate tiers reduced by delayering exercises, communication lines between the strategic centre and frontline delivery shortened and distinctions between internal and external boundaries blurred (Benington, 1995). 'The authority builds a network of relationships and partnerships with outside organisations in the public, private, voluntary and community sectors' (Benington, 1995, p 3). The chief executive – not now the lawyer town clerk of the traditional authority, nor the treasurer of the corporate authority, nor the business manager of the contract authority – might define the role as a 'change agent' (Benington, 1995). Experienced perhaps in economic or community development, the Chief Executive might see the defining question as: 'how to maintain cohesion and commitment to the authority's strategic goals and priorities through the culture and values of the whole local authority rather than through traditional management control mechanisms' (Benington, 1995, p 4).

An organogram of overlapping and interpenetrating circles now describes the structure of a local authority such as Solihull for example; some of the cultural values may have persisted but the typical chart of a Weberian bureaucracy belongs to a different age.

There can, of course, be terrible problems in managing a network and some have speculated on how government might express and achieve its purpose through a rag-bag of networks, partnerships and structured markets. However, the Blair commitment to joined-up government for joined-up problems virtually guarantees the further development of the networked organisation as the basis for public service delivery in the medium term; effective resolution of any strategic and operational difficulties will be demanded of managers as an early priority.

CONCLUSIONS

Politics does matter, especially for public service managers for whom political management assumes greater salience than for many of their counterparts in business. This chapter has sought, in the context of post-war Britain, to explore how broad political themes are reflected in the delivery of public services. Such effects are not only of abstract, academic interest, for they have very real consequences for those working in public service organisations as well as for service users.

The magnitude of cultural change within public service organisations has been immense. When the city treasurer of a local authority in North East England retired in 1993 at the age of 55, he publicly reflected in a local newspaper on his years of local government service – remembering how, as a junior clerk in the rates department in 1955, his duties had included charging the inkwells and the coal fires. When the books were balanced, he would be sent out to buy an apple for each of the staff. The largesse apart, it all has a whiff of Bob Cratchit's workplace about it. Forty years on – having negotiated all the thrills of the Community Charge and the Council Tax as well as the particular delights of capping, targets, penalties, clawback, holdback and super holdback – the sorely pressed treasurer had a budget of £400 million which was the means by which a large authority, in a high-technology, globalised, intensely competitive and wholly transformed environment could play its part in satisfying the aspirations of over a quarter of a million variously demanding people. To visualise another local government treasurer, the celebrated Lake District guide, 'A.W.' (Wainwright), in a modern local authority would be virtually inconceivable.

Cultural change is not, of course, unique to public services. Working practices have been revolutionised in many areas of activity, such as the manufacturing and service sectors for example. What perhaps characterises the intensity of the public sector revolution is that many of the assumptions defining and underpinning the very notion of a public service have also been undermined or knocked away. Not only have public servants had to embrace continuous innovation in information technology, for example, or to meet the demands of evaluative government, they also have needed to engage with changing fundamentals, such as the role of government, the nature of welfare, redefinitions of public and private and the place of a public service professional.

In order to make sense of the complexity – not least in order to avert personal catastrophe – some sort of analytical framework is necessary if all the information and critical reflection is to be organised. This chapter has taken the retreat from the so-called post-war consensus, which imparted so much stability for so long, as its organising theme. In that process of retreat, the UK stands at a critical point. Tony Blair may have committed to change but for the public services his election has seemed to offer more of the same, only more so. Take the introduction of tuition fees in higher education as an example. Mrs Thatcher would have approved. Mr Major would neither have dared nor have wished to. Labour, in opposition, would have been apoplectic had he sought to. Yet, in government, New Labour – despite denial of any such plans only weeks before the General Election – responded to the Dearing Report by their introduction. New Britain, new charges. The neo-liberalism of the 1980s appears not to have been routed by the election of New Labour. By a delicious irony Mrs Thatcher, the scourge of consensus politics, may have authored the new consensus. As Wilding (1992) observed, her most lasting accomplishment may have been to change the nature of the Labour Party.

The question yet to be definitively answered is whether Mr Blair stands in a line of political succession from Mrs Thatcher or from Mr Callaghan? Or neither?

ACKNOWLEDEGEMENTS

Earlier versions of some of the material in this chapter were contained in:

- Hartas, B and Harrop, K (1991) 'Patterns of Change in Local Government since 1945', *Teaching Public Administration*, 9(1), pp 25–36.
- Fenwick, J and Harrop, K (1997) 'La privatizzazione dei servizi pubblici locali nel Regno Unito' in Monaco, F R (ed) *Sussidiarietà e Pubbliche Amministrazioni*. Rimini: Università degli Studi di Bologna/Maggioli Editore. Translated as 'The privatisation of local public services in the United Kingdom', it is based on a conference paper at the University of Bologna (September 1995) and is available in published form only in Italian.

I am grateful to Bill Hartas and to John Fenwick for our earlier collaboration, as well as to all other colleagues in Government and Politics at the University of Northumbria. Special thanks are also due to Kerry Douglas, Deborah Goodall, Bob McKee and Aidan Rose.

REFERENCES

Allison, G T (1979) *Public and Private Management: are they fundamentally alike in all unimportant respects?*. Washington DC: Brookings Institution.

Audit Commission (1989) *Losing an Empire, Finding a Role: The LEA of the Future*, Occasional Paper No. 10.

Bains, M (1972) *The New Local Authorities: Management and Structure*. London: The Stationery Office.

Benington, J (1995) *Skyscrapers, Pyramids, Hypermarkets and Networks. The impact of changing information needs, systems and technologies on the organisation and culture of local government*. Warwick: The Local Government Centre, University of Warwick.

Blair, A (1998) *Leading the way: a new vision for local government*. London: Institute for Public Policy Research.

'Conservative Party Manifesto' (1979). London: The Stationery Office.

Cole, J (1995) *As It Seems to Me: Political Memoirs*. London: Weidenfeld & Nicolson.

Dinan, D (1994) *Ever Closer Union? An Introduction to the European Community*. Basingstoke: Macmillan.

Dror, Y (1968) *Public Policy Making Re-examined*. Scranton, Penn: Chandler Publishing.

Elcock, H J (1983) 'Disabling Professionalism: the Real Threat to Local Democracy', *Public Money*, 3, pp 23–7.

Finer, S E (1980) *The Changing British Party System, 1945–1979*. Washington, DC: The American Enterprise Institute for Public Policy Research.

Garrett, J (1972) *The Management of Government*. Harmondsworth: Pelican.

Greenwood, R, Hinings, C R, Ranson, S and Walsh, K (1976) *In Pursuit of Corporate Rationality: organisational developments in the post-reorganisation period*. Birmingham: University of Birmingham, Institute of Local Government Studies.

Greenwood, R and Stewart J D (eds) (1974) *Corporate Planning in English Local Government*. Croydon: Knight.

Hambleton, R (1978) *Policy Planning and Local Government*. London: Hutchinson.

Harrison, A (ed.) (1993) *From Hierarchy to Contract*. Newbury, Berks: Policy Journals.

Healey, D (1990) *The Time of My Life*. Harmondsworth: Penguin.

Hennessy, P (1992) *Never Again. Britain 1945–1951*. London: Jonathan Cape. (Page references are to the 1993 Vintage edition.)

Hoggett, P and Hambleton, R (1987) *Decentralisation and Democracy. Localising public services*. Bristol: University of Bristol, School for Advanced Urban Studies, Occasional Paper No. 28.

Holtby, W (1936) *South Riding*. London: Collins.

Hood, C (1991) 'A Public Management For All Seasons?', *Public Administration*, 69, pp 3–19.

Hood, C and Dunleavy, P (1994) 'From Old Public Administration to New Public Management', *Public Money and Management*, July–September, pp 9–16.

Jackson, W E (1945) *Local Government in England and Wales*. Harmondsworth: Pelican.

Jacques, M (1994) 'Where lies the moving spirit of the Nineties?', *Independent*, 26 October.

Jenkins Commission (1998) *The Report of the Independent Commission on the Voting System*. London: The Stationery Office.

Kavanagh, D (1996) *British Politics. Continuities and Change* (3rd edn). Oxford: Oxford University Press.

Kavanagh, D and Morris, P (1994) *Consensus Politics, from A to Thatcher* (2nd edn). Oxford: Basil Blackwell.

Kavanagh, D and Pimlott, B (1989) 'Is the post-war consensus a myth?', *Contemporary Record*, Summer.

Loughlin, M (1982) 'Recent Developments in Central-Local Government Fiscal Relations', *Journal of Law and Society*, 9(2), pp 253–65.

Mallabar, N (1991) *Local Government Administration – in a time of change*. Sunderland: Business Education Publishers.

Midwinter, A (1990) 'What New Managerialism?', *Public Policy and Administration*, 5(1).

Ranson, S and Stewart, J (1989) 'Citizenship and Government: the challenge for management in the public domain', *Political Studies*, 37 (1), pp 5–24.

Rhodes, R A W (1979) 'Ordering urban change: corporate planning in the government of English cities' in Lagroye, J and Wright, V (eds) *Local Government in Britain and France: problems and prospects*. London: Allen and Unwin.

Rodgers, W (1982) *The Politics of Change*. London: Secker & Warburg.

Rutter, L (1980) *The Essential Community: local government in the year 2000*. Washington, DC: International City Management Association.

Sampson, A (1983) *The Changing Anatomy of Britain*. London: Coronet.

Seldon, A (1994) 'The Rise and Fall (and Rise Again?) of the Post-war Consensus' in Jones, B (ed.) (1984) *Politics UK* (2nd edn). Hemel Hempstead: Harvester Wheatsheaf.

Sked, A and Cook, C (1993) *Post-War Britain. A Political History* (4th edn). Harmondsworth: Penguin.

Skidelsky, R (1990) *Guardian*, 21 December, quoted in Wilding, P (1992).

Stanyer, J (1976) *Understanding Local Government*. London: Fontana.

Starling, G (1993) *Managing the Public Sector*. Belmont, Ca: Wadsworth.

Stewart, J. D (1971) *Management in Local Government: A Viewpoint*. Croydon: Charles Knight.

Stewart, J and Ranson, S (1988) 'Management in the Public Domain', *Public Money and Management*, Spring/Summer, pp 13–19.

Stewart, J and Stoker, G (1989) *The Future of Local Government*. Basingstoke: Macmillan.

Wildavsky, A (1974) *The Politics of the Budgetary Process*. Boston: Little Brown.

Wilding, P (1992) 'The British Welfare State: Thatcherism's enduring legacy', *Policy and Politics*, 20(3), pp 202–12.

Willcocks, L and Harrow, J (eds) (1992) *Rediscovering Public Services Management*. Maidenhead: McGraw-Hill.

Young, H (1994) 'Blair runs away with consensus and clichés', *Guardian*, 29 September.

Young, J. W (1991) *Cold War Europe, 1945–1989. A Political History*, Edward Arnold.

QUESTIONS AND DISCUSSION TOPICS

1 How does the political environment influence the public service manager's professional life and to what extent?

2 To what extent do public service organisations reflect their political, economic and social context?

3 Does the concept of the so-called post-war consensus provide a useful starting point for understanding the public service revolution which has swept the UK and spread elsewhere during the past generation?

4 How significant were the 1970s for the changing culture of public service delivery in post-war Britain?

5 How relevant will Thatcherism be judged to be in the search for a lasting paradigm to replace Keynesianism?

6 In the 1997 British General Election, the electorate apparently voted in large numbers for New Labour's agenda of modernisation and radical change. Which is more prominent on the public service agenda since that election, change or continuity?

7 In October 1998 *Marxism Today*, the journal credited with introducing the term 'Thatcherism', came out of retirement to reflect upon the nature of 'Blairism'. For public service users, does Blairism offer new hope for a new millennium?

2 The social and economic context

Ian Worthington

INTRODUCTION

Change is an enduring feature of organisational life. Few, if any, currently working in the public, private or voluntary sectors can claim to have been untouched by either the pace or direction of organisational change in recent years. Managers responsible for shaping and implementing changes to the structure, culture or management of the organisation find that the management of change represents a particular challenge and is one which requires the individuals involved to demonstrate a high degree of skill and sensitivity in their dealings with colleagues if the process of change is to be managed successfully.

In the literature of organisation theory and corporate strategy, the concept of change has long been recognised as a legitimate area of study and has been an important subdiscipline in its own right (Wilson, 1992). In the early 1950s, for example, Kurt Lewin characterised organisational change as an imbalance between the forces 'driving' change (e.g. changing markets, social transformations, new technology) and those 'restraining' it (e.g. individual inertia, organisational culture, structural rigidity). Lewin's basic contention was that organisations tended towards a kind of equilibrium or status quo in the face of countervailing forces acting on both individuals and the organisation. For change to take place there needed to be an 'unfreezing' of the status quo: reducing resistance to change by helping people to understand both the need for it and the benefits to be gained from it. The resultant imbalance between the pressures for change and those against it would permit change to take place and this could be followed by a 'refreezing' or consolidation of the new state (Lewin, 1951).

Recent studies of change have tended to adopt a more holistic and dynamic approach by focusing on the process of changing within a temporal and contextual setting. Thus

Pettigrew *et al.* (1992) have argued that research on organisational change should examine the relationship between the context, process and content of change. These refer broadly to the 'why' (context), 'what' (content) and 'how' (process) aspects of change. In relation to the context of change they draw an analytical distinction between the organisation's 'inner' and 'outer' contexts. The former refers to ongoing internal aspects such as strategy, structure, culture and management which help to shape the processes through which ideas for change proceed. The latter denotes the broad economic, political and social environment in which organisations exist and operate, together with perceptions, actions and interpretations of policies and events by decision makers operating at different spatial levels. For Pettigrew *et al.*, explaining why change occurs largely requires an analysis of an organisation's inner and outer contexts and the dynamics of the relationship between them.

This focus on the contextual aspects of change has much in common with the systems approach to organisational analysis which portrays any one organisation as an interdependent part of a much larger whole. Under this approach organisations are seen generically as transformers of inputs (e.g. materials, labour, technology) into outputs (e.g. goods, services, information), with all aspects of the transformation process taking place within a complex, multifaceted, spatially diverse and often changing environment (Worthington and Britton, 1997). This environment is normally presented as having two aspects, internal and external, equivalent to Pettigrew's inner and outer contexts, with the latter being seen as an important factor that shapes the internal characteristics and actions of the internal organisation. It is this dynamic relationship between the organisation's internal and external environment which provides a useful framework for analysing why change occurs. Successful organisations are generally characterised as those which are constantly able to adapt in order to maintain a 'strategic fit' between the organisation's internal resources and capabilities and the threats and opportunities it faces in its external environment.

To illustrate this interplay of the internal and external environments in a public sector context, this chapter focuses on two key environmental variables: social and economic. Using a longitudinal analysis of key changes in the social and economic contexts of public sector organisations, the chapter demonstrates how environmental change has important implications for the way in which the public services are managed. For analytical purposes the social and economic environments are treated separately in the discussion below; in practice the picture is much more complex, with interactions occurring between external variables, each of which tends to operate at a variety of spatial levels.

THE SOCIAL CONTEXT OF CHANGE

People are vital to all organisations: they provide the organisation's workforce and management and are the customers or clients who consume its output. From both a demand and supply point of view, then, an organisation's social environment is of critical importance to its well-being both now and in the future.

Demographic change is one aspect of the social context of public sector organisations. Changes in the size, structure, social and ethnic composition or location of the population can have significant consequences for an organisation, affecting, for example, its ability to recruit the right quantity or quality of staff and/or the number of clients requiring its services. Monitoring both the extent and direction of demographic change is as important an ingredient in planning for the public services as it is for other types of organisation.

Changes in society are not simply restricted to population developments; people's values, attitudes, preferences, beliefs and lifestyles are also subject to change over time and these, too, can sometimes have profound consequences for the public, as well as the private, sector. At the macro level, one important indicator of changing social conditions has been the labour market, which has reflected some of the broader social, economic and technological influences affecting advanced capitalist economies in the late twentieth century. At the level of the individual organisation, these influences have been felt in areas as diverse as recruitment, management style and service provision. They may ultimately have a fundamental impact on the extent of resource allocation by government. For the public sector as a whole, changing public sentiments and predispositions, whatever their root cause, could challenge or sustain the whole basis of future welfare provision, giving rise to either a depleted or an enhanced pattern of services funded from the public purse.

One change that has occurred in recent years has been the rise in the expectations of members of the public about public services. As Osborne and Gaebler have put it, 'one size fits all' government is no longer appropriate since American society has been transformed from a mass society to 'a mosaic society with great cultural diversity, even with the middle class. We have come to expect products and services customized to our own styles and tastes, from television networks to restaurants and beer' (1992, p 168). This demand for choice extends to public services in both the USA and the UK and is reflected in the Charter movement which we discuss in Chapter 16.

Demographic change

Information on the size and structure of a country's population is vital for an understanding of many aspects of society including the labour market and the general composition of households; it also provides a valuable insight into the demand for various public services including education, health and social security benefits.

An examination of actual and projected demographic change in the United Kingdom in the period 1971–2031 reveals a picture familiar in much of the developed world, that of a growing and ageing population. In 1971 the UK population was estimated to be just under 56 million people; it rose to over 58 million by 1994. Projections for the next century suggest that there will be almost 60 million people in the UK by 2001 and that this figure will grow to a little over 62 million by 2031 (*see* Table 2.1).

Table 2.1 UK population trends: Mid-year estimates and projections (millions)

1971	1981	1991	2001	2031
55.93	56.35	57.81	59.80*	62.24*

*projections.
Source: Based on *Social Trends 1996*.

Clear evidence of an ageing population is provided by an analysis of age distribution over the same time period (*see* Table 2.2). In 1971 around a quarter of the UK population was under the age of 16 and approximately 13 per cent were over 65. By 1994 the respective figures were 21 per cent and 16 per cent, with a quarter (4 per cent) of the latter figure being people aged 80 or over. This trend is projected to continue well into the twenty-first century, with the under-16s expected to make up just under 18 per cent of the population by 2031; those over 65 will comprise around 23 per cent, a third of whom will be aged 80 or over.

Table 2.2 UK population by age distribution: estimates and projections (percentages)

	Under 16 (%)	16–64 (%)	65–79 (%)	80 and over (%)
1971	25	61	11	2
1981	22	63	12	3
1991	20	64	12	4
1994	21	64	12	4
2001*	21	64	11	4
2031*	18	58	16	7

*projections.
Source: Based on *Social Trends 1996*.

The reasons for such changes in the age structure of the UK population are well known and include the downward trend in the number of live births since the 'baby boom' in the 1960s and the increasing longevity resulting from a combination of social, economic and medical developments. As far as the rising elderly population is concerned, it is estimated that those aged 60 or over have increased by over a third since 1961 and now number 12 million; by 2031 the figure is expected to be around 18 million. Moreover within this group there has been a much sharper increase in the numbers of very elderly people, with the proportion of the over 60s who are aged 80 or over rising from 11 per cent in 1961 to 19 per cent in 1994 and projected to increase to 22 per cent by 2031. As politicians and economists have come to recognise, these actual and projected increases could have very significant implications for the provision of pensions and health care in the foreseeable future.

The proportion of the population over retirement age, together with those under working age, constitutes what is known as the 'dependent population', a crude measure of the number of people within the population who are supported economically by those of working age. Figures produced by the Government Actuary's Department suggest that whereas child dependency is likely to fall in future as a result of the fall in the birth rate, elderly dependency will grow significantly by 2031 following a period of relative stability. As a consequence, although overall dependency (i.e. child dependency plus elderly dependency) should fall from around 64 per cent of the working population in 1994 to 58 per cent by 2021, it is expected to rise quickly to 68 per cent by 2031 and to rise even further in subsequent years (*see* Table 2.3), placing an increased burden on the economically active proportion of the population as well as on the public services.

Socio-cultural change

Whereas demographic change lends itself, by and large, to statistical measurement, analysing social and cultural changes often tends to be more nebulous and impressionistic and is usually based on observed trends in the structure and characteristics of households and families and on opinion poll findings. That said, it is still important to gain an understanding of changes in the social composition of the population and in its attitudes and values since both can have an impact on the extent and pattern of public service provision.

Table 2.3 UK projected dependency rates (percentages)

	Child dependency (%)	Elderly dependency (%)	Overall dependency (%)
1994	34	30	64
2001	33	29	62
2031	29	39	68
2061	29	44	73

Source: Government Actuary's Department (adapted).

CASE STUDY 2.1

Demographic trends have important implications for economic and social policy makers. One international trend that we have already is the ageing population that is affecting most industrialised nations. The policy consequences are a matter for debate at national and supra-national level and have implications for the role of government and the use of markets for delivering support for the ageing.

PENSIONS TIMEBOMB

By Jonathan Guthrie

The European Commission seems to be getting very concerned about pensions provision within Europe. What's the problem? The main problem is a falling birth rate. European pensioners get the bulk of their pension income from state schemes run on a pay-as-you-go (PAYG) basis. This means the money comes from taxation of people who are working. That is fine as long as the ratio of pensioners to workers is declining or static.

But longevity is increasing and birth rates are dropping, partly because generous state pensions support old people more comfortably than big families ever did. This means a shrinking number of working people have to support a growing number of elderly.

Currently there are four people of working age for every pensioner in the European Union. By 2040 it is estimated there will be just two. The result is a growing strain on some EU economies as the tax burden rockets.

Which countries are worst affected and why? Those where birth rates have fallen, or are falling, from a relatively high base. The pain is intensified when a big proportion of pensioners' income is paid by state PAYG schemes. Countries in this group include Germany, Italy and France. For example, Germany's state pension system was reportedly DM10bn (£3.5bn) in deficit in 1995, when contributions were increased to a steep 19.2 per cent of taxable earnings.

It may get worse. By 2030 pension payouts will have risen to a hefty 15 to 20 per cent of gross domestic product in all three countries if maintained at present levels. Both France and Italy have cut state pensions and introduced measures to encourage more private provision. The cost was rioting in the streets and a watering down of the reforms.

Will the UK be affected too? The bulge in the proportion of elderly in the population is not expected to strain the UK's public finances too badly. That is partly because the birth rate has not fallen heavily. Moreover state PAYG schemes account for a relatively small part of pensioners' income. For example, the UK basic state pension is worth only 12 per cent of average adult male earnings. An equivalent German scheme is worth 60 per cent of average adult male earnings.

If state provision is so low, where do UK pensioners get their income? Many get a big chunk of it from private funded pension schemes. The beauty of the schemes is that each new generation – typically with assistance from employers – provides for its own retirement by investing in tradeable assets, such as shares. These rise in value over time, reducing the amount of contributions required.

Bill Birmingham of the National Association of Pension Funds, a trade body, estimates the UK has £600bn in private pension assets, a huge bulwark against future needs. The Republic of Ireland and the Netherlands also have big funded pension systems, and are also thus relatively immune from the financial squeeze affecting some other EU nations.

What is the European Commission doing to sort out the problems of those states squeezed by big unfunded pension liabilities? The commission is making belated attempts to encourage them to increase funded provision. The greater the proportion of pensions that can be provided by this means, the lower the tax burden on future generations of workers to support pensioners.

Are there any pitfalls? The snag of shifting from PAYG to a funded system is that one generation of workers has to pay twice: once through taxation used to pay pensions to their parents' generation; and once in contributions to their own retirement funds.

There is another difficulty with funded schemes. Governments can raid them – in a roundabout way – to finance public spending. The preferred method is to impose restrictions on pension funds' investments that force them to buy government bonds.

This captive market allows the government to lower its cost of borrowing at the expense of funds' long-term returns. Funded schemes can thereby become tributaries of a PAYG system. For example, Belgium requires 15 per cent of pension fund assets to be in Belgian government bonds. Other states merely specify a percentage of assets that have to be held in the local currency, referred to as 'currency matching'. That has a similar affect, given the fondness of continental investment managers for sovereign bonds.

But isn't one of the main aims of the EU that capital should be able to slosh freely over national borders? Quite so. There are suggestions that the Commission could challenge national investment restrictions through a test case in the European Court of Justice, in which it would argue they contravene the Treaty of Rome, on which the EU is founded.

Meanwhile, it has published a consultative document, which makes the case for freeing pension funds to seek the best rate of return on assets, both in the EU and outside it. The paper suggests a system of prudential regulation for pension funds, with the aim of putting paid to member states' claims that investment restrictions are needed to protect funds from taking excessive risks.

Legislation may follow.

Source: *Financial Times*, 12 June 1997. Reprinted with permission.

Questions on the case study

1 Describe the policy alternatives for reducing the commitment of the state to provide pensions.

2 The European Commission has no responsibility for paying pensions. Why should it be concerned about the issue?

3 What values can, and in your opinion should, underpin the policy choices made about future pension provision?

Looking at households and families first, there is clear evidence of quite a dramatic shift in UK experience over the last generation, comparable to that in some other parts of Europe and elsewhere. Summarised briefly, data produced by government sources show that since the early 1970s there has been:

● a fall in average household size and a marked increase in the number of one-person households;

- a decline in the proportion of 'traditional' one-family households comprising a couple with children;
- a dramatic rise in the proportion of dependent children in one-parent families;
- a substantial fall in the number of first marriages and a significant increase in the number of divorces and in the incidence of cohabiting.

Not only are many of these trends interrelated (e.g. more divorces increases the number of one-parent families), but they are a result of a complex array of social, demographic and economic changes which will inevitably alter and intensify patterns of need and which are said to be changing the constituency of welfare services in Britain and beyond as we approach the next millennium (Benington and Taylor, 1993). As Hills' work (1993) on the future of the welfare state has indicated, there is good reason to suppose that many of the present structures of welfare provision in the UK may no longer be appropriate since they are based on assumptions about social and economic conditions, many of which no longer pertain.

Alongside the above changes – and in some cases related to them – there has been a perceived shift in social attitudes and values. According to Isaac-Henry *et al.* (1997, p 5):

> People are becoming more sophisticated, discriminating, assertive and less subservient to official views and actions. They are demanding not only more services but also better quality provisions. . . [T]hey, and the interest groups representing them, are questioning the motives, values and competence of bureaucrats and professionals. They are beginning to act more like 'customers' than 'clients'.

This growth in public expectations of both the quality and quantity of service provision has given rise to a discernible degree of stakeholder conflict. Thus, although public service managers are understandably keen to meet client expectations by providing sensitive and responsive services, they are invariably being called upon to do so in a regime which promotes increased efficiency and cost savings and in which the onus appears to be on rationing rather than on meeting public demand. Squaring this circle is by no means an easy task and is one which is likely to be accompanied by a considerable degree of misunderstanding, resentment and frustration on the part of those individuals seeking access to public services and those empowered to provide them.

The changing labour market

Historically the traditional perception of work in the UK has been largely one of full-time, male occupation based predominantly on employment and on a much more modest level of self-employment and this has provided an important part of the context in which the public services, and particularly the welfare services, have been established and developed. This paradigm is increasingly looking out of date: the labour market in the 1990s is a very different place from the labour market of the past (Worthington and Britton, 1997, p 138).

Organisations in both the public and private sectors have changed their configurations, their structures and the employer–employee relationship. Many organisations now have different kinds of employees on different kinds of contracts. Will Hutton (1995) has defined the 30: 30: 40: society, which consists of the disadvantaged: the marginalised and insecure: the privileged. Hutton argues that it is only the privileged 40 per cent who have some security in the job market. He argues that two-thirds of all new jobs offered to the unemployed are part time or temporary. This change in the composition of society will have an effect on the relationship between the organisation and its employees. Analysis of labour market statistics indicates that the traditional pattern has been upset in a variety of ways:

1 Unemployment levels in the last twenty years have often been substantially above what might have been expected and there has been a significant growth in the incidence of long-term unemployment.
2 As female participation has continued to grow there has been a marked convergence between the level of male and female economic activity.
3 There has been a notable decline in the number of full-time jobs in the economy and a growth in part-time employment.
4 Self-employment has increased as has the number of individuals holding more than one job.
5 Organisations have begun to make increased use of temporary and short-term contracts.
6 Individuals now face greater job insecurity.

As indicated above, these changes raise important questions about the relevance of existing structures and practices; equally, they seem destined to have some effect upon the experiences of those employed in the public services. In a working environment in which the watchwords have become efficiency, flexibility and devolved responsibility and in which staff have frequently had to contend with threats of 'downsizing', 'restructuring' or 're-engineering', the process of change appears to have generated a growing level of uncertainty and stress, particularly at middle management level (Rigg and Trehan, 1997). For many organisations, dealing with the human aspects of change has represented a substantial challenge at a time when the concept of managing people has itself been changing.

THE ECONOMIC CONTEXT OF CHANGE

As a glance at any quality newspaper will verify, economic factors have an impact on organisations of all sizes and in all sectors of the economy. Firms producing and selling consumer durables, for instance, will be affected by such variables as interest rate changes, unemployment trends, consumer confidence, domestic and external competition and the general level of economic activity. These, together with a host of other influences at both the micro and the macro level, provide an important part of the context in which the individual decisions of consumers, producers and distributors occur in a market-based economy.

When we examine the economic environment in which the public services have developed over the last twenty to thirty years, four factors seem to have been of particular relevance:

● the changing structure of the economy;
● changing attitudes to state provision;
● increased public expenditure restraint;
● changing economic orthodoxies.

These factors are, of course, interrelated. Moreover in the case of the last three, successive governments – under pressure from a variety of sources – have played a major role in driving through change and their impact in shaping public attitudes to the role of the state in a market economy has been undeniably significant. Early indications are that the new Labour administration under Tony Blair is unlikely to disturb the status quo.

The changing structure of the economy

A country's economic structure is determined by the mix of industries which produce its output of goods and services and employ its population. These industries and the broad sectors in which they tend to be grouped represent the component parts of the economy and these are subject to change over time as a result of changes in such factors as income and tastes, demography, technology, resource availability and international competition (*see*, for example, Griffiths and Wall, 1997). It is changes in the relative size of an economy's component elements, whatever their origin, which govern the shape and direction of structural change.

It is common to distinguish between the primary sector which is made up of activities related to natural resources, the secondary sector which comprises activities concerned with the production of goods and the tertiary sector which is concerned with services, both public and private. An analysis of output and employment figures for the UK economy over the last thirty years or so illustrates how quickly the country's economic structure has been transformed (*see* Table 2.4). In 1964 the secondary sector contributed two-fifths of the economy's output and employed around 11 million workers, with manufacturing alone being responsible for 30 per cent of gross domestic product (GDP) and almost nine million jobs. By 1995 secondary industries accounted for less than 30 per cent of GDP and under 5 million jobs, with manufacturing now contributing only about one-fifth of GDP and employing less than 4 million workers. In employment terms alone, manufacturing's contribution fell from around 40 per cent of total employment in 1964 to less than 20 per cent by 1995, representing a loss of five million manufacturing jobs in the economy.

Table 2.4 Employment by sector (percentages)

	1964	1973	1990	1995
Primary	5.1	3.4	2.1	1.7
Secondary	46.9	42.4	26.6	22.6
Tertiary	47.8	54.4	71.3	75.4

Note: Figures are rounded.
Source: Central Statistical Office.

The picture in the tertiary sector is somewhat different. Between 1964 and 1995 the sector's share of GDP rose from just over one half to two-thirds, whereas employment grew from around 11 million jobs to over 16 million, with the majority of the expansion in the financial sector and in various professional and scientific services. By 1995 employment in the public and private services had grown from a little under 50 per cent of total employment to just over 75 per cent, an increase of between five and six million service jobs.

This relative decline in the significance of industrial output and employment as compared to the service sector is by no means unique to the UK. Figures produced by the European Union and by the Organisation for Economic Co-operation and Development show a similar picture in other advanced industrial economies, although the scale of change varies between countries (*see* e.g. European Commission, 1996). The significant fact as far as the British economy is concerned is that for much of the 1980s and 1990s the decline in the secondary sector, and in particular in manufacturing, has been absolute as well as relative and recent improvements in manufacturing output have done little to improve the situation – which has largely been one of negligible growth. Moreover, whereas the substantial job loss in the manufacturing sector has been accompanied by job gains in the service sector, the net effect for the period as a whole has been one of net job loss at a time when the number of people in the labour force has been steadily increasing. Leaving aside the question of whether redundant miners or steel workers could expect to take advantage of the new jobs in banking, information technology or the insurance industry, it is clear that the UK economy has suffered a significant loss of jobs as a result of structural and technological changes and this has posed important problems for the public services, not least for those involved in education and training, the social services and in the administration of social security benefits.

Academic explanations of the underlying causes of structural change vary considerably. For some the process of industrial decline and restructuring is linked to the stage of economic development, with the relative maturity of the economy resulting inevitably in a shift in emphasis towards services and away from manufacturing as demand conditions change. Some writers see this as a natural response to a process of wider economic and industrial change taking place in Western society, encapsulated in the terms 'post-Fordism' and 'post-modernism' (*see*, *inter alia* Harvey, 1989; Healey *et al.*, 1995). Others tend to take a less all-embracing view, pointing to such influences as the effects of North Sea oil on the exchange rate and hence on trade in manufactures or the problem of low-wage competition from lesser-developed economies. A third explanation blames the decline of British industry on the growth in the non-market public sector (e.g. health care and education). Under this view, popularised by Bacon and Eltis (1976), a burgeoning public sector was seen as responsible for 'crowding out' the market sector by consuming resources which the private sector could have used, but without producing any marketable output in return. Although this latter thesis has been subject to considerable criticism since it first appeared, there is little doubt that the proposition that the rapid growth in the non-market public sector was responsible for many of the economy's problems (e.g. higher taxes, higher interest rates, low investment, inflation, balance of payments) found considerable support in political circles and helped to provide the intellectual backing to the Conservative government's approach to fiscal policies after 1979.

Changing attitudes to state provision

Table 2.5 compares levels of government expenditure and government employment in a number of selected developed countries. Differing political histories and attitudes to the role of the state as a provider of services are among the factors that explain the large differences in levels of public expenditure as a percentage of national income. Similar differences can be observed when one compares government employment as a percentage of total employment. The contrast is at its most stark when we compare Sweden with Japan; this reflects Sweden's post-war social democratic welfare policy background.

The process of intergenerational economic change in the United Kingdom has also been marked by a significant measure of state disengagement from economic activity, commonly referred to as 'privatisation'. When the Conservatives took office under the leadership of Mrs Thatcher in 1979, large parts of British industry – including energy,

Table 2.5 Comparative government expenditure and employment, 1995

	Current general government expenditure (% of GDP)	Government employment (% of total employment)
France	50.9	24.8
Germany	46.7	15.9
Ireland	40.4 [b]	13.4 [a]
Japan	27.0 [a]	6.0 [a]
Sweden	66.4	32.0
United Kingdom	42.3 [a]	14.4
USA	35.8 [b]	14.0 [a]

Notes:
[a] 1994 figures.
[b] 1993 figures.
Source: Based on OECD (1997), *National Accounts*. Paris: OECD.

water, transport and communications – were under state ownership and control and government was responsible for providing a wide range of publicly funded services at national, regional and local level. Almost two decades later, most of the former public corporations and nationalised industries are now private sector organisations (e.g. gas, the electricity generating and supply industries, the water authorities and telecommunications), operating on a commercial basis in an increasingly competitive and deregulated marketplace. In addition, central government has required or allowed local authorities to sell off some of their assets (e.g. council houses, playing fields), has introduced competitive tendering and 'market testing' in the public sector, privatised a number of government agencies (e.g. Her Majesty's Inspectors of Education), permitted private funding of major capital projects normally funded by the taxpayer (e.g. hospitals and roads) and has established internal markets in the health service. 'Experiments' of this kind have occurred in most countries, including the former planned economies of eastern Europe, and the Chinese government has recently announced a substantial programme of privatisation involving the sale of loss-making state industries.

It is widely accepted that the roots of privatisation policy lie in an attempt by the Thatcher government to tackle the perceived deficiencies in the supply side of the UK economy. Central to the government's philosophy was the belief that the free market was a superior method of allocating economic resources and that large-scale state involvement in business activity hampered economic progress. 'Rolling back the frontiers of the state' by reducing the size of the public sector was seen as a key component in improving the country's economic performance at both national and international level.

The government's case for privatisation centred on the claim that the sale of state-owned businesses would improve their efficiency and general performance and would, through increased competition, help to broaden consumer choice. Under state ownership and control, it was felt that businesses had no incentive to strive for efficiency or to respond to consumer preferences since many of them lacked any direct competition and all of them could turn to government for financial support if revenue was insufficient to meet operating costs. In contrast, firms which were exposed to the 'test of the market' would have to satisfy both the consumer and the financial markets if they were to survive or to avoid take-over by more efficient and competitive organisations.

Allied to this was the proposition that privatisation would improve the performance of an organisation's management and workers. Freed from the need to meet objectives laid down by politicians and civil servants, management could concentrate on commercial goals such as profitability, improved productivity and cost reduction, and on encouraging greater flexibility, technical innovation and a more customer-centred approach. Implicit in these claims was an acceptance that a considerable degree of restructuring would need to occur in each privatised organisation and that this was likely to act as an incentive to the workforce to improve its performance. Additional encouragement was also expected to derive from the introduction of employee share-ownership schemes which would give employees a financial stake in the organisation's future.

The sale of shares to employees and to the public generally was also presented as a benefit of privatisation in that it helped to encourage wider share ownership and to create a 'share-owning democracy' with increased sympathies towards capitalist modes of production (and possibly the Conservative government). Concomitantly, the sale of state assets also served to reduce the size of the Public Sector Borrowing Requirement (PSBR), since revenue from sales was treated as negative public expenditure, and this would help to reduce the size of the government's debt and to take some of the pressure off interest rates, as well as releasing funds for use by the private sector.

As far as the non-industrial public sector is concerned, the presumed benefits of state disengagement appear to have been limited and the government has been restricted by both technical and political constraints in extending privatisation to the mainstream public services. Apart from the introduction of contracting out, the decision to allow council house sales and attempts to privatise pensions, state disengagement in this area has largely been 'tokenism', exemplified by the government's efforts to encourage schools to opt out of local authority control and hospitals to become self-governing trusts. Even the much-vaunted Private Financing Initiative (PFI) has done little to reduce state involvement in funding capital projects, as the private sector has remained cautious in committing its money to projects where the anticipated rate of return on investment can be difficult to calculate (*see* Cook, 1996).

Public expenditure restraint

Public expenditure has a tendency to increase over time. For much of the period since the end of the Second World War spending by UK central and local government has risen in both money and 'real' terms and on average has grown as a percentage of national income. Current estimates suggest that in 1996/7 the government intended to spend around £306 billion, representing about 40 per cent of gross national product (GNP) at factor cost. Of this, almost half was to be spent on health, personal social services and social security programmes.

Part of the explanation for the upward trend in public expenditure lies in the approach adopted by successive post-war governments to the management of the economy. In essence until the early 1970s macroeconomic policy making tended to be based on broadly 'Keynesian' principles which advocated the management of aggregate demand as the means of achieving the government's policy objectives, particularly the creation and maintenance of full employment. Under this interventionist approach, fiscal policy – the manipulation of government expenditure and/or taxation – assumed primary importance and increases in public spending became one of the government's key weapons in the fight against unemployment.

Doubts about the wisdom of this 'fine tuning' approach to economic management began to emerge in the early 1970s as a combination of adverse economic circumstances and new orthodoxies called into question the policy of short-term fiscal intervention. Although economic historians may differ in their interpretations of this period, there appears to be general agreement that the key pressures for change included:

● the growing perception in official circles that fiscal intervention was increasingly unable to deal with the twin problems of rising unemployment and rising inflation;
● the effects of the oil crisis in 1974 which appeared to undermine the assumed relationships and trade-offs between policy objectives;
● the impact of new schools of economic thought, such as monetarism, which emphasised the importance of the supply side of the economy and the need to control public expenditure as part of a longer-term strategy of monetary control.

The sterling crisis of 1976 and the subsequent demand by the International Monetary Fund (IMF) that the UK government should seek to control the growth in the money supply as a precondition for a $3.9 billion loan gave the process of change a further push and, with hindsight, heralded the start of a new approach to the management of the economy and to the role played by public spending and taxation in determining performance at both the macro and micro level.

It is no coincidence that when the Conservatives returned to office in 1979 they were elected on two major policy platforms: to cut public spending as part of a monetarist approach to the control of inflation and to reduce the perceived dead-weight effect of income tax on incentives to enterprise. As far as the former was concerned, the new government argued that a Medium-Term Financial Strategy (MTFS) was required which would help to constrain the growth in the money supply and hence the tendency to inflation in the economy. Since there was felt to be a close relationship between the money supply and the PSBR, reductions in the size of the PSBR, mainly by reducing public expenditure, were seen as fundamental to the success of the new approach. In effect, fiscal policy was to be subordinated to the needs of monetary policy – which was to become the government's main policy instrument.

Although the record shows that since 1979 successive administrations have found it difficult to halt the rise in public spending as demand-led expenditures (e.g. pensions, social security benefits) have grown, the evidence indicates that there has been slightly more success in recent years in cutting spending as a proportion of GDP. How far this is attributable to recent growth in the economy or to changes in procedures (e.g. the introduction of new control totals for the majority of general government expenditure) or to the influence of supranational developments (e.g. the Maastricht criteria for EU fiscal convergence) is difficult to say and it remains to be seen whether the downward trend will continue, particularly if future growth rates do not reach anticipated levels. What does seem likely, however, is that present and future administrations will continue to regard public expenditure restraint as an important element of macroeconomic policy and this will have implications for the public services as social and demographic circumstances change.

Changing ideological perspectives

As indicated above, changing official attitudes to public expenditure reflected in part the development of alternative economic orthodoxies. To what extent the new thinking was a cause or an effect of economic change is debatable, but there seems little doubt that it has had a formative effect on decision makers at the highest levels of government. Isaac-Henry *et al.* (1997) have argued that a combination of changing economic circumstances – including the decline of the UK's industrial base and the increasing problem of public sector finance – provided the conditions in which a new approach could take root and gain acceptability. The theoretical basis on which this new approach was founded owed much to the work of Hayek and Friedman and to the public choice theorists.

The essence of what has become loosely known as 'New Right' thinking, which contains a mixture of ideas and prescriptions, is that given a free choice rational politicians and bureaucrats are likely to act in their own self-interest and seek expansion, since this will enhance their status. One implication of this behaviour is that pressure groups will tend to organise to promote expansionist public spending. Consequently, state expenditure is likely to be much higher than might otherwise be the case and the state is destined to be more active in economic affairs and in the general management of the economy. In *The Road to Serfdom* (1944) Hayek had argued that growing state intervention and state decision making would eventually result in a lack of choice by individuals and would give rise to a 'dependency culture', whereas the free market provided the basis of individual economic and political freedom. Friedman (Friedman and Friedman, 1980) has been equally critical of the role of the state, arguing that high levels of public expenditure pose a threat to freedom and democracy and has called on government to direct its attention to controlling inflation via controlling the money supply, rather than seek to manage demand through fiscal intervention.

All the evidence indicates that ideas such as these, and those put forward by right-wing 'think tanks' (e.g. the Institute of Economic Affairs; the Adam Smith Institute), struck a chord with the new leaders of the Conservative party after 1975 and when the party was returned to office in 1979 Mrs Thatcher and her senior advisers – particularly Keith Joseph – set about the reform of both institutions and attitudes. As Norman Flynn (1993) has suggested, although the Thatcher government's radical intentions proved difficult to implement in practice, a number of reforms were made and it is possible to identify at least four themes which illustrate the influence of 'new right' (or 'new liberal') ideas, namely that:

- market mechanisms should be used wherever possible;
- competition should be encouraged between providers, and customers should be given more choice;
- individualism and individual choice are preferable to collective action;
- state provision should be kept to a minimum.

Alongside this new ideological stance, the new government attempted to introduce a more 'managerial' approach to public administration, using leading industrialists as advisers on how to bring private sector approaches to the management of the public sector and introducing a number of initiatives designed to improve managerial efficiency and cost control.

Although there is some doubt in academic circles as to whether the period after 1979 represented a 'step change' in policy towards the welfare state (*see*, for example, Jordan and Ashford, 1993; Marsh and Rhodes, 1992), it would be wrong to underestimate the degree to which the belief in the innate superiority of the market, as a means of allocating resources and as a guarantor of economic and political freedom, has come to hold sway. This has had important implications for long-cherished principles such as universality and access to services. As suggested above, the recent change of government appears to have done little to alter either attitudes or rhetoric, with choice and efficiency remaining key concepts and the need to control public expenditure in order to reduce levels of taxation a central plank of the Blair administration's economic policy. Perhaps, as some have suggested, the essential legacy of Thatcherism lies not in the wholesale restructuring of the welfare state but in its contribution to attitudes, ideas and approaches; this does not make it any less considerable (Wilding, 1992).

IMPLICATIONS FOR PUBLIC SERVICE MANAGERS

In what ways have the changes outlined above affected managers working in the public services?

Although the answer to this question depends to some degree on the service concerned, and within a service may vary in different geographical locations, it is possible to identify a number of major themes which appear to apply across the public services generally and which look likely to continue to be relevant in the foreseeable future.

Pressure for budgetary restraint

Changing demographic and economic circumstances have played a major role in increasing the level of public expenditure, particularly on welfare services, and this has put the national budget under considerable strain. In political circles a consensus seems to have emerged concerning the need to restrain the growth in public spending relative to GDP in order to ensure that the country remains internationally competitive and can qualify for membership of the single European currency. For those public services faced with a combination of increasing demand and growing expectations, a policy of restraint – however justifiable this may be in macroeconomic terms – normally means a 'real' reduction in funding and this will tend to have implications for the level of service provided and/or the people employed to provide it.

Managers operating in an environment where budgets are cut, or where the demand for services is growing while budgets remain static, can face some difficult choices. Should the volume of services be reduced so that everyone gets a lower standard of provision or should fewer people receive the service than previously was the case? Alternatively, should the staff providing the service be asked to work harder by increasing their workload for the same pay or should they be paid less, either through a reduction in rates of pay or in staff numbers? Whichever solution or combination of solutions managers may choose, the choice is destined to be unpopular among the stakeholder groups adversely affected by the change.

The implications for the working environment are not difficult to imagine. Apart from any political unpopularity which is likely to result from a cut in service provision, the withdrawal of services from people who previously received them is bound to generate some public hostility which will be felt throughout the organisation concerned and particularly by those who interface directly with the public. Although managers may be to some extent insulated from the immediate effects of public anger, any consequences of such a reaction for employee morale and motivation cannot be ignored by those responsible for the effective deployment of resources, especially when there are implications for the level of staff absenteeism or retention.

Looking for efficiency savings by reductions in staff numbers or pay or by requiring workers to increase their output can also have an impact on employee motivation and morale, making it more difficult for managers to retain staff, especially when conditions in other sectors appear more favourable. In addition to the cost implications of increased staff turnover, a demoralised and demotivated workforce clearly makes the job of managing human resources considerably more difficult and threatens to undermine the whole basis of effective service provision in the public sector.

The move towards a more competitive market environment

The idea that markets are a better way of allocating resources than the traditional planning process, and that they should be introduced wherever possible, is one of the underlying themes in public sector reform over the last twenty years. Proponents of markets have argued that compared to bureaucratic rules the market mechanism offers a far more efficient and effective means of resource allocation since it matches supply to demand, reduces waste and inefficiency and improves consumer choice through competitiveness. Promoting the introduction of markets in the public sector, along with the calls for more private provision (e.g. private pensions or health care), has assumed therefore an ideological aspect which is likely to prove more enduring than many of the reforms that have ultimately been implemented.

Although it is beyond the scope of this chapter to undertake a detailed examination of the market solutions applied across the public services, such as the introduction of internal or quasi-markets for welfare provision (*see*, for example, Le Grand, 1990; Ferlie, 1994), it is worth noting that they have taken a variety of forms and have engendered different degrees of competitiveness in different parts of the public sector, factors which clearly have implications for the task confronting managers. As Flynn (1997, p 123) has noted, the structure of a market on both the demand and supply side provides the context in which managers operate and is an important determinant of managerial responses. For example, where a market arrangement is in the form of a supplier–customer relationship *within* an organisation and competition is absent, the essential task of management in supplier organisations is to define the nature of the services being provided and to calculate unit costs. As the degree of competition increases and as purchasers become more able to choose between alternative suppliers, managers have to pay more attention to the behaviour of competitors and to those aspects of service provision which can give the organisation a competitive advantage in the marketplace (e.g. price or quality or cost reduction).

The impact on public service managers of the move towards a more market-oriented environment is exemplified by some of the changes which have occurred in attitudes and perceptions. As well as having their traditional bureaucratic and professional concerns, many managers now see their task as being to produce a 'product' which they hope will be more appealing to customers/clients than any alternative 'offering' from a competitor. Like their counterparts in the private sector, managers in public service organisations now increasingly talk of 'market strategies' and of promoting favourable 'images' or of 'beating the opposition'. The language of the accountant and the marketer have, in effect, become part of the everyday pattern of communication between managers and their staff and concerns over the revenue and cost implications of different strategies and decisions have become important preoccupations in organisations as varied as schools and health centres.

The requirement that managers embrace a paradigm more typical of a consumer market can, of course, have its drawbacks. In an environment where organisations are increasingly seen as in competition with each other and where survival may ultimately depend on attracting sufficient customers and/or on controlling costs, managers are less likely to collaborate with organisations now perceived as competitors and this may result in a loss of some of the synergistic benefits of former joint ventures (e.g. between schools). Equally there is a danger that temporary changes in consumer demand may provoke managers to look for cost savings, particularly on the staffing budget, and this may significantly weaken an organisation's ability to respond if market conditions improve. Whereas changing market conditions can provide managers (and, for that matter, politicians) with a convenient scapegoat for reductions in staffing levels, they may also help to encourage a short-term and cost-centred approach to problem solving. This is unlikely to prove effective in the longer term, particularly if the problem lies on the demand side of service provision.

Changes in management methods and practice

The move towards a competitive market environment has brought with it a more business-like approach to management based on private sector practices. Devolved budgets, cost centres, management information systems and performance indicators have become familiar features in public sector organisations and mark a move towards more accountable forms of management. Like their counterparts in the private sector, public service managers now tend to look on clients as 'customers' and are increasingly called on to introduce procedures and systems which can help to identify consumer attitudes and preferences. The vocabulary of public service management – with its talk of greater efficiency, flexibility, value for money, customer orientation and citizens' charters – underlines the development of a business culture; professional values and ethos are no longer a sufficient guide to management action and decision.

The requirement on managers to adapt to a changing managerial environment and to develop new attitudes and skills is evident across a range of public service organisations, as Pollitt (1993, p 181) found in relation to District Health Authorities (DHAs):

> DHAs had to invent the purchaser role – to become what the then Secretary of State for Health famously termed 'the people's champion'. Social Service Departments (SSDs) had to learn about contracting and needed to set up comprehensive systems for assessing individual clients' needs. Hospitals were obliged to 'market' themselves as high quality providers. Head teachers also had to 'sell' their schools as well as looking very carefully at the costs of employing above-average proportions of senior, experienced staff. Many professionals were thus propelled into roles they had never trained for and often did not relish.

In local government, for example, Whitehall's attempts to bring market disciplines into the operation of local authorities by the introduction of compulsory competitive tendering has helped to create a more commercial environment, exemplified by the requirement to operate on a trading basis (see, for example, Walsh, 1989; Wilson and Game, 1994). As local government has taken on more of an enabling role, the emphasis in the management task has shifted towards the specification of services to be provided by contractors and to checking that the services are provided in accordance with the specifications. For many this has meant the need to develop new skills in contract writing, negotiation and supervision, within a partnership framework involving external, private, voluntary and not-for-profit organisations (Lawton and McKevitt, 1995).

CONCLUSIONS

For those involved in the public services the combined effects of socio-cultural, demographic and economic change have undoubtedly posed, and will continue to pose, a considerable challenge. Whether in future this challenge can be met to the satisfaction of all the stakeholders involved depends not only on the attitudes and competences of those responsible for policy making and administration, but also on the ability of an increasingly service-based economy to provide enough resources to meet the demands of an ageing and growing dependent population while remaining internationally competitive. To put it another way, can a post-industrial economy, operating in an increasingly competitive global marketplace, generate a sufficient and sustained level of non-inflationary economic growth to support the seemingly inexorable demand for public services?

Although this may appear an academic question, for those concerned with the management of the public services the problem of resourcing is vital. At a time when demands appear to be increasing and public expectations are growing, any constraint on funding by central government – however justifiable in macroeconomic terms – will normally have an effect on the quantity and/or quality of service provision. Apart from the problem of maintaining staff morale at a time when resources are tight and when customers/clients tend to become more hostile, managers in these circumstances tend to be faced with a perennial demand to make efficiency savings. Such a demand not only may have implications for the structure or functions of the organisation, but also may challenge some of the basic principles on which it is founded and may help to develop an organisational culture which assumes that performance is best measured in crude input/output terms rather than customer satisfaction or some other form of outcome.

In the final analysis, how far the public services will continue to be affected by the changes examined above remains something of an open question. Hills (1993) has argued that concerns about a ticking 'demographic time-bomb' have been considerably exaggerated and that the purely demographic pressures in areas such as social security, health and education may now be easing. Like Hills, many observers believe that a combination of policy changes (e.g. increasing the numbers going into higher education) and economic developments, particularly any tendency to recession and growing unemployment, are likely to be as important – as sources of upward pressure on the public services – as an ageing and an increasingly consumer-conscious population.

REFERENCES

Bacon, R and Eltis, W (1976) *Britain's Economic Problem – Too Few Producers*. London: Macmillan.

Benington, J and Taylor, M (1993) 'Changes and challenges facing the UK welfare state in the Europe of the 1990s', *Policy and Politics*, 21 (2), pp 121–34.

Cook, G C (1996) *Economics Update*. Leicester: Sterling Books.

European Commission (1996) *European Economy*, 61. Brussels: European Commission.

Ferlie, E (1994) 'The creation and evolution of quasi markets in the public sector: early evidence from the National Health Service', *Policy and Politics*, 22 (2), pp 105–12.

Flynn, N (1994) *Public Sector Management* (2nd edn). Hemel Hempstead: Prentice-Hall/Harvester Wheatsheaf.

Flynn, N (1997) *Public Sector Management* (3rd edn). Hemel Hempstead: Prentice-Hall/Harvester Wheatsheaf.

Friedman, M and Friedman, R (1980) *Free to Choose: A Personal Statement*. Harmondsworth: Penguin.

Griffiths, A and Wall, S (eds) (1997) *Applied Economics* (7th edn). Harlow: Longman.

Harvey, D (1989) *The Condition of Postmodernity: An Enquiry into the Origins of Cultural Change*. Oxford: Blackwell.

Hayek, F A (1944) *The Road to Serfdom*. London: Routledge.

Healey, P, Cameron, S, Davoudi, S, Graham, S and Madani-Pour, A (eds) (1995) *Managing Cities: The New Urban Context*. Chichester: John Wiley.

Hills, J (1993) *The Future of Welfare: A Guide to the Debate*. York: Joseph Rowntree Foundation.

Hutton, W (1996) *The State We're In*. London: Vintage.

Isaac-Henry, K, Painter, C and Barnes, C. (eds) (1997) *Management in the Public Sector: Challenge and Change* (2nd edn). London: International Thomson Business Press.

Jordan, G and Ashford, N (1993) *Public Policy and the Nature of the New Right*. London: Pinter.

Lawton, A and McKevitt, D (1995) 'Strategic change in local government management', *Local Government Studies*, 21(1), Spring, pp 46–64.

Le Grand, J (1990) 'Quasi-markets and social policy', *Studies in Decentralisation and Quasi-Markets*, 1. Bristol: School of Advanced Urban Studies.

Lewin, K (1951) *Field Theory in Social Science*. New York: Harper & Row.

Marsh, D and Rhodes, R A W (1992) *Implementing Thatcherite Policies*. Buckingham: Open University Press.

Osborne, D and Gaebler, T (1992) *Reinventing Government: How the Entrepreneurial Spirit is transforming the Public Sector*. Reading, MA: Addison-Wesley.

Pettigrew, A, Ferlie, E and McKee, L (1992) *Shaping Strategic Change: Making Change in a Large Organisation. The Case of the National Health Service*. London: Sage.

Pollitt, C (1993) *Managerialism and the Public Services* (2nd edn). Oxford: Blackwell.

Rigg, C and Trehan, K (1997) 'Changing management and employment in local government', in Isaac-Henry, K, Painter, C and Barnes, C (eds) *op. cit*.

Skelcher, C (1992) *Managing for Service Quality*. Harlow: Longman.

Walsh, K (1989) 'Competition and service in local government' in Stewart, J and Stoker, G (eds), *The Future of Local Government*. London: Macmillan.

Wilding, P (1992) 'The British welfare state: Thatcherism's enduring legacy', *Policy and Politics*, 20 (3), pp 201–12.

Wilson, D. C (1992) *A Strategy of Change: Concepts and Controversies in the Management of Change*. London: Routledge.

Wilson, D and Game, C (1994) *Local Government in the United Kingdom*. Basingstoke: Macmillan.

Worthington, I and Britton, C (1997) *The Business Environment*, 2nd edn. London: Financial Times Pitman Publishing.

QUESTIONS AND DISCUSSION TOPICS

1 Distinguish between the 'context', 'content' and 'process' of change. How does the 'internal context' differ from the 'external context'?

2 What are the main forces driving organisational change? What factors are likely to determine whether the forces for organisational change or stability will ultimately prevail?

3 Examine the major social and demographic changes that have affected public service organisations over the last two decades.

4 In your opinion what are the key economic influences which have affected the development of the public services since the mid-1970s?

5 Identify some of the ways in which the job of a manager in the public services has been affected by social and economic change.

3 New technologies and public management:
issues for the information age

J A Taylor

AIMS

This chapter will:

- enable the reader to understand the critical importance of information and communication to public management;

- assess the impact of information and communication technologies in government and for new models of governance;

- adopt a critical perspective on the role of new technologies in the formation and implementation of public policies;

- evaluate the role of citizens and consumers in using new technologies and their implications for democracy.

INTRODUCTION

Set apart from mainstream perspectives on reform and change in public management, has been a distinctive, conceptually radical approach to the study of contemporary public management. It is a perspective yet to achieve widespread recognition and acceptance in the academic study of public management, but it is one that is extensively understood within the practitioner communities of government and governance. The word *informatization* (Frissen and Snellen, 1990) provides us with a conceptual entry to this approach. 'Informatisation' enables us to describe, classify and analyse contemporary public management by reference to a specific combination of changes that are occurring. The first of these is a wave of technological change, that of information and communication technologies (ICTs), and the second is a wave of innovations around the development and use of information and communication. 'Informatisation' combines the view that new ICTs are vital to our appreciation and understanding of contemporary public management with a strong emphasis on the massive intensification that is occurring in the uses and flows of information in and around organisations of governance.

Public management has always been concerned with information – its collection, storage and application. Before the era of computers vast manual filing systems were in use in

45

almost every sphere of government activity. It is not surprising, therefore, that governments are among the largest users of computers. Nor is it surprising that 'back-recording' of information is currently allowing public service organisations to compile very large-scale computerised databases which combine historical and current data in new information systems.

Computers form only one of the elements of ICTs. Telecommunications is the other, and government organisations are prodigious users of these too. Governments, at both central and sub-central levels, lease and manage major voice and data networks that allow for the transmission of data and information both within their jurisdictions and, in some cases, between jurisdictions. The term ICTs thus becomes of central importance to our understanding, for it is in the technological convergence of computers and telecommunications that much of the significance of the informatisation perspective lies. It is the electronic flows of information in digital form that make up the bloodstream of contemporary government structures. As one author (Negroponte, 1995) has said: 'As one industry after another looks at itself in the mirror and asks about its future it is driven almost 100% by the ability of that company's products or services to be rendered in a digital form.' Almost all of the activities of public management comprise the management of data and information. Public management is, therefore, supremely amenable to an analysis which places information and communication at its core. Moreover, public management is also an 'industry' supremely amenable to having its administration and services 'rendered in digital form'. Once this is accepted, it follows that digital, information-bearing technologies should also be central in any analysis of public management.

'INFORMATISATION' IN ITS CONTEXT

The informatisation perspective needs further refinement before we can be entirely certain of its central importance to the study of public management. First, we must look again at ICTs and ask what *new* qualities they bring with them to information handling. Second, we must look beyond the technological context of ICTs and at their political and managerial context, if we are fully to understand the power of this perspective for contemporary public management.

How different are ICTs?

In his discussion of the emergent 'network society', Castells (1996) discusses five core features of what he terms the 'information technology paradigm'. Two general features are:

1 The pervasiveness of ICTs. These are technologies that can be deployed in all business and social contexts. They can be found in the factory and the office, the small firm or the large public bureaucracy. They pervade all business functions, from finance and personnel to service functions such as housing and social services. They are deployed in the home as well as in the voluntary organisation and small community group.

2 ICTs are *convergent* technologies. It is the combination of computers and telecommunications, in the form of computer networks, which makes these technologies so powerful. This convergence has occurred because both computers and telecommunications are now digital technologies. It is a convergence that is often referred to as 'telematics'. The next stage of technological convergence is approaching fast, as

broadcast pictures come to be rendered in digital form and as the device through which we capture them, the TV set, in effect becomes a computer.

Three other features of the network society, adduced by Castells, lend further weight to the importance of the informatisation perspective and help us elucidate it further. These three features are 'reflexivity', 'connexity' and flexibility.

Reflexivity

In the present era of profound technological change, unlike previous ones, technologies act upon information rather than simply being a response to it. Information has always under-pinned technological innovation. In the current information age a very different additional aspect has emerged. That is, the information which first produces our innovations is then itself the subject of them. Our understanding of a particular activity in public management will thus derive from the information resources that are available to us about that activity. In subjecting those information resources to critical appraisal, public managers then seek to innovate with new systems, correcting the deficiencies of the old, either by developing entirely new information resources or by subjecting existing information to new forms of analysis. Thus, it is informational innovation that fundamentally differentiates ICTs from other types of technology. Zuboff (1988) has allowed us to understand this point clearly by arguing that the contribution of these new information-bearing technologies lies in the ways in which they add an extra element of reflexivity: it makes its contribution to the product (or service) but it also reflects back on its activities and on the system of activities to which it is related. In contrast to other technologies, ICTs permit reflection upon the organisation into which they are introduced. That reflective process thereby changes human perceptions of the organisational context in both intended and unintended ways. These technologies cannot be interpreted simply as production technologies, therefore, designed to speed up and otherwise improve production and administrative processes. Whereas they might well be formally designed to bring greater velocity to transaction processing, the crucial inno-vatory importance of ICTs lies in their reflexivity. The example of circulation and control systems in public libraries makes this point clearer. From the late 1980s onwards public libraries have sought to improve their book-handling capabilities, particularly in respect of lending and returning activities. To do so they have introduced computer systems that allow them both to speed up and to make more accurate their recording of such transactions. Thus, in effect, they have automated their existing procedures. What these systems also allowed, however, was to go beyond simple automation and into informatisation, for they enabled librarians to produce a higher quality service to their consumers, based upon their improved information resources. Data captured on the circulation and control system are reworked so as to identify the book preferences of different consumer groups, for example, as well as allowing stock purchasing to be managed better by reference to actual con-sumption patterns. Moreover, informatisation also has an effect upon the nature of the work processes through which public service provisions such as libraries are delivered. As we shall see below this effect can be ambiguous. In the case of libraries, in many instances the professional workforce is released from many of the more routine aspects of its work and enabled through these new computer systems to exploit professional knowledge to a higher degree.

'Connexity'

ICTs bring a *networking logic* into the organisational world. 'Connexity' (Mulgan, 1997) thus becomes inherent in society and organisation, bringing new forms of relatedness, perhaps loose textured, even anarchic, on the one hand, or highly structured, on the other. Public management does not escape this new connexity, as we shall show below. Nor, however, are such new electronic linkages devoid of ambiguity. To be connected, to be networked electronically, is not necessarily advantageous. Networks link the powerful to the weak, the producer to the consumer, the citizen to the state. Although they may seem to convey advantages to one or other side of these relationships, or even to both sides simultaneously, it is not easy to ascertain whether ultimately they convey desirable outcomes. Information flows on these networks are flows of power and control. By design or by unintended consequence, employees or citizens can be either empowered or disempowered in their relationships with their employer or with the state. Information networks provide opportunities wherein benefits and advantages in a relationship are sought, gained and lost. To return briefly to the earlier example of librarians, new networked information systems might provide the basis for job enhancement and professional empowerment. Equally, it might provide the basis for a new relationship between the employee and the manager, a relationship in which the computer system is used to exert greater control over employed staff. Computer systems are designed around the accomplishment of specific tasks, measuring them usually with a view to speeding them up. The information they make available can enable employers and managers to exercise new forms of control as they are enabled to 'see' their organisation and the work rates of their employees in new ways.

Flexibility

Organisational and business *flexibilities* are inherent features of the network society. The growth, both of teleworking (employees working remotely, often from their homes) and 'call centre' (the emergence of large-scale telephone-based, customer-serving 'service factories'), provides two examples of this flexibility which have now become commonplace. In the network society organisational formations and relationships thus, in principle, become entirely malleable, susceptible to recasting, even to 're-engineering'. Equally, organisational outputs – the products and services of organisations – can themselves be made flexible and shaped and tailored to specific consumer groups so as to meet particular requirements. New forms of organisational integration, both functional and consumer oriented, thus become the norm.

To return once more to our example of public libraries, what we can expect to see, according to this analysis, is the development of new relationships between the strategic managers of a public library system, a system which might cover a wide geographical area and include numerous individual libraries, and the operational staff. There is already evidence that services are becoming differentiated and made more flexible, with individual libraries in a group of libraries specialising in particular areas. For the consumer, such flexibilities promise much. Not least, they promise that consumer preferences will shape local bookstocks in a new consumer-responsive mode of delivery rather than delivery being shaped by a producer-dominated service.

Each of these features of the 'network society', when taken separately, has important practical implications for public management. When taken together, these features suggest new and profound imperatives for the practice of public management. They suggest that the intrinsic value of information should be exploited to its optimum so as to secure the public good, however defined. Moreover, they suggest that new connections should be realised between producers and consumers within the polity and that innovations in organisational forms and service deliveries should be sought from the inherent flexibilities that the technologies bring to bear. Table 3.1 seeks to capture these imperatives as they apply specifically to public management. It suggests that new 'principles of management' are unfolding as the information age comes upon us, principles that reflect the information intensiveness which is coming to characterise our systems of public management.

Table 3.1 Information-age principles for public management

Traditional principles of old public administration	Emergent principles of the new public management
1 Uniformity of provision	Targeted provision in search of economy, efficiency and effectiveness – *the business principle*
2 Hierarchical structure in bureaucratic organisation – *the top-down control principle*	Flexible structure in an enabling public – *the network management principle*
3 Division of work – the dominance of *the functional principle*	The convergence of services – the growing significance of the *integrative principle*
4 Paternalisitic relationships to clients – *the professional principle*	Responsive relationships to customers and citizens – the *'whole person' principle*

Source: Taylor (1992).

NEW TECHNOLOGIES – FOR GOOD OR ILL?

What we must avoid as we take on this informatisation perspective is the tendency displayed in so much of the literature on the information age. Thus there is a common predisposition towards extreme simplifications whereby these technologies are seen as heralding either a new golden age, or Utopia, or a dire and wretched Orwellian nightmare of control. A preferable, and more balanced, view is that the character of these technologies is such that they have little in the way of intrinsic propensity that can lead in either of these directions. On this view the technologies hold in their application the simultaneous potential for both 'Big Brother' and 'Soft Sister'. For example, whereas officials might use computer systems to manage their own caseloads better and thus be released from much tedium and mundanity, a networked machine is also capable of providing management with information about the work rates of employees. Equally, the citizen of a state might be supplied with empowering forms of information through these technologies yet, simultaneously, the movements and transactions of the citizen might become more amenable to tracking and control.

The new ICTs introduce new capabilities into public management, but they do not determine specific outcomes, one way or the other. To take a prior position on the impact of ICTs, as many academic commentators have done, is misguided. Polarised views have high value in bringing forward specific issues for celebration, investigation, vigil and condemnation. They have low value if their effect is to pre-form our understanding. There is a danger that the power of these opposing ways of understanding technology in organisations may lock successive generations of students and researchers into ideas that will crowd out the development of new ways of thinking about information and its communication. This is a danger which we must avoid.

PUBLIC MANAGEMENT IN AN INFORMATION POLITY

Public management sits at the centre of a network of relationships that comprise the polity or political system. As new ICTs come to be more and more at the core of public management so informatisation becomes a useful concept through which to explore public management in the polity. It is for this reason that we can use the concept of the 'information polity' (Taylor and Williams, 1991). The information polity should be interpreted as a set of relationships within the political milieu of public management that are information intensive; that are profoundly amenable to exploitation through new ICTs; and that are an arena for innovations in the use of new ICTs.

The relationships to be found in the polity are many and varied. Four sets of relationships that lie at the core of the information polity are analysed (Bellamy and Taylor, 1998). The first three of these relationships are recognisably the analytical stuff of mainstream public management, though they are approached here from the informatisation perspective. The fourth is more specific to information-age public management, for it concerns the provision of the technologies, in particular the 'superhighways', through which the first three relationships are increasingly being conducted. Whereas public management has always been concerned with the provision of an enabling infrastructure for its own service delivery, what is different here is that the electronic infrastructures of the information age are not specific to particular outputs of government. Rather, they are generic, serving to underpin all kinds of public management activities. Dependence on these infrastructures is widespread, and growing, across the organisations of government.

Internal relationships in the machinery of government

The internal relationships of the machinery of government are both 'horizontal' across units, departments or ministries, and 'vertical' between levels of government, central ministries and agencies, regional administration and local administration. Many of these relationships represent highly sequential processes in public administration. One such is that of the criminal justice system which takes an accused person through the multi-agency 'funnel', from police arrest, through appearances in the courts, to prison, probation, or both. Here the funnel combines central departments and agencies with locally administered services in a pattern of vertical and horizontal relationships.

What is striking in relationships such as these is the combination of informational interdependency and independence in this complex institutional setting. Thus the various actors and agencies of the criminal justice system are both operationally independent of each other and engaged with the system as a whole through data and information exchanges. Criminal courts, the Home Office, the Lord Chancellor's Department, the

Crown Prosecution Service, the 51 local police forces in Britain, the locally organised probation services and over 100 prisons all have common data needs within the criminal justice system. The operational independence of these organisations is sustained by long-standing constitutional separations, separations that in turn give rise to normative and cultural differences between them. Each stakeholder organisation in the criminal justice system in effect translates these normative and cultural differences into their own 'information domain', thereby ensuring that the definitions and meanings attached to individual parts of the system remain distinctive. Informatisation has brought challenges to these historic separations yet it has not done so overwhelmingly. The evidence that we have about the computerisation of the criminal justice system is that existing organisational and informational domains are extremely resistant to the potential for integration which the technologies introduce (Bellamy and Taylor, 1996). Although there may be a strategic case and a desire for changes in the collection and sharing of information across a system there is also a case to be made against it and in favour of constitutional separations and separate information domains.

This analysis bears the echoes of the movement for the 'reinvention of government' that has begun to emerge in the 1990s (Osborne and Gaebler, 1992). Indeed, in the United States, where this line of argument began, it has been closely linked for the most part with the potential of ICTs for effecting this reinvention. The reinvention debate is thus intimately linked to the arguments about re-engineering organisations, through techniques such as Business Process Re-engineering (BPR). British governments have taken up the theme of re-engineering in recent years, with ICTs being seen as crucial tools in its realisation. The bureaucracies of government, with their origins in the nineteenth century, are increasingly being criticised as inappropriate for the coming information age.

This movement to reinvent and re-engineer organisational structures is examined again at the end of this chapter. It is critical to understand at this point that information and communication play vital roles in how governments do their business internally, for the machinery of government is essentially a set of informational relationships and domains. It is not surprising that once this point of view is adopted, new arguments are brought forward to reinvent and re-engineer government organisation through alterations to these flows and domains.

Government relationships with consumers

Government relationships with consumers in the polity are the subject of innovations in relation to the use of ICTs in a number of ways, some highly visible, and some less so. Realising the potential that accompanies the extensive diffusion of ICTs, with its potential for electronic service delivery (ESD), has become a major preoccupation of governments, not least the UK's Conservative government to 1 May 1997. It published Green Papers under the rubric of *government.direct*. This preoccupation should not interpreted as being linked to political party preferences in any strong sense. The new Labour government in the UK, for example, is proving to be at least as enthusiastic a proponent of ICT applications to improve the quality and efficiency of government as was its predecessor.

CASE STUDY 3.1

This chapter considers in detail attempts by government to use electronic forms of communication to interact with citizens. This article describes an initiative announced by the Conservative Government in 1997.

PILOT PROJECTS PROVIDE ELECTRONIC INFORMATION

By Alasdair Barron

New delivery systems offer substantial savings compared to paper-based information.

The UK government's vision of user-friendly government services to be delivered direct to citizens in their homes and public places is set out in the recent Green Paper, entitled 'Government direct'.

The technology now exists 'to bring government to the people, giving them access at a time and place convenient to them,' says Roger Freeman, public service minister.

With the benefit of private and public links, the UK government will be accessible to businesses and to members of the public, 24 hours a day, seven days a week, with instant responses in many cases.

'We believe that many people will prefer to use these systems, rather than paper, and that it will be possible to offer secure access to government so that people can check their private information in the same way that balances can be checked at a cash machine', he says. Three new pilot projects have been set up in order to assess the success of electronic information delivery to the public.

'Direct Access Government' brings together official forms and regulatory guidance from all the main government departments to provide a 'one-stop regulation shop'. The service is available free of charge from trial locations, as well as via the Internet.

The information displayed on a recipient's screen can be printed out, but as yet there is no way to return forms electronically. This is expected to follow soon when issues such as establishing the validity of electronic signatures have been solved.

A 'touch screen' pilot will provide information on tax, VAT and national insurance; and in Scotland, the Scottish Land Information Service pilot provides information to individuals and businesses. According to Graham Jordan, director of the Central Information Technology Unit, Citu, the government hopes to use the expertise of the private sector to deliver electronic services which will provide substantial cost savings over paper systems.

Those savings will finance electronic delivery in future. The use of a number of delivery systems to provide services is being considered. For example, existing financial networks could be used to make services available through public access points. 'It's vital to make our electronic communications as user-friendly as possible, and one of our aims is to use responsive dialogue with prompts, as an aid to filling in forms correctly,' says Mr Jordan.

The Green Paper is the first to be published in CD-Rom form. It is a visually attractive product with graphics, video, and word-searchable text. Pre-prepared questions with space for user-comment are provided.

Making the Green Paper available free over the Internet, and in CD-Rom form for £4.25 from the CCTA (Central Computer and Telecommunications Agency), will have income implications for HMSO which supply the traditional printed version for £6.85 through HMSO bookshops.

One of the reasons for a planned review of Crown copyright issues later this year is the need to open the way to expand these electronic information services.

The Green Paper was produced by Citu, part of the Cabinet Office which was established a year ago to harness the latest technology, to improve co-ordination across government, and the effective delivery of services to the public.

One of the driving forces behind the move to electronic services is a commitment to improving 'national competitiveness', particularly by giving businesses better access to information.

According to the Cabinet Office, the number of comments received so far on the Green Paper is high – and half of them were received electronically.

Source: Financial Times, 5 March 1997. Reprinted with permission.

Questions on the case study

1 Who are the primary audiences for these forms of communication?

2 To what extent can this development be seen as a development in democratic government as opposed to a development in efficient government interaction with business?

3 Can you identify how you, as a citizen or a user of public services, have used information and communication technologies to interact with government?

Some examples of contemporary innovations in ESD are:

- the computerisation of paper records, leading to increased efficiency in dealing with consumer enquiries, such as in the registration of land, for example, enabling speedier property purchases;
- information kiosk facilities to apply for licences, passports etc.
- 'smart cards', which are used to cut costs as well as to improve service quality when dealing with requests for information or when conducting some welfare transactions;
- on-line services which enable job searching and the running of business partnerships;
- call centre innovations using 'computer-integrated telephony', enabling fast and efficient help in progressing consumer enquiries;
- multimedia applications enabling the enhancement of service provisions such as in telemedicine, aspects of social welfare and education.

Examples such as these raise profound organisational issues, for the optimal realisation of the potential gains of these innovations is by no means a simple technical matter. There is no technological determinism in innovations such as these. Their success will lie in organisational adjustments and recastings of the kind that the following key questions raise for public management:

- How can departmentalised arrangements become more integrated, so as to produce the seamlessness of government that is usually offered as a distinctive benefit to the consumer of public services in the information age?
- Can government accounting systems, focused on discrete business units, be shaped so as to encourage and support this desirable integration, rather than, as at present, to support differentiated provision?
- Can narrowly focused 'business case' methodologies for systems developments become broader in their orientation? New systems can be risky ventures, with their gains to a significant extent being amenable only to qualitative, not quantitative evaluation. Current business case methods tend to be risk averse, and, as the product of bureaucratic organisations, they are precluded from taking advantage of the high potential for qualitative improvements which new systems offer.
- Can mutually beneficial strategic alliances between public, private and voluntary sectors be encouraged into existence as public management moves from a government to a governance setting? Vertically integrated government is being replaced by a fragmented governance system whose success will depend in large measure on horizontal integration among the players. As we shall see below, without such strong alliances the business case for improved telecommunications infrastructure investment, upon which so much of information-age government depends, will be lost.

- Can a cash-constrained public service offer the levels of remuneration required to retain staff? There is at present a dearth of ICT skills, and it is predicted that this shortage will become increasingly acute up to and beyond the millennium.
- Can public management adequately handle the data privacy issues that emerge from these scenarios? Those who wish to realise the proleptic visions of the information age advocate data matching, data sharing, data donors and new surveillance systems in urban spaces. Yet each of these raises enormous problems for good public management, in relation, in particular, to the privacies which have become normatively embedded in liberal democracies.
- Can digital, broadband telecommunications, together with common network standards and protocols, be put in place universally so as to secure these potential gains for public management?

The success of public management of ESD requires that conditions such as these be realised. The success of ESD must also be judged against the nature of the relationship between the state and the consumer of services that it embodies. To what extent is that relationship one in which the consumer of public services becomes ascendant over the producer? To what extent is the service provider responsive to the needs and wants of the consumer, and are new forms of electronic communications both facilitating and realising that responsiveness? These are questions to be re-visited in later sections of this chapter.

New electronic relationships between government and citizens

The new electronic relationships between government and citizens have been the subject of intense debate for more than twenty years. Debates about 'teledemocracy', as with so many of the debates that involve ICTs, are oscillatory. That is, they ebb and flow between unbridled enthusiasm for new possibilities for direct democracy that these technologies appear to convey – a new Athenian democracy – and deep pessimism, as these same technologies are interpreted as being implicated in variants of social control – the Orwellian nightmare of the Big Brother state (Van de Donk and Tops, 1992; Van de Donk, Snellen and Tops, 1995). Optimism has risen at each technological turn of events. In the 1960s and 1970s the technical possibility of enabling the citizen to sit at the television set and vote electronically on the issues of the day seemed profoundly innovative and energising in democratic terms. In the 1990s the Internet seems capable, too, of enabling the citizen to engage in democratic processes in ways previously beyond belief. Now, rather than simply offering the prospect of more intensive voting activity, the Internet promises a more sustained citizen voice, one that can be heard in a variety of ways, as some of the examples below suggest. These examples illustrate some ways in which ICTs are involved in democratic processes. They also show how varied our conception of democracy can be, for ICTs are being used in the expectation that they can offer voice to the citizen in many different ways.

1 *Consumption is citizenship*. Capturing information about consumer preferences for public services potentially creates a more responsive system of public management. For some commentators there is an elision between consumerism, meaning the consumption of public services, and citizenship, meaning the expression of democratic voice (Corrigan, 1996). If the modern citizen is, effectively, the consumer of services,

then information about services consumption captured on computer systems can provide the perfect expression of citizen preferences. We have already seen in this chapter how public services are being informatised to become more responsive to consumer preferences.

2 *Computer-supported representative democracy.* There is at present in the UK and Europe a concern that public representatives should be supported in their information and communications needs by ICTs. At present, and taken as a whole, this support is patchy, though in some places there has been a strong effort to support public representatives in this way. In British local government a few authorities stand out as leading the way. For example, the City and County of Swansea is the pioneer in providing councillors with computers at home, electronic mail and remote access to departmental data.

3 *Direct democracy and citizenship.* Historically ICTs designed to provide enhanced voting opportunities for citizens have been one of the strongest application areas for ICTs in democracy. Much of this teledemocratic zeal has come from a view that ICTs can support more active forms of citizenship and thereby a much enhanced form of democracy. Altogether simple voting applications, pioneered in the USA in the 1960s and 1970s are now less favoured, new concepts have emerged such as the City Talks project in Amsterdam. There, citizen panels are technologically enabled to vote on specific issues immediately after watching proceedings on television. The extent to which their vote is taken into account by public representatives is described at best as uncertain.

4 *The Internet as the realisation of cyberdemocracy.* The Internet has rapidly become the centrepiece of the information age and, for many, a *sine qua non* of modern democracy. The Internet is not only encouraging active citizenship in enabling a culture of 'fetch' rather than of provision in respect of information, it also enables vast electronic mail networks supporting new forms of citizen dialogue and discussion.

5 *Democracy as 'Netizenship'.* The Internet is currently the source of innovations in addition to those discussed above. Governments, including UK central and local government, for example, have encouraged its use through the establishment of vast information resources, available over the World Wide Web (for example through www.open.gov.uk). Others are becoming more radical in their application areas as they relate to democracy. In Luxembourg, for example, citizens can vote on the performance of their Members of Parliament as well as expressing (in 'preferenda') broad policy preferences on issues of the day.

Criticising the application of new ICTs to public management

The above listing of some of the electronic innovations occurring in relation to the themes of democracy and citizenship raise many, varied questions, both about the actual innovations themselves and about the potential of ICTs to make significant gains for democratic governance. Among these questions are the following:

1 Are ICTs and the information they make available, fuelling the consumer society rather than the democratic polity? As public management becomes more knowledgeable about consumer preferences, especially from actual consumption data, does the traditional role of the elected politician begin to reduce? Are business managers in public administration now more equipped to manage day to day without the 'encumbrance' of representative democracy?

2 Why is the potential of ICTs for strengthening the role of elected politicians in decision and policy-making processes not being exploited within public management systems? Recent evidence (Taylor and Whiteside, 1998) shows that fewer than 20 per cent of British local governments have computer support for councillors as a high priority. Is the information age confirming what many critics of public management have argued for many years, that managerial values override democratic values?

3 Can electronic forms of direct democracy succeed in giving stronger voice to citizens? The evidence to date on this question at best is mixed and at worst suggests that ICTs act mainly as an apparent rather than a real adjunct to democratic activity. In the Dutch example of City Talks, cited above, it remains unclear whether the views of a citizen panel are taken into account in the making of decisions. Moreover, there is no consensus on whether citizens' views elicited in this way should be taken into account. The representativeness of citizen panels seems likely always to be questioned. Therefore the significance of their votes cannot be high.

4 Although the Internet may well provide for a range of innovations, from the provision of large amounts of data to the encouragement of citizen feedback and citizen-to-citizen discourse, concerns abound about how it should be interpreted as a vehicle for democratic expression. Information is an artefact; its provision is, it follows, constructed. It may be argued therefore that the simple provision of large quantities of information on the 'net' may not be terribly interesting if the most beneficial information in democratic terms remains neither formed nor disseminated. Moreover, experiments such as the 'preferenda' of Luxembourg, an opportunity for citizens to express policy preferences on the Web, provide the age-old problem of any plebiscitary democracy; who controls and orders the questions being asked?

5 Finally, and in contrast to the 'netizen' claims that the Internet is a potential fount of democratic expression, the problem of social exclusion returns to haunt the information age. In the UK approximately 25 per cent of households have a personal computer somewhere within them. Fewer than 5 per cent of households have a modem, however. Access to the Internet from workplaces remains the most common way of using the net, but it is clear from the data that the Internet is, as yet, far from being a mature technology which can enhance considerably the expressive needs of the democratic polity.

The ultimate judgement on ICTs as a force for democracy cannot be made unless and until we are clear about what kind of democracy we want. These new technologies will not deliver democracy of themselves. Rather, the technologies must be applied towards the realisation of a particular democratic theory. Do we want to engage citizens in political debate and voting from their homes? Do we want to strengthen the role of elected politicians through the provision of information resources? Do we wish to unleash the expressive, even anarchic, qualities of the Internet? The answers to questions such as these will shape the democratic applications of ICTs that develop. These answers will also be profoundly important for the critical investment decisions that are being made to enable the furtherance of the information age. We now turn to this last point.

Wiring up public management for the information age is increasingly contingent on the presence of digital telecommunications infrastructures. Economic developers have recognised for some time the central importance of high quality telecommunications infrastructures in attracting business firms and public bodies to relocate. Indeed there is strong evidence that the third major consideration in the location strategies of large business firms, after political stability and the availability of suitable skills, is advanced telecommunications infrastructure. It is equally increasingly clear that telecommunications is fast achieving the status of public governance infrastructure – an underlying foundation and basic framework upon and within which modern governance can be most effective (Dutton *et al.*, 1994; Bellamy and Taylor, 1998). Whether it is in the provision of information to citizens, the opening up of new possibilities for transacting electronically with consumers, innovation in the provision of services, or the re-shaping of the ways in which democratic communications occur, there is a profound dependence on high quality telecommunications infrastructure (Taylor, 1994; Taylor and Williams, 1995; Taylor and Webster, 1996).

Four key, interrelated questions are raised by this general point:

1 What is the quality of telecommunications infrastructure in particular places?
2 What is the meaning of 'universal service' provision in telecommunications, in particular, and in public services more generally?
3 What, in practice, is the 'reach' of telecommunications infrastructure as it supports strategies for electronic service delivery?
4 What is the extent of social inclusion and exclusion in the information age?

The first question concerns the quality of telecommunications infrastructure available to organisations of governance. To put the situation simply, investment in modern digital telecommunications by the main network operators in the UK is spatially uneven. In places of high business demand in cities the Telecommunications Operators (TOs) invest heavily in digital switches and optical fibre networks. In areas of comparatively low business demand most of the TOs have only limited presence or none at all and, in the case of BT's network, 'pseudo-digital' switches are still to be found in some rural areas and copper wire abounds throughout the network. This situation of unevenness in the quality of the infrastructure of telecommunications is further aggravated by the uneven presence of competition. Thus if, for example, we look at the presence of the cable TV companies, most of which now offer telephone services, we find large urban areas where there is not a cable franchise or where, if a franchise has been awarded, plans to cable are being stalled. Moreover, in the case of cable, there is uneven interest amongst franchise holders in the provision of telecommunications services, and doubts have been raised too about the capabilities of cable infrastructure to handle high bandwidth for interactive multimedia applications of the kind which is central to the enhancement of some public services.

Second, there is the regulatory issue of 'universal service in telecommunications'. The universal service obligation can be interpreted in many ways. Perhaps the weakest of these is the one that has prevailed in the UK for the largest part of the twentieth century. On this interpretation of universal service, all citizens should have access to 'simple telephony' at the same cost of access. At the other end of the continuum some have argued that this principle should, in the information age, be one which affords universal access to high quality, broadband telecommunications at an affordable and equal price regardless of location. This latter interpretation has enormous cost implications for the TOs and, in the UK, the telecommunications regulator, OFTEL, has recently taken a middle course in its review (OFTEL, 1994; 1995a, 1995b). OFTEL has proposed that the definition of universal service be changed to incorporate some network services that are directly a consequence of the advent of digital telecommunications. Thus universal service would be reinterpreted to mean access for all customers to digital telecommunications (though not broadband), with some free services such as itemised billing as standard. OFTEL has also advocated raising the standard of universal service to one whereby some selected public service units, such as schools, should have a right to be connected to affordable wide-band service levels (OFTEL, 1995b). Indeed, such a network is currently being developed for the UK's educational system at school level.

Third, the specific circumstances of individual governance structures must be evaluated in the light of these points. For effective governance, knowledge of the telecommunications infrastructure that is in place becomes paramount (Taylor and Whiteside, 1998). The quality of that infrastructure, the bandwidth that it will support and, most importantly of all, the geographical spread, or reach, of that infrastructure, are critical in considering strategic options for developments in services and public communications. Public management has always been concerned with its own interpretations of the principle of universalism. Reaching the consumer and the citizen at some relevant point of delivery or access has always been a central concern. Thus, to provide electronically enhanced services across variable infrastructures is to provide services whose universal consumption cannot be guaranteed.

Fourth, there is the issue of a new rich and poor for the information age which is emerging over the question of access to modern communications. As public management becomes more and more reliant on telecommunications for the delivery of services and for improved communications, so the problem of those who are unconnected to electronic networks arises. One indicator of this connectedness is the rate of penetration of basic telephony. In the UK, this is not especially high: household penetration stands at about 93 per cent (OFTEL, 1994). In Sweden the equivalent figure is *circa* 126 per cent. Added to this is the variable nature of regional penetration, with that for households in the northern region of England, for example, being at around 85 per cent. Moreover, in some small areas of cities, telephone penetration is lower than 50 per cent (Graham and Marvin, 1996). Furthermore, BT has recently revealed that it removes its connections from between 20 000 and 30 000 households each month due to bad debt (OFTEL, 1995b). Access to basic telephony remains a basic standard against which to measure electronic public management for the information age. The promise of electronic service delivery and electronically enhanced citizenship pales once we see that many of the citizens who a priori are those most in need of public services are also those with less opportunity to access them. Nor can we take satisfaction in this respect from the rapidly accelerating growth in use of the Internet, for fewer than 5 per cent of UK households have the modem, the first requirement for access from the home. As public services become more and more dependent on the presence of electronic infrastructures so these questions of access to the network for consumers and citizens are a matter for concern.

A primary concern for public managers, therefore, is awareness of the quality and presence of the infrastructures in their areas of responsibility, in particular the telecommunications infrastructure. Most infrastructures, such as transportation infrastructures, are highly visible and their quality relatively self evident. Others, and telecommunications is perhaps the supreme example, are hidden from view and little is understood about their quality, apart from what is known to the TOs themselves. As government is replaced by governance, a word that captures the complex organisational networks through which both public services and democratic processes are respectively provided and played out, so public management must be aware of both telecommunications infrastructures and the likely pattern of social inclusion and exclusion arising from information age innovations. For these reasons the involvement of telecommunications operators in the new partnerships of governance is becoming crucial, yet recent research shows that, at best, only one in three local governments has a strategic partnership with a telecommunications operator (Taylor and Whiteside, 1998).

CAN PUBLIC MANAGEMENT CHANGE FOR THE INFORMATION AGE?

> Today's and tomorrow's choices are shaped by the past. And the past can only be made intelligible as a story of institutional evolution (North, 1990).

This quotation captures the essential thrust of an approach that signals caution against the heady optimism that often accompanies discussions of the information age. It is an approach that places a major emphasis on continuities and the slowness of change in social, political and economic life, rather than glibly assuming that we are captured within a technological tidal wave of irresistible change.

Much of this chapter has been predicated upon the commonly assumed need for profound changes to occur in the way in which public management is conducted in the information age. Indeed the necessity of change is an aspect of so much of the debate about our governance processes that is taken for granted. This section looks not at the case for change, for that has already been done, but at the amenability of the public management system to change. It asks whether the public management system can be changed so as to take forward the promise of information age government. In the next section the equally intriguing question is asked of whether public management systems *should* be changed.

A corpus of work on the 'information polity' (Taylor and Williams, 1991; Bellamy and Taylor, 1998) has stressed the political and institutional influences which have shaped, and continue to shape, the polity and the relationships which it embraces. From this perspective, visions of the future which are replete with either Utopian zeal, or its opposite, over the power of new ICTs to reinvent the basic processes of, and relationships around, governance should be treated sceptically. The technological determinism at the core of these visions is at odds with the confusions, sub-optimisations, contradictions and even the systems disasters that characterise the empirical world. This realisation should lead to us to stress the social, political and institutional shaping of the technologies and their use. It should lead us too, to the understanding that the 'information age' can promise little more than incremental changes, or even perversions in electronic form, of what has gone before. The quotation that follows provides one piece of anecdotal evidence that this institutionalist perspective is valid. It shows how an existing set of procedures continues to be used despite the fundamental challenge to them which new technology introduces. It is only a single anecdote and, of itself, has limited utility as evidence in support of this perspective. What is clear from research findings, however, is that this perspective is further strengthened once detailed studies are undertaken.

When in April 1995 the Minister for the Office of Public Service and Science (OPSS) publicly announced his electronic mail address, a journalist sent perhaps the first electronic mail message to a UK Minister from a member of the public. At a PICT/ESRC conference on Information Technology and Social Change two months later, he asked the head of the CCTA, Roy Dibble, why he had not had a reply. Now that citizens were talking to governments when were governments going to talk to citizens? Roy Dibble replied that the journalist's questions were currently sitting on his desk. When the Minister received the electronic message it had been printed off and sent to Roy Dibble by post. One of his staff had written to the relevant agency heads with a request for information; their staff would prepare this information and send it back to Roy Dibble's office where it would be collated and returned to the Minister's office. He will check the information and one of his staff would type it on to electronic mail and transmit it to the journalist. This evidence of how new methods of communication can flounder when having to interface with existing administrative operations is not isolated; an employee of a Next Steps Agency observed in 1995 that as a matter of procedure all electronic messages sent to the agency were printed off and filed (Margetts, 1995).

Here then we can begin to see the emergence of a situation that is very different from that envisaged by those who foresee a dramatically new era unfolding for public management. Now we can see that:

1 We should not expect dramatic organisational or management changes to occur as a direct consequence of the uptake of these apparently revolutionary information and communication technologies.
2 Academics should divest themselves of the tacitly deterministic thinking that has so pervaded our field. The claims of both Utopian and dystopian commentators on ICTs in governance derive from a mistaken, technologically determinist perspective.
3 Academics should focus their work *primarily* upon the nature of information flows around the polity, and *secondarily* upon the technologies of the information age. Once they do so the prospect for dramatic organisational and managerial change begins to ebb away. Information is an artefact created by organisational actors. The meanings attached to it are therefore value laden; they are essentially political. New forms and flows of information will, it follows, excite organisational politics. In turn, organisational politics will tend to push towards the existing ways of doing things rather than towards new practices. Evidence from the project to computerise the criminal justice system, cited earlier, sustains this view.
4 Once the distinctive informational content of new technologies has been understood then Utopian and dystopian assumptions fall away, to permit less hidebound examination of the institutionalised settings that are the true shapers of the information polity.
5 In opening up the polity to this institutionalist analysis, academics must focus on both the complex formal and the informal content of institutionalised environments, on their respective influence in shaping management and policy outcomes and, most importantly, on their amenability to change.

Douglass North's (1990) leitmotif for institutionalism, with which this section of this chapter is headed, provides a summation of this perspective. Institutions are a set of formal and informal rules, norms, expectations and conventions that provide for stability in everyday life, setting a framework both for action and innovation and for the reduction of uncertainty. By establishing this framework for action, institutions provide an environment for the exercise of bounded rationality, for they are, in effect, a 'set of readinesses to distinguish some aspects of a situation rather than others and to classify and value these in this way rather than that' (Vickers, 1965).

In short, an institutionalised environment provides for the development of two vital characteristics of complex organisational settings. In the first place it establishes the routines and repertoires (Nelson and Winter, 1982) by which decision taking is directly facilitated, the recognised 'ways of doing' in the organisation. Second, the institutionalised environment is characterised by the existence within it of long-term 'epistemic communities', the professional workforces that guard, protect and promote a specific way of valuing their particular interpretation of the organisational world. Information processing is central to both of these characteristics for, in both, the institution acts so as to specify the need for information as well as the manner of its use and interpretation.

CONCLUSIONS

The polity is a settled ordering of politics and government in a society. Aristotle advised that the polity was a *stable* system of government. When it becomes an *information* polity, through the adoption of new and extensive informational and communications capabilities, it does so in ways that are inclined to replicate rather than rupture existing practice. The relationships at the heart of the polity, between the agencies of governance on the one hand and between them and citizens of the state, on the other, are highly institutionalised relationships. In consequence, we should expect any changes that might occur within these relationships to be characterised by only a gradual shift. The heroic and simplified images of new governance structures in the information age should be abandoned.

A focus on informatisation provides both the student and practitioner of public management with a unique perspective. It is through an informatisation perspective that research and understanding of the body politic can be approached from the inside outwards, rather than, as in traditional study, from the outside inwards. Flows of information around the essential relationships of the polity are the bloodstream of public administration. To understand the nature, specification and use of that information is, in effect, to be able to diagnose the condition of the relationships that comprise the polity, those between governments and citizens, those between executive and legislature and those between political leadership and bureaucracy. To ignore the power of this informatisation perspective is to remain purblind to understanding the nature of changes and continuities in the core relationships of the polity. We can now understand these relationships in a more complete way than public administration has ever before afforded.

A new perspective for the study of public management in the information age lies in an understanding of the core relationships of the polity, one that interprets them as essentially informational relationships. It is an understanding that seeks to interpret those relationships as relationships through systematic examination of the dams, reservoirs and flows of information in the polity, thereby centring the investigation of scholars and students upon what might usefully be termed the *information polity*.

Students of the information polity must break away from the mainstream literatures of public management. In those information is ignored altogether; or is presented in a determinist way which centres on the shaping power of new technologies; or deals with information and new technologies as one element only in an understanding of public management and the wider polity. For the student of informatisation in public management, information is the centrepiece of our understanding and, from that understanding we can research and understand public management to a level which has previously been impossible to achieve.

REFERENCES

Bellamy, C and Taylor, J A (1996) 'New information and communication technologies and institutional change: the case of the UK criminal justice system', *International Journal of Public Sector Management*, 9(4), pp 51–69.

Bellamy, C and Taylor, J A (1998) *Governing in the Information Age.* Buckingham: Open University Press.

Castells, M (1996) *The Rise of the Network Society. Economy, Society and Culture.* Oxford: Blackwell.

Corrigan, P (1996) *No More Big Brother.* Fabian Pamphlet 578. London: Fabian Society.

Dutton, W H, Blumler, J, Garnham, N, Mansell, R, Cornford, J and Peltu, M (1994) *The Information Superhighway. Britain's Response.* PICT Policy Research Paper 29. Uxbridge: ESRC/PICT.

Frissen, P and Snellen, I (1990) *Informatization Strategies in Public Administration.* Amsterdam: Elsevier.

Graham, S and Marvin, S (1996) *Telecommunications and the city. Electronic Spaces, Urban Places.* London: Routledge.

Margetts, I-I (1995) 'The automated state', *Public Policy and Administration*, 10(2), pp 88–103.

Mulgan, G (1997) *Connexity: How We Should Live in the 21st Century.* London: Chatto & Windus.

Negroponte, N (1995) *Being Digital.* London: Hodder and Stoughton.

Nelson, R R and Winter, S G (1982) *An Evolutionary Theory of Economic Change.* Belknapp: Harvard.

North, D (1990) *Institutions, Institutional Change and Economic Performance.* Cambridge: Cambridge University Press.

OFTEL (1994) *Households Without a Telephone.* London: OFTEL.

OFTEL (1995a) *Effective Competition: Framework for Action. A Statement on the Future of Interconnection.* London: OFTEL.

OFTEL (1995b) *Universal Telecommunication Services. A Consultative Document on Universal Service in the UK from 1997.* London: OFTEL.

Osbome, D and Gaebler, T (1992) *Reinventing Government. How the Entrepreneurial Spirit is Transforming the Public Sector.* Reading, MA: Addison-Wesley.

Taylor, J A (1992) 'Information networking in government', *International Review of Administrative Sciences*, 69, pp 375–89.

Taylor, J A (1994) 'Telecommunications infrastructure and public policy development. Evidence and inference', *Informatization and the Public Sector*, 3 (I), pp 63–73.

Taylor, J A and Webster, C.W.R (1996) 'Universalism, public services and citizenship in the information age', *Information Infrastructure and Policy*, 5(3), pp 217–33.

Taylor, J A and Whiteside, L (1998) *Local Governance in the Information Age, Innovations and the Development of Communications Infrastructure.* Glasgow: Glasgow Caledonian University.

Taylor, J A and Williams, H (1991) 'Public administration and the information polity', *Public Administration*, 69, pp 171–90.

Taylor, J A and Williams, H (1995) 'Superhighways or superlow-ways', *Flux. The International Journal on Telecommunications*, 19, pp 45–54.

Van de Donk, W B H J, Snellen, I and Tops, P (1995) *Orwell in Athens: A Perspective on Informatization and Democracy.* Amsterdam: IOS Press.

Van de Donk, W B H J and Tops, P W (1992) 'Informatization and democracy: Orwell or Athens. A review of the literature', *Informatization and the Public Sector*, 2, pp 169–96.

Vickers, G (1965) *The Art of Judgement. A Study of Policy Making.* London: Chapman and Hall.

Zuboff, S (1988) *In the Age of the Smart Machine: The Future of Work and Power.* Oxford: Heinemann.

QUESTIONS AND DISCUSSION TOPICS

1 How significant is 'informatisation' for public management?

2 In what ways are new technologies being used in the core relationships of the polity?

3 Can new technologies bring about necessary change in public management?

4 The distinctiveness of public management

Aidan Rose

AIMS

This chapter will:

- enable you to understand the role that public services play in a liberal democracy;
- present the changing agenda for public managers;
- assist in an understanding of the perspective of those arguing that management is either a generic or a contingent activity;
- help you to come to a point of view about that nature of management in specific public services.

INTRODUCTION

This chapter introduces the debate about the distinctiveness of the public services and analyses the nature of public service work. It also discusses the role of public managers and the condition under which they work. This chapter does not come to any firm conclusions about the distinctiveness debate. Instead, it should put you in a position where you can come to a personal point of view about how distinctive public services management is. Reference is made to a wide range of public services. It should be borne in mind that the context of each of these services will differ and this may influence the conclusion that you come to in the debate about distinctiveness.

A number of themes raised here will be pursued in more detail in later chapters. Where relevant, references are made to more detailed debates contained later in the book. However, it is not necessary to follow these links at this stage as one of the key purposes of this chapter is to provide an overview and contextual information that will be essential when considering the managerial task in detail in Part 2 of the book.

THE SOCIAL ROLE OF THE PUBLIC SERVICES

Public service organisations often owe their existence to the social policy goals of government. Indeed, many texts on public management focus exclusively on the management of the welfare state (Cutler and Waine, 1994). This begs the question about what the objectives of social policy are. Research conducted for the Department for International

Development offers a number of, albeit overlapping, frameworks for understanding social policy. They are:

- social policy as 'welfare through redistribution', where the long-term welfare of citizens is served through transfer payments such as cash benefits to those judged to be in need;
- social policy as human resource development, where the welfare of the population is served by provision of, for example, health care and education;
- social policy as safety net, where the destitute and vulnerable in the population are assisted by a variety of programmes including targeted benefits;
- social policy as social integration which, the authors say, differs from the other three frameworks in that its concern is less with compensating for the consequences of economic policy than with governance. The authors quote the declaration of the 1995 World Summit for Social Development held in Copenhagen which stated that societies exhibiting social integration are 'stable, safe and just and based on the promotion and protection of all human rights, and on non-discrimination, tolerance, respect for diversity, equality of opportunity, solidarity, security and participation of all people, including disadvantaged and vulnerable groups and persons' (Overseas Development Administration, 1995, p 17).

Thus we can see that in analysing the role of social policy, the relationship between social policy and economic policy is called into question. Is it the role of social policy to follow the consequences of economic policy or is it inextricably linked with economic policy in achieving societal goals?

Kieron Walsh (1995) set out the case for the public sector intervening in the provision of public services due to the failure of the market economy to provide them. Drawing on economic theory, he argued that markets can fail for a number of reasons.

Public goods

The production of certain goods and services may result in externalities. That is, they may provide benefits to others than those who purchase them. For example, it can be argued that we all benefit from street lighting and that it is impossible to provide it to selected individuals only (*see* Flynn, 1997, p 14). Such goods should therefore be provided on a basis where they are paid for as well as consumed collectively. This raises the question of which goods fall into this category. Higher education has in recent years been the subject of debate in this context. Graduates are an important input to a successful skills-based economy and it is argued that they are therefore of benefit to society. On the other hand, graduates tend to earn higher salaries than non-graduates and the argument follows that they are in a position to pay for their tuition fees and living expenses once they enter the labour market. In the United Kingdom this was a focus of the debate following the publication of the Dearing report on the future of higher education (Dearing, 1997).

Increasing returns to scale

Certain services, often part of the infrastructure, may have decreasing unit costs as production increases. For example, the cost of the provision of water is expected to reduce as the scale of its provision increases. Therefore it may be inefficient to have two parallel systems in one city. This results in an argument for monopoly provision. Economists have concerns about monopolies in that they are often inefficient, they may exploit that monopoly and they may generate super profits. This raises a number of questions about the locus of such services in either the public or private sectors and the role of regulation.

Merit goods

Merit goods are goods which provide benefits to society as a whole and which individuals, if left to choose for themselves, may underconsume. An example may be education, which provides society with an educated and skilled labour force and which may also contribute to civil society. As Walsh argues, the state can intervene to ensure that access is not restricted to those that have the purchasing power and inclination to obtain it.

Information asymmetrics

Public services working in areas such as health, education and social welfare employ large armies of professionals. Professional status is achieved through extended training and education, with rigorous examination of competence in the given technical area. This process revolves around the profession having claim to a body of expertise such as, for example, medicine or law. According to Wrigley and McKevitt (1994), such professionals as producers of services have access to large amounts of complex information which is difficult to transfer to the user. Taking the example of medicine, they argue that a doctor is 'not merely the provider of medicine, but also, necessarily, an agent of the client in providing information . . . In the decision to acquire health care, the sick cannot stand alone' (1994, p 75).

Thus, they argue, the doctor has two roles: one as a provider of health care and another as an agent of the patient. This enables us to question the applicability of market models to areas where professionals have disproportionate amounts of information under their control. Markets assume that purchasers are well informed and their experience enables them to make informed repeat purchases. However, one can argue that in the private sector there are many examples of professionals who may operate under similar conditions. This may enable us to identify a continuum stretching from public to private and one stretching from monopoly to competition.

POLITICAL CHOICES

The arguments set out above, mostly drawing on economics for their rationale, offer a case for state intervention to either provide or regulate goods and services. However, decisions about whether there is intervention by the state is a matter of political choice. Thus, the rationale for regulation or public sector provision may rest on a set of politically determined criteria rather than purely economic criteria. An example of such criteria for deciding on whether the public sector should intervene was provided by the Conservative administration in the United Kingdom in 1997.

> Does the work need to be done at all? If not, the work should be abolished. If the work is necessary, does the government need to be responsible for it? If not, privatisation should be considered.
>
> If the government does need to be responsible, does the work have to be performed by civil servants, or could it be delivered more efficiently and effectively by the private sector? A competition should be held to establish who can deliver the service in the most efficient and effective way. The basis of the decision will always be best value for money.

> Where the job must be carried out within government, is the organisation properly structured and focused on the task? The Next Steps principles of clear accountability and delegation should be applied. A range of techniques may be applied to improve efficiency (OECD, 1997, p 277).

Of course, positions of government can change. Following the General Election in 1997, the new Minister for Local Government and Housing introduced a policy change concerning the management of local authorities. This involved a shift from the extensive use of compulsory competitive tendering for the allocation of work to the public, private and voluntary sectors to reliance on the concept of best value. We will examine best value elsewhere (*see* Chapter 16), but here our concern is with the principle underpinning the shift. Armstrong stated to Parliament that 'We have an open mind on whether services are delivered by the private sector or directly within the public sector. Either way there needs to be an effective partnership, and fair and open competition where this is called for' (Armstrong, 1997, Col 50). Hence the shift is one from an ideological belief in the use of the private sector to one where competition is used as one of a range of management tools to drive quality and efficiency up.

CHANGE: THE CHANGING AGENDA FOR PUBLIC MANAGERS

In Chapter 6 we examine the fundamental shift that has taken place in the organisational form in which many public service managers operate: the shift from bureaucratic organisations to ones based on markets. We acknowledge that shift, but we can also examine the debate that has taken place about the nature of the managerial task. Essentially, there are two views. The first is that the nature of the work of public service managers is distinctive from private sector management. The second view is that it is broadly similar to private sector management. This chapter does not propose a point of view about this debate. Instead, it takes the view that the evidence needs critical evaluation and that firm conclusions are difficult to arrive at.

The generic case

The Griffiths inquiry into the management of the National Health Service (NHS) offered one position on this debate. It is important to recall that Sir Roy Griffiths was a managing director of the supermarket, Sainsbury's, and that it was the intention of government to allow him to bring his experience of retail management to bear on the NHS. He took a particular view about the management of publicly provided health care:

> We have been told that the NHS is different in management terms, not least because the NHS is not concerned with the profit motive and must be judged by wider social standards which cannot be measured.
>
> The clear similarities between NHS management and business management are much more important. In many organisations in the private sector, profits do not impinge on large numbers of people below board level. They are concerned with levels of service, quality of product, meeting budgets, cost improvement, productivity, motivating and rewarding staff, and the long-term viability of the undertaking. All these things Parliament is urging on the NHS (Griffiths, 1983, p 10).

Writing almost a century ago, F W Taylor, an American engineer and manager, developed the principles of what is known as scientific management. He drew upon the principles of science and applied them to work activity. He argues the case for a generic approach to management:

> The best management is a true science, resting upon clearly defined laws, rules and principles . . . the fundamental principles of scientific management are applicable to all kinds of human activities, from our simplest individual acts to the work of our greatest corporations (Taylor, 1967, p 7).

As the name scientific management suggests, this approach is concerned with the application of the methods and techniques of science to organisations. It is the belief that universal and general principles can be applied to every organisation. The approach suggests that organisations can be viewed as essentially the same and that there are few differences between organisations that cannot be overcome by the application of general principles. Two of the leading exponents of this approach to organisations were F W Taylor and H Fayol. Unlike Weber, however, whose approach was academic, Taylor and Fayol were not content just to analyse organisations. Both were concerned to offer prescriptions as to how organisations should be run with a view to particular management ends, in particular how to improve performance.

Taylor was an engineer by training and his approach to understanding organisations reflected both his scientific background and the belief in science as the solution to society's problems that was so characteristic of the late nineteenth century. Taylor (1967) examined the traditional working methods of individual workers in a number of studies covering such simple tasks as bricklaying and shovelling materials. He believed that it was possible to apply scientific principles to each task which would replace the old rule-of-thumb method of working. He believed that the workforce should be selected on the same scientific basis. Such an approach would lead to a more efficient worker and hence to a more profitable organisation. He also believed that the worker was rational and would respond to financial incentives as a way of increasing productivity. Hence the payment by piece-rate for the individual worker. Taylor believed in the division of labour, with tasks being broken down into simple repetitive jobs. This would allow the individual to specialise in a particular job and the division of labour would lead to a clear distinction between management and the workforce. The modern versions of Taylorism are expressed in terms of job design and work study.

Similarly, the concepts of the division of labour and organisation through specialisation still hold sway within many organisations. Indeed, Pollitt (1990, p 177) describes the approaches to public management adopted by President Reagan in the USA and Mrs Thatcher in the UK as neo-Taylorist: 'The chief feature of both classic Taylorism and its 1980s descendant were that they were, above all, concerned with *control* and that this control was to be achieved through an essentially *administrative* approach the fixing of effort levels that were to be expressed in quantitative terms.'

Although Taylor carried out his research at the beginning of the century and despite the fact that his conclusions did not meet with the universal approval of either the workers or the management he left an important legacy on which later theorists have built:

- the application of universal scientific principles;
- specialisation;
- division of labour;
- clear hierarchies;
- ethos of management control.

Those familiar with either central or local government in Britain will, no doubt, recognise some of these features as characteristic of their own experiences:

- emphasis upon routine tasks;
- clearly defined tasks;
- clear hierarchical control.

The concern with the scientific approach to organisations was developed by Henri Fayol (1949), whose scientific background was in biology rather than engineering. He was apt to use biological metaphors to explain the workings of organisations. His principles of management were as follows:

- the division of labour and the emphasis on the advantages that such specialisation brings;
- the emphasis on authority;
- the emphasis on discipline and the penalties incurred when discipline broke down;
- the concept of the unity of command, and a belief that a dual-command system leads to dissension and chaos;
- the unity of direction since, to use one of Fayol's biological metaphors, 'a body with two heads is a monster';
- the subordination of individual interests to those of the organisation as a whole;
- the fair remuneration for the workforce: like Taylor, Fayol believed in the motivating force of money;
- the principle of centralisation: according to Fayol centralisation, like the division of labour, is a feature of the natural world;
- a scalar chain or line of authority, both vertically and horizontally;
- a concern with order: this is the idea that there is a place for everyone and everything;
- equity, in the form of equitable treatment for the workers;
- initiative;
- stability of tenure;
- *esprit de corps*: this is the notion that union is strength. The modern-day equivalent of this is the idea of an organisation having a corporate image which all members of the organisation can respond to and identify with.

Fayol suggested that management is concerned with planning, with organisation, with command, co-ordination and control and with an emphasis on formal authority.

There is a sense in which scientific management is concerned with a way of thinking about organisations irrespective of the individual prescriptions of particular writers and researchers. It links into organisational structure in so far as structure is concerned with:

- specialisation;
- standardisation of rules and procedures;
- standardisation of employment practices;
- formalisation of clearly specified rules;
- centralisation;
- configuration, that is, whether the chain of command is long or short.

The advantage of this formal approach to organisations is that it shows how organisational objectives can be reached.

1 It enables formal allocation of people and resources. Individuals may feel happier if they have a clearly specified job in the organisation and know exactly where they fit into the workings of the organisation. It helps if people know where to go for formal approval of decisions, or know who is responsible for what. Accountability and responsibility can be clearly located.

2 Such an approach also clearly specifies operating procedures and mechanisms which may be laid down in a formal manual, for example. In local government the existence of standing orders, codes of conduct and conditions of service clearly stipulate what can and cannot be done in certain circumstances. This is particularly important in view of the fact that much of the work of government is legal in nature, involving the carrying out of statutory responsibilities.

3 It also indicates the decision-making procedures which show how and where decisions are made in organisations. Again, the formal committee structure of local government indicates where authority is located. We shall see later, though, that in practice this may not always be where power is located.

It is significant that this school of thought about management has been so enduring, both as a theoretical position about management and as an influence on the nature of management in practice. The Griffiths Report gave rise to the introduction of general management in the NHS (*see* Powell, 1997, pp 76–7) and was mirrored by a rise of managerialism as a phenomenon in the public services in general. The increased authority accorded to managers as opposed to administrators was reflected in the change of name of the relevant professional body from the Institute of Health Service Administrators to the Institute of Health Service Management.

The case for distinctiveness

The case that management of public services is distinctive rests on a number of propositions which we will examine in turn. When looking at these claims, one needs to bear a few points in mind. First, arguments need to be evidence driven. Many claims made about the distinctive nature of public services are not backed up by well marshalled evidence. Instead we often see assertions which fail to draw upon research. Second, we need to question whether arguments are applicable to all public services or whether they apply to some services to a greater degree than others. For example, the case for 'publicness' may apply to a greater degree to services such as education or health care rather than, say, highways maintenance. Third, as this book continues to emphasise, public services are subject to particularly high levels of change and therefore arguments that were applicable twenty years ago may not necessarily be applicable today. The initiatives of the Conservative government under Mrs Thatcher sought to introduce market mechanisms to a wide range of public services, thus changing the operating conditions and attempting to produce lasting cultural change. The Labour government which took power in 1997 has continued to bring people from the private sector into the management of public services.

Claim 1: Distinctive purpose, conditions and task

The claim made by Griffiths is that management below board level is to all intents and purposes the same in the private and public sectors. As we saw above, he rests his case on the common range of activities that managers in the public and private sectors are expected to perform. An alternative perspective is offered by Stewart and Ranson (1988) who argue that public services have distinctive purposes, conditions and tasks (*see* Table 4.1). Elsewhere they argue that public organisations are given responsibilities which should be carried out with public purpose. If this is not appreciated then they maintain that the political process could be seen as a constraint rather than an expression of political legitimacy. Equally, they argue that private sector models which employ the term 'customer' are inadequate as they do not take account of the role of the public as those for whom the services are provided and those to whom local authorities are accountable (*see* Leach *et al.*, 1994, pp 3–4).

Table 4.1 Stewart and Ranson's public domain model

Private sector model	*Public sector model*
Individual choice in the market	Collective choice in the polity
Demand and price	Need for resources
Closure for private action	Openness for public action
The equity of the market	The equity of need
The search for market satisfaction	The search for justice
Customer sovereignty	Citizenship
Competition as the instrument of the market	Collective action as the instrument of the polity
Exit as the stimulus	Voice as the condition

Source: Stewart and Ranson, 1988. Reproduced with permission.

One needs to bear in mind that the authors referred to above write from a local government perspective. All of them are based at the Institute of Local Government Studies at the University of Birmingham. The work of local authorities is subject to relatively immediate political scrutiny, with locally elected councillors overseeing it, and local users of services and taxpayers having access to meetings and key papers. Therefore, one could argue that many of the features of 'publicness' are more commonly found in local government services, particularly such politically sensitive services as education and social services than in other parts of the public services which are less exposed to such scrutiny. Thus, there may be varying degrees of 'publicness' in the public services. Perhaps there may be more than one model of public service management.

Eliassen (1993) draws attention to one of the dimensions raised by Stewart and Ranson, the role of the manager *vis-à-vis* politicians and bureaucrats. Politicians are charged with the responsibility of setting goals, and bureaucrats and professionals are responsible for implementing them. Managers are placed in the middle and need particular skills for dealing with this situation. Eliassen argues that 'Public managers need to react to sudden shifts in the priorities of the political leadership, their numerous and often conflicting goals, and their short term perspective which is defined by the number of years in which they hold office' (Eliassen, 1993, p 271).

Claim 2: Equity

One issue that arises out of Stewart and Ranson's analysis is the question of equity. They point out that in the private sector model equity is determined by the market. This is the justification used by those supporting the large pay rises enjoyed by senior managers of privatised industries. In the public sector model, they argue, equity is based on the concept of need. Earlier in this chapter we considered the implications of market failure and the case for public intervention. To take the example of housing, we can contrast methods of allocation used in private and public services. In the private sector housing is priced according to supply and demand, taking account of market trends. Participation in this market depends on the individual's ability to pay. Allocation of local authority housing takes place in line with social criteria, and takes account of housing need.

The concept of equity raises questions about the distribution of services. Moore (1996) argues that competing claims for resources may be made by differing geographical areas, ethnic groups and other groups in society. Claims for resources may be made according to different principles. For example, market efficiency may be advanced as a criterion, as might an allocation mechanism which ensures the maximum possible outcomes. On the other hand, resources might be directed to those groups which already make an effort, as an incentive to maintain private contributions (Moore, 1996, p 49). Resources may be allocated to the areas in the most need or equally to all areas. This raises questions of whether decision makers wish to see equity of inputs or outputs.

An example of city regeneration policy under the Conservative government in the UK was the Single Regeneration Budget, which required local authorities to form partnerships with other local organisations, particularly training and education councils, to marshal resources to develop bids to central government's regional offices which decided on resource allocation. Hence the criterion of need alone was set aside in favour of a mechanism which required resources to be contributed from the local level in order to secure central government funding.

We examine the question of equity in relation to human resources management in Chapter 8.

Claim 3: The Allison claim – fundamentally alike in all unimportant respects

Allison's work (Allison, 1983) is based on interviews with two top level managers in the United States, one based in the manufacturing sector, the other working in a federal government agency. He contrasted the nature of the managerial tasks faced by the two managers on the basis of a number of managerial functions as set out in Exhibit 4.1.

Allison found that the public service manager had decisions of the type, 'What business are we in?' made for him by the legislature whereas the private sector manager had a high degree of control over these decisions. Both managers reported that staffing was a major concern. However, the public manager faced predetermined organisational structures and a highly developed system of civil service rules designed to meet equity considerations and to ensure that due processes were followed, whereas the private manager had a high degree of discretion in making even major decisions.

In addressing the external environment, the public manager had to deal with a large number of external constituencies which had an interest in the activities of his agency. These included Congressional committees and other bodies with which he was required to consult and which could frustrate him in his pursuit of the organisation's mission.

Exhibit 4.1

Functions of general management

● **Strategy**: establishing objectives and priorities; devising operational plans.

● **Managing internal components**: organising and staffing; directing personnel and the personnel management system; controlling performance.

● **Managing external constituencies**: dealing with external units; dealing with independent organisations; dealing with the process and public.

Source: Allison, 1983, p 76.

Allison reports that for the private sector manager the 'bottom line was profit, market share and the long-term competitive position of the organisation' (1983, p 86), whereas the public manager did not face such a simple results-based measure. We examine this claim about private sector management in Claim 5 below, and in Chapter 7 we assess the changing nature of public services management.

There are three points to make about Allison's work. First, it is now dated and the sharp distinctions that existed in the early 1980s may not exist today. Second, it is a comparison of managers in the United States and such comparisons may not transfer to other contexts. Third, as Allison himself recognised, the comparisons are not 'pursued systematically' and further research is required.

Claim 4: That there is a distinctive public service ethos

Reference is commonly made to the existence of a distinctive public service ethos. Research by Pratchett and Wingfield (1994) shows that explicit reference to such an ethos in local government is relatively recent. This could be explained by a number of reasons, the most persuasive in their view being that 'there are certain deep-rooted values that underpin the culture of local government and inform the day-to-day activities of those employed in it' (1994, p 31). However, they acknowledge that these values 'have always been, and remain, ill-defined, confused and ambiguous' (1994, p 31).

Within this ethos they identify differentiations based on the various functions that local government performs and the nature of professionalisation. They report that professional bodies are a primary source of the values that make up the public service ethos and that these values may vary from profession to profession. Also they point to the role that highly politicised authorities play in making up the environment in which the ethos exists. Authorities which adopted a radical position, either supporting or opposing reforms, had staff who offered a 'more definitive interpretation of the public service ethos' (1994, p 33). They also highlight a number of factors which have led to an erosion of this ethos:

● the introduction of new, contractual forms of accountability;
● the decline in formal bureaucratic rules;
● the fragmentation of organisations into business units and cost centres.

In assessing the changes that local government has faced during the 1980s and 1990s, Pratchett and Wingfield conclude that 'changes in the public service ethos threaten to be the least conspicuous but most profound in their impact' (1994, p 34).

Claim 5: Public service organisations have complex and often competing objectives

We saw earlier the claim in the Griffiths Report (1983) that below board level, management in public and private sectors is a broadly similar activity. Early writing about private sector management revolved around a concern to improve organisational efficiency and this has continued throughout managerial thought this century. The contested area has been the debate about what methods should be employed to improve efficiency. The view offered by those seeking to assert public service distinctiveness is that private sector organisations have simpler and more clearly understood objectives. This is contrasted with the public services where objectives are more complex and often competing. Consider the observations of Metcalfe and Richards (1987, p 33) about management in British central government:

> In government, objectives are notoriously difficult to define, are frequently in conflict and are often subject to change. Coping effectively with ambiguity, conflict and instability are strategic tasks of public management that cannot be assumed away . . . [G]oalsetting is a particular problem of public management because it is an inter-organisational process and not just an intra-organisational process.

This raises two crucial issues: complex and competing objectives and management as an interorganisational process. Taking the issue of competing objectives, Hood (1991) identifies three competing families of values that govern the work of public managers. These relate broadly to efficiency, robustness and equity. He argues that there are tensions between these values and that during the 1980s in the United Kingdom efficiency issues dominated. Even within a family of values there are tensions. For example the cluster of concepts that make up the efficiency family include economy, efficiency and effectiveness. We will deal with these concepts in detail in Chapter 12. For the moment, we can illustrate this tension by pointing out that a drive for efficiency may mean that, say a college may teach more students per lecturer but they may not be taught as effectively.

The second concern relates to management as an interorganisational process, Metcalfe and Richards argue that '[p]ublic management is getting things done through other organisations' (1987, p 220). Nutt and Backoff regard the public service context as pluralistic, with numerous stakeholders making competing demands on public managers. Thus the public managerial task revolves around consensus building, with obvious concerns about equity. Hence, for them, '[p]rivate sector approaches to strategic management cannot cope with this pluralism and new methods are needed' (Nutt and Backoff, 1992, p 47). A contrary view is offered by Cyert and March (1992) who argue, contrary to conventional economic thinking, that there is no such clarity of goals in private firms. Instead they maintain that within organisations there is a wide range of different and often conflicting positions about the goals of the organisation and the means to attain them.

Claim 6: The public services are subject to high degrees of external controls

It is often asserted that public services operate in a 'goldfish bowl', with multiple stakeholders having an interest in the processes and outputs of those services. Leach *et al.* (1994) point to the importance of public purpose and responsiveness for local government. Local authorities are political institutions with democratically elected and locally accountable politicians responsible for making local choices about priorities. Additionally, the activities of local authorities are heavily circumscribed by legislation which dictates not only what can and cannot be done but also, in many cases, exactly how things should be done. In the NHS there are numerous instances where priorities are subject to change to meet the short-term requirements of politicians, often at variance with rational resource-allocation mechanisms aimed to meet health needs.

ASSESSING THE PUBLIC–PRIVATE INTERFACE

Public services do not and have never operated in complete isolation. Despite the Fulton Report (Fulton, 1968), which criticised the civil service for being isolated from the rest of society, ideas from the private sector and abroad have permeated the thinking of public services. Trends in public service reform often reflect trends in wider society. For example, the trend in the early 1970s towards large organisations was mirrored in the reorganisation of central government departments, local authorities and health authorities into fewer, larger organisations. The 1980s witnessed the fragmentation of organisations into smaller units, with competition being used as an instrument for driving behaviour.

Academic thinking about organisations has been influential in shaping public service organisations. For example, the rise of systems theory, arguing that organisations need to make the best fit with their environment, was influential in the structural and managerial reforms of the 1970s (Bains, 1972; Stewart, 1971). Popular managerial thinking such as the 'Excellence' model developed by Peters and Waterman (1982) permeated public service thinking in the 1980s resulting in publications such as the Local Government Training Board discussion paper (1985). This was paralleled by the development of the public service orientation which focused on the relationship between organisations and their publics (Local Government Training Board, 1987). More recently work on entrepreneurial government published by two American authors, Osborne and Gaebler (1992) has influenced thinking at both central government policy-making and local government levels.

In addition, all parts of the public services are making increasing use of consultants for a variety of purposes including policy reviews, restructuring, quality initiatives and benchmarking. The 1997 annual report of the Management Consultancies Association notes that in the year following the general election 'fees coming from central government work rose by over 90 per cent to £157 million' (Management Consultancies Association, 1998).

Later chapters of this book look at the role of partnerships between public service organisations and agencies in the private and not-for-profit sectors. Privatisation and quasi-privatisation, in the form of contracting out and agency provision, have meant an increasing interface with non-public-sector organisations. Part of the rationale for this development is that these organisations have expertise and competences which are not as well developed in the public sector. This has facilitated the transfer of technologies such as business process re-engineering and the business excellence model.

CASE STUDY 4.1

Public services are making increasing use of private sector organisations to provide both core and peripheral services. Case study 4.1 shows how this is being done in one of the organisations at the core of welfare delivery, the Benefits Agency.

PRIVATE SECTOR TO ADVISE BENEFITS AGENCY

By Liam Halligan

The Benefits Agency is to open its offices to private sector managers, it emerged yesterday, in a move viewed by trade unions 'as the beginning of the privatisation of the benefits system'.

Three private sector consortia are to provide a year's free consultancy to the agency – the semi-independent government body that annually administers social security payments of £76bn – in an effort to deliver benefits more efficiently.

The consortia, which comprise Electronic Data Services, AT&T and Sema group as the prime contractors, with National Westminster Bank, Price Waterhouse, Manpower and Group 4 among the sub-contractors, will be in a strong position to bid for lucrative contracts if private sector involvement is extended.

The three consortia will partner the agency in East London and Anglia, Yorkshire and the West Country respectively. Each is expected to provide about 40 consultants at a cost of £6m.

Mr Frank Field, minister for welfare reform, said: 'We're asking the private sector to take a look at how we do our work in a bid to deliver to taxpayers the best possible benefits service.'

But the move brought 'profound concern' from the Civil and Public Service Union, which represents the majority of the 77,000 Benefit Agency staff. 'We are worried about jobs cuts and staff morale,' it said. 'These firms will come in and cherry-pick the best work.'

Mr Iain Duncan-Smith, shadow social security secretary, was 'disturbed' that the announcement was made during the parliamentary recess. 'This marks the beginning of a major rethink on the delivery of benefits,' he said. 'Why is it being sneaked out over the summer?'

Mr Marwan Rifka, chief executive of the EDS-led consortium, said: 'The government wants to tap into private sector know-how, and is effectively getting help for free.'

He stressed there was no guarantee of a contract at the end of the 'experimental' attachments, but said: 'I don't think the government would do this unless it was serious.'

Mr Field denied the Benefits Agency would be privatised. 'There is no question of ending agency status,' he said.

He also stressed the partnership scheme would only be extended 'if the private sector shows it can make a real improvement'.

Source: Financial Times, 13 August 1997. Reprinted with permission.

Questions on the case study

1 What benefits may be derived from the use of private sector organisations?

2 What are the dangers of such approaches?

CONCLUSIONS

This chapter has assessed differences between the public services and the private sector. We do not, at this stage, seek to offer a firm conclusion. Instead, we merely seek to state that the debate is one where many assumptions are contested. Furthermore, this is a fluid area. Public services are subject to continuing change and the interface between the public and private sectors is a dynamic one, with new modes of engagement continuing to emerge. Later chapters of this book examine many of the issues raised in this chapter in more detail.

One issue that emerges from the debate is that of the role of the public manager. Clearly the role is changing. Managers are having to learn new skills as the public services develop new roles and new modes of service provision. For example, new types of people management and financial management skills are required. Splits between purchasers and providers mean a new focus on strategy for some and operations for others. Competition, both within the public sector and against the private and not-for-profit sectors, means that managers need marketing skills. These are issues that we raise in Part 2 of this book.

Public service managers must recognise that distinctive elements remain. These elements include the relationship with politicians and the public as well as the professional nature of public services.

REFERENCES

Allison, G T (1983) 'Public and private management: are they fundamentally alike in all unimportant respects?' in Perry, J L and Kramer, K L (eds) *Public Management: Public and Private Perspectives*. Palo Alto, CA: Mayfield.

Armstrong, H (1997) Written Answers for 2 June 1997, *Hansard*, Cols 49–50, London: The Stationery Office.

Bains Committee (1972) *The New Local Authorities: Management and Structure*. London: Department of the Environment.

Cutler, T and Waine, B (1994) *Managing the Welfare State: The Politics of Public Sector Management*. Oxford: Berg.

Cyert, R M and March, J G (1992) *Behavioural Theory of the Firm*. Oxford: Blackwell.

Dearing, Sir Ron (1997) *Higher Education in the Learning Society*. Committee of Inquiry into Higher Education. London: HMSO.

Eliassen, K A (1993) 'Conclusions' in Eliassen, K A and Kooiman, J (eds) *Managing Public Organisations: Lessons from Contemporary European Experience*. London: Sage.

Fayol, H (1949) *General and Industrial Management*. London: Pitman Publishing.

Flynn, N (1997) *Public Sector Management*. Hemel Hempstead: Prentice Hall/Harvester Wheatsheaf.

Fulton, Lord (1968) *The Civil Service*, Vol. 1, Report of the Committee. London: HMSO (Cmnd. 3638).

Griffiths, Sir Roy (1983) *Inquiry into NHS Management*. London: HMSO.

Hood, C (1991) 'A public management for all seasons?', *Public Administration*, 69, pp 3–19.

Leach, S, Stewart, J and Walsh, K (1994) *The Changing Organisation and Management of Local Government*. Basingstoke: Macmillan.

Local Government Training Board (1985) *'Excellence' and Local Government*. Luton: LGTB.

Local Government Training Board (1987) *Getting Closer to the Public*. Luton: LGTB.

Management Consultancies Association (1998) *Annual Report, 1997*. London: Management Consultancies Association.

Metcalfe, L and Richards, S (1987) *Improving Public Management*. London: Sage.

Moore, M (1996) *Creating Public Value: Strategic Management in Government*. London: Harvard University Press.

Nutt, C and Backoff, R W (1992) *Strategic Management of Public and Third Sector Organisations: A Handbook for Leaders*. San Francisco: Jossey-Bass.

OECD (1997) *Issues and Developments in Public Management: Survey 1996–1997*. Paris: OECD.

Osborne, D and Gaebler, T (1992) *Reinventing Government: How The Entrepreneurial Spirit is Transforming the Public Sector*. Reading, MA: Addison-Wesley.

Overseas Development Administration (1995) 'Social Policy Research for Development', unpublished paper. London: ODA.

Peters, T J and Waterman, R H (1982) *In Search of Excellence*. New York: Harper & Row.

Pollitt, C (1990) *Managerialism and the Public Services: the Anglo-American Experience*. Oxford: Blackwell.

Powell, M A (1997) *Evaluating the National Health Service*. Buckingham: Open University Press.

Pratchett, L and Wingfield, M (1994) *The Public Service Ethos in Local Government: A Research Report*. London: Commission for Local Democracy Ltd. in association with the Institute of Chartered Secretaries and Administrators.

Stewart, J (1971) *Management in Local Government: A Viewpoint*. London: Charles Knight.

Stewart, J and Ranson, S (1988) 'Management in the public domain', *Public Money and Management*, Spring/Summer, pp 13–19.

Taylor, F W (1967) *The Principles of Scientific Management*. New York: Norton.

Walsh K (1995) *Public Services and Market Mechanisms: competition, contracting and the new public management*. Basingstoke: Macmillan.

Wrigley, L and McKevitt, D (1994) 'Professional ethics, government agenda, and differential information' in McKevitt, D and Lawton, A (eds) *Public Sector Management: Theory, Critique and Practice*. London: Sage.

QUESTIONS AND DISCUSSION TOPICS

1 After the public management reform since the 1980s, is there still a valid case for the proposition that public services are distinctive?

2 In what ways have the public services learnt from the private sector?

3 Can the private sector learn from the public sector?

4 What new skills does the public sector manager need in order to operate in the contemporary public service environment?

5   Accountabilities

Jennifer Law

AIMS

This chapter will:

- explain the meaning of accountability;
- examine the distinctions between accountability in the public services and in private organisations;
- identify four traditional models of accountability – political, managerial, legal and professional – and examine some of the evidence concerning their effectiveness;
- assess some of the changes in accountability brought about by the 'New Public Management'.

INTRODUCTION

Accountability is a complex, multidimensional concept. Accountability operates in all environments, including the political arena, the public services and the private sector.

In the political arena accountability has been of significance in the United Kingdom in recent years. One of the primary causes for concern has been the growth of quasi-governmental agencies, with concomitant disquiet about their conduct and accountability. The controversy surrounding these organisations is not new, but was fuelled by scandals affecting organisations such as the Welsh Development Agency which was found to have misused £2 million on staff 'perks' (Public Accounts Committee, 1993). However, concern about accountability has not been limited to un-elected bodies. There is also a long-standing debate about the accountability of both central and local government, and there are suggestions that there is an 'impending crisis in accountability' (Stewart, 1992). Recent scandals have also affected central government, such as the 'brief entanglement' of the provision of aid to the Pergau Dam scheme (in Malaysia) with arms sales, and the investigation of the 'Arms to Iraq affair' by Mr Justice Scott. These have increased disquiet over the standards of conduct in public life. The Nolan Committee was appointed in October 1994 as a response to this and set out seven principles for public life. These were selflessness, integrity, objectivity, openness, honesty, leadership and accountability. The extent of the problem of accountability is indicated by the wide remit of the committee, which covers central and local government, health authorities, housing associations and grant-maintained schools.

Accountability operates in a variety of ways throughout the public services. For example, professionals such as doctors are accountable to their professional association, and local government managers and politicians are accountable to the Ombudsman. These methods of accounting for performance, or mechanisms of accountability, may change over time and reflect, among other things, the ideology of the government. The 'New Right' ideology of recent Conservative governments has stressed the importance of the market. Part of this strategy has included reforms to improve accountability to the consumer (Common and Flynn, 1993). For example, parents are allowed to choose a school for their child (subject to the availability of places), and are provided with information which supposedly helps them to do this, in the form of examination league tables. Thus in recent years we have experienced a number of changes in accountability:

1 There has been a shift in focus from traditional mechanisms of accountability, such as through the political process, to accountability through the market.
2 There is an increased emphasis on holding individuals and organisations to account for results through the use of performance indicators, rather than adherence to procedures.
3 Non-elected bodies, which are not directly politically accountable, play an increasingly important role in the governance of the public sector.

This chapter first attempts to explain the complex concept of accountability, and then examines the extent to which its meaning and operation differ in the public services and in the private sector. The next section identifies traditional aspects of accountability (political, managerial, legal and professional) and examines some of the evidence concerning their effectiveness. This discussion is followed by illustrations of the many meanings of accountability in public services organisations. The final section analyses the changes in accountability brought about by the Conservative governments of the 1980s and the first half of the 1990s. A number of the reforms considered here are a part of what is described as the 'New Public Management'. The analysis covers changes in organisational structures, mechanisms of accountability and performance measurement.

THE CONCEPT OF ACCOUNTABILITY

Accountability is a complex and difficult concept (Day and Klein, 1987). A simple definition is that to be accountable is to be required to explain or justify one's actions or behaviour. Hence the concept of accountability is closely connected to responsibility, as those who have been given responsibilities or duties are asked to account for their performance. For example, we may give responsibility for the operation of local government to elected councillors. We would then expect them to be accountable to us for their performance.

Stewart suggests that accountability is made up of two parts, the 'element of account' and the 'holding to account'. The element of account is the 'need for information, including the right to question, and debate that information as a basis for forming judgements' (1984, p 15). When an account of performance is given, information is provided which may be verbal or written, formal or informal and may or may not be governed by strict rules. Attempts to improve accountability have often involved an increase in the amount, and/or a change in the type, of information provided, for example the Citizen's Charter. This has led to debates about openness. Questions that have been raised include how much information should be made available? Should there be a Freedom of Information Act? There has also been debate about the *type* of information that should be provided. Information is provided to enable performance to be judged, but it is often difficult to measure the performance of public services organisations (as we shall see in the next section). There may also be conflict between groups over the appropriate measure of performance. For example education professionals are frequently hostile to the use of examination results as a measure of performance. Many argue that the results need to take account of the socio-economic circumstances of the children involved to have any validity.

However, accountability involves more than simply giving an account. The information will be evaluated and performance will be assessed and if it is not satisfactory then action may be taken. The capacity for action and the potential to impose sanctions is what Stewart (1984) calls the element of holding to account. Dunsire (1978, p 41) also argues that this is important:

> The answer when given, or the account when rendered, is to be evaluated by the superior body, measured against some standard or some expectation, and the difference noted; and then praise or blame are to be meted out or sanctions applied. It is the coupling of information with its evaluation and application of sanctions that gives 'accountability' or 'answerability' or 'responsibility' their full sense in ordinary organisational usage.

This definition of accountability, which assumes that there is some authority to call to account, will be used in this chapter.

One of the prerequisites of effective accountability is that those given responsibility know to whom they are accountable, and for what aspect of performance. Similarly, those who delegate authority know whom to hold to account. Stewart (1984, p 16) argues that 'the relationship of accountability, involving both the account and the holding to account can be analysed as a bond linking the one who accounts and is held to account, to the one who holds to account . . . For accountability to be clear and enforceable the bond must be clear'. This theme of clarity was evident in the proposals for the reorganisation of local government in the early 1990s. The Welsh Office consultation paper claimed that a structure of unitary authorities in Wales would bring 'clearer accountability to the electorate', which implies that the public did not understand the division of responsibilities between the two tiers of counties and districts (Welsh Office, 1991). In addition to clarity there also needs to be agreement on the process and content of the account. Day and Klein (1987, p 5) state that accountability 'presupposes agreement both about what constitutes an acceptable performance and about the language of justification to be used by actors in defending their conduct'.

Accountability in the public services operates through a variety of mechanisms. These include:

- the audit of central government departments by the Auditor General;
- parents holding a headteacher to account for examination performance in their school;
- a professional association such as the British Medical Association holding an individual doctor to account for his or her performance;
- citizens holding their elected representatives to account through local elections.

To understand the concept fully we need to consider questions such as who is accountable, to whom, for what aspect of performance and how they are accountable? A further question is how well accountability operates.

ACCOUNTABILITY IN PUBLIC SERVICES ORGANISATIONS AND PRIVATE ORGANISATIONS

Accountability is an important issue for both public and private organisations. The current concern about accountability in the public services is mirrored by similar disquiet in the private sector. The recent increase in emphasis on corporate governance and accountability in the private sector may be linked to the business scandals involving the Bank of Credit and Commerce International (BCCI) and the Maxwell Group (Stiles and Taylor, 1993). The Cadbury Committee was formed in 1991 to examine corporate governance. The Cadbury Report (1992) highlighted three fundamental principles of corporate governance: openness, integrity and accountability. Corporate governance was defined as the system by which companies are directed and controlled. The Report recommended a Code of Best Practice. The Code was neither mandatory nor prescriptive; corporate boards were required to state in their annual reports how far they had complied with the Code and to give reasons for non-compliance. The Committee considered that, on the whole, companies would see it as in their interests to comply. The Committee felt that compliance would indicate publicly that the company had met the standards now expected of well-run businesses. It has been argued that the Cadbury Report is important because it addresses concerns that are equally relevant to the public sector (Evans, 1995 cited in Hodges *et al.*, 1996). So is accountability different in the public services?

Private sector organisations and their managers are accountable to a number of stakeholders, including the board of directors, shareholders, employees and central government. They may be accountable for different aspects of performance to the different stakeholders; for example, accountability to central government may be for compliance with health and safety legislation. However, the aspect of performance with which shareholders will primarily be concerned will be the financial performance of the organisation, and the dividend that they obtain. Farnham and Horton (1996) suggest that accountability is simpler for organisations in the private sector as their goals are less complex than those of public services organisations. Although they may be concerned with meeting a number of goals their ultimate aim is to make a profit. Hence the measurement of performance is straightforward as the extent to which the goals have been met can be assessed. In contrast, the goals of public services organisations are likely to be complex. The objectives of the organisation, set by politicians, may be ill defined. The objective of raising educational standards, for example, is unclear. What are educational standards and how can they be assessed? Even if the objectives are defined it is still difficult to measure some aspects of public services performance. The difficulty of measuring aspects of performance such as effectiveness and equity have led in the past to an emphasis on measuring the measurable.

The primary distinction between accountability in the public services and accountability in private organisations is that the basis of accountability in the former is democratic. One of the defining features of many public services organisations is that they are funded through general taxation. Hence the public has an interest in that organisation, and expects some accountability, not necessarily directly, but through their elected representatives. Although there is debate about the characteristics of a democracy (*see*, for example, Held, 1993), one of the most important is public accountability.

Lively (1975) suggests that a system which does not include direct, participatory democracy, or allow for the accountability of rulers to the ruled, cannot be called democratic. Simey (1984, p 17) similarly illustrates the importance of accountability: 'In a democracy it is only by the consent of the people that authority to govern can be delegated and that consent is given on one condition, that all those who then act on our behalf will hold themselves accountable for their stewardship.' Public services organisations as a result have more extensive forms of accountability to the wider community, in addition to consumers and providers of resources. Of course, some public services organisations, such as government trading agencies which are not funded through general taxation, may argue that this more extensive form of accountability is inappropriate and too constraining for them.

CASE STUDY 5.1

Case study 5.1 examines one of the tensions facing the Labour government elected in 1997. Accountability of public service organisations was a continuing issue under the Conservatives, as was the relationship between central and local government. At issue here is the extent to which new regional development agencies for England will be accountable locally or centrally.

LABOUR-CONTROLLED COUNCIL BODY TO DEMAND MORE ACCOUNTABILITY FOR REGIONAL AGENCIES

By Alan Pike

Ministers will next month face their first public clash with the Labour-controlled Local Government Association as council leaders demand more accountability in the English regions.

The association is to campaign for amendments to the bill setting up nine English regional development agencies, due for its second reading soon after Parliament's Christmas recess. It wants to make RDAs more answerable to regional chambers of councillors and other local interests.

'It is essential that RDAs are regional institutions rather than an arm of central government in the regions,' said Sir Jeremy Beecham, Labour leader of the LGA. 'They must be part of a move away from old fashioned centralism.'

Sir Jeremy said the LGA would approach ministers and MPs early in the new year 'in a bid to ensure a stronger, more effective voice for the English regions'. The campaign has all-party support in the association.

Since the general election, John Prescott, the Deputy Prime Minister, and his team at the Department of the Environment, Transport and the Regions have been working to improve central government's relations with local government. Their proposals for RDAs have been broadly welcomed, but many councillors are concerned that the government as a whole may be insufficiently committed to replacing quangos answerable to ministers with locally accountable bodies.

The government's RDA white paper proposes that the agencies should 'have regard' to views of regional chambers when preparing economic strategies, and consult chambers on corporate plans. Council leaders want this strengthened so that RDA's economic development strategies and business plans have to be approved by chambers, with RDAs required to work within chambers' broad regional strategies.

A paper from the LGA to the Common Environment, Transport and Regions committee says that without such changes RDAs were in danger of being seen as arms of national government in the regions and would 'not secure a more coherent, regionally responsive approach to regional economic policy and regeneration'.

The government is expected to begin advertising for members of RDA boards soon. This will generate another disagreement with the LGA.

Local authorities will qualify for four of the 12 seats on each board. But the government says that to ensure continuity individual councillors would not be required to resign from RDA boards if they lost their local electoral mandate.

LGA leaders intend to challenge this. The association will tell its member councils that elected representatives should resign if defeated at the polls and will suggest that authorities obtain a commitment to this policy from potential nominees.

Source: *Financial Times*, 30 December 1997. Reprinted with permission.

Questions on the case study

1 What are the arguments in favour of bodies that are more locally accountable?

2 Why might central government be reluctant to make these bodies more locally accountable?

DIFFERENT DIMENSIONS OF ACCOUNTABILITY

One way of clarifying the complex concept of accountability is to identify different models of accountability. A number of these models have been developed by, for example, Day and Klein (1987), Oliver (1991), Ranson (1986), and Kogan (1986). There are some differences of classification and nomenclature, but four of the main traditional models – political, managerial, professional and legal accountability – are discussed below.

Political accountability

There are two aspects of political accountability relevant to public services organisations. These are illustrated in Table 5.1.

Table 5.1 Two aspects of political accountability

	Accountability to the public	Accountability to Parliament
Who is accountable?	Politicians	Government: (Cabinet, ministers)
To whom?	Public	Parliament
For what?	Responsiveness: all aspects of performance	Efficiency, probity
How?	Election	Parliamentary questions, Select Committees

In a system of representative democracy the accountability of politicians to the public is paramount. In this model politicians give an account to the citizens, who may impose sanctions through the ballot box. The public hold their representatives to account and have the opportunity to 'throw the rascals out' if they are dissatisfied with their performance. There is some debate about the effectiveness of this as a mechanism of accountability, particularly at the local level. Evidence shows, for example, that the number of people who vote in local elections is on average between 40 and 45 per cent (Rallings and Thrasher, 1991). This suggests that only a minority of the electorate holds their representatives to account. Another concern about the accountability of local politicians is the lack of effective party competition. Elkins (1974) argues that the chance or probability of turnover is vital for accountability and is the most relevant interpretation of party competition. There must be some possibility that government can be replaced, and recent evidence suggests that there is a higher level of party competition in local government than had previously been believed (Boyne and Ashworth, 1997). Another factor crucial to the operation of political accountability is the provision of information. The public need to have information in order to make judgements on the performance of their politicians. Sources of information include manifestos, the media, annual reports and the Citizen's Charter. However, there has been criticism of the quality of some of the information provided (*see*, for example, Boyne and Law, 1991 on annual reports). Also important for accountability are principles such as the freedom of the media to report on matters of public interest, and public right of access to official information. Concern at the state of local democracy led to the launch of the Commission for Local Democracy in 1993 which made a number of proposals to improve democracy and accountability, such as the introduction of elected mayors. The proposal for elected mayors has been acted upon by government: in May 1998 a successful referendum was held for an elected mayor for London and the idea is proposed for authorities outside London in the 1998 local government White Paper (Department of the Environment, Transport and the Regions, 1998).

The second aspect of political accountability is the accountability of the government to Parliament. This has traditionally operated through the doctrine of ministerial and Cabinet responsibility. Ministers are accountable to Parliament for the operation of their departments: 'The traditional view, exemplified in the famous Crichel Down case is that Ministers are responsible and accountable to Parliament for all that occurs in their departments. It follows that if a significant mistake is made by the department, the Minister should resign' (Select Committee on the Treasury and Civil Service, 1986). However, as Day and Klein (1987) point out, the way in which ministerial responsibility has developed has stressed the concept of answerability rather than accountability. This is partly because of the huge growth in the work of the public sector. The principle of ministerial responsibility may have been effective when the scale of public services was small. However, the thousands of operational decisions made by government departments means that ministers cannot be held accountable for each individual problem. The issue of ministerial responsibility and what ministers can be held accountable for arose in the mid-1990s in the Scott Report. The investigation by Mr Justice Scott was initiated after the collapse of the Matrix Churchill trial concerning the possibility that arms components had been illegally exported to Iraq and the subsequent allegations that ministers had been aware of the possible use of the machine tools (used to produce the components), and had prevented the defence from accessing information by using Public Interest Immunity Certificates. Sir Richard Scott concluded that accountability involved the 'obligation of ministers to give information about the actions and omissions of their civil servants'. Bogdanor (1996) suggests that ministers may be held to account for more than this and cites Roger Freeman, Chancellor of the Duchy of Lancaster, who stated:

> Ministers take responsibility for five fundamental areas: the policies of their departments; the framework within which those policies are delivered; the resources allocated; such implementation decisions as the framework documents for agencies may require to be referred to them or agreed with them; and their response to major failures or expressions of parliamentary or public concern, in the sense of demonstrating what action they have taken to correct a mistake and prevent its recurrence (cited in Bogdanor, 1996, p 603).

The principle of ministerial responsibility has been under attack for some time (*see* Jordan, 1994), particularly the effectiveness of sanctions. Bogdanor suggests that it is difficult to enforce ministerial accountability as the House of Commons is dominated by party politics and whereas 'in theory the House of Commons can enforce the resignation of a minister who has breached the code, under modern conditions of strict party discipline, that will hardly ever occur' (1996, p 603). Many have commented on the declining accountability of the executive to the House of Commons – one aspect being the accountability of the Prime Minister to the Commons. Dunleavy and Jones (1993) suggest that direct parliamentary accountability of the Prime Minister has fallen sharply since 1868, especially since the early 1980s. Partly as a result of problems with ministerial responsibility as a mechanism of accountability, new systems have been adopted, such as the introduction of Parliamentary Select Committees in 1979. These were introduced to enable all MPs 'to exercise effective control and stewardship over Ministers and the expanding bureaucracy of the modern state for which they are answerable, and to make the decisions of Parliament and Government more responsive to the wishes of the electorate' (HC 588, 1977–78, quoted in Oliver, 1991, p 42). The issue of ministerial responsibility is illustrated in relation to the Prisons Service in Exhibit 5.1.

Exhibit 5.1

The Prisons Service Next Steps Agency

The Prisons Service 'Next Steps' Agency was established on 1 April 1993. Its Chief Executive, Derek Lewis, was in charge of approximately 39 000 staff and a budget of £1.6bn (in 1994–5). The aim of 'Next Steps' was to separate the policy and executive functions of the civil service and emphasise the importance of the management in the executive agencies. After the escape from Parkhurst prison (Isle of Wight) of three inmates on 3 January 1995 the Learmont Inquiry was set up to examine Prisons Service security. Subsequent to their report Derek Lewis was sacked by the Home Secretary, Michael Howard.

The framework document of the Prisons Service states: 'The Home Secretary is accountable to Parliament for the Prisons Service. The Home Secretary allocates resources to the Prisons Service and approves its corporate and business plans including its key targets' (quoted in Talbot, 1996). The debate after the Learmont Report concerned the extent to which the Home Secretary was responsible and hence accountable for the breakout. His argument was that it was clearly an operational matter. However Derek Lewis suggested that there was no clear-cut division between policy and operational matters, and that the Home Secretary was deeply involved in the operational role of the Prisons Service. The Learmont Report indicated the extent of involvement when it established that between October 1994 and January 1995 'just over 1000 documents had been submitted, relating to life sentence prisoners, appointment of Boards of Visitors, parliamentary cases, briefing on incidents, reports on media stories with "lines to take", briefings for visits and meetings, and briefing on specific prisoners or prisons' (para 3.83, quoted in Talbot, 1995a). The Learmont Report shows that the clear distinction between policy and operational matters does not exist in practice. The framework document also indicates this – 'The Home Secretary will not normally become involved in day-to-day management of the Prisons Service but will expect to be consulted by the Director General on the handling of operational matters which could give rise to grave public or parliamentary concern'. It also states that 'The Director General is responsible for the day-to-day management of the Prisons Service and is also the Home Secretary's principal policy advisor on matters relating to the Prisons Service' (HMPS FD 1993:3, quoted in Talbot, 1996).

Thus key issues are raised, concerning:

- the extent to which there can be a clear-cut division between policy and operational matters;
- the location of responsibility and hence accountability.

The confusion of roles in the example given in Exhibit 5.1 creates problems of accountability. As was stated earlier in the chapter, clarity of responsibility is an important prerequisite for effective accountability. If the location of responsibility is not clear, it is difficult to know who should be held to account. It also illustrates the debate on ministerial responsibility. Talbot (1995a, p 7) argues:

> Ministers have developed a curious doctrine which argues that 'accountability' cannot be delegated to Chief Executives but that 'responsibility' can . . . This 'limited liability' defence is being deployed with increasing frequency by Ministers to avoid criticism for particular failings. It does not apply to successes however and any 'operational' initiative to improve services by an agency is invariably a Ministerial announcement, press conference and photo-opportunity.

A number of organisations have only indirect political accountability to the general public. These include Hospital and Health Service Trusts, Training and Enterprise Councils and Urban Development Corporations. These organisations are accountable through the relevant minister to Parliament. These non-elected organisations operate at a local as well as national level, and a wide definition would include organisations such as housing associations. Whereas these quasi-governmental agencies may be appropriate for providing national services and operating in a relatively entrepreneurial manner, many people are concerned at their lack of accountability. Political accountability operates through ministers for many of these agencies but there is little chance for the general public to hold them to account.

Managerial accountability

Managerial accountability has also been described as internal accountability (Birch, 1974). In contrast to political accountability, which has an outward emphasis, managerial accountability concerns the accountability of staff within the organisation. Stewart defines it as 'the accountability of a subordinate to a superior in an organisation' (Stewart, 1984, p 18). In a traditional model of public sector management this would operate through a hierarchy. In local government, for example, those at the lowest level account to their superior and so on through the ranks, until the chief officer accounts to the politicians. This hierarchical accountability is in some cases giving way to new forms of accountability as new internal structures are put in place in many public services organisations. The creation of business or devolved units, and internal markets within organisations, has led to the fragmentation of traditional bureaucratic organisations. The objective of many of these changes was to give managers 'freedom to manage'. More and more managers are in control of their own budgets under systems of devolved management and are accountable for their performance. These systems of devolved management have sometimes been imposed, for example by the Education Reform Act 1988 and the NHS and Community Care Act 1990. In other cases pressure for change has come from within the organisation. Some of the advantages of these new structures are said to be increased efficiency, responsiveness and accountability.

Managerial accountability may be carried out by a number of groups. For many staff it will be exercised by their line managers. For senior managers this may involve being held to account by politicians. Managerial accountability is illustrated in Table 5.2. The table shows that managerial accountability encompasses a wide range of activities and a number of different stakeholders.

Table 5.2 Managerial accountability

	Accountability
Who is accountable?	Managers, staff
To whom?	Politicians, line managers
For what?	Economy, efficiency, effectiveness; administrative propriety; outputs; policy advice
How?	Reporting mechanisms, performance indicators

Day and Klein (1987) state that the concept of managerial accountability has its origins in the notion of stewardship and that it is an essential prerequisite of political accountability. The link between political and managerial accountability is important – to account to the people effectively (political or external accountability) representatives must be able to exercise managerial or internal accountability. They must be able to hold the service deliverers to account: 'public accountability, in the sense of the accountability of a government or council for activities undertaken in the public sector, can depend on the existence of managerial accountability within the departments of government' (Stewart, 1984, p 18). The operation of managerial accountability was comparatively straightforward when the public sector was small, but the problem of control obviously becomes greater as services become numerous and more complex. Hence it becomes increasingly difficult to control those providing services.

The issue of control and accountability is long-standing in relation to public services. Birch (1974, p 54) describes the operation of managerial accountability in local government in the following way:

> The principles of public accountability and stewardship are so fundamental and basic to local government that there has evolved within each authority an elaborate system of rules, regulations and procedures. This has been accompanied by the development of internal control and by the imposition of sets of checks and balances to ensure that rules are not broken, that regulations are adhered to and that procedures are followed. Thus has developed internal accountability in local authorities.

Gradually the emphasis has shifted from adherence to procedures to measurement of outputs as a mechanism of managerial accountability. A more 'managerial' rather than 'administrative' approach has developed. For example the Maud Report (1967) suggested that local authority members should set the objectives of the authority and review performance, whereas officers would deal with the day-to-day administration. As Day and Klein (1987, p 47) state, the report was suggesting that 'councillors should be more concerned with outputs and less concerned with inputs or process'. Developments of this type were not unique to local government. Reforms such as the Financial Management Initiative (FMI) in central government were designed to improve managerial accountability through the provision of information. Objectives were to be set, against which performance could be assessed. Gray and Jenkins (1986, p 56) suggest that 'The FMI . . .

aims to influence not only lower-level department operations but also ministerial conduct. The latter point may not be clear immediately but undoubtedly the intention is that ministers should be principal beneficiaries of the change: i.e. the information system should enhance ministerial capacity both for control and resource allocation.' Similar reforms have been recently developed and form a central part of what is described as the 'New Public Management'. This approach to managerial accountability includes an increased emphasis on strategic control through the measurement and evaluation of performance.

There has also been criticism of these new approaches to managerial accountability. Keen and Murphy state that devolved management 'is largely "hype" and rhetoric with little having changed, apart from the terminology, and that it promotes the interests, mainly, of an elite group of "new managerialists", rather than "customers" or "less senior staff"' (1996, p 39). Although the accountability and responsibility of middle managers appear to have increased there is often no corresponding increase in authority and autonomy. Middle managers do not always have real control over resource deployment. Humphrey *et al.* (1993) suggest that 'accountable management' appeals to some groups in an organisation more than others. This differential appeal, they argue, depends 'largely on the extent to which individuals perceive themselves as either being in control of the reforms or being able to use the reforms better to protect their own positions and/or enhance organisational performance' (1993, p 18).

Legal accountability

Public services organisations are also held to account for their actions through the legal system. This is illustrated in Table 5.3. Individuals may bring a civil action against an organisation, but issues of public law are mainly considered through statutory appeal procedures and judicial review. Woodhouse (1995) notes the increase in judicial review (from 525 applications in 1980 to 2089 in 1991), with 25 per cent of the applications related to central government. Part of the increase in applications for judicial review is because the system has become less heavily weighted against the applicant. Woodhouse also suggests that the judiciary is now increasingly willing to play a more significant role in public administration. Many statutes provide leave for appeal to the courts by individuals, and where this is not provided, individuals can seek an application for judicial review. The legal accountability of public services organisations is different from that of private sector organisations. For example local government operates under the doctrine of *ultra vires*, that is, councils may do only that which they are specifically empowered to do. In addition, if they are held to account in court through judicial review the criteria by which they may

Table 5.3 Legal accountability

	Accountability
Who is accountable?	Staff, politicians
To whom?	Courts
For what?	Legality, propriety, 'rationality'
How?	Judicial review, statutory appeals

Exhibit 5.2

Government accountability

On October 1992 the Secretary of State for Trade and Industry, Michael Heseltine announced his decision to close 31 collieries. Subsequently, on October 19 this was amended to a decision to close 10 of the collieries and review the future of the remaining 21. This decision was found to be unlawful, as the decisions had been made without any consultations with unions, in breach of section 99 of the Employment Protection Act. The ruling was that the unions were entitled to a declaration that British Coal should not reach a decision on the closure of any of the collieries until there has been a review procedure that included some form of independent scrutiny.

Source: Law Report, *The Times*, 30 December 1992.

---

be judged include not just legality, but also procedural propriety and 'rationality' on the part of the decision makers. A high-profile case of the government being held to account is illustrated in Exhibit 5.2.

Loughlin (1992, p 119) argues that local government is now more susceptible to control through legal processes and that the central government is transforming the legal relationship between local authorities and their consumers by giving, for example 'tenants a broad catalogue of rights which may be exercised against their landlord or by strengthening the rights of parents in matters of school placement and school government'. As we indicated above, it is certainly the case that the use of judicial review has increased substantially in recent years. However, the cases in which leave to review is sought are largely housing and immigration cases and, apart from these, the number of judicial review proceedings is actually very small (Sunkin *et al.*, 1993, cited in Drewry, 1995). An important aspect of legal accountability is that the remedies and sanctions are coercive. Hence public services organisations can be compelled to act in certain ways (Oliver, 1991).

There have been many criticisms of the operation of legal accountability. Concern has been expressed that the doctrine of *ultra vires* unduly restricts local government. It has been suggested that this hampers the development of local government and discourages enterprise. A solution to this may be a power of general competence, as currently exists in the 'free commune' experiments in the Scandinavian countries. This means that those local authorities may perform any function that they consider to be in the interests of their area, as long as it has not been expressly forbidden, or has been assigned to another authority.

There have also been criticisms of the system of judicial review. One is that 'the courts have been too willing to accept pleas of "public interest immunity" which means that government documents need not be disclosed to applicants for judicial review if sensitive issues of national security are in issue' (Oliver, 1991, p 113). The political salience of public interest immunity has increased since the Matrix Churchill trial, which centred on accusations of the illegal exportation of arms components to Iraq, as discussed above. Criticisms have also been made of the lack of a statutory basis of grounds for judicial review. Some have suggested that the grounds are too narrow, and others that they are too broad (*see* Oliver, 1991, pp. 112–13). Loughlin (1992, pp 121–2) sums up these criticisms, suggesting that:

The courts seem ill-equipped to handle the challenges with which they have been faced in the 1980's. They continue to invoke anachronistic doctrines, such as that of a fiduciary duty owed by a local authority to its ratepayers, they seem unable to devise principles concerning the exercise by the local authority of its dominion powers and simply requiring local authorities to 'bite the bullet' in matters of public finance may be viewed as an abnegation of judicial responsibility. The courts often seem incapable even of articulating the issues properly, let alone adjudicating on them in an appropriate manner.

Professional accountability

Professionalism can be defined in a number of ways and there is a substantial literature which addresses this question. One definition suggests that a profession is a group that has the following characteristics: possession of a body of systematic knowledge, a commitment to the client, an occupational association which grants rights to practise, and exclusive entry based on recognised credentials. Another definition is that a profession is an occupational group that has succeeded in pressing a claim to substantial autonomy for its members in the workplace (Laffin, 1990). The process of delivering public services has traditionally been perceived as so complex that a heavy reliance was placed on professional judgement, which had the result that only professionals could hold other professionals to account. This concept of accountability is illustrated in Table 5.4. Professional accountability is achieved through a variety of mechanisms.

First, the occupational association defines and monitors standards and has the authority to withdraw a right to practise. There was, for example, support for the creation of a General Teaching Council, a professional body for teachers, which would seek to improve standards and act as a regulating body (*Guardian*, 21 January 1997).

Second, standards are monitored through inspections such as those by Her Majesty's Inspectorate in education and the Social Services Inspectorate. The primary role of these inspectors is to promote good practice through advice and support. Attempts have been made to change this role with, for example, the requirement that one member of a school inspection team must be a lay person.

The third mechanism is an internal or moral sense of accountability to the values of the profession. These are inculcated through the long training necessary to obtain professional status. The value system, which places a commitment to the client before other considerations, is one of the defining characteristics of professionalism. Such accountability is not unique to professionals, however. One of the features of many voluntary organisations is an accountability to values rather than operations. In these organisations there is 'little attempt to account for decisions in terms of literal rules, concerted attempts are made to account for decisions in terms of substantial ethics' (Rothschild-Whitt, 1979, as quoted in Taylor, 1996). Problems may arise when these values clash with those of politicians and/or managers who are in charge of the organisation. This has been well documented in the reformed National Health Service where the doctor's duty of care to the individual patient may clash with the manager's efforts to improve efficiency.

Table 5.4 Professional accountability

	Accountability
Who is accountable?	Professionals
To whom?	Other professionals
For what?	Process, conduct
How?	Self-evaluation, occupational association

Conflict may also arise over attempts to introduce new methods of measuring performance. Sockett (1980, p 11) suggests that the view of education professionals is that 'the question they debate is not whether certain results have been achieved, but whether certain standards of integrity and practice have been adhered to'. Recent attempts by central government to introduce the publication of school test and examination results led to conflict with the teaching profession. Scott (1994) argues that the tensions between the professional and market models of accountability can be identified in the debate over the national curriculum and assessment regulations, particularly the appropriate method of assessing performance.

There have been a number of criticisms of professional accountability. One is that the emphasis on accountability to other professionals means there is insufficient responsiveness to the consumer. This was part of the rationale behind the introduction of reforms such as the Citizen's Charter and the introduction of a 'market' in education and health. William Waldegrave, the Minister responsible, stated that 'the key point in the argument is not whether those who run our public services are elected, but whether they are producer-responsive or consumer-responsive' (Waldegrave, 1993, p 13, quoted in Stoker, 1996). In general, the Conservative governments of the 1980s and 1990s were critical of professionals and hence, as Gray and Jenkins argue, 'the thrust of the reform agenda is almost unhesitatingly hostile to the values of traditional public sector professionals' (1995, p 81).

CHANGES IN ACCOUNTABILITY

The approach of Conservative governments of the 1980s and 1990s to public service reform is often referred to as 'managerialism' or the 'New Public Management'. Hood (1991) suggests that it has the following main points: hands-on professional management, explicit standards and measures of performance, greater emphasis on output controls, a shift to disaggragation of units, a shift to greater competition, a stress on private-sector styles of management practice and a stress on greater discipline and parsimony in resource use. This section examines a number of these changes and identifies the impact that they have had on accountability.

Structures

A wide range of structural changes to public services organisations have taken place, many imposed by the centre. These have had a major impact on accountability. One type of structural change has been the growth in quasi-governmental agencies, particularly at a local level. The extent of this growth has been debated (*see* Davies, 1995) but most would accept that there has been an increase in non-elected bodies. Charter 88 identified as many as 5521 such bodies with executive functions in the UK in 1994. Some of these organisations have taken over responsibility for functions that were once under the control of local government, for example Urban Development Corporations. In the field of education there have been suggestions that the Local Education Authority (LEA) has been marginalised and now has only a residual role (Ranson, 1995). Now schools can opt for grant-maintained status and thus to be out of LEA control. The Funding Agency for schools will allocate funds to those schools and will also plan schools places in areas which have more than 75 per cent of pupils in grant-maintained schools. Other new quasi-governmental agencies in this field are city technology colleges, further education and sixth form colleges, further and higher education funding councils and the Office for Standards in Education (OFSTED). This growth has been mirrored in other service areas such as housing and health.

The increase in these organisations has led to what has been described as 'the new magistracy' (Stewart, 1993) and to suggestions that we should more accurately use the term governance, rather than government (Stoker, 1996). Many would argue that one of the results of these developments has been a reduction in accountability. These organisations are not subject to local electoral control, and at best have indirect political accountability through ministers to Parliament. Although elections do not guarantee accountability, there are other requirements for local authorities that are not applicable to these non-elected bodies. Davies and Stewart (1993) show in their study of ten major types of quasi-governmental agency that none of the members is liable to surcharge, most are not required to hold meetings in public, some make their own arrangements for audit and most are not subject to the same requirements of public access to information as local government. Although political accountability has been reduced, some of these reforms were introduced with the aim of improving accountability to the consumer. This argument is considered later in this section.

Another change in the structure of many public services organisations is the disaggregation of what are perceived as large producer-dominated bureaucracies into a number of small units. These units, and the managers in charge, can be held to account through the use of performance targets, service level agreements and contracts. The use of legal contracts means that there can also be accountability to the courts. As our earlier discussion of managerial accountability indicates, the theory of devolved management does not always accord with reality. For example Ferlie *et al.* (1996) suggest that devolved management in the NHS has been accompanied by tighter line management hierarchies, which are necessary to implement top-down change. Hence it is unclear whether accountability has altered.

Similar structural changes have also taken place in the civil service, where executive functions have been devolved to 'Next Steps' Agencies. The aim of these reforms was to separate policy and executive functions in order to improve management and to reduce the workload of ministers. There are 109 agencies (*Next Steps Review*, 1995), for which complex governmental organisation is necessary. This development has also led to questions about the accountability of these agencies. As the Prisons Service example shows, it is difficult if not impossible to distinguish between policy and operational issues. These structural changes can lead to tensions, one of which is the role of the departmental Permanent Secretary. Massey (1995) suggests this tension is largely to do with a lack of clarity over accountability to Parliament. Permanent Secretaries, as departmental accounting officers, may be asked about agencies, and agency chief executives, as agency accounting officers, may be asked about strategic policy. Despite these problems, 'there is no doubt among officials that the Next Steps reforms have contributed to the ability of managers to manage well, efficiently, effectively and to be held accountable. Their annual reports, their targets and their overall performance are visible both to ministers and to parliament' (Massey, 1995, p 26). However, although it is true that there is an increase in information, there has been serious criticism of the quality of that information. Talbot (1995b, p 23) states that there is an absence of basic data that relate outputs to agency objectives, with the result that 'it is almost impossible to derive really meaningful information about "performance" from agency annual reports or from anywhere else'.

A final structural reform is the reorganisation of local government in Wales, England and Scotland. Whereas Wales and Scotland now have a single-tier system, England has a mixture of single and two-tier local authorities. The rationale for reorganisation in the Welsh Office consultation paper specified a number of criteria for a local government system, one of which was accountability. In addition, unitary authorities were said to provide 'clearer accountability to the electorate' (Welsh Office, 1991). As discussed above, the assumption is that the public does not understand the division of responsibilities in the two-tier system, and hence cannot hold the correct organisation to account. Some of the local authority submissions to the Welsh Office used this argument and provided survey evidence. For example: 'Cardiff residents are highly aware of many of the services provided by Cardiff City Council . . . however, residents are much less aware of the County Council as a provider'. The districts argued that they were already mistakenly being held accountable for many of the services which were provided by county councils (Boyne and Law, 1993). If we accept that the electorate was confused by the old system, we should expect clarity of accountability to improve in Scotland, Wales and parts of England. However, the likelihood is that the new authorities will be too small to directly provide specialist services, which will need to be provided through some form of joint arrangement. Obviously these will not be directly elected bodies. As a result accountability may be further confused. A number of other factors combine to reduce or weaken accountability in a unitary system. These include the reduction in the number of councillors in the new system, the lack of opportunity for the electorate to pass separate judgements on the performance of county and district councils and the increased opportunity for central government to control the smaller number of authorities (Boyne *et al.*, 1995).

Mechanisms

One of the main features of the reforms has been the introduction of competition in the production of public services. This has been achieved through policies such as compulsory competitive tendering (CCT), market testing and the creation of 'quasi-markets', for example in the health service. The emphasis in these reforms is that accountability will be achieved through the market. In a market-oriented model accountability is to the consumer, rather than to line managers, professionals or politicians. In such a system producer organisations are accountable to the consumer who chooses whether to consume their product or an alternative available in the marketplace. In order for the market to operate effectively information needs to be made available so consumers know the full specifications of the product they are 'buying'. Organisations need to respond to the demands of the marketplace or they face the possibility of going out of business. This is illustrated in Table 5.5.

Table 5.5 Market accountability

	Accountability
Who is accountable?	Service providers (e.g. schools)
To whom?	Consumers (e.g. parents and children)
For what?	Outputs (e.g. examination results)
How?	Market forces

The concept presented in Table 5.5 can be illustrated using the example of education. Feintuck (1994, p 88) states that the 'ultimate objective expressed by the proponents of the ERA (Education Reform Act 1988) and subsequent reforms was the enhancement of educational standards in schools, as a result of the introduction of mechanisms of accountability deriving from the exercise of market forces'. Decisions that were made via local democratic processes were to be replaced by market forces. The introduction of open enrolment in the Education Reform Act 1988 meant that parents could choose a school for their child, and the LEA could not determine admission levels. Grant-maintained schools and city technology colleges were also introduced, giving more choice by providing a differentiated product. The choice of school is informed by the publication of performance indicators such as examination results and truancy rates. School funding on the basis of pupil numbers was a central part of the Education Reform Act and the introduction of a market. Popular schools are now financially rewarded for attracting more pupils. Conversely, unpopular schools face major financial penalties, and may ultimately go out of business. The market as a mechanism of accountability has also been used in the NHS. In this case a 'quasi-market' operates as a result of the reforms introduced in the National Health Service and Community Care Act 1990. The Act separated the purchasing and providing of health services. The purchasing agents – health authorities and GP fundholders – developed contracts with the providers – hospitals and community services. Providers had an incentive to attract customers, as money followed patients; hence in theory providers could go out of business if they were unsuccessful. However, whereas the NHS operated through market accountability, this is not the type of accountability that many groups in the NHS perceived to be important. As stated earlier, professionals such as doctors tend to see themselves as accountable to the patient and their professional association. Ferlie *et al.* (1996) found that health authority members felt accountable to a number of groups. In contrast to the findings of Day and Klein's (1987) earlier study, members felt accountable upwards, through the hierarchy to the chairman of the board. Others felt accountable to the community. The concept of accountability through the market was hardly ever mentioned by the respondents in their study. Levaggi (1995) argues that accountability through the market has brought a number of benefits such as the drawing up of contracts and the increased clarity over standards and targets that this involves. Nevertheless, the market as it operated had a number of problems of accountability, primarily involving GP fundholders who were virtually unaccountable (Levaggi, 1995).

In the field of education, schools were made to be responsive by giving parents and children choice. In principle they have power to 'take their custom elsewhere', but in reality this course of action is heavily circumscribed by the availability of places. However choice is not available in all services, so reforms which introduced fixed standards and mechanisms of redress have been developed to encourage responsiveness. The primary example of this is the Citizen's Charter which is discussed in detail in Chapter 16. The aim of this Charter was to improve public services through quality, choice, standards and value and the provision of information to the public.

Accounting to the consumer may be more difficult for public services organisations than for private organisations, as it can be difficult to identify the customer. For example, who is the consumer of the police service? It may be a person held in custody, the Crown Prosecution Service, a victim of crime, or society in general. The consumer may be all or one of the above, at different times and in different circumstances.

The rise of market accountability has been mirrored by changes in other mechanisms. Professional accountability has clearly been under attack, and the increase in non-elected bodies has meant that the traditional emphasis on political accountability through the ballot box has declined. A major development has been the rise of managerial accountability with its mechanisms of performance targets and audit. These are discussed in the next section.

Performance measurement

One of the main characteristics of the reforms described as the 'new public management' has been the emphasis on performance measurement as a mechanism of control and accountability. Reforms such as the Citizen's Charter, the Financial Management Initiative, the publication of examination and truancy rates in school 'league tables', and the Next Steps initiative all fit this conception of accountability. Stone (1995, p 513) suggests that managerialism has led to 'an emphasis on strategic, rather than detailed control; an emphasis on agency self-evaluation and reporting plus periodic, formal external evaluation; and a "rationalisation" of agency responsiveness'. Instead of the traditional detailed control based on adherence to rules and procedures, a strategic approach is utilised, where the emphasis is on the setting of objectives and assessment of performance. The Next Steps Agencies, for example, have a framework document which contains broad policy objectives and key performance indicators which are approved by ministers. Often the mechanism of accountability is enforced self-evaluation and reporting by the agency concerned. Hence Next Steps Agencies, and local authorities, have to produce an annual report.

The emphasis in the majority of the reforms is on improving the quality of information available to evaluators, who may be the public, ministers, Parliament, or the Audit Commission. Stone (1995) argues that information is improved through stricter reporting requirements and outside involvement in the choice of performance indicators. As Stewart (1984) notes, for local authority services the external involvement comes from central government, which specifies the form of account and the information to be provided, in addition to details such as when and how it is to be published. One other characteristic of the managerialist approach to accountability is the 'rationalisation' of evaluation. Instead, for example, of being responsive to political demands as in the parliamentary control model, the organisation can be controlled through the measurement and evaluation of performance (Stone, 1995). There is an assumption in these reforms that objective indicators can be set which enable an assessment of performance. These and other issues relating to performance management are discussed in detail in Chapter 12.

CONCLUSIONS

One of the features of public services organisations is the complexity of accountability, which arises partially because of the large number of stakeholders involved. For example Chief Constables will be accountable to their Police Authority. They will also be accountable to the Home Office which provides 51 per cent of the funding for the police service and sets national standards and targets. In addition, they will be accountable to their staff, the community through liaison committees, and also to organisations such as the Audit Commission and the Police Complaints Authority. Each of these groups may be interested in a different aspect of performance, for example efficiency or propriety, which further complicates accountability. Problems may arise when there are conflicts of accountability. For example, the introduction of accountability through the market in education has led to an emphasis on examination results which conflicts with the traditional professional emphasis on the process of education. Similarly, the medical profession may face conflicting pressures in accounting to their professional association and accounting for their actions through the legal system.

The issue of accountability is obviously vital to public services organisations. They are held to account by a number of different groups and for many aspects of performance – from probity and legality to efficiency and effectiveness. The way in which public services organisations are accountable has undergone substantial change as part of the reforms of the New Public Management. These reforms have introduced accountability to the consumer through market mechanisms in areas such as health and education. They have also introduced a type of managerial accountability which emphasises the measurement of results through performance indicators, rather than adherence to procedures. Structural reform has also taken place in many organisations, involving disaggregation into small devolved units which can be held to account for their performance. Public services organisations have higher levels of legal accountability than private organisations and, in particular, make more frequent use of judicial review. The increase in these aspects of accountability has often been at the expense of more traditional methods of accountability. The principal control mechanisms were once political and professional, but these have to some extent been superseded by the mechanisms identified above. The increased role for non-elected bodies in the governance of public services means that direct political accountability has been reduced. The other traditional form of accountability under attack is professional accountability. A number of reforms have been imposed which introduce 'objective' standards and targets over areas which were once subject to professional evaluation alone.

These changes have had a major impact on those working in public services organisations, as they are held to account in new and different ways. For example, although the publication of the Citizen's Charter indicators does not currently command widespread public interest, this situation may change and these indicators may become central to the way in which the performance of public services organisations is judged. It has been suggested that the Labour Party may allocate funds to local authorities on the basis of performance on these indicators. These changes in mechanisms of accountability may, however, be resisted. Although accountability through the market has been introduced in education, a study of LEA perceptions of accountability in the period since the enactment of the Education Reform Act 1988 showed that the ethos of accountability was professional, and that officers and members attempt to minimise the impact of the reforms.

Although they operate within the legislative framework of market accountability, one councillor suggested that the strategy of the LEA was one of 'reducing the damage, as far as possible, by trying to reduce the influence of the market' (Farrell and Law, 1995, p 20).

Despite the changes outlined above, the issue of accountability will continue to be of profound importance as long as there are public services. The basis of the accountability of public services organisations is democratic, with most being funded through general taxation. The public therefore expect that those organisations will be accountable to them. Using the definition of accountability developed in this chapter, this will involve:

- the provision of information and the right to debate and question that information; and
- the capacity to impose sanctions if performance is felt to be unsatisfactory.

Each of the four traditional models of accountability, that is, political, managerial, legal and professional, has limitations. How effective can political accountability be if only 40–50 per cent of the electorate vote in local elections? How can politicians be accountable to the public if they are unable to control those who provide services? Is judicial review a useful mechanism for holding politicians to account? Does emphasising accountability to other professionals mean that there is insufficient responsiveness to the consumer?

Some of the reforms which are part of the 'New Public Management' were introduced to attempt to resolve these problems. However, they also have limitations. The example of the Prisons Service shows that the creation of Executive Agencies does not always clarify responsibility and accountability.

Accountability through the market does not work effectively if, for example, there is no real choice of school. Similarly, the emphasis on the easily measured aspects of performance in published sets of indicators such as the Citizen's Charter does not significantly enhance accountability.

REFERENCES

Birch, F (1974) 'Internal accountability in local government', *Public Administration Bulletin*, 17.

Bogdanor, V (1996) 'The Scott Report', *Public Administration*, 74(4), pp 593–611.

Boyne, G and Ashworth, R (1997) 'Party competition in local government: an empirical analysis of English counties 1974–1995', *Policy and Politics*, 25(2), pp 129–42.

Boyne, G, Jordan, A G and McVicar, M (1995) *Local Government Reform: A Review of the Process in Scotland and Wales*. London: Local Government Council and Joseph Rowntree Foundation.

Boyne, G and Law, J (1991) 'Accountability and local authority annual reports: The case of Welsh District Councils', *Financial Accountability and Management*, 7(3), pp 179–94.

Boyne, G and Law, J (1993) 'Bidding for unitary status: The contest in Wales', *Local Government Studies*, 19(4), pp 537–57.

Cadbury Report (1992) *Report of the Committee on the Financial Aspects of Corporate Governance*. Oxford: Gee Publishing.

The Citizen's Charter: Raising the Standard (1991) Cmnd. 1599. London: The Stationery Office.

Common, R and Flynn, N (1993) *Decentralisation and Competition*. Oxford: Butterworth Heinemann.

Connolly, M, Law, J and Topping, I (1996) 'Policing Structures and Public Accountability in Northern Ireland', *Local Government Studies*, 22(4), pp 229–44.

Davies, H (1995) *Inlogov Informs on Quangos*. Birmingham: Inlogov.

Davies, H and Stewart, J (1993) *The Growth of Government by Appointment: Implications for Local Democracy*. Luton: Local Government Management Board.

Day, P and Klein, R (1987) *Accountabilities. Five Public Services.* London: Tavistock.

Department of the Environment, Transport and the Regions (1998) *Modern Local Government: In Touch with the People.* London: The Stationery Office.

Drewry, G (1995) 'Public law', *Public Administration,* 73(1), pp 41–57.

Dunleavy, P and Jones, G with Burnham, J, Elgie, R and Fysh, P (1993) 'Leaders, politics and institutional change: The decline of prime ministerial accountability to the House of Commons, 1860–1990', *British Journal of Political Science,* 23(3), pp 267–98.

Dunsire, A (1978) *Control in a Bureaucracy. The Execution Process,* vol. 2. Oxford: Martin Robertson.

Elkins, D (1974) 'The measurement of party competition', *American Political Science Review,* 68, pp 682–700.

Farrell, C and Law, J (1995) *Educational Accountability in Wales.* York: Joseph Rowntree Foundation.

Farnham, S and Horton, D (eds) (1996) *Managing the New Public Services.* London: Macmillan.

Feintuck, M (1994) *Accountability and Choice in Schooling.* Milton Keynes: Open University Press.

Ferlie, E, FitzGerald, L and Ashburner, L (1996) 'Corporate governance in the post-1990 NHS: The role of the board', *Public Money and Management,* 16(2), pp 15–21.

Gray, A and Jenkins, B (1986) 'Accountable management in British central government: some reflections on the financial management initiative', *Financial Accountability and Management,* 2(3), pp 171–86.

Gray, A and Jenkins, B (1995) 'From public administration to public management: Reassessing a revolution', *Public Administration,* 73(1), pp 75–99.

Held, D (1993) *Prospects for Democracy: North, South, East and West.* Cambridge: Polity Press.

Hodges, R, Wright, M and Keasey, K (1996) 'Corporate governance in the public services: Concepts and issues', *Public Money and Management,* 16(2), pp 7–13.

Hood, C (1991) 'A public management for all seasons?', *Public Administration,* 69(1), pp 3–19.

Humphrey, C, Millar, P and Scapens, R (1993) 'Accountability and accountable management in the UK public sector', *Accounting, Auditing and Accountability,* 6(3), pp 7–30.

Jordan, G (1994) *The British Administrative System.* London: Routledge.

Keen, L and Murphy, M P (1996) 'Devolved budgetary management in local government – lessons from a shire county', *Financial Management and Accountability,* 12(3), pp 37–52.

Kogan, M (1986) *Educational Accountability. An Analytic Overview.* London: Hutchinson.

Laffin, M (1990) *Professionalism in Local Government.* Harlow: Longman.

Levaggi, R (1995) 'Accountability and the internal market', *Financial Accountability and Management,* 11(4), pp 283–96.

Lively, J (1975) *Democracy.* Oxford: Blackwell.

Loughlin, M (1992) *Administrative Accountability in Local Government.* York: Joseph Rowntree Foundation.

Massey, A (1995) 'Civil Service reform and accountability', *Public Policy and Administration,* 10(1), pp 16–33.

Maud, Sir John (1967) *Report of the Committee on the Management of Local Government,* Vol. 1. London: The Stationery Office.

Next Steps Review (1995). London: The Stationery Office.

Oliver, D (1991) *Government in the United Kingdom.* Milton Keynes: Open University Press.

Public Accounts Committee (1993) *Welsh Development Agency Accounts 1991–92, 4th Report.* London: The Stationery Office.

Rallings, C and Thrasher, M (1991) 'Local elections: the changing scene', *Social Studies Review,* 5(4), pp 163–6.

Ranson, S (1986) 'Towards a political theory of public accountability in education', *Local Government Studies,* 4, pp 77–98.

Ranson, S (1995) 'From reform to restructuring of education' in Stewart, J and Stoker, G (eds) *Local Government in the 1990s.* London: Macmillan.

Scott, D (1994) 'Making schools accountable: Assessment policy and the Education Reform Act' in Scott, D (ed.) *Accountability and Control in Educational Settings.* London: Cassell.

Simey, M (1984) *Government By Consent. The Principle and Practice of Accountability in Local Government.* London: Bedford Square Press.

Sockett, H (1980) 'Accountability – The contemporary issues' in Sockett, H (ed.) *Accountability in the English Educational System.* London: Hodder & Stoughton.

Stewart, J (1984) 'The role of information in public accountability' in Hopwood, A and Tomkins, C (eds) *Issues in Public Sector Accounting.* Oxford: Phillip Alan.

Stewart, J (1993) 'Advance of the new magistracy', *Local Government Management*, Summer, pp 18–19.

Stewart, J D (1992) *Accountability to the Public*. London: European Policy Forum for British and European Market Studies.

Stiles, P and Taylor, B (1993) 'Maxwell; the failure of corporate governance', *Corporate Governance*, 1(1), pp 34–45.

Stoker, G (1996) 'The struggle to reform local government: 1970–1995', *Public Money and Management*, 16(1), pp 17–21.

Stone, B (1995) 'Administrative accountability in the 'Westminster' democracies: Towards a new conceptual framework', *Governance*, 8(4), pp 505–26.

Talbot, C (1995a) 'The prison service: a framework of irresponsibility', *Public Finance Foundation Review*, November.

Talbot, C (1995b) 'Ministers and Agencies: Responsibility and Performance', submission to the Public Services Committee.

Talbot, C (1996) 'The prison service: A framework of irresponsibility', *Public Money and Management*, 16(1), pp 5–8.

Taylor, M (1996) 'Between public and private: Accountability in voluntary organisations', *Policy and Politics*, 24(1), pp 57–72.

Treasury and Civil Service Committee (1986) Seventh Report 1985–86, 'Civil Servants and Ministers: Duties and responsibilities', HC 42. London: The Stationery Office.

Welsh Office (1991) *The Structure of Local Government in Wales*. Cardiff: HMSO.

Woodhouse, D (1995) 'Public administration and the courts: a clash of values?', *Public Money and Management*, January/March, pp 53–9.

QUESTIONS AND DISCUSSION TOPICS

1 What are the implications of the Westminster model of government for the political accountability of public services?

2 In what ways are public services managers more accountable than those in the private sector?

3 Does there remain a case for expert professional bodies to hold their members accountable for the standards of their work?

6 Bureaucracy and markets

Aidan Rose and Alan Lawton

AIMS

This chapter will:

- examine changes in the public services and the consequences of those changes;
- discuss the consequences of those changes for structure, power and values of organisations;
- assess the criteria by which an organisation adopts one particular structural configuration rather than another;
- discuss the impact of structural change on people and processes.

INTRODUCTION

Like organisations in the private sector, public service organisations are facing a more dynamic and more turbulent environment. Writing from a generic perspective, the American management theorist Rosabeth Moss Kanter (1990, p 20) has argued that:

> If the new game of business is indeed like Alice-in-Wonderland croquet, then winning it requires faster action, more creative manoeuvring, more flexibility, and closer partnerships with employees and customers than was typical in the traditional corporate bureaucracy. It requires more agile, limber management that pursues opportunity without being bogged down by cumbersome structures or weighty procedures that impede action. Corporate giants, in short, must learn how to dance.

Similar sentiments have been expressed in a public service context by Osborne and Gaebler (1992) in their work on American public services. In their call to 'reinvent government' they argue that the adoption of ten principles can transform a bureaucratic government into an innovative one:

1. Government should seek to act as a catalyst to allow other organisations to provide services. It should seek to steer rather than to row.
2. Citizens should be empowered by transferring control from bureaucracies to the community.
3. Government should promote competition between service providers.
4. Government should be driven by its mission – what it is there to do – rather than by rules and regulations.
5. The performance of government should be judged by the outcomes – what it achieves – rather than by the inputs – what it swallows up.

6 By focusing on the customer, government will ensure that the needs of the customer and not the bureaucracy are being met.

7 Government should become an enterprise, earning rather than spending money.

8 Government should be proactive rather than reactive, looking to prevent problems rather than to cure them.

9 Government should be decentralised and participatory management should be encouraged.

10 Market mechanisms should be preferred to bureaucratic mechanisms

In this environment, public services managers are enjoined to be more responsive, more flexible, more entrepreneurial and innovative. At the same time, it is argued, structures must support these new roles and organisations will require flatter, more flexible and customer-responsive organisations, where decentralisation will have a key role to play.

There are a number of assumptions evident in such arguments:

1 Public service organisations should be responsive, flexible and innovative and, as public service organisations are bureaucratic they are unsuitable vehicles for delivering public services.

2 Bureaucracy is essentially seen as, in some sense, a bad thing.

3 The key value of public service organisations should be responsive to customers through the marketplace and traditional values of accountability, probity and procedural justice enshrined in a hierarchical structure are of diminishing importance.

The merits of bureaucratic structure have been questioned because of their costs, their lack of responsiveness and their 'deadening' effect on staff motivation and morale. Flatter organisations will allow, so it is argued, a quicker and more flexible response to the outside environment. We shall examine the status of these arguments, and the assumptions upon which they are based, throughout this chapter.

BUREAUCRACY AND THE PUBLIC SERVICES

However, before we move on, we need to examine briefly the status of bureaucracy. Discussions of bureaucracy start with Max Weber. Beetham (1987, pp 11–12) summarises the basic features of a bureaucratic system as propounded by Weber:

Hierarchy: each official has a clearly defined competence within a hierarchical division of labour, and is answerable for its performance to a superior;

Continuity: the office constitutes a full-time salaried occupation, with a career structure which offers the prospect of regular advancement;

Impersonality: the work is conducted according to prescribed rules, without arbitrariness or favouritism, and a written record is kept of each transaction;

Expertise: officials are selected according to merit, are trained for their function, and control access to the knowledge stored in the files.

According to Weber, bureaucracy has the potential to be more efficient than any other form of organisational structure. Bureaucracies ensure control, uniform treatment, consistency and clarity in applying rules and reduce arbitrary decision making. However, in the period since the Second World War a substantial body of literature emerged showing that as well as producing intended consequences, bureaucracies also produced unintended consequences. These are also known as the dysfunctions of bureaucracy. These include:

1 Rules can become ends in themselves; managers may hide behind them and use them as an excuse for not exercising judgement. 'I was only following the rules' does not remove the need for individual judgement (*see* Merton, 1940).

2 Rules can increase the power of public officials, who may use the knowledge of the rules to circumscribe the desires of politicians. In this sense it is argued that bureaucracy undermines the democratic process. Bureaucracy is not a neutral machine for the transmission of politicians' wishes into public policies (*see* Thompson, 1983).

3 Rules can lead to rigidity and to lack of motivation among staff, particularly where, for example, promotion is based on seniority and position in the hierarchy rather than ability (*see* Gouldner, 1954 and Crozier, 1964).

4 Informal rules may be more efficient for achieving organisational goals; sometimes rules can be too rigid and not allow the discretion necessary for officials to make decisions. 'Red tape' sometimes has to be by-passed (*see* Blau, 1963).

CASE STUDY 6.1

The Financial Times *article reproduced below illustrates the problems of a 'bloated' bureaucracy.*

A BATTLE TO CUT BUREAUCRACY

By David Lane

According to legend, Italians are burdened with 150 000 laws and regulations. Whether or not this figure is correct, few would dispute Italy's claim to the slowest, most complex and contorted bureaucracy and legal system in western Europe.

Even where these are aimed at the citizens' benefit, such as traffic laws covering one-way streets, pedestrian crossings and seat belts, they are flouted. Such law-breakers are not infrequently the uniformed servants of state and city. The average Italian's lack of respect for authority is understandable, and so is the fragile trust between citizen and state.

If Mr Franco Bassanini, the civil service and regional affairs minister, has his way, relations between Italians and authority will change radically and for the better. Mr Bassanini has been busy since becoming a minister one year ago.

While not confirming the existence of 150 000 laws and regulations, Mr Bassanini, a former university professor of constitutional law, admits that Italy is far too regulated. 'There are many more laws and regulations than in other countries, and an enormous number of them are obsolete. A thorough clean-out is needed,' he says, describing the present situation as 'Byzantine'.

'Do people know that official permission is needed to donate books to school libraries or computers to parish youth clubs?' he asks. This requirement dates from laws enacted in 1855 and 1896 and has led to numerous absurdities, such as the pulping of 250 000 books that a publisher wanted to donate to public libraries in Piedmont. Each book would have had to be valued and be given approval for donation, an enormous cost in terms of time and money that neither donor nor recipient was willing to incur.

Mr Bassanini has three main objectives. First, he wants to deregulate by reducing the number of rules that impinge both on the private sector and business, and on the civil service itself. 'Rules paralyse the public administration as well as business,' he notes.

Administrative federalism, under which responsibilities are decentralised and local administrations take a greater role, should help to improve efficiency and make the system more user-friendly.

Second, he seeks a lesser role for government which continues to be swollen, in spite of privatisations. Highly publicised sell-offs involving banks, the ENI state energy group and subsidiaries of the IRI state holding corporation have barely scraped the surface.

Probably few Italians know that spectacles and rope factories are among the industrial assets owned by the ministry of defence. A national dredging service is operated at great cost and with great inefficiency by the transport ministry.

'The public sector should concentrate on its core business. This means privatising and outsourcing,' says Mr Bassanini. He sees no reason why Italy should have a national body for certifying the safety of lifts, an activity which, like motor car testing, could be better and less expensively done by the private sector.

The third objective is the simplification of procedures. Anyone familiar with the Italian bureaucracy, whether central or local, knows that the system's aim often seems to be the creation of difficulties and obstacles for users. The vexing bureaucratic perseverance tests to which businessmen wishing to build factories or expand existing operations are subject are one reason why Italy has been a loser in attracting inward investment.

Little wonder that Italian businessmen are enthusiastic supporters of Mr Bassanini's reforms. Mr Guidalberto Guidi, a director of the Confindustria industrialists' association, said that the minister's aims are completely in line with what business seeks. He described the reforms as courageous. But Mr Guidi is less optimistic than Mr Bassanini about the number of laws and rules to which Italians are subject: he puts the figure at 612 000.

The annual cost to business of the time needed to satisfy bureaucracy's requirements amounts to L20.2 trillion (L20 200bn), according to Confindustria. An employee must be engaged for more than a day in order to register a lorry. Delays mean that permits for factory expansion can take up to 6 years to arrive. And the posts? 'Business has given up on the postal service. Fax and private courier have taken over completely,' says Mr Guidi.

Scathing about the posts, which he described as making work for the unemployed, Mr Guidi is also critical of the national employment service. 'The employment offices are useless. Business would not notice if they were shut tomorrow.'

Mr Bassanini may have these in mind when he says that 30 000 of Italy's 50 000 public bodies should be closed down.

Few have illusions that implementing the reforms will be easy, however. The bureaucratic mentality is an enormous obstacle. 'Civil servants have difficulty in conceiving that new is better than old, that being free is better than being a state employee,' says Mr Guidi.

The minister agrees. 'The real problem is changing the culture. Traditional bureaucracy resists change. There will be enormous resistance,' he says. While trade union leaders such as Mr Guglielmo Epifani of the leftwing CGIL organisation fully support Mr Bassanini's reforms, objections arise on the extreme right and left of the political spectrum.

Source: Financial Times, 21 July 1997. Reprinted with permission.

Questions on the case study

1 What are the problems of an over-bureaucratic state?

2 What do you think should be the core business of the public sector?

What is clear, however, is that discussions of structure turn on an assumption that it is closely linked with strategy. We will discuss strategy in detail in Part 2. For the moment, we need to be aware that an organisation's goals need to be supported by its structures and that as goals change then it is likely that there will be pressure for structural change.

STRATEGY AND STRUCTURE

Public service organisations define themselves in different ways. For example, local authorities can play the role of direct service provider, they can adopt a commercial approach or a neighbourhood approach or define themselves in terms of community government. Each role may require a different organisational structure as the following analysis indicates.

1 Direct service provider may be based on traditional departments carrying out a particular function such as education or social services. Control may be located in the hands of professionals at the top of a hierarchical structure (*see* Leach *et al.*, 1994, pp 239–40).

2 The commercial-style organisation may deliver services through a range of other bodies all kept at arm's length on a contractual basis. A strong central core will be concerned with contract specifications, tendering and monitoring functions (*see* Leach *et al.*, 1994, pp 241–2).

3 A neighbourhood approach may require power to be devolved to neighbourhood offices at the local level, with a small central core (*see* Leach *et al.*, 1994, pp 242–3).

4 A community approach may require that the organisation be structured on matrix lines where programme teams rather than departments deliver services which cut across traditional departmental or geographical boundaries.

The key issue is what the organisation does and how its structures can best support it.

Strategy is concerned with where an organisation is going and structures are concerned with how to get the organisation there. Strategy is not a given and strategic processes are iterative in nature.

Let us return to the example of bureaucracy and compare it with an alternative structure, with what Kanter (1990) calls 'post-entrepreneurialism' (*see* Table 6.1).

Table 6.1 Bureaucracy and Kanter's 'post-entrepreneurialism'

	Bureaucracy	*Corporate ideal*
Authority system	Position centred, status or rank critical	Person centred, authority derives from expertise and/or relationships
Task focus	Repetition oriented	Creation oriented, seeks innovation and efficiency
Orientation	Rules oriented	Results oriented
Reward system	Payment for status	Payment for contribution and value added
Information flows	Formal structures, restricting information	Communication and coalitions
Style	Creates mandates and territories	Opportunities developed by network relations
Direction	Seeks ownership and control	Seeks leverage and experimentation

One conclusion that we can draw from the analysis presented in Table 6.1 is that bureaucracy as an organisational form may be suited to a particular context. Thus it may be appropriate where, for example, large amounts of information need to be stored for long periods of time, where organisational tasks are repetitive and the external context of the organisation is stable and likely to remain so.

Structures do not stand alone but involve people, processes, outcomes and tasks. Kanter's post-entrepreneurial model implies that organisations need to move from:

- an emphasis on hierarchical decision making to an approach stressing delegation and personal responsibility;
- a focus on quantity to a focus on quality;
- being a service provider to having a user orientation;
- an emphasis on internal procedures to an emphasis on outcomes;
- an emphasis on professional judgement to an emphasis on management of contracts and trading relationships within an internal market;
- stability and conformity to innovation and diversity.

Internal strategies and structures

The classical management theorists were concerned with the enduring principles of organisation structure. From Taylor onwards, through Fayol to Burns and Stalker (*see* Lawton and Rose, 1994), structures have reflected a concern with:

- rules, processes and work tasks;
- division and specialisation of labour;
- allocation of duties and responsibilities;
- relationships between the centre and departments and/or field offices in terms of control;
- communication;
- configuration in terms of size, functions, clients, place, knowledge and skills;
- vertical and horizontal integration;
- co-ordination.

One of the key internal roles of structure is to ensure co-ordination between the different parts of the organisation. Traditional approaches to public services assume that an organisation structured in hierarchical terms, such as a bureaucracy, is best placed to achieve this. According to Mitchell (1993, p 12):

> Hierarchy is a structural mechanism for bringing about co-ordination, of running a large and complex organisation, of making a large number of individuals act together for a collective purpose, of producing desired end results, in short it is a way of 'getting things done'.

Whether co-ordination is best carried out by hierarchy is, however, open to question and later in the chapter we examine the role of markets in co-ordination. However, many organisations have tinkered with their structure and then found a rationale for so doing; strategy has followed structure. Under the guise of speedier decision making, or encouraging and empowering frontline staff, organisations have sought to cut costs by 'de-layering'. Tiers of middle management have disappeared. Advocates argue that de-layering gets rid of unnecessary tiers of management and empowers staff to take on more responsibility and become more involved in organisation decisions. Others argue that de-layering expands responsibilities but often not resources, reduces career opportunities and leads to bigger workloads and increased stress. Whatever the arguments, it is clear that the workplace is changing.

The Local Government Management Board (1996) argued for:

- smaller corporate management teams;
- the appointment of specialist policy advisers to support decision making;
- decentralisation and a move towards multifunctional directorates;
- the establishment of contracting units staffed by councillors with a remit to seek value for money and service quality;
- increased use of joint officer/member working groups;
- partnerships and alliances with a variety of organisations.

Equally obvious are the costs involved in changing from one form of structure to another. Kanter argues that there are many by-products of significant organisational restructuring, including discontinuity, disorder and distraction.

> If mismanaged, restructuring can all too easily make people feel helpless, anxious, startled, embarrassed, dumb, overworked, cynical, hostile or hurt. Restructuring thus produces a window of vulnerability at a time when exposure to disease is increased at precisely the same time as the corporate body is temporarily weakened. This threatens not only current productivity, but also the foundation of the future, the organisation's credibility, culminating in a *crisis of commitment and a need for people to reaffirm their membership*. Every time the basis of the relationship of employee and company changes, a recommitment is necessary. It is especially ironic that more commitment is needed at the very time when the basis for commitment itself is temporarily weakened (Kanter, 1990, p 63, emphasis in original).

NEW DECENTRALISED ORGANISATIONS

Organisations are not value neutral; that is, a belief in efficiency, responsiveness, control or whatever is not just about improving organisational effectiveness but is also a concern with a preferred way of conducting business. As we saw above, advocates of de-layering argue that it is a good thing in so far as it empowers frontline workers. Values are an enduring feature of public services organisations and one expression of these is in terms of the balance between political ideals (in Western countries, the ideals of democracy) and organisational effectiveness. Those who support decentralisation argue that not only does it encourage the organisation to be more flexible and responsive but it is also more democratic. For example, Burns *et al.* (1994, p 28) argue that 'Decentralisation offers glimpses of a new vision for local government which is rather different from the current obsession with markets and quasi-markets'.

Decentralisation is seen as strengthening 'voice' in local government by:

- improving representative democracy through voter registration drives, open government, giving citizens rights at meetings and providing better support for councillors;
- extending representative democracy in area committees of councillors based on wards or groups, and strengthening parish councils;
- fusing representative with participatory democracy by co-option on to committees, neighbourhood committees and user groups;
- extending participatory democracy through the funding of non-statutory groups,

community development and user groups and valuing grass-roots participation (*see* Burns *et al.*, 1994, p 35).

Jeffrey (1997) argues that the traditional local authority committee is an inappropriate vehicle for participation. She says that local authorities which have widened the scope of participatory democracy through the encouragement of community involvement in decision making have become dominated by a community élite. Jeffrey argues that structures tend to limit committee membership, that discussion has often taken place elsewhere, that papers are only circulated to key members and that the local authority committee cycle means that time is a key constraint. She concludes (1997, p 30) that 'The cumulative effect of the way the structures operate is to reinforce the creation of a community elite of "gatekeepers" into the system. They become pseudo-councillors, but with none of the councillor's requirements of accountability and adherence to a party manifesto.' This illustrates the way in which structures can be used to further individual ends. Structures, ideally, will support strategy. Organisations are not, however, rational bodies, but places where power is played out.

Decentralisation can be seen in terms of power transferred from a central body to sub-units or operational agencies. The centre gives up some of its power and decisions are taken lower down the organisational hierarchy. In contrast, deconcentration is carried out for administrative reasons where it is considered that a service could be more effectively administered by local or regional bodies; power is still held at the centre. Local bodies become more effective in carrying out national policies rather than determining policies for themselves. Mintzberg (1983, p 99) identifies three different types of decentralisation:

1 *Vertical decentralisation*, where power is located down the chain of command.
2 *Horizontal decentralisation*, where decision-making powers are transferred to people outside the line structure.
3 *Dispersal*, involving the physical relocation of services. This is often referred to as field administration.

However, even administrative relocation may not be 'power neutral', as new regional offices of central government may conflict with local government or may impose greater central control over local government, for example, through Single Regeneration Budget allocations.

The two cases presented in Case study 6.2 are of fictional local authorities in an inner city in England. Both have similar demographic features; they have a similar population size (100 000) and sizeable ethnic minorities (15 per cent); both areas are socially and economically deprived, with high unemployment and with almost 40 per cent of the population in rented council accommodation.

Both councils are Labour-controlled, with a handful of Liberal Democrats and Independents.

| CASE STUDY 6.2 | **DECENTRALISATION** |

Case A

Interest in decentralisation goes back to the 1970s. In its 1982 election manifesto the Labour Party made a commitment to decentralisation but without specifying the form that it might take. The Labour Party saw decentralisation as part of a broader strategy of constructing a 'community in struggle' against the central government controlled by the Conservative Party. However, neighbourhood offices were created and put in place in 1983. Local residents were initially wary, particularly as tenants associations already existed, with their own negotiating machinery, but they had not been consulted over the precise roles of the neighbourhood offices. Staff were put into neighbourhood offices without consultation. Despite the attempts of workers in the neighbourhood offices to respond to the local communities, progress seemed to be slow and achievements thin on the ground. Workers felt under a great deal of pressure to 'fire-fight' crises – which arose frequently – but felt that they had little support and few resources; staff felt isolated. Each neighbourhood office had its professional staff but they tended to look to their parent departments, which still existed, rather than to the locality. Departmental interests still seemed to dominate the authority and the neighbourhood offices seemed to mirror existing structures and the interests of the centre, which changed little.

Political support seemed to ebb and wane as councillors perceived power to be located in existing service committees, which had a vested interest in preserving departmental structures. Decentralisation issues were dealt with by a subcommittee of the central Policy and Resources Committee.

Case B

In this authority neighbourhood offices were also created but the background was very different. There were no existing local offices of any description. After extensive consultation with local citizens and with its staff the local authority decided to create neighbourhood offices at the same time as it restructured the rest of the authority. Many of the existing departments were abolished and multidisciplinary teams were created at all levels. Resources were put into staff training and development, particularly in making staff and services more user friendly. Resources were devolved to neighbourhood offices, which opened at hours to suit local citizens. Each office consisted of interdisciplinary teams who drew up action plans with neighbourhood involvement to decide on local needs and local priorities. The authority invested in a management information system which linked up the offices with each other and the centre.

What are the lessons from the two cases?

1 Whereas localisation may be relatively easy to achieve in terms of the physical relocation of services from a centralised to a neighbourhood level, location is not enough.

2 A change in culture is required, not just by managers, but also by citizens.

3 Relations with the centre need to be worked through.

4 New working practices need to be adopted: more flexible forms of management need to be achieved through multidisciplinary teams drawing on a multiskilled workforce.

5 The involvement of key stakeholders both inside and outside the organisation may help to overcome entrenched interests.

As we saw in the two cases presented in Case study 6.2 on decentralisation, a number of problems were encountered. These include fears about deskilling and worries about redundancy, on the part of staff, and an unwillingness of areas to take on functions. Often there is a perception that insufficient resources are being devolved with the responsibility. Factors leading to success include devolving functions only when it is clearly cost effective to do so and the development of improved management information systems. Management of the area to which functions are devolved must accept the responsibility and their accountability for performance. Quality control should be provided, together with feedback. Customer care strategies also need to be developed.

So far we have concentrated on decentralisation in terms of area. It is also possible to reorganise on the basis of function, and it is this which underpins the creation of business or trading units. Consider the advantages and disadvantages of creating a direct service organisation (DSO) (*see* Exhibit 6.1).

Exhibit 6.1

Direct service organisation: functional decentralisation

Advantages
- large enough to recruit competent managers;
- large enough to influence the rest of the authority in the pursuit of its interest;
- economies of scale;
- ability to use its staff flexibly;
- easier to identify and allocate the cost of DSO services;
- easier to allocate capital, buildings and land;
- easier to allocate central overheads.

Disadvantages
- it may become too dominant in the affairs of the authority;
- possible duplication of functions and staff;
- establishing a radically different structure will involve considerable disruption to the authority;
- possible difficulty in recruiting managers to manage large DSOs;
- it will contain a very wide range of functions that may bear little relationship to each other.

Source: Local Government Training Board, 1988, p 8.

Decentralisation has been experimented with throughout liberal democracies. In Australia, for example, the public sector has undergone major reforms in recent years. One aspect of this reform has been the creation of devolved agencies at all levels of government. The Management Advisory Board conducted a comprehensive survey of decentralisation in central government. Its findings are set out in Exhibit 6.2 overleaf.

Exhibit 6.2

Advantages and disadvantages of decentralisation

Benefits

- Devolution is a powerful tool to promote and implement change.
- Managers are more in control of achieving outcomes.
- Managers become more familiar with corporate management issues.
- Managers have more scope in determining the level and type of service delivery and the method of delivery.
- Managers can be more responsive to stakeholders.
- Service providers are closer to their clients and have a better understanding of needs.
- There are opportunities for increased job satisfaction.
- Managers have the opportunity to acquire new and marketable skills.

Costs

- Loss of quality and increased inconsistency in decision making.
- Loss of purchasing power and other economies of scale.
- Duplication of tasks or functions.
- Reduction in number of people skilled in providing corporate services.
- Diminution of expertise, for example in personnel matters.
- Loss of corporate identity.

Findings

1 Commitment from the Chief Executive is crucial.
2 Communication, transparency and openness are needed.
3 Training for all staff is crucial.
4 Appropriate time must be allowed, plus monitoring and evaluation.
5 Line managers must be given real choices about how they will obtain or undertake corporate service functions.
6 Accountability must be taken into consideration.
7 There is no one best way; each agency needs to find its own way.
8 There is a need for good management information systems.
9 Trust line managers.

Source: Management Advisory Board, 1992.

THE CORE AND THE PERIPHERY

In the rhetoric surrounding decentralisation it is easy to forget that there are certain advantages in centralisation. These include:

- easier implementation of a common policy for the organisation as a whole;
- prevention of subunits becoming too independent;
- easier co-ordination;
- improving economies of scale and a reduction in overhead costs;
- greater use of specialisation;
- improved decision making, which might otherwise be slower and a result of compromise because of differentiated authority;
- uniform and equitable treatment of clients.

Some local authorities are experimenting with the development of a stronger strategic core which is responsible for controlling the core values of the organisation and the strategies which it wishes to pursue. Service units are controlled through strict performance management systems. Thus there appear to be two trends: one with a strong corporate centre and another in which organisations are being encouraged to change their structures in favour of giving responsibility (though not always power) to those lower down the organisation. Winstanley *et al.* (1995) describe public services restructuring as involving change from:

- centralised management to local management of service provision;
- direct hierarchical control to arm's length regulation;
- a smaller number of large hierarchies to more complex networks of organisations;
- being state owned and run to being characterised by a contracting out of services, CCT and the development of quasi-markets;
- a unified service to a splitting of the purchaser and provider roles.

Such changes are deemed to be desirable. Consider the LGMB's view of good management in local government (1993, pp 42–3):

The well-managed authority is one which:
- undertakes structural change only when it has established a real need for it and avoids cosmetic changes;
- establishes a relatively small management team of officers (five to eight members) whose primary role is strategic and encourages a strong sense of corporate identity;
- relies on informal networks of staff throughout the organisation to deal with corporate problems and spread corporate messages;
- develops a clear view of the role of the centre of the organisation in the new local government context;
- achieves a balance between central direction and devolution of managerial control.

Whether such authorities exist is a moot point. Research carried out by Rao and Young found that:

There were also indications that regrouping the authority around a set of trading units exposed the lacunae in the overall strategic management of authorities. The externalisation of parts of technical services, or the loss of a competitive bid by an in-house team under CCT, could have an impact on the authorities' central departments as they reduce the customer base. In one authority it was recognised that while certain aspects of central service provision would be carried out externally, such as payroll, accountancy, legal and personnel advice, and personnel records, the authority should seek to retain a significant proportion of the central support services 'to enable the client and regulatory services to carry out its statutory, democratic and strategic functions' (1995, p 43).

Of course, such structural changes are not 'people neutral' in their effects. Charles Handy (1990) uses the imagery of the shamrock to show how organisations may be composed of three different kinds of staff:

1 The first leaf is the core professionals; it is shrinking.
2 Non-essential work is contracted out so that much of the work of an organisation is carried out by people not in the organisation. The risks are thus outside the organisation.
3 Flexible labour force, part-timers and temporary staff.

Each group of people will have a different kind of commitment to the organisation, a different contractual arrangement and a different set of expectations. A core group, whose contribution is deemed to be essential and which would be difficult to replace, will sit alongside others who are more peripheral, in the sense of being more easily replaceable or whose work adds little extra value to the organisation.

Much of what has been happening in public services organisations in recent years poses questions for the boundary of the organisation. These relate to the practice of outsourcing, where an organisation contracts to another supplier work that was previously done in house. Under competitive tendering, many authorities have outsourced activities such as payroll, catering, security, cleaning, IT services. One driving factor is legislation, but other reasons include political motivations, so as to give, for example, at least the illusion of reducing the size of the public sector; a belief in the private sector; or a requirement to cut costs. Invariably the contracting out of work provides an incentive for firms to win contracts through offering lower tender prices, often based on lower labour costs. It may also allow access to specialist services, or may eliminate peripheral activities which distract from the core business.

The issues for management in outsourcing include contract negotiation, confidentiality and risk sharing. Outsourcing may result in the loss of expertise in certain areas which is difficult to recover. There is a danger of 'hollowing out' the organisation, the loss of core capabilities, leaving nothing in their place.

According to Bahrami (1992, p 38):

> The emerging organizational system of high-technology firms is more akin to a 'federation' or a 'constellation' of business units that are typically interdependent, relying on one another for critical expertise and know-how. Moreover they have a peer-to-peer relationship with the center. The center's role is to orchestrate the broad strategic vision, develop the shared organizational and administrative infrastructure, and create the cultural glue which can create synergies, and ensure unity of mission and purpose.

FROM HIERARCHY TO MARKETS

As indicated above, outsourcing or contracting out can be given an economic justification. Before we turn to consider that aspect, however, let us consider the role of hierarchies in organisations. It is assumed that hierarchy should give way to either markets or networks as a means of organising the delivery of public services. Jaques (1990, p 127) offers an alternative view: 'managerial hierarchy is the most efficient, the hardiest, and in fact the most natural structure ever devised for large organisations'.

According to Jaques, a hierarchy meets four fundamental needs:

1 To add value to work as it moves through the organisation.
2 To identify and nail down accountability at each stage of the value-adding process.
3 To place people with the necessary competence at each organisational layer.
4 To build a general consensus and an acceptance of the managerial structure that achieves these ends.

He argues that the managerial role has three key features. First, every manager must be held accountable for the work of subordinates and for adding value to their work. Second, every manager must be held accountable for sustaining a team of subordinates capable of doing this work. Third, every manager must be held accountable for setting a direction and getting subordinates to follow willingly.

There are boundaries between successive managerial layers and these have a time-span element to them. The more distant the time-span, the heavier the weight of responsibility. Senior managers are looking at a direction for the next three years, the production supervisor at a direction for the next three months. Jaques argues that managerial boundaries occur at a specific time-span increment. Similarly, the higher up the hierarchy, the more complex are the problems to be solved. Jaques (1990, p 133) argues that 'What we need is not some new kind of organization. What we need is managerial hierarchy that understands its own nature and purpose.'

However, Leach *et al.* (1994, p 124) argue that the public services have moved from hierarchy to markets: 'The relationship between the centre and direct service providers has moved from one of distribution on the basis of command, towards allocation on the basis of exchange, that is, from hierarchy towards market processes.'

The centre no longer retains control through hierarchy but through a mixture of subcontracting, franchising and partnership arrangements. Williamson (1975) contrasts the co-ordinating role of the market, in contrast to hierarchy, and provides a theoretical underpinning for contracting out. Williamson argues that hierarchical co-ordination is more efficient under certain conditions:

1 Where there is insufficient information to specify a market contract, that is, where *bounded rationality* exists, with the result that future contingencies cannot be specified or it is costly to do so.
2 Where *opportunism* exists, so that parties to a contract will try and take advantage of any loopholes. By internalising the transaction the firm gains more information. Also, where there are a large number of competitors, opportunists would have more difficulty in renewing contracts than where there is no alternative.
3 Where *asset specificity* (specialised equipment or skills) exists, that is, where resources are committed to a specific activity and have little value in any alternative use. A small number of suppliers and buyers increases asset specificity since there are few alternatives and price can be affected. A component supplier would charge a higher price to compensate for the risk of the investment.

Where these conditions are internal to an organisation risks are reduced and transaction costs are lowered. Williamson argues that a firm has a role to play in the economic system if transactions can be organised within the firm at less cost than if the same transactions were carried out through the market. The limit to the size of the firm is reached when the costs of organising additional transactions within the firm exceed the costs of carrying out the same transactions through the market. Transaction costs economics adopts a comparative contractual approach to the study of economic organisation in which the transaction is made the basic unit of analysis.

This approach employs two critical behavioural assumptions:

1 Human agents are assumed to be independently rational but only in a limited way. Bounded rationality means that comprehensive contracting is not feasible.
2 Human agents are given to opportunism. Therefore costs of safeguards may be high.

Bartlett (1991) examines contracting in the NHS using the transaction costs approach. He argues that the NHS reforms move away from vertical integration to more market-like considerations. It is, though, a quasi-market in which consumers' decisions are mediated through a variety of intervening agents, the District Health Authority or fundholding GPs.

Bartlett argues that many of the defects of market exchange associated with uncertainty, bounded rationality, opportunism and asset specificity apply to the NHS. He examines different types of contract – block, cost per case, cost and volume (a mixture of the other two):

1 Complete contracts, which cater for every possible act of nature, are difficult and costly to write, implement and enforce. Therefore transaction costs will be relatively high.
2 Incomplete block contracts (which the NHS prefers) are the answer, but they do allow opportunistic strategies and they shift the risk on to the provider unit.

However, as Stewart (1993) points out, contracting for the public services involves more than economic considerations. He considers the advantages claimed for the contract model:

1 It separates the political process of determination of objectives from their delivery, removing the conflict of interest which occurs when those specifying a service are also its deliverers.
2 It reduces the public choice phenomenon of lobbying for bureaucratic expansion by introducing built-in competitive pressures.
3 It strengthens opportunities for quality control.
4 It makes funding transparent.
5 It regularises relationships between central government, local authorities and competing agencies.
6 It establishes a set of guarantees with reciprocal responsibilities.

Could any of these be achieved without contracts or with existing relationships? Stewart accepts that, in the past, public services have been too much producer led. Yet is government by contract the only response?

It cannot be assumed that the introduction of contracts into public services is unproblematic or that contracts can play the same role in relation to public services as they do in the private sector. They have to be judged by criteria grounded in government. The local council, for example, is responsible for everything done in its name; the DSO or a business unit is not in the same legal position. Stewart (1993, p 12) argues that:

> The process of government has its distinctive role as the arena of collective action in society on which the functioning of society depends. In the public domain the process of government enables values to be realized and purposes pursued that are beyond the capacity of private action. Insofar as contracts enable that process, they can promote governmental effectiveness as well as efficiency of service delivery, but there are limits. Government cannot be reduced to a series of contracts.

Public sector organisations, particularly in the NHS, tend to operate in quasi-markets where the boundary between public and private is blurred. The existence of hybrid organisations which both provide tax-supported services and rely on income from the commercial market leads, according to Paton (1993), to a dual logic. The logic of the quasi-market is different from that of the commercial market. Quasi-markets involve:

- a fixed pot of tax finance, now distributed more on the basis of competitive bidding;
- a mixed bag of competition and collaboration;
- fragmentation of the organisation and agreement between units in terms of service-level agreements (internal contracts);
- continued existence as non-profit organisations.

Hybrid managers compete in two markets – quasi and the real thing! Paton identifies a number of key questions. First, how much of the resources of the organisation are to be devoted to the two sides? Second, where are funds reinvested? Third, what products are developed? Fourth, what pricing policy is appropriate? Fifth, what are the internal transfer prices?

Rather than enhance responsiveness, it could be argued that the introduction of markets creates increased organisational formality. Services are more strictly specified, payment systems are precisely defined – involving orders and invoices. Record systems are central to the management of contracts. There also needs to be a system of arbitration for the resolution of differences between the parties. All of this leads to increased costs. Does transaction costs analysis cater for this? There are also the costs of disruption and the costs to morale that Kanter (1990) highlighted and which are described above.

CONCLUSIONS

Organisational structure is not a given and it is not just concerned with centralisation or decentralisation, hierarchies or markets. It is more problematic and involves people, power, culture, processes and so on. In the NHS management by hierarchy has been replaced by management by contract. This may shift the fundamental rationale of the organisation from being based upon a division of labour to being based on a division of knowledge and power – that is, who has the purchasing power. With any change we can ask who has lost and who has won in terms of power, resources, or status.

In local government we have seen the division of role between client and contractor but also the need to develop a greater capacity for strategy and cohesion. How fragmentation has taken place and what has been its effect on strategy are key questions. Has the role of the core strategic management cadre been reinforced at the expense of service professionals? To what extent is the centre driven by a resource-led view rather than any consideration of public service? Is the relationship between members and officers now one of contract specification, penalty points and service monitoring?

In education there are some signs of a return to centralised provision, particularly in specialist education services, curriculum advice, the careers service, education psychology. This seems likely to have occurred as a result of pressures to streamline services.

However, in general, where central services have been retained their provision has been subject to service-level agreements with user departments.

A concern with structure cannot be separated from power; Winstanley *et al.* (1995) identify restructuring as resulting in a restriction of local political accountability, an attack on the monopoly power of the provider professions and an emphasis on consumer power. They define two aspects to power:

1 *Criteria power* is concerned with the ability of stakeholders to define aims and purposes, design overall systems, set or influence performance criteria and evaluate performance on the basis of these.

2 *Operational power* is concerned with the ability to provide the service and change the way the service is delivered, allocating limited resources and using knowledge and key skills.

They provide a power matrix and map various services on this matrix (*see* Fig. 6.1).

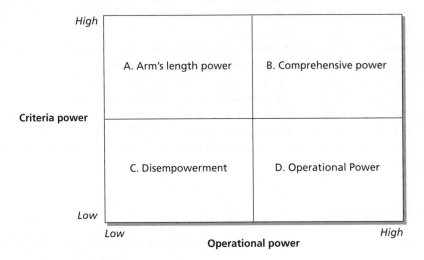

Fig. 6.1 Power matrix

Source: Winstanley *et al.* (1995). Reproduced with permission.

Thus, in the NHS restructuring, regional health authorities have reduced criteria power since they have become regional offices of the NHS. They have retained accountability for purchasers and monitor trusts. District health authorities have become commissioning agencies and have increased their power in setting local criteria for service delivery but have lost direct operational power.

In much the same way, other public services could be mapped, to show that local education authorities (LEAs) have moved from B to C. In other words what are the implications of structural change from a power/stakeholder perspective? Generally, Winstanley *et al.* (1995) consider that government will move from B to C and from A to D.

Of course the devolution of power may be more evident in rhetoric than in reality. In the NHS, the creation of clinical directorates could be seen as an example of forcing the medical profession to make unpalatable decisions concerning rationing.

Paton (1993, p 106) contends that:

> Decentralisation and devolution may be strategies to pass responsibility for the management of limited resources to those providers responsible for using them. This has been an interpretation by some sceptical doctors of the policy to establish clinical directorates. It is in effect an attenuated example from the developed world of a phenomenon rife in healthcare systems within the developing world – decentralization to communities as a means of admitting that resources do not exist at the central level to allow a nationally planned system.

The discussion of power illustrates the tensions and paradoxes that exist within organisations. Structures are part of the tension. These tensions pull in different directions:

- central control and decentralisation;
- integration and differentiation, reflecting the problems of co-ordination mechanisms, strategy and operations when the roles of purchaser and provider are differentiated;
- management and democracy;
- continuity and flexibility, knowing what to discard and what to retain;
- uniformity and diversity;
- specialisation and generalisation, and the relationship between professionals and managers.

Organisational balance is crucial. Some of these tensions are captured by the chief executive of an American corporation quoted by Bahrami (1992, p 37):

> We want an environment that enhances individual creativity, but we do not want chaos . . . we want people involved in decisions that affect their work and we want teamwork, yet we want our employees to have a bias towards action . . . we want small groups of dedicated workers (decentralization) but such groups may feel aimless or may be charging in the wrong direction with hidden agendas . . . we want people to stretch to reach tough goals, so our real emphasis is on easily-measured short-term growth and profits – but we should also have time to develop our employees for the longer haul, to promote from within, to monitor the atmosphere for creativity.

Contradictory demands are made upon employees. There are institutionalised inequalities of power and opportunity. We respect individuality but also expect conformity. Organisational structures will need to reflect these contradictions!

REFERENCES

Bahrami, H (1992) 'The emerging flexible organization: Perspectives from Silicon Valley', *California Management Review*, 34(4), pp 33–51.

Bartlett, W (1991) 'Quasi-markets and contracts: a markets and hierarchies perspective on NHS reforms', *Public Money & Management,* Autumn, pp 53–61.

Beetham, D (1987) *Bureaucracy.* Milton Keynes: Open University Press.

Blau, P M (1963) *The Dynamics of Bureaucracy: A Study of Interpersonal Relations in Two Government Agencies.* Chicago: University of Chicago Press.

Burns, D, Hambleton, R and Hoggett, P (1994) *The Politics of Decentralisation: Revitalising Local Democracy.* Basingstoke: Macmillan.

Crozier, M (1964) *The Bureaucratic Phenomena.* London: Tavistock.

Gouldner, A W (1954) *Patterns of Industrial Bureaucracy.* New York: The Free Press.

Handy, C (1990) *The Age of Unreason.* London: Arrow.

Jaques, E (1990) 'In praise of hierarchy', *Harvard Business Review,* January/February, pp 127–33.

Jeffrey, B (1997) 'Creating participatory structures in local government', *Local Government Policy Making,* 23(4), pp 25–31.

Kanter, R M (1990) *When Giants Learn to Dance: Mastering the Challenges of Strategy, Management and Careers in the 1990s.* London: Unwin Paperbacks.

Lawton, A and Rose, A G (1994) *Organisation and Management in the Public Sector* (2nd edn). London: Pitman Publishing.

Leach, S, Stewart, J and Walsh, K (1994) *The Changing Organisation and Management of Local Government.* Basingstoke: Macmillan.

Local Government Management Board (1993) *Challenge and Change: Characteristics of Good Management in Local Government*. Luton: LGMB.

Local Government Management Board (1996) *Portrait of Change 1995*. Luton: LGMB.

Local Government Training Board (1988) *Competition and Local Authorities: Organising for Competition*. Luton: LGTB.

Management Advisory Board (1992) *Devolution of Corporate Services*. Canberra: Australian Government Publishing Service.

Merton, R K (1940) 'Bureaucratic Structure and Personality', *Social Forces*, 18, pp 560–8.

Mintzberg, H (1983) *Structure in Fives: Designing Effective Organizations*. Englewood Cliffs, NJ: Prentice-Hall.

Mitchell, J (1993) 'Co-ordination by hierarchy' in Maidment and Thompson 1993.

Osborne, D and Gaebler, T (1992) *Reinventing Government: How the Entrepreneurial Spirit is Transforming the Public Sector*. Reading, MA: Addison-Wesley.

Paton, C (1993) 'Devolution and Centralism in the National Health Service', *Social Policy and Administration*, 27(2), pp 83–108.

Rao, N and Young, K (1995) *Competition, Contracts and Change: The Local Authority Experience of CCT*. York: Joseph Rowntree Foundation.

Stewart, J (1993) 'The Limitations of Government by Contract', *Public Money & Management*, July–September, pp 7–12.

Thompson, D F (1983) 'Bureaucracy and democracy', in Duncan, G (ed.) *Democratic Theory and Practice*. Cambridge: Cambridge University Press.

Williamson, O (ed.) (1975) *Markets and Hierarchies: Analysis and Antitrust Implications*. New York: Macmillan Press.

Winstanley, D, Sorabji, D and Dawson, S (1995) 'When the pieces don't fit: A stakeholder power matrix to analyse public sector restructuring', *Public Money & Management*, April– June, pp 19–26.

QUESTIONS AND DISCUSSION TOPICS

1 Under what conditions is bureaucracy the most appropriate form of organisational structure?

2 How does structural change impact upon people and processes?

PART 2

The manager's task

Part 1 examined the context of public services management. Stewart and Ranson (1988) argued that the distinctiveness of public services and their management rests upon the specific nature of the conditions and purpose which we examined in Part 1 and the tasks to be completed. This part of the book addresses the question of the managerial task. We are concerned with how managers can respond to the context examined in Part 1. We also provide an analysis of how specific elements of management manifest themselves in a public service context.

Thus, our focus is upon the key tasks involved in managing public services including financial and human resources, managing change and performance. Chapter 7 links Part 1 to Part 2 and underpins the discussion in the remaining chapters in Part 2. It does so by providing an overarching introduction to the functional and process aspect of public services management.

Strategic management describes how an organisation's capabilities and capacities can be managed to respond to, and shape, the organisation's environment. Grant (1995, p 26) considers that successful strategies consist of four ingredients:

1 They are directed towards unambiguous long-term goals.

2 They are based on insightful understanding of the external environment.

3 They are based on intimate self-knowledge by the organisation or individual of internal capabilities.

4 They are implemented with resolution, co-ordination, and effective harnessing of the capabilities and commitment of all members of the organisation.

Thus we consider competing models of strategic management and we examine the key issues using a case study of strategy in a local authority. It is recommended that you read Chapter 7 before reading the subsequent chapters in Part 2.

The remaining chapters in Part 2 explore the implications of these ingredients in terms of financial and human resources, marketing, performance and change and managing stakeholders across organisational boundaries.

Chapter 8 examines the changing nature of human resource management (HRM). Drawing heavily on organisation theory, it provides the reader with an understanding of contemporary approaches to the management of people in organisations. This is done by examining competing theories of motivation, rewards and leadership – aspects which are widely considered to be important for an organisation's success.

Chapter 9 examines public service financial management. Increasingly, public service managers need to acquire new financial management skills to succeed in a resource-scarce environment. This chapter examines recent developments which are illustrated using practical examples that show the implications of change for managers in a variety of contexts.

Marketing is traditionally associated with private sector organisations. However, as public services move into competitive environments, organisations need to address questions of effective marketing of their services. Chapter 10 examines the contribution that marketing can make to an organisation's strategy.

As we saw in Chapter 6, the concept of the monolithic public sector bureaucracy is obsolete. New environments and legislative demands require managers to achieve tasks through other organisations and other people. Chapter 11 uses cases of professional networks to illustrate the implications of these contextual shifts and examines how managers can respond to these shifts.

Chapter 12 examines the management of performance. Public services are subject to increasing amounts of measurement, both internally and externally driven. This chapter addresses the question of what is and what should be measured and how this process is managed.

Perhaps the underlying theme of all the chapters in both Parts 1 and 2 is change. Chapter 13 brings together the issues set out in earlier chapters and analyses them with reference to theories of change.

REFERENCES

Stewart, J and Ranson, S (1988) 'Management in the Public Domain', *Public Money and Management*, Spring/Summer, pp 13–18.

Grant, R M (1995) *Contemporary Strategy Analysis* (2nd edn). Oxford: Blackwell.

7 Strategic management

Alan Lawton

AIMS

This chapter will:

- form a link between the context-setting chapters of Part 1 of the book and the more detailed examination of the internal workings of organisations in Part 2;

- introduce and evaluate models of strategic management;

- examine strategic issues which include the relationship between the formulation and the implementation of policy, the role of politicians in the strategy process and the environmental constraints under which the public services manager operates;

- examine the role of the strategist and the nature of the core competences that are required for strategy;

- analyse the notion that strategy depends upon a fit between the external environment and the internal organisational capability.

INTRODUCTION

The concept of strategic management has long been seen as a key to understanding and prescribing the role of senior managers in organisations, particularly those in the private sector. Most Masters in Business Administration (MBA) courses include the study of strategic management as a core course. Its importance is recognised for a number of reasons;

1 The concept of strategy is assumed to be concerned with the organisation as a whole.
2 It is taken to be concerned with the long-term direction of an organisation.
3 It is distinguished from operational matters which are deemed to be concerned with day-to-day aspects of running an organisation.
4 The skills of strategic management are considered to be of a high order and are often assumed to be found at senior levels within organisations.

Echoing the definition of strategy that we used in the introduction to Part 2, Bowman and Asch (1987, p 4) state that:

Strategic management is the process of making and implementing strategic decisions . . . [it] is about the process of strategic change. [It is] the match an organization makes between its own resources and the threats and risks and opportunities created by the external environment in which it operates. So strategy can be seen as a key link between what the organisation wants to achieve – its objectives – and the policies adopted to guide its activities.

Although they recognise that many of the features of strategy occur in both private and public sector organisations, Ranson and Stewart (1994) argue that the conditions facing the public services manager are different in so far as, first, public organisations do not face market choices. They may well be required to provide services because of market failure. Second, they do not respond to market signals but to voices raised in the arena of public discourse. Third, public services organisations usually have no choice about location.

We discuss, in Chapter 4, whether such a distinction between public and private sector organisations is sustainable. However, Bozeman and Straussman (1990) in their work on public sector strategy offer a middle way and suggest that public management is most like business management at the operational level and least like it at the strategic level. They argue that strategic public management is guided by four principles:

● concern with long-term goals;
● the integration of goals and objectives into a coherent hierarchy;
● the recognition that strategy is not self-implementing;
● an external emphasis on anticipating and shaping environmental change rather than just responding to it.

However, the extent to which these four principles could also be applied to any organisation in any sector is a moot point. Without wishing to revisit earlier debates, this chapter will draw upon both private and public sector experiences to examine the nature of strategic management.

THE STRATEGIC APPROACH

From our brief discussion thus far it appears that strategic decisions are likely to be concerned with the following:

● The scope of the organisation's activities, for example, which markets to serve and in which geographical areas. Public sector organisations might be faced with different decisions but they will still involve fundamental questions concerning the organisation's role.
● How an organisation responds to its external environment. It is, therefore, concerned with change in so far as its external environment is changing.
● The long-term direction of the organisation rather than the day-to-day issues. In public service organisations this is complicated by the relatively short-term horizon of the electoral cycle.
● Matching the organisation's activities to its resource capability.

There are a number of different ways in which strategy can be approached, and these are discussed below.

Strategy as a plan

Strategy as a plan is concerned with a comprehensive, rational and linear approach to objective setting, implementation and appraisal, proceeding in a logical manner. Strategic or corporate planning continues to be popular, particularly within local government, with a time-frame built in that reflects the annual priorities of the authority concerned. It is important to note that the authorities also develop a strategy for the next three to four years. Table 7.1 shows the similarities between a classical strategic plan as advocated by Argenti (1980) and that adopted by Liverpool City Council.

Table 7.1 Strategic planning: theory and practice

Argenti model	Liverpool City Council
1 Target setting • clarify corporate objectives • set target levels of objectives	**1 Needs of city** Analysis of key problems and needs (May)
2 Gap analysis • forecast future performance on current strategies • identify gaps between forecasts and targets	**2 Vision and key aims/objectives** The kind of place councillors aim to make Liverpool and major changes needed (June)
3 Strategic appraisal • external (environmental) appraisal • internal appraisal • identify competitive advantage • redefine targets in the light of stage 3 • information for service plans	**3 Corporate strategy statement** Purpose and direction of major priorities. Framework; 3–4 year perspective (July)
4 Strategy formulation • generate strategic options • evaluate strategic options (against targets and internal/external appraisals)	**4 Service plans** Councillors agree service policy brief and approve 3–4 year strategy take strategic decision (September)
5 Strategy implementation • draw up action plans and budgets • monitor and control	**5 Budget process** Councillors allocate resources through capital and revenue expenditure (October to March)
	6 Action plans Councillors agree 1-year action plan including levels of service and key tasks (not later than April)
	7 Performance review Committees monitor performance, measure results against targets and review policies

Source: Based on Argenti (1980) and Chape and Davies (1993).

On a continuum between *deliberate* and *emergent* strategy, strategic planning is at the deliberate end of the continuum (*see* Mintzberg and Waters, 1985). Deliberate strategy is consciously intended, planned and controlled in contrast to emergent strategy which is uncontrolled or unintended. It is argued that the more stable the environment and the more centralised the control, the more appropriate may it be to employ a deliberate strategy. The less stable the environment the more appropriate may be an emergent strategy. According to McKevitt (1992, p 35):

Planned strategy emphasises direction and control of the organisation and it is thus more suited to a predictable external environment. Emergent strategy, including logical incrementalism, puts the emphasis on organizational learning whereby corrective action can be taken to alter strategic direction and to experiment, adapt and revise the original decision in the context of changing circumstances.

According to Quinn (1980) logical incrementalism is a cohesive, step-by-step approach towards goals which are broadly conceived but which are constantly refined and reshaped in the light of new information. An emergent strategy does not imply that the organisation is out of control, but that it takes one step at a time, is flexible and responsive. This is particularly important when the environment is turbulent or complex. Different approaches might be used at different times in an organisation's existence so that, according to Mintzberg and Waters, 'Strategy formation walks on two feet; the one deliberate, the other emergent' (1985, p 17).

The concept of an *umbrella* strategy captures the thrust for both deliberate and emergent strategies, where a broad direction is determined centrally with key policies in place but with broad parameters of action so that the detailed implementation is left to those lower down the organisation.

We can explore the notion of strategy more fully through a case study.

STRATEGIC CHANGE AT NEWVILLE COUNCIL

The environment

Newville has a population of 150 000 most of whom live around Southbury, the ancient capital. The town relies on tourism, some light engineering and the service sector. Elsewhere in Newville, the farming population is slowly declining and unemployment is higher than the national average. Young people find difficulty in getting work and in buying their own homes. Many rural properties are second homes for wealthy professionals working in London.

The population is ageing and the younger generations are moving away from the area to find work and housing. The percentage of elderly and very elderly people within the resident population has risen significantly. There is an increasing concentration of people who are dependent on state and council benefits in one form or another.

Newville Council is made up of 15 Conservatives, 12 Liberal Democrats, 4 Labour and 6 Independents. Many of the members consider themselves to be above party politics.

Facts
- 29 per cent of households comprise single persons living alone;
- 4 per cent of households are one-parent households;
- 30 per cent of households contain one or more pensioners;
- 17 per cent of households contain single pensioners;
- 20 per cent of households rent their house from the local authority;
- the unemployment rate is 12 per cent;
- the unemployment rate for males aged 18–24 is 30 per cent;
- 35 per cent of the population is wholly or mainly dependent upon welfare benefits of one kind or another.

Change in the 1990s
Along with every other local authority in the UK, Newville has been subject to the impact of central government legislation, changing public expectations and changing ideas concerning the role of the local authority. Change in a number of areas has affected Newville Council:

- government legislation has meant the introduction of competitive tendering, community care, local management of schools, and has led to local government reorganisation;
- increasing public expectations, and a growing awareness of, and demands for, choice, quality, value for money and efficiency;
- demographic changes such as an ageing population;
- increasing importance of 'green' issues including recycling of waste;
- changing leisure patterns;
- continued impacts of new technology;
- European economic, political and social integration;
- no real increase in budgets and tight controls on capital spending;
- increasing politicisation of some local authorities with the decline in the number of Independents and an increase in the number of one-party controlled authorities;
- conflict within authorities between those managers who wish to have more responsibility and be more entrepreneurial and those who favour the status quo;
- clear direction from the Audit Commission which identified the need for local authorities to understand their customers; respond to the electorate; set, and pursue, consistent and achievable objectives; assign clear management responsibilities; train and motivate people; communicate effectively; monitor results; and adapt to change;
- continuing support for the enabling authority and the growing importance of networks and partnerships.

The story

Christine Brown, newly appointed Director of Strategic Management at Newville Council, a unitary authority, sat in her office overlooking the ancient city walls and wondered what she had let herself in for. She had just returned from an 'away day' with leading members of the council and the senior management team.

Before joining the Authority, Christine had worked for a large retail company and gone into consultancy during the late 1980s and acquired an MBA. More and more of her work had involved facilitating team development in local authorities. She had liked the people she had met in local government and recognised the potentially rewarding career that local government could offer. Christine had been approached by the Chief Executive of Newville after she had given a conference paper on managing strategically. The Chief Executive, Robert Smith, told Christine that the authority was seeking to recruit a Director of Strategic Management. Christine was impressed by Robert's enthusiasm and obvious commitment to Newville; Christine applied for the post and after two days of interviewing was offered the job and duly accepted.

However, it became apparent at the 'away day' that not much thought had been given to strategic management or how to bring about change. Indeed the enthusiasm for change appeared to emanate from Robert Smith and one or two leading members and officers. Some senior managers and members were sceptical of strategic management and change. Typical comments from the sceptics were:

'There are too many variables over which we have no control – we are constrained by central government every which way we turn.'

'We are a traditional authority and always will be. As a member I don't want to spend all my time looking at the "Grand Vision" – I want to get involved in the so-called trivia, in the nuts and bolts. That's why I entered local politics, to help local people.'

'My constituents are interested in what is happening in their own street, with schooling or the environment, not in some management jargon called strategy.'

'I have been working in local government for thirty years and my legal training is essential for making sure that this authority acts within the legislation and with probity.'

'These new-fangled business techniques and MBAs are not relevant.'

'Does this mean that we have to go through another reorganisation?'

'Change is all very well, but what will it cost?'

It was at this point that Christine realised the uphill battle that she faced and that her appointment was not universally approved of. However, she was heartened by some comments:

'We have to let the officers get on with the day-to-day running of the authority. That is what they are there for. We should be trying to steer and I do hope that we steer in the right direction.'

'The important thing is that members do not get bogged down in the detail.'

And one of the senior managers argued:

'We have to be much more proactive. OK, we have to operate within a legal environment but we do have discretion in, for example, leisure, community work, economic development.'

Christine was made fully aware of her responsibilities when, later that day, one of the Council's middle managers came to see her. Jim Adkins had worked his way up the management ladder after joining the authority some ten years earlier, after leaving school. He had no professional qualifications but had obtained a degree through part-time study and was now studying for his Diploma in Management. Jim had called in to introduce himself and had stayed to chat. His view of the authority was that it was a frustrating place to work. He was keen to take on responsibility and to be allowed greater scope in the Community and Leisure Department. He indicated that for too long the authority had been dominated by professional cadres fighting their corners with no thought given to the overall aims of the authority. Newville was riven with the debris of countless departmental battles. Jim argued that a growing number of middle managers like himself were becoming disillusioned, particularly when they met colleagues from other authorities who appeared to be responding positively to all the changes that had taken place in local government in the previous 15 years. Jim felt that Newville was going to be left behind in the new competitive world of local government. Jim conceded that the authority was a friendly place to work and had always prided itself on doing well by its citizens – it had come third in the 'Bloom in Britain' contest five years earlier. However, Jim argued that the authority could be doing a lot more and certainly opinion down at his local pub was that more should be done on the economic development side.

Jim felt that Newville was missing out on opportunities offered by the Single Regeneration Budget and the Private Finance Initiative. He knew that joint working was not too familiar to most members and managers in the authority.

Christine decided to call a meeting of the senior management team. The purpose of the meeting was to introduce her view of strategic change and to seek the views of her colleagues. Christine wanted the meeting to focus on the following questions:

1 What are some of the key strategic issues facing the authority and what specific competences are needed?

2 How can Newville formulate a strategic direction which will address these issues and accommodate relevant stakeholders?

We shall see how Christine gets on later in this chapter.

We now return to the example of Liverpool City Council that we visited earlier (*see* Table 7.1) to determine the need for strategic management. It is worth recalling the troubled history of Liverpool City Council in the 1980s and its domination by a small and powerful political faction, the Militant Tendency, which refused to accept some aspects of central government legislation. According to Chape and Davies (1993, p 4) the need for strategic management arose because of the need to:

- assert the prime role of the City Council as meeting the needs of the people of Liverpool;
- develop a strategic view of the objectives and priorities of the council;
- address the imbalance between available resources and financial commitments;
- establish an effective management structure and management processes;
- establish quantified performance targets and the monitoring of performance against such targets;
- review the partnership between members and officers;
- support and develop the role of members and to make the best use of the Council's workforce;
- address issues relating to the image of Liverpool.

The focus adopted is on both the internal issues and stakeholders and the need to interact with the wider environment.

STRATEGIC ANALYSIS

A number of techniques are available to managers to help them make sense of the external environment. The background information that we supplied in the Newville case can be analysed in terms of a STEP analysis, that is, a consideration of the Social, Technical, Economic and Political environment:

1 *Social*: At a general level these will include demographic features such as an ageing population, more fragmented families, smaller households, less community-minded citizens, rising expectations, changing lifestyles and so on.
2 *Technical*: These might include new opportunities provided by information technology such as the 'electronic village', new developments in medical technology such as new genetic techniques as in DNA testing which could also be used in crime fighting.
3 *Economic*: This refers to changes in the economy generally but also to widening disparities in income, higher male unemployment with geographical concentrations of unemployment, more flexible working patterns, diminishing resources and so on.
4 *Political*: This includes changing legislation and the demands that this puts on public service organisations whether it be in education, community care or health care. It will also be bound by political values perhaps expressed in the balance between state and private funding, the adoption of quasi-business methods or techniques such as those required by the dynamics of the internal market.

The use of a technique such as a STEP analysis helps the manager make sense of a complex environment; it does not tell the manager how to act but is a precursor to strategic action. A second, popular and simple tool, is a SWOT analysis, which examines Strengths, Weaknesses, Opportunities and Threats.

We use the example of a further education (FE) college as a vehicle for exploring this type of analysis further:

1 *Strengths*: These might include the quality of the staff, its links with local industry and the local community, its library facilities, its reputation as a friendly, caring college and its success in achieving examination passes in national qualifications. It might also include its open access policy, its computing facilities and so on.
2 *Weaknesses*: These might include the lack of a strategic focus, the lack of facilities in

certain subjects which do not allow for expansion, poor security on an open site, limited parking, no crèche or play group for staff and students, inflexible start times of courses or uncertainty over funding.

3 *Opportunities*: These could include developing franchising arrangements with the local university, extending the college year, offering more full-cost courses to local employers, developing the adult market, merging or collaborating with sixth form colleges and generally seeking to expand its portfolio of courses.

4 *Threats*: These might come from private providers, increased competition, changing legislation, increased demands on staff which they are not equipped to carry out, e.g. financial management or marketing, vandalism and poor security etc. (*see* Rayner, 1996).

A SWOT analysis is both internally and externally focused, and it identifies areas for action. In the case of the FE college this might be developing the adult education market and offering more flexible start times to fit around students with families.

Porter's Five Force model

One tool of analysis that is favoured by those within a competitive environment is Michael Porter's Five Force model for analysing a particular industry. Porter (1979) argues that there are five forces which impact upon the competitive environment:

1 Threat of entry of new competitors.
2 The bargaining power of customers.
3 The threat of substitute products or services.
4 The bargaining power of supplying.
5 Industry jockeying for position among many competitors.

Threat of entry of new competitors

Increasingly, many parts of the public services are having to compete with the private and voluntary sectors. In the FE college example used above, private providers or sixth form colleges could compete for those courses which have traditionally been offered by FE colleges. Competition, whether it be in education, health services, prison services, transport, utilities etc., is now an established part of the landscape of public services not just in the UK but worldwide.

The bargaining power of customers

The customers of, say, Sainsburys can always go elsewhere to another food retailer. Can the customers of public services go elsewhere if they are not happy with the services they receive? How much consumer power do they have? The rhetoric of successive Conservative governments was one of increasing citizen choice through the use of competition and markets whether through deregulation of transport and the utilities or the introduction of fundholding GPs. The reality has delivered less than the rhetoric promised despite the adoption of 'Citizens Charters' for a wide range of services.

The threat of substitute products or services

It is more difficult to see how the threat of substitute products or services might apply in the public services. Are there alternatives in the provision of education or health?

Alternative medicine might be one such substitute for more standard health care but it has not had a great deal of impact in terms of the total expenditure on health care.

The bargaining power of suppliers

At one time the public services were heavily criticised for being producer led, in so far as decisions were often based on professional or bureaucratic rationales rather than on what was, necessarily, in the best interests of the consumer. The nearest application to the public services of this competitive force might be, therefore, in terms of the power of those who actually supply services on behalf of the public sector, whether they be teachers, doctors, social workers or members of a whole host of other professional bodies. However, a key feature of the 1980s and 1990s has been the undermining of professional power by central government.

Industry jockeying for position among many competitors

As indicated above the public services operate in an increasingly competitive world, where survival is a key aim. Public services can 'go out of business', as those who worked in local authorities such as Cleveland County Council found out following the recent local government reorganisation in England. Competition to stay alive was every bit as fierce as that between rival private sector companies.

Strategic choice

Research on private sector organisations has developed a number of models to help companies make strategic choices. We shall describe these and then discuss their relevance for public services organisations. Porter described a number of generic strategies to cope with the competitive forces outlined above.

1 *Cost leadership*: This requires a low overall cost position and often a high market share. In the case of our FE college which competes with similar-sized colleges nearby, a low-cost position might be difficult to adopt. Staff costs are usually high, some 80 per cent of total budget. One solution might be to appoint more part-time staff on short-term contracts. Private trainers often pay their staff less and it is unlikely that the college could compete on cost grounds. Funding is based on student numbers and what may be attractive to students are quality courses and personal tuition rather than fewer staff and larger class sizes.

   Similarly, a low-cost strategy will not be an option for certain aspects of provision, especially safety in relation to fire prevention or transport.

2 *Differentiation*: A differentiated strategy involves offering a differentiated product, creating something which is perceived to be unique. Differentiation may inspire brand loyalty. A differentiation strategy requires a number of skills and resources such as strong marketing abilities, a reputation for quality and a long tradition in the industry. For our FE college, if students perceive that they are receiving a quality product they may feel loyal to the college and stay to do other courses at the college.

3 *Focus*: A focus strategy involves concentrating upon a limited number of lucrative products. A college could pull out of low demand areas or areas which are expensive to deliver in favour of full-cost courses which are more lucrative. The college could also seek to expand its franchising functions.

However, we should not assume that establishing a strategic direction for public services is straightforward. Commenting upon strategy in higher education, Robertson (1993) argues that it may require a fundamental shift in educational values which will include a much greater awareness of the student as customer. It will require a challenge to prevailing concepts of the self-regulating profession. Robertson indicates that course development will become a matter of product positioning. Perhaps a more fundamental point, however, is that 'The goals of higher education are concerned as much with process as with outcome . . . these goals concern the intellectual development of individuals, manifested in person, social and economically-relevant attributes' (Robertson, 1993, p 49).

Organisations may offer a range of products or adopt a portfolio approach to its strategy. The best-known model of a portfolio approach is that developed by the Boston Consulting Group in the 1970s, the Boston Matrix, which examines products and services from two perspectives, market share and growth potential. Products or services are characterised as:

- *Stars* – high-growth and high-share business which generates substantial cash but needs large investments if market share is to be maintained.
- *Cash cows* – low-growth and high-share business which generates large cash flows and requires little investment, and the profits of which can be used elsewhere.
- *Dogs* – low-growth and low-share business generating little cash.
- *Problem children* – high-growth but low-share business which could become a star or a cash cow but involves risks.

Nutt and Backoff (1992) have developed a similar matrix model for examining issues in public services organisations involving the amount of stakeholder support for an issue and the possibility of dealing with that issue. Tractability indicates the prospect that an issue can be successfully attacked by the organisation. The degree of tractability depends on technical problems, target group mix, or the extent to which a target group is expected to change. They have characterised issues as:

- *angry tigers* – these issues, such as hard-core unemployment or inflation, arouse considerable public interest but are difficult to deal with;
- *sitting ducks* – these include public health programmes or transport safety issues and are easy to manage since they have high public support;
- *dark horses* – such as providing life management skills for people with learning difficulties; issues of this type can be dealt with successfully but often have low public support;
- *sleeping dogs* – which are neither high on the public agenda, nor easy to deal with, such as AIDS treatment.

In terms of strategic choices we have identified services or products and issues as being key variables. But there is also an organisational dimension. According to Miles and Snow (1978) organisations can be characterised as being of four different strategic types:

- *Defender* – which operates best in stable, well-defined markets, where prevailing beliefs are essentially conservative and well-tried solutions are valued.
- *Prospector* – which seeks out new products, services and opportunities and where high-risk strategies are valued.
- *Analyser* – which consists of a combination of both defender and prospector, maintaining existing markets while seeking new ones. There is the possibility of conflict between the two approaches. We can speculate about the possible tensions in, say, a

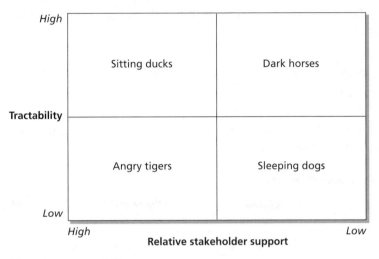

Fig. 7.1 Issue portfolio

Source: Reprinted with permission from P C Nutt and R W Backoff (1992, p 103). *Strategic Management of Public and Third Sector Organizations: A Handbook for Leaders*. Copyright © 1992 Jossey-Bass, Inc., Publishers, 350 Sansome Street, San Francisco, CA.

local authority where part of the authority is driven by statute, as in welfare provision, whereas another part of the organisation is driven to seek new opportunities such as in economic development. We consider a clash of organisational cultures in Chapter 14.

- *Reactor* – fails to act effectively in any field, it is bold when it should be cautious and vice versa.

According to Miles and Snow only the first two strategic types are sustainable. They argue that different types of organisation will respond differently even in the same environment, and that the strategies that organisations pursue are better accounted for by prevailing beliefs than by environmental stimuli.

This view is supported by Johnson, who argues that managers may believe that they are responding to the external environment but that in fact they are reinterpreting it in terms of their own values and beliefs. This he calls a paradigm and describes it as:

> the set of beliefs and assumptions, held relatively common through the organisation, taken for granted, and discernible in the stories and explanations of the managers, which plays a central role in the interpretation of environmental stimuli and configuration of organisationally relevant strategic responses (1989, p 45).

Paradigms resist change and, according to Johnson, are preserved and legitimated in the cultural web of an organisation in terms of rituals and myths, symbols, power structures, organisational structures, control structures and routines. Over time there is strategic drift between environmental change and strategic change because of this reinterpretation.

For a local authority, the strategic choices may include:

- the extent to which the authority wishes to exercise a wider role of local governance going beyond its service responsibilities;
- the degree to which it wishes to introduce market mechanisms;
- the relative importance it gives to services to individuals (and/or households) or to communities.

Thus the Local Government Management Board sees local authorities fulfilling four possible roles:

- direct service provision;
- commercialism;
- community government;
- neighbourhood approach.

Boyne *et al.* (1991) mapped differences between different local authorities on a range of different issues (*see* Table 7.2).

Table 7.2 The mapping exercise

	Enabler (market)	Traditional (direct provider)	Enabler (participatory)
Role emphasis	X Town Plc	Direct service provision	Community government
Role culture	Competitive	Reactive	Proactive
Strategic planning	Parameters set by market	Scale and priorities by services	Response to community
Basis of service provision	Mixed economy	Professionally based	Variety of community provision
Basis of internal organisation	Contract specification negotiation	Service departments	Matrix, decentralised
Political management structures	Executive Management Board	Professionals as gatekeepers	Area committees
Accountability	Mutual responsibilities	Members and committees	To locate people
Scope for discretion	By negotiation	Depends upon professional autonomy	High in response to local preferences
Basis of relations with other authorities	Ring holder	Self-sufficient	Strong commitment
Basis of relations with other bodies	Ring holder	Self-sufficient	Strong commitment to local groups

Source: Boyne et al. (1991). Reprinted with permission.

Richards and Rodrigues (1993) argue that there are two types of strategies in public services:

1 *Type A*, driven by central planning and control with implementation within tight specifications.
2 *Type B*, driven by market considerations.

Type A typifies the NHS, under the illusion of an internal market. In effect, more control is put in the hands of managers. The Financial Management Initiative in central government was similarly driven by central control. Richards and Rodrigues argue that Type A has been used most often because of the pursuit of efficiency and the need to curtail public expenditure. They argue that Type B has now been used for civil service reform in the form of market testing.

IMPLEMENTATION ISSUES

To separate strategic choice from the processes used to implement that choice is, in many ways, artificial. The relationship between the two is iterative, particularly when strategy is viewed as a process or is emergent rather than deliberate or planned. However, let us return to our case study, Newville local authority, to discover how Christine is faring.

CASE STUDY 7.2

IMPLEMENTING NEWVILLE'S STRATEGY

The senior management team and the leading members have met and produced a strategic plan to take Newville into the twenty-first century. The summary of the strategic plan is reproduced below.

Newville's mission

To become a caring, competitive and attractive employer which will recruit, retain and develop staff to work in a high performance organisation providing quality, accessible services to all sections in the community in a way that is competitive, gives value for money, and meets our customers' expressed needs.

In order to achieve our mission and respond to change, we need to develop a high-performance culture which has the following core values:

- customers first
- service quality
- staff development
- innovation
- value for money
- flexibility
- achievement
- high performance

In short we are looking to build an organisation which is:

- Accountable
- Customer-oriented
- Effective

In order to develop an organisation which is ACE we need to recruit, select and develop staff who show PRIDE in their work, that is, staff who show:

- Professionalism
- Responsiveness
- Initiative
- Decisiveness
- Enterprise

Christine recognised that producing a mission statement was only the first step on a long road to strategic change. She knew that some members and officers expected the mission to achieve itself. Others thought that the mission statement could be put on a shelf and gather dust while life proceeded pretty much as normal. Christine believed that implementation was even more important than the drawing up of strategy and she wanted to keep the momentum going. She decided to organise another away day for members and managers. It was, after all, six months since the last one and six months is a long time in the local government world. She sent out a briefing paper to members and officers detailing implementation issues and she asked for responses to a number of questions.

1 We now have a mission statement but what does this mean in operational terms?

2 How can the authority meet its objectives?

3 What should our priorities be?

The case study introduces a number of strategic issues concerning the specific circumstances of local authorities:

1 What role do political parties play?
2 Does it require a change in relationship between officers and members?
3 What will be the relationship between leading members and backbenchers?
4 How should the community be involved?
5 How can the requirements to be entrepreneurial sit alongside a hierarchical structure?
6 Are there dangers that different departments will move in different directions depending on the extent to which they are bound by statutory requirements or have the 'freedom to manage'?
7 Is the enabling type of authority the best suited for a strategic approach?

A strategic authority will need to work out the role of the centre. It will need to work out the nature of its relationships with external stakeholders. Are citizens to be encouraged to participate? What are its priorities and where is accountability located? A local authority may consider itself to be strategic but it still has to address these basic issues. Thus, there will be a number of key questions to be asked:

1 How effective is the link between operational and strategic management?
2 Is there a human resource strategy consistent with the overall strategy?
3 Has enough attention been paid to the skills of managers and those charged with implementation?
4 What is the role of the centre in each authority or department to be?
5 Is strategy compatible with the planning and budgetary cycles adopted by the authority?
6 Are there measures for success and is evaluation built into the strategic process?

According to Bryson:

At a minimum, any organization that wishes to engage in strategic planning should have: (1) a process sponsor(s) in a position of power to legitimise the process; (2) a 'champion' to push the process along; (3) a strategic planning team; (4) an expectation that there will be disruptions and delays; (5) a willingness to be flexible about what constitutes a strategic plan; (6) an ability to pull information and people together at key points for important discussions and decisions; and (7) a willingness to construct and consider arguments geared to very different evaluative criteria (1988, p 18).

At the same time we must recognise, along with McKevitt, that:

Just as the classical strategy models underestimate (or ignore) the influence of an unpredictable environment on the organisation's capacity to plan its future, so too do the traditional policy implementation models of public sector decision making fail to capture the ambiguity and uncertainty in the policy making process (1992, p 38).

Strategic management and core competences

In the introduction to this chapter we indicated that it is with senior management that strategy is located, but that is essentially a top-down approach to strategy. Strategy formulation, in organisations that rely heavily on professionals, as in much of the public services, may be occurring at the point of delivery of services. The delivery of public services requires discretion on the part of professionals and frontline staff and what impacts upon their decisions may be client demands or technical innovations rather than an analysis of social, political or economic forces. The relationship between formulation and implementation may be an interactive one and there may be no clear-cut distinction between the two. This view of strategy is consistent with the demise of a belief in the politics–administration dichotomy which characterised much of the early work in public administration.

However, according to Choo (1992) the fundamental tasks of strategic management are:

1 *Environmental analysis*: This involves monitoring the external and internal environments to identify present and future strengths, weaknesses, threats and opportunities, as discussed above.
2 *Developing a corporate vision*: This involves infusing the organisation with a sense of purpose, providing long-term direction, and establishing a mission and objectives, as Christine did in Newville.
3 *Strategy formulation*: This involves crafting a strategy that leads to the attainment of organisational objectives.
4 *Strategy implementation*: This involves executing the chosen strategy efficiently and effectively.
5 *Strategic control*: This involves evaluating performance, reviewing the situation and initiating further action.

Berman and Maxwell (1986, pp 251–2) argue that successful strategic managers were seen to require the following qualities:

1 A mixture of sensitivity and toughness – the former to be able to gauge both the external and internal environments and to assess the risks of failure, and the latter to persist with the strategies selected to ensure that the organisation is moving in a purposeful direction.
2 The wisdom to refrain from managing the components of the organisation but rather to provide leadership in two principal areas: interpreting the environment to the organisation and the organisation to the environment, and managing the interplay between tasks and processes when change is required.
3 The skill to spot the leading edge of an activity – the new opportunity for the organisation – and its peak and decline, so that the institution can engage and disengage to maximum advantage. In effect this means recognising life cycles in the way that any fashion industry has had to learn to do.

4 A commitment to the importance of organisational learning to demonstrate how they can create success out of crisis or failure. Leaders must provide the environment, motivation and vision for learning. They must also build the internal capability to cope with continuing uncertainty and unforeseen situations.

According to Hamel and Prahalad (1993), long-term competitiveness depends on managers' willingness to challenge continually their managerial values and frames of reference, their paradigms. Hamel and Prahalad argue that leveraging resources is as important as allocating them. They use the notion of 'strategy as stretch' which applies where there is a significant gap between an organisation's resources and its aspirations. A large organisation may have a scarcity of ambition and may be less successful than a smaller more ambitious organisation. Why do comparable local authorities seem to be leaders or laggards? The gap can be bridged through the leverage of limited resources and capabilities. Resource leverage is essentially energising with a 'bigger bang for the buck'. Hamel and Prahalad argue that downsizing is essentially demoralising where the buck paid for the bang is reduced. Management can lever resources in five basic ways:

1 Concentrating resources effectively on strategic goals.
2 Accumulating resources more efficiently (extracting and borrowing).
3 Complementing one kind of resource with another to create higher-order value.
4 Conserving resources wherever possible.
5 Recovering resources from the marketplace in the shortest possible time.

Hamel and Prahalad argue that every company is a reservoir of experiences but some companies are better than others at extracting that experience. Furthermore, risk recedes as knowledge grows, and with it so does the company's capacity to advance. Strategy as stretch recognises the essential paradox of competition: leadership cannot be planned for, but neither can it happen without a grand and well-considered aspiration.

This view of strategy is depicted as 'strategy as revolution' by Hamel (1996). Hamel argues that strategy making must challenge existing assumptions and that revolutionaries exist in every company; that strategy making must be democratic in the sense that anyone can be a 'strategy activist'. Hamel argues that:

> To invite new voices into the strategy-making process, to encourage new perspectives, to start new conversations that span organizational boundaries, and then to help synthesise unconventional options into a point of view about corporate direction – those are the challenges for senior executives who believe that strategy must be revolution (1996, p 82).

The challenge for managers in the public services, from this perspective, is to involve a range of stakeholders both inside and outside the organisation in the strategic process. Where public services are delivered increasingly across organisational boundaries, as we investigate in Chapter 11, managers in public services organisations will, invariably, need to engage in dialogue outside existing organisational boundaries. We now return to the Case study 7.3. By now you should have recognised some of the challenges that Christine faces.

The last point is an important one and we investigate it further in Chapter 13. Any change is bound to have costs and it should not be assumed that developing a strategic approach is not without difficulties.

There is, as yet, little systematic research on strategy in UK public services. What does exist tends to be in the form of case studies. Evidence concerning strategic processes elsewhere is discussed in Exhibit 7.1.

CASE STUDY 7.3

THE CHALLENGES FOR CHRISTINE

What are the challenges that face Christine in her efforts to introduce a strategic perspective to Newville?

1 The need to involve key stakeholders such as politicians, staff and the community. She will have to work out ways of engaging them in the process, perhaps through area committees or user panels.
2 The need for a dedicated staff which will involve a strategic management champion.
3 The recognition that staff ownership is crucial and the need to encourage employees to see beyond their unit or departmental interests.
4 The need to identify good practice elsewhere.
5 The need to recognise that the process will not happen overnight.
6 The need to recognise the importance of political commitment.
7 The need to consider how appropriate a 'big bang' approach is, compared to a gradual approach.
8 The need to recognise that culture change may be necessary and that this will involve values which must be articulated and shared.
9 The need to recognise that processes and implementation are just as important as the content of strategy.
10 The need to be prepared for casualties.

Exhibit 4.1

Strategic planning in USA state agencies

Berry (1994) carried out a longitudinal study of nine types of state agency in the USA from 1970 to 1991. The study involved 987 state agencies, which were surveyed in 1992, with a response rate of 56 per cent or 548 agencies. Berry was interested in the experience of strategic planning of these state agencies and was concerned with when strategic planning was introduced, the perceived outcomes, the extent of internal and external participation and so on. Strategic planning was seen as a management process that combines four basic features:

1 A clear statement of the organisation's mission.

2 The identification of the agency's external constituencies or stakeholders and the determination of the agency's purposes and operations.

3 The delineation of the agency's strategic goals and objectives, typically in a three to five year plan.
4 The development of strategies to achieve them.

Berry sought to test a number of hypotheses.

● *Hypothesis 1: The fiscal health of an agency affects the likelihood of the agency adopting strategic planning.*
   The findings support the hypothesis that fiscally healthy agencies are more likely to be innovators in adopting strategic planning than are financially weak agencies and that it is not used as a tool in cutback management.

● *Hypothesis 2: The larger an agency the more likely it is to adopt strategic planning.*
   The size of the agency appeared to have little impact.

● *Hypothesis 3: In the political administration cycle, agencies are most likely to adopt strategic planning in the year after a new governor is elected, second most likely in the year immediately after a governor is re-elected, and least likely in the year of an election.*

Exhibit 7.1 *cont.*

> The probability of adopting strategic planning decreases almost threefold from the first year of a new governor's term to an election year.
>
> ● *Hypothesis 4: Agencies that work closely with private sector businesses are more likely to adopt strategic planning than agencies that do not.*
> There was mixed evidence in support of this hypothesis.
>
> ● *Hypothesis 5: The greater the extent to which an agency delivers its services directly to citizens as opposed to delivering to other state agencies or local governments, the more likely it is to adopt strategic planning.*
> There was equally strong evidence whether the customers are citizens or other government workers.
>
> ● *Hypothesis 6: Agencies are more likely to adopt strategic planning as the number of 'sister' agencies in neighbouring states that have adopted strategic planning increases.*
> This was a positive finding. Agency leaders did seem to learn from their neighbours.

CONCLUSIONS

The findings of the study reported in Exhibit 7.1 demonstrate the importance of the political cycle, the importance of learning from others and the difficulty of embarking on strategic planning when faced with resource constraints.

However, the belief in the need for a strategic approach can come from a number of different sources:

1 It can be driven along by a charismatic champion, usually either a senior politician or senior manager.
2 The impetus for it could be a single external event which forces organisations to examine closely what they are about, perhaps a piece of legislation such as that which took further education colleges and polytechnics out of Local Education Authority control.
3 It may arise as a result of a general feeling of discontent within the organisation and a belief that the organisation can do better.

According to Bryson (1988, p 18), 'An effective strategy must meet several criteria. It must be technically workable, politically acceptable to key stakeholders, and must accord with the organisation's philosophy and core values.'

In other words, strategy must be suitable, feasible and acceptable, particularly to key stakeholders.

According to Choo (1992), the potential benefits of strategic management involve:

● creating a capacity to be proactive and to respond positively to change in the environment;
● optimising organisational performance and results;
● institutionalising a rigorous process of decision making and environmental analysis;
● identifying different strategic options;
● identifying, prioritising and exploiting opportunities and threats;
● developing a framework for improved co-ordination, effective decision making and control of activities;
● reducing bureaucracy and the duplication of work;

- providing a basis for clarification of individual responsibilities;
- encouraging forward thinking;
- increasing responsiveness to change;
- allowing the empowerment of employees.

It is concerned with questions such as 'Where are we going?', 'How do we get there?', 'Who and what do we need to get us there?', 'Do we have an implementation plan?' and 'How do we know if we are on track?'

The remaining chapters in Part 2 seek to explore the resources that organisations have at their disposal and to begin to grapple with some of these questions.

REFERENCES

Argenti, J (1980) *Practical Corporate Planning*. London: Allen and Unwin.

Berman, P C and Maxwell, R J (1986) 'Managers as Strategists', *Hospital and Health Services Review*, November, pp 247–52.

Berry, F S (1994) 'Innovation in Public Management: The Adoption of Strategic Planning', *Public Administration Review*, July/August, vol. 54, pp 322–30.

Bowman, C and Asch, D (1987) *Strategic Management*. Basingstoke: Macmillan.

Boyne, G A, Griffiths, M P, Lawton, A and Law, J (1991) *Local Government in Wales: its Role and Functions*. York: Joseph Rowntree Foundation.

Bozeman, B and Straussman, J D (1990) *Public Management Strategies: Guidelines for Managerial Effectiveness*. San Francisco: Jossey-Bass.

Bryson, J M (1988) 'A Strategic Planning Process for Public and Non-profit Organizations', *Long Range Planning*, 21(1), pp 11–19.

Chape, A and Davies, P (1993) 'Implementing strategic management in local government: Liverpool City Council as a case study', *Local Government Policy Making*, 20(3) December, pp 3–10.

Choo, K L (1992) 'Strategic management in local government – guiding principles for effective action', *Local Government Policy Making*, 19(3), pp 42–9.

Grant, R M (1995) *Contemporary Strategy Analysis* (2nd edn). Oxford: Blackwell.

Hamel, G (1996) 'Strategy as Revolution', *Harvard Business Review*, July–August, pp 69–82.

Hamel, G and Prahalad, C K (1993) 'Strategy as Stretch and Leverage', *Harvard Business Review*, March–April, pp 75–84.

Johnson, G (1989) 'Rethinking Incrementalism' in Asch, D and Bowman, C (eds) *Readings in Strategic Management*. Basingstoke: Macmillan, in Association with the Open University.

Local Government Management Board (1993) 'Fitness for purpose', Luton: LGMB.

McKevitt, D (1992) 'Strategic Management in Public Services' in Willcocks, L and Harrow, J (eds) *Rediscovering Public Services Management*. Maidenhead: McGraw-Hill.

Miles, R E and Snow, C C (1978) *Organisational Strategy, Structure and Process*. New York: McGraw-Hill.

Mintzberg, H and Waters, J H (1985) 'Of Strategies Deliberate and Emergent', *Strategic Management Journal* vol. 6, pp 257–72.

Nutt, P C and Backoff, R W (1992) *Strategic Management of Public and Third Sector Organizations: A Handbook For Leaders*. San Francisco: Jossey-Bass.

Porter, M (1979) 'How Competitive Forces Shape Strategy', *Harvard Business Review*, March/April, pp 137–45.

Porter, M (1980) *Competitive Strategy: Techniques for Analyzing Industries and Competitors*. New York: Free Press.

Quinn, J B (1980) 'Managing Strategic Change', *Sloan Management Review*, Summer, pp 3–20.

Ranson, S and Stewart, J (1994) *Management for the Public Domain: Enabling the Learning Society*. Basingstoke: Macmillan.

Rayner, J (1996) 'Strategic Change at Kirby College' in Lawton, A and McKevitt, D (1996) *Case Studies in Public Services Management*. Oxford: Blackwell.

Richards, S and Rodrigues, J (1993) 'Strategies for Management in the Civil Service: Change of Direction', *Public Money & Management*, April–June, pp 33–8.

Robertson, D (1993) 'Establishing Strategic Direction in Higher Education Institutions', *Public Money & Management*, July–September, pp 45–51.

QUESTIONS AND DISCUSSION TOPICS

1 What are the key strategic issues that face public services organisations?

2 What are the advantages and disadvantages of senior managers formulating strategy?

3 What are the differences between strategy as a plan and strategy as a process?

8 Managing human resources

Michael Dempsey

AIMS

This chapter will:

- enable the reader to understand the key concepts in human resource management (HRM) and the controversies surrounding them;

- locate within an HRM context some of the core considerations in managing people in the public services, namely, motivation, rewards and leadership;

- examine these considerations in a way in which their interrelationship can be clearly understood;

- analyse the role of trade unions in the public services and their place within a developing UK model of HRM.

INTRODUCTION

It has become a truism that people are an organisation's greatest asset and much of the manager's day is taken up with managing people. Despite this, managing human resources remains complex and difficult. This chapter unravels some of the complexity and examines some of the key issues. Keep (1989, p 110) observes that:

> If the term 'human resource management' is to be taken as something more than an empty 'buzz phrase', then the word 'human', in this context, can only relate to the employees, past and present, of the enterprise. The use of the word 'resource' as opposed to commodity or cost, implies investment therein. The word 'management', for its part, implies that strategies aimed at the motivation, development and deployment of this resource and its associated investment will be directed in such a way as to maximise its potential. Training is a prime investment in human resources that plays a vital role in securing these goals. Companies that, for whatever reasons, are inclined to treat their employees as a cost or a commodity and who hence fail to invest in training and development activity cannot meaningfully be said to be practising human resource management.

From the perspective of a manager committed to achieving the potential of people at work, this definition encapsulates all that, in the late 1980s, was exciting about this new approach to managing people. However, there are almost as many definitions of HRM as there are writers. Storey (1992) presents an integrated model which helps to clarify the position. He suggests that there is a continuum of meanings. At one end of the continuum is a 'weak' meaning where the term is used as a synonym for personnel management. The continuum passes through the idea that personnel management techniques should be used in a more integrated way, to a position where HRM is 'fully attuned and integrated with a wider business strategy'. The continuum ends at a position where not only is HRM fully integrated but it is directed, for example, at fostering employee commitment to the organisation and its strategy. At the same time he suggests that HRM manifests two versions, a 'hard' version which stresses the rational quality of the word 'resource' and a 'soft' version which stresses the implications of the word 'human' and the consequent people orientation of the concept.

There are, as Legge (1989) points out, some critical differences between HRM and personnel management. The first is hinted at above – the fact that in most HRM models managers manage and HR staff are a resource to facilitate the process rather than the repository of bureaucratic rules to constrain their freedom to manage. The second is that organisational culture is seen as a critical element in the process of HRM. It offers a sense of direction and purpose, and encourages staff involvement, where the role of senior management in giving a strategic focus is crucial.

The idea that culture is there to be managed rather like the organisation's complaints procedure is a controversial one. Anthropologists believe that a concept developed for very different circumstances has been hijacked by management writers (*see*, for example, Peters and Waterman, 1982) in support of senior managers' goals of endeavouring to ensure that everyone in the organisation shares their own values. But the power and importance of organisational culture is impossible to deny.

In the public services, there has been widespread adoption of various models of HRM as part of a process of managing change. The context is one of sustained financial pressure from government, structural changes which brought management of public institutions of, for example, schools and hospitals down to local level, compulsory competitive tendering and an ethos in which public services values were seen as inferior to those of the private sector. As Derek Lewis, formerly Director of the Prison Service, said: 'The public service ethos has not yet been lost but it has been put at risk because civil servants feel they are not as valued as they used to be' (*Newsnight*, 25 July 1996).

With its prescriptions for devolution of responsibility to line management, HRM offered a potentially rich source of techniques and tools. As in the private sector, however, these were used in widely differing ways and with widely differing results. For example, both in a large local authority (Keen and Vickerstaff, 1996) and in a social work department (Buck and May, 1996), contradictions were found between the rhetoric of HRM (autonomy, use of initiative and increase in commitment) with the reality (central control of resources and alienative management practices which led some staff to wonder 'whether we work for the computer'). Case study 8.1 discusses these issues.

PEOPLE AT WORK AND MOTIVATION

Something is up

One public manager realised there was something about human relations that he did not understand. This realisation came on a short course run by the Industrial Society on action-centred leadership. Students were required to complete a questionnaire in which they

CASE STUDY
8.1

THE TRADITIONAL CAREER MAY ENJOY A REVIVAL

By Andrew Bolger

Human resource managers believe that the new Labour government will give them greater scope to pursue what might be described as soft management issues in their companies, according to a consensus drawn from a weekend conference run by the Human Resource Forum.

A mood of optimism that the career in its traditional sense may indeed have a future after years of downsizing emerged from some 400 HR delegates gathered at the forum held on the cruise ship *Canberra*. Stephen Wells, an independent consultant, summarising part of a discussion on the implications of the Labour government for HR, talked about 'a renewed sense of self-confidence about the HR function'. Fellow HR managers, he said, 'foresee a greater role for "soft" people issues – which HR was always interested in, but have been crushed under the heel of the finance people'.

Penny Horner, another consultant summarising discussion groups, pointed to a new willingness of personnel specialists to challenge supposed truisms – such as there no longer being any jobs for life. 'People were asking: "Why not – if it suits both the employer and the employee?",' she said.

Horner said that companies had begun to learn the lessons of downsizing – one being that it was important not to lose too many experienced staff.

'People are looking at how to retain the interest and motivation of employees aged over 45, such as through the progressive use of job shares and special projects.'

Wells found that many delegates believed it was also time to start challenging the prevalent office culture that encourages the workaholic. 'HR professionals need to take a stand on dissuading people from working long hours, if they are doing so for "macho" reasons or because of peer group pressure,' he said.

But there was also scepticism about how much workplace change could be achieved, regardless of the change of government. 'One Monday morning, I will go back to the office and the chief executive will be asking the same tough questions about payroll and costs – as he has been for years,' said one HR director.

Opening the conference, Will Hutton, editor of the *Observer*, forecast that Labour could have won a big enough victory to see them through two terms of office.

'That is going to shape the policy and the legal framework in which our companies and our financial institutions do business. After a hesitant start, I think we will see a more confident move to the kind of ideas loosely called stakeholding,' he said.

Hutton said employees would always be attracted to good employers – and companies such as Marks and Spencer and Unipart had shown this could be a source of competitive advantage.

The only real exceptions to the positive mood was among public sector delegates. Executives in the National Health Service, police and local authorities admitted to feeling bruised – trapped between members of the public, unhappy with the standards of service, and hostile politicians quick to pillory managers as bureaucrats.

Delegates from the private sector, however, remained unconvinced about how much Labour can alter the commercial pressures HR people face – or the extent to which it wishes to. Perhaps beginning to address the gulf in status and morale between the public and private sectors is a more realistic and achievable goal for the new government

Source: *Financial Times*, 4 June 1997. Reprinted with permission.

Questions on the case study

1 What is the impact of government on HRM?

2 Do you think that there are differences in HRM in the public and private sectors?

had to rank factors which were the most important in motivating, first, themselves and, second, their subordinates. In the report-back session, the tutor first put up a chart plotting the results of this activity in a 'large UK organisation'. This showed that throughout the organisation, people thought that those above them and those below them were motivated by money whereas they were motivated by achievement. When the results of the course members' questionnaires were reported back, the manager in question saw that not only had he answered in the same way, so had most of his colleagues. Plainly, something was up.

This incident occurred in the early 1980s. In 1998 the public service trade union UNISON undertook a survey which reported that 85 per cent of members regarded work as interesting and enjoyable and over 80 per cent as something that made them feel they had accomplished things. Even in the turbulent world of public management today, people's wishes to fulfil themselves at work are a paramount consideration.

These conclusions would have come as no surprise to Elton Mayo (1971), one of the seminal forces in the human relations school of management. Between 1927 and 1932 a team led by Mayo undertook the now well-known Hawthorne experiments. A series of changes were made in the working conditions of a group of industrial workers. Some of these were 'hard' – for example, changes in incentives, some 'soft' – for example, more rests and some negative – for example, longer hours. All were introduced in ways which fully involved the workers. All the changes, of whatever character, increased production. Mayo's conclusion was that it was the increased sense of participation which the workers had over their environments, the feeling of importance which that brought and the cohesive nature of the group which developed throughout the experiment which were major contributors to the work satisfaction of the workers and the increases in production which they achieved.

This work emphasises the key role of managers in achieving the job satisfaction of their staff. Yet managers have their own value systems and have widely differing approaches to those whom they manage. Two writers in particular focus on these differences. Likert (1961) distinguished between supervisors who were 'job centred' and those who were 'employee centred'. The former saw themselves as 'getting the job done' in ways which regarded employees as functions of production. These supervisors presided, Likert found, over areas of low efficiency. The latter engaged with the human issues of management – the value of individuals and the importance of effective working groups – and were participative in approach. These supervisors were responsible for much more efficient and productive functions. Arising from this research, Likert provided a model of four systems of management. System 1 represents the authoritarian manager; system 2 the benevolent manager; system 3 the consultative manager and system 4 the participative manager. Likert believed that system 4 produced the most effective results, as well as recognising the value of individuals.

Better known is the work of McGregor (1960) who postulated the notions of Theory X and Theory Y management (*see* Exhibit 8.1). McGregor believed that Theory X embodied the assumptions about human motivation implicit in the traditional view of the manager as controller. These were that humans inherently dislike work, that therefore the role of management was to direct and to provide incentives for the work process in ways which led unwilling subjects to perform to target, under pain of sanction. Security, the theory goes, is more important than ambition. Theory Y, by contrast, assumes that people can and do obtain satisfaction from their work, that they welcome responsibility and will exercise it creatively in the right circumstances to achieve things to which they are committed, in the process giving themselves the opportunity of achieving their potential.

Exhibit 8.1

Theory X and Theory Y in practice

The Director of Education had the open plan office space organised so that, from her room, she could see everyone. She believed that if anyone was outside her line of sight, they would be likely to start skiving. And she resisted giving junior staff telephones because she thought they would make private calls. Her successor managed a move of offices into largely cellular accommodation. He instituted regular progress and training needs assessment interviews between managers and staff so that there was objective information on how people were doing. Morale and creativity soared.

There is a significant body of research that supports the proposition that most people seek achievement at work and that therefore it is an important managerial role to enable them to do so. In the public sector, Livingstone and Wilkie (1981) conducted research in the civil service. They found that the most important factors leading to work satisfaction among junior and middle managers were a sense of achievement, recognition, decent colleagues, the physical environment and autonomy over their work. Relatively junior staff did not shirk opportunities for taking responsibility when the opportunity was there. In a bureaucratic organisation where material reward for success is not part of the culture, this provides significant support for the proposition.

Theories of motivation

In looking at theories about motivation which have been developed it is helpful to put them in context. Randell's equilibrium, or steady state, theory – a motivational structure for performance reviews – usefully does this in diagram form, *see* Fig. 8.1.

The model in Fig. 8.1 demonstrates how complex the issue of motivation is. Entry involves the question of whether a person has the capacity and inclination to do the work. Plainly, efforts to motivate someone for whom the answer is 'no' are likely to be fruitless. If the answer is 'some', then the model suggests that job design is the next issue to address to utilise the person's capacity and build on their inclination.

On the right hand side of the model are job-related issues having a significant effect on performance. On the left, on a time dimension, are the person-centred aspects of motivation. The model suggests that these range from the immediate things which a manager should be doing, like giving praise, to long-term growth and achievement. Finally, the question is asked whether the individual's and the organisation's goals are met. In either case, 'the model is a loop in which the actors are continually changing and, therefore, the needs, inclinations and capacities are also changing. It is the manager's task to make sense of these for the benefit both of the players and the organisation at large' (Tyson and Jackson, 1992).

(i) Now

For the purposes of this discussion, let us start on the left of the model, with the people. Skinner's (1980) work in behavioural psychology is concerned with rewards and asserts that a manager must continuously recognise and reward good behaviour, in his or her terms by giving praise and positive feedback. The obvious question here is, 'What about negative feedback?' This is an equally important part of the managerial role but Skinner would say that if positive behaviour is recognised and rewarded, then negative outcomes are less likely.

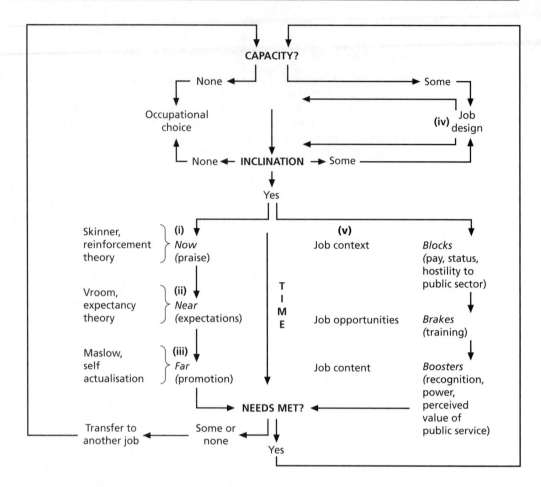

Fig. 8.1 A motivational structure for performance reviews

Note: The Roman numerals in the figure relate to the numbered subsections of the text.

Source: Adapted with permission from Tyson and Jackson (1992).

(ii) Near

Further down the time dimension is expectancy – what people expect will be the future reward they will receive for their work. Here we meet the first important motivation theories. Expectancy theory, developed by Vroom (1964) seeks to make the point that, no matter what the reward which will actually result from a particular course of action, people will not be motivated to make the effort to perform in a way which will win that reward if they do not believe that the reward will result from their performance.

In coming to that conclusion, there are three essential causal links. First, a person must understand that increased effort will lead to improved performance (this is known as *expectancy*). Planning officers who can achieve targets in casework output are unlikely to continue to exert effort to achieve this if the administration is incapable of processing the casework in a way that their achievement is reflected in the section's turnaround figures. Second, a person must understand that the increased performance will lead to positive outcomes (this is known as *instrumentality*). A hospital receptionist who acquires public recognition for the quality of her or his service is unlikely to be motivated to maintain that standard of performance if it is known that the person who will win the employee of the month award will be the one who is of indifferent calibre but who is extremely friendly with the general manager. Third, the outcome or reward must be attractive so that the person must desire that outcome or to avoid a negative outcome (this is known as *valence*). An air traffic controller whose parents live in Athens is unlikely to be motivated to perform well enough to win a holiday in Northern Cyprus if she or he knows that the passport stamp from that visit will mean that it will never again be possible to enter Greece.

This analysis probably strikes a chord because it reflects so closely most of our own experiences. It is intuitively sound. Another theory which does likewise is equity theory, based on the proposition that people wish to be treated equitably (Adams 1965). This says that people intuitively compare the effort which they put into their work and the outcomes which they obtain with the effort and outcomes of other people. Where people perceive (and it is perception that is important here; a person's perception is their reality) that other people's ratio of input to effort is not equal – that the other person's efforts are less or their rewards more – then inequity exists. It follows that it is quite possible that a person perceiving inequity will become demotivated and will exert less effort because that implicitly seems a way of restoring equity. Exhibit 8.2 illustrates such a situation.

Exhibit 8.2

A failure to understand perceptions of equity

In the 1970s, three solicitors embarked on the reorganisation of a local authority legal department. As was the fashion of the time, everything was to be scaled up, both in terms of numbers and many grades. But the creation of a strong administration function with the librarian, a new and untried member of staff, upgraded to run it did not go down at all well with the Legal Executives who saw their status eroded. The promotion of the Chief Solicitor's secretary, not renowned for having the work ethic, also grated. Differentials were affected by other proposals. Morale plummeted and it took a considerable time for it to recover. The solicitors, untrained managers, could not understand what the fuss was all about. So many people were doing so well out of it.

(iii) Far

We move from perceptions of values to Maslow's (1943) hierarchy of needs. Maslow suggests that individuals have a hierarchy of psychological needs and that only when the lower-level needs are satisfied do the higher-level needs become important.

- Level 1: *Physiological* needs such as the material need for food, drink and shelter.
- Level 2: *Safety* needs such as protection from danger.
- Level 3: *Belonging* needs such as friendship and social compatibility.
- Level 4: *Esteem* needs for respect, reputation and autonomy.
- Level 5: *Self-actualisation* needs expressed as the realisation of one's potential.

The implications of the hierarchy of needs are that only when the basic needs of life are attended to, perhaps as a result of the material rewards from work, only when we become a valued part of the community and enjoy the respect of peers, can full potential be achieved. Maslow's work is not organisation specific and it is worth making the point that many people achieve their potential outside work, but there are obvious lessons for managers in this theory.

(iv) Job design

The next stage in our model is the design of jobs. This is something which needs to be considered early in the employment process, particularly in analysing whether a person has the capacity to do a job or whether the design of the job is at fault. The bridge between our previous discussion and the role of job design in motivating individuals is provided by Herzberg (1966). His two-factor theory arose from research among 90 male engineers and accountants in the USA whom he asked to recount incidents which made them feel good and those which made them feel bad. Thus, he developed a theory which described 'satisfiers' and 'dissatisfiers' at work. Dissatisfiers, known as hygiene or maintenance factors, have great potential for creating dissatisfaction or demotivation but do not motivate. Satisfiers have the potential to motivate. Hygiene factors, it should be noted, are extrinsic to the job itself whereas the satisfying or motivating factors are intrinsic to the job. Table 8.1 presents examples of satisfiers and disatisfiers.

Table 8.1 Hertzberg's two-factor theory of job design

	Dissatisfiers	Satisfiers
Factor	Hygiene or maintenance	Motivation
Relationship to the job	Extrinsic	Intrinsic
Examples	Interpersonal relations	Achievement
	Working conditions	Recognition
	Supervision	Work itself
	Policy and administration	Responsibility
	Salary	Advancement

Herzberg and others tried over many years to replicate the results of his research, without success. Tyson and Jackson (1992) suggest that the reason for this might be the different economic circumstances in which the original research was carried out, not to mention the limited character of the sample of employees researched. Nevertheless, the work opens up significant areas for discussion, not least the role of money as a motivator – to which we shall return below. The work led Herzberg to advocate that jobs should be enriched to include the motivating factors, to the benefit of individuals and organisations. This would be achieved by the following seven principles:

1 Removing some controls while retaining accountability.
2 Increasing individuals' accountability for their own work.
3 Giving a person a complete, natural unit of work.
4 Giving an employee additional authority.
5 Reporting downwards directly to the employee rather than to the supervisor.
6 Introducing new and more challenging tasks.
7 Giving individuals specific or specialised tasks so that they become experts.

Peter Warr (1987) looked at job characteristics and the way in which they had an impact on mental health. He looked not only at work-related health but also at what he called 'context-free' mental health, relating to 'feelings and processes in a life space more generally'. After reviewing a number of research traditions, he proposed nine principal job features which, he said, influenced mental health. These are shown in Table 8.2.

Table 8.2 Warr's nine factor approach to job-related mental health

Factor	Feature
1 Opportunity for control	Low levels of personal control in a job are psychologically harmful and, depending on the level, greater control is associated with better mental health.
2 Opportunity for skill use	The opportunity to use or extend skills is known to be associated with mental health.
3 Goals and task demands	Excessively low demands give low opportunity for control and skills use. High levels are associated with low job satisfaction, job-related anxiety and exhaustion.
4 Variety	Repetitive work gives rise to low job satisfaction.
5 Environmental clarity	People need to understand their environment and predict what will happen to them. Low levels of clarity are detrimental to mental health.
6 Availability of money	There is a positive relationship between standard of living and mental health.
7 Physical security	This is related to poor working conditions where it is suggested, for example, that a job-induced deterioration in physical health arising from a poor environment can have an effect on mental condition.
8 Opportunity for interpersonal contact	Friendship opportunities at work are associated with job-related mental health. Where people undertaking repetitive tasks have been deprived of the opportunity for daydreaming, there was increased proclivity to mental breakdown.
9 Valued social position	Perceived social value has a significant effect on job-related mental health.

Source: Warr (1987).

A number of issues arising from Warr's factors are relevant to our discussion of motivation.

1 Delegation and empowerment are central to giving people greater control over their work. Delegation – giving responsibility to a subordinate to undertake a task for which the manager remains ultimately accountable – is one of the most challenging and rewarding of management tasks and it is consistent with Herzberg's principles of job enrichment. It is often done badly – dumping things on subordinates and blaming them for failure instead of treating delegation as an opportunity for learning and growth. Empowerment is arguably not a term of art but a description of ways of working

which result in people having a sense of self-worth as a result of the opportunities afforded them – 'a sense of freedom we feel inside' (Evans and Russell, 1989).

2 Job redesign initiatives in the 1970s improved employees' abilities to make use of their judgement, skills and abilities. Although this was then the cause of some controversy in that it breached job demarcations and produced a more flexible approach to job descriptions, it is now commonplace. Other initiatives such as quality circles – groups which meet several times a month with management commitment and support to discuss ways of improving the service – enable employees to contribute their knowledge and skills to the work of an organisation.

3 Job enlargement exercises can have an impact on the levels of demands made on employees and consequently on their state of health.

4 Job rotation (for example in a social services team where members rotate between geographical 'patches' or specialisms) can increase variety of work and improve job satisfaction.

5 Regular two-way communication with staff can improve environmental clarity and improve job satisfaction.

6 The idea that the public sector is valued within society would contribute to job satisfaction and mental health. This is referred to below.

(v) Job context, opportunities and content

The right-hand side of the model in Fig. 8.1 (*see* p 146) directs us to the job itself, to what it calls blocks, brakes and boosters. To some extent, the previous discussion has ranged over these issues. Blocks, however, include status; brakes include security and boosters include recognition and responsibility. Hostility to the public sector is a block in motivational terms; the perceived social value of public service a booster. The extent to which developments in public sector management offer the opportunity to enable people to achieve their potential at work is therefore an important contextual issue.

Much of the discussion on people at work has involved issues of autonomy, responsibility, self-esteem, self-worth, control and so on. Arguably, a public service context in which responsibilities have been devolved and in which individual accountability and responsibility have a much higher priority (even if the perceived social value of the work may be more difficult to establish), offers the public service manager far greater opportunities to use her or his responsibilities in ways which can achieve the potential of staff than was ever the case in the days of monolithic, unresponsive bureaucracies. The UNISON survey referred to earlier in this chapter found that 70 per cent of those public sector staff surveyed believed that they had a say in how the work was done and over 50 per cent believed that their job enabled them to learn new skills and develop their abilities. Many public sector managers seem, on this evidence, to be performing this task well. As this section has demonstrated, it is a complex task. But it is a task that is vital to any manager given responsibility for any part of the lives of people at work.

REWARDS

One of the manifestations of government policy towards public service management in the 1980s and 1990s had been the pressure it has exerted for, and its own implementation of, performance-related pay (PRP). Managerial and political issues have played their part. On the managerial side, most forms of HRM assert that there should be integration of a rewards strategy with the other elements of HR and business strategies. Since, as we have seen, cultural management is often one of the distinguishing features of HRM, developing a culture in which high performance is demanded and rewarded is not an unreasonable goal.

On the political side, the increased individualism in society is mirrored in moves away from collective bargaining and national pay scales towards personal, often fixed-term, contracts, marginalisation of trades unions and individualised rewards.

In discussing theories of motivation, we have indicated that the importance of money as a motivator is not universally accepted. We have seen that Herzberg (1966) considered it to be a 'hygiene factor' which did not motivate at all. Money can be described as an 'extrinsic' motivator and, according to expectancy theory, in order to motivate there must be links between effort, reward and valued outcome.

Table 8.3 shows some examples of different payment systems and comments on some of the characteristics of these systems. It will be seen that the further down the table one goes, the more influence managers have over the rewards resulting from the system. This again is consistent with the trend towards devolution of greater responsibility to individual managers.

Table 8.3 Some examples of payment systems

Systems	Examples	Public sector	Comments
Time systems	Payment by hourly, weekly or annual rate	Incremental advancement. Rewards more highly for experience/length of service. Overtime payable to all but highest grades.	Consistent with national bargaining. Managerial control related to placement on grades by job evaluation or individual decision.
Incentive pay	Merit pay Individual bonus Team bonus	Merit increments part of most national white collar schemes. Bonus criteria usually devised locally.	Incentives often grafted on to national schemes at local level and give some managerial control.
Payment by results	Piecework	Probably not common in a shrunken public sector which does not produce goods.	Common in production line work. May be effective in terms of expectancy theory.
Performance-related pay	The trend towards performance rather than merit assessment is a trend towards rewarding output rather than input (Fowler, 1988)	Requires measurable performance indicators.	Strong managerial control; efficacy often questioned.

Clearly, payment systems are important – as much because of their ability to frustrate organisational objectives as because of their efficacy. For example, one incentive scheme rewarded local authority lawyers on the basis of the number of County Court judgments they obtained. This probably increased cash flow but it did absolutely nothing for customer care, particularly as there was no incentive to settle cases before hearing. Performance indicators are required to manage a scheme such as this and if they are not adequately linked to strategy, disaster is threatened. One of the most fraught issues for debate concerns the place of individual rewards alongside working practices which increasingly value teamwork. Kinnie and Lowe (1990) report a comment made to them that 'we talk about teamwork at training sessions and then destroy it in the compensation system'. There is a paradox at the heart of this dilemma. On the one hand individual incentives in a team context can be divisive and dysfunctional; on the other hand, team incentives, unless they are carefully specified, can be problematic in terms of expectancy theory, in that they may not involve a sufficiently strong link between effort, reward and valued outcome.

Table 8.3 highlights one other issue faced by many public sector managers – the lack of influence they often have in relation to rewards. Merit increments and bonuses were often virtually the only levers available to them in an environment where 'downsizing' and 'delayering' meant that they were being told of the importance of managers accepting devolved responsibility for a wider range of decisions. It is not surprising that PRP was often welcomed, in particular because it was often they who benefited from it. (However, there is little evidence that linking performance to pay has a positive impact on motivation.)

As will therefore be appreciated, PRP remains an extremely controversial issue. To say the least, the evidence of its efficacy is mixed. Kohn (1993) believes that PRP can *never* work, except in the short term. He lists six reasons why this is so:

1 Pay is not a motivator.
2 Rewards are a covert form of punishment.
3 Rewards disrupt teamwork.
4 Other things affect performance.
5 PRP discourages risk taking.
6 Rewards undermine interest.

A survey by Richardson and Marsden (1992) in the Inland Revenue is totally consistent with this. It found that not only did PRP have little impact on motivation and performance, it had in some cases led to demotivation. Clark's (1996) survey found that PRP will be most effective in workplaces where prevailing values are closest to those assumed in the underlying theory – that is, where values are individualistic and calculative. Many public sector organisations may not meet this criterion. Indeed, some would say that teamworking and a belief in the community and its development are part of the public sector ethos – *see* Exhibit 8.3.

Exhibit 8.3

The cost of PRP

The fact that the cost and benefit of PRP is often a difficult equation to balance is demonstrated by the case of an English county council which in the early 1990s adopted new grades for managerial staff based on systems devised by a well-known firm of management consultants. The grades had performance-related elements. In the second year of implementation, these grades showed an increase over 3 per cent more than those awarded to the rest of the staff. The Chief Executive wrote to managers asking them on financial grounds 'seriously to consider accepting a phased implementation'. This was accepted but the following year an early warning was received that a similar outturn was likely. 'I had hoped that the method would deliver a level which had better regard to the general levels of settlements, but this is not to be.' A further phased increase was proposed. In the event, this was not necessary but two years later the scheme was abandoned along with the link with performance.

Table 8.4 Perceptions of performance-related pay

Perceived advantages	Perceived disadvantages
Consistent with creating a performance culture	Difficult to establish link with performance
Devolves responsibility to managers	Requires considerable management time and specialist expertise
Capable of adaptation to local circumstances	May distort appraisal schemes which focus on individual development
Flexible and capable of encouraging flexibility	Requires precise performance indicators to measure performance
Consistent with moves away from collective bargaining	Requires precise performance indicators to measure performance
May help with recruitment and retention of staff	Potentially divisive
	Potentially expensive

The perceived advantages and disadvantages of PRP are summarised in Table 8.4. We are not likely to be able to provide here answers to all the questions raised by this discussion. What is important is that these issues are approached critically, taking into account the extensive research on motivation and the public sector context. Nowhere is there a better demonstration that the uncritical adoption of models and prescriptions of management theory, particularly where the experience of them has been principally in quite a different context, can be at best risky and at worst downright dangerous.

LEADERSHIP

The inclusion of leadership in this chapter reflects the fact that, whatever disagreements there are about the precise definition of the term, it is indubitably about people and the extent to which they can be motivated to behave in particular ways. The relationship of leadership with management is more difficult to pin down.

At a conference in 1996, John Adair, the author of the concept of action-centred leadership, distinguished between leaders and managers. He talked of twenty-first-century leaders requiring vision, empathy and concern for people and issues, lack of reliance on position and rank for status and the ability to be a team builder and team maintainer. He identified Gail Rebuck, the Chief Executive of Random House and Nelson Mandela as twenty-first-century leaders; John Major, he said, was a day-to-day manager of crises. John Monks, General Secretary of the Trades Union Congress, expressed similar thoughts when he said that leadership was listening, inspiring and morale building. One public service manager has his team work to the CHILTERN principles of leadership: communication, honesty, involvement, listening, trust, enthusiasm, results and no games!

So perhaps leadership is merely a subset of the more general management role? Field Marshal Lord Slim used to say that leadership involved people whereas management was concerned with money and materials. This is certainly one way of looking at it. Another is that management is related to formal organisational authority whereas leadership is a deeper concept related to the personal qualities of the leader (Ackerman, 1985) – a thought that is succinctly expressed in the phrase 'Emperors rule; leaders motivate' (Marshall cited in Evans and Russell, 1989). This approach is consistent with the reality in many modern organisations where lateral rather than vertical relations are common and ability to influence across boundaries is consequently important. There are many writers (for example, Kossen, 1983) who argue that leadership involves a process of legitimate influence. Kossen defines leadership as 'the ability to influence the behaviour of others to go in a certain direction'.

This wide definition at least has the merit of giving us a starting point. If leaders are exercising influence to achieve goals, then the abilities and qualities they need to deploy may include those identified by Adair and Monks. The problem then is how those abilities and qualities are gained.

Trait theories

If there are, as we suggested earlier, people who believe that management cannot be taught there are even more people who believe that leadership is an inbuilt trait which a person either possesses or does not, and which cannot be learned – 'Leaders are born not made' as the old saying has it.

If one does believe this, then one has the responsibility of identifying the traits that do define a leader. On this matter there is little agreement. Intelligence, initiative and self-assurance are three traits which have often been identified but these are obviously incomplete and difficult to measure objectively. In the public sector, qualities such as vision, resilience, charisma (Local Government Training Board, 1987), emotional stability and maturity (Chapman, 1984) have been suggested. These are, however, subject to the same reservation.

It is excessively idealistic to believe that anyone is capable of learning leadership skills. The voluntary sector, including trade unions, has often suffered from the mistaken belief that commitment guarantees performance. One of the best examples of the development of the role of the public sector manager is the changes that have taken place in the role of the local authority chief executive. The Bains Report published in 1972 formed the foundation of the modern corporate approach to managing local authorities which turned the historic role of town clerk into that of chief executive. Bains described the role in the following way: 'His first task is to gain the respect and esteem of his colleagues, because his true powers will come more from his own qualities and character than from anything written into his terms of appointment'. (Cited in Widdicombe, 1986, p 143.)

Style theories

If, then, leadership skills can be taught, perhaps the teaching should be directed towards leadership behaviour since it is the behaviour that leaders manifest towards those whom they are leading which will be instrumental in achieving their objectives. This was the origin of 'style' theories of leadership and within this body of writing the human relations approach, exemplified by Mayo whom we encountered earlier in this chapter, has been very influential. White and Lippitt (1953), for example, undertook research in a boys' club where they experimented with three styles – autocratic, *laissez-faire* and democratic. The *laissez-faire* approach was unsuccessful by any criteria and whereas the autocratic style led to the highest productivity, this was only while the leader was actually present. The democratic style was the most popular and the one which produced the most consistent quality and productivity.

Contingency theories

It is almost always wise to be sceptical about any management writer who claims to have identified one best way of doing something. Contingency theories of leadership recognise that in the real world there are likely to be different situations in which different approaches will be appropriate.

Two contingency approaches are particularly important. The first is that of Fiedler. His researches identified two principal leadership styles; task oriented and relationship oriented. Both of these styles, Fiedler (1967) believes, can be appropriate provided the circumstances are right and those circumstances are defined on three dimensions:

- *leader–member relations*: if a leader is liked and respected by the people who are being led, Fiedler believes that the leader will have more influence with them;
- *task structure*: clearly defined tasks will give the leader more influence than those which are inchoate or vague;
- *position power*: leaders who have substantial position power are in a more favourable situation than those who have not.

Where one or more of these elements exist, Fiedler believes that the situation is likely to be favourable to the leader. Task-oriented leaders are likely to perform better where the situation is either highly favourable or unfavourable – where, presumably, the achievement of the task transcends other considerations. Relationship-oriented leaders performed better, he found, in situations which were less easy to define as favourable or unfavourable – where, perhaps, they were less clear-cut.

The other contingency model is that of Tannenbaum and Schmidt (1973). They produced a continuum of leadership styles which is shown in Fig. 8.2.

There are, according to Tannenbaum and Schmidt (1973) four variables which will determine the appropriate leadership style to adopt – the leader, the led, the task and the context. It is common to analyse situations by the use of 'best-fit' diagrams which enable one to see whether there is a 'fit' between the various components of a situation and to determine how to manage the situation if there is no 'fit'.

It is important, in trying to understand this concept, to try to envisage practical situations which will illuminate it. First, the *leader*. Nobody comes to a leadership situation without bringing with them their own values, personality, experience and education. There is no clean sheet. One of the most common criticisms of contingency theories is that they overestimate the extent to which people are likely to be able easily to alter their core values. But understanding that different situations require different approaches can help leaders to behave in ways which offer the best chance of success.

Next the *led*. They also bring their historically and culturally influenced expectations to any situation and will be likely to respond to styles of leadership which fit those expectations. But their expectations will also be defined by the *task* and the context. A bounded task such as taking a patient's temperature and blood pressure would normally be

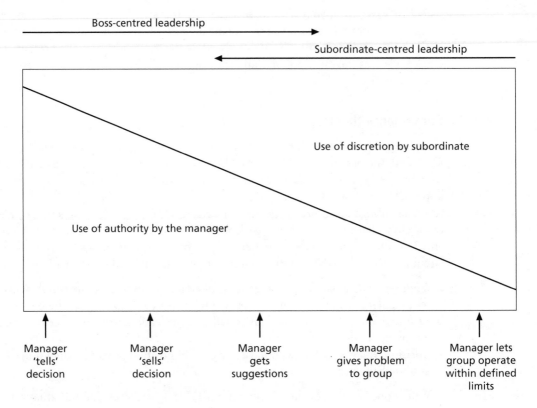

Fig. 8.2 A continuum of leadership styles

Source: Reprinted by permission of *Harvard Business Review* from an exhibit from R Tannenbaum and W H Schmidt, 'How to choose a leadership pattern', *Harvard Business Review*, May–June 1973. Copyright © 1973 by the President and Fellows of Harvard College; all rights reserved.

appropriate for a more directive style – 'Could you do it, please.' A more open task, such as deciding why that patient had difficulty in breathing, is likely to involve a much higher degree of discretion for the health worker involved.

The *context* is equally important. Chapter 14 deals in details with culture, an area the importance of which should never be underestimated. The culture of a social services department is likely to involve expectations of a more democratic style of leadership than that of an engineering department. But a social services manager may find that the culture in a residential home may not be the same as that in the office in which he or she works and tasks there may need to be achieved using a different leadership approach.

The cultural context was equally important in the development of the local authority chief executive. The deep cultural traditions of local government meant that they were *primus inter pares* rather than chief executives in the sense in which the term was understood in the private sector. This, however, changed over the years and the Widdicombe Inquiry into the conduct of local authority business (1986) called for the role to be enhanced, by taking overall managerial authority. A clear leadership role was thus mapped out, as culture changed.

Situational leadership

An alternative approach is that of situational leadership, developed by Hersey and Blanchard (1977). The key to this is four levels of job-related development of those who are led, the developmental level being the competence to undertake particular tasks without supervision. A low level of development in relation to a specific task indicates a directive style; a moderate level of development a 'coaching' style involving high direction but also high supportive behaviour. Where there is a higher level of development a 'supporting' style may be appropriate, involving high support but low direction. Where there is a high level of development, then a delegating style is indicated.

One of the key issues for managers is the question of when and what to delegate. A leadership model which takes that into account is likely to find resonance with managers in all sectors. However, the monitoring systems which are an essential part of any delegation have to take into account whether that leadership style is still appropriate. If leadership style is changed, there must be an open and honest explanation of this if the manager is to avoid accusations of inconsistency.

Action-centred leadership

Action-centred leadership has been mentioned several times in this chapter and deserves explanation at least partly because it was a concept which was very influential in the public sector not very long ago. It is less a leadership theory than a framework within which managers exercise leadership, a framework most commonly illustrated by three circles, shown in Fig. 8.3 (Adair, 1983). The idea is that a leader has to bring together the three variables illustrated, the task, the team and the individual.

Adair proposes eight elements of the leadership role. These are:

- defining the task
- planning
- briefing

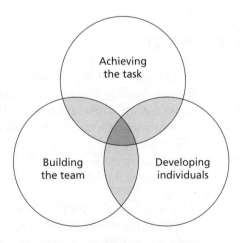

Fig. 8.3 Action-centred leadership

Source: Adair (1983).

- controlling
- evaluating
- motivating
- organising
- setting an example

Although this view of the leadership role at first sight seems a far cry from some of the more visionary approaches we have considered earlier, the concept is very much based on the need to inspire the team and the individuals who are the responsibility of the leader. A checklist used in training includes items such as valuing people, caring about their well-being, listening and praising. Whatever the model, one comes back to the qualities which we intuitively recognise as being characteristic of effective leaders.

In a report in 1989, the Audit Commission emphasised the importance of that leadership role, emphasising that a strong chief executive can provide much of the leadership local government needed to restore a sense of direction. The description of the responsibilities of the post provide a useful framework for this discussion of leadership because they bring together in a coherent way some of the ambiguities which, it might be thought, need to be resolved for a manager to exercise leadership responsibility in the public sector:

1 Manage the interfaces between politics and management and also, increasingly, between clients and contractors.
2 Convert policy into strategy and then into action.
3 Develop processes, people and management skills to ensure that the authority is, and will continue to be, capable of delivering its strategy.
4 Review performance against stated objectives.
5 Think and plan ahead. (1989, p 8)

A chief executive undertaking these responsibilities will certainly be engaged in processes of legitimate influence and will arguably be engaged in action-centred leadership – the similarities with these ideas are striking. But the exercise of that leadership will still, arguably, be contingent on a range of contextual issues and on the situational factors identified by Hersey and Blanchard (1977). Plainly, there is no 'one best way' of leading.

TRADE UNIONS AND HUMAN RESOURCES

Public services in the UK have traditionally been characterised by high levels of trade union membership. However since the late 1970s, membership levels have declined though reduction in union density has not been as marked in the public sector as in other sectors. In 1992, around 72 per cent of workers in the public sector were members of unions, with figures for membership ranging from nearly 90 per cent in the railways to around 55 per cent in the fire service, the police and the defence industry. The fact of decline, however, has to be acknowledged and new working and managerial methods, including the practice of HRM, have probably contributed to that decline.

There are three main areas where unions have to engage with HR. The first, and the least often noted, is in their role as employers. This area is outside the scope of this chapter although it might be noted that if unions exist to help their members achieve their potential and to be treated fairly and equitably at work, then one should not be surprised to learn that they were equally concerned for the interests of their own staff. Whether this has always been manifested in the past is a matter for some conjecture but there is now much more interest in managing unions in ways which exemplify best practice, as suggested by the foundation in 1996 of a Centre for Strategic Trade Union Management at Cranfield School of Management, Cranfield University.

Working with human resources

The second way in which unions engage with HR is in reacting to changes in working practices which have effects both on union organisation, in the increased individualism of the workplace, and on individual union members. In reacting, they have the additional difficulty of defining exactly with what form of HR they are dealing.

HRM originated in the USA and its emergence, as Claydon (1994) points out, was closely linked to the decline in trade union organisation and rejection by managers of established patterns of industrial relations. He identifies deep-seated anti-union values among management, exacerbated by a legislative climate in which employers were free to oppose unionisation and a widening of the wage differential between union and non-union workers which gave employers an economic incentive to open non-union operations. This took place in a tradition where, in contrast to the UK, trade unions and collective bargaining had a precarious existence.

It is not surprising, therefore, that American forms of HRM incorporate strong anti-union and unitarist elements. Kochan and Cappelli (1984) argue that the American approach to HRM focused upon psychology-based and individual-oriented personnel policies which are antithetical to the labour relations approach. The idea that American HR has a primary focus of anti-unionism is supported by other commentators. Claydon notes that fully developed HR is almost as rare in the USA as anywhere else, with employers picking and mixing from a fashionable set of ideas and prescriptions; Guest concludes further that 'the main impact of HRM in the USA may have been to provide a smokescreen behind which management can introduce non-unionism or obtain significant concessions from trade unions' (1990, p 389).

To follow a similar route to that taken by their American counterparts is a temptation which some employers in the UK find it difficult to resist. A consultant working with the personnel director of a Health Service Trust on a staff survey discovered after the event that the survey was being used as a prelude to union de-recognition. When a meeting was held for the consultant to protest, she noted that the director's bookshelf prominently displayed various American HR text books.

Yet the tradition of union membership and collective bargaining is very different in the UK, particularly in the public sector. Workplace Industrial Relations Survey researchers found that the more comprehensive the use of recognisable HRM techniques, the more likely the organisation was to recognise unions. There are examples of models of HR in the UK which take this into account. Storey (1992) reviewed the practice of HRM in a variety of areas. In the public sector he looked (*inter alia*) at Bradford Metropolitan Council and the National Health Service. At Bradford he found that the employers were committed to treating the unions as 'partners', providing a union-linked approach to HRM in the British context. In the National Health Service the situation was less clear-cut, no doubt because of its diversity. Storey found proliferations of tools such as team building, inter-personal skills, an emphasis on communication and team involvement processes. These, it should be noted, are not necessarily anti-union. Managers who in the 1970s relied on unions to communicate with their employees were arguably not doing their jobs, even in a culture that was heavily collectively organised.

Consequently, unions have a dilemma. They too may have to pick and mix, depending on the model of HRM they are using. As John Edmonds, General Secretary of the General, Municipal and Boilermakers Union, said (Storey *et al.*, 1993): 'Let us use some of the attractive ideas of HRM. But let us also run them fully through and expose any inconsistencies between the underlying principles and actual practice'. Bacon and Storey (1996) have produced a 'ladder' of union co-operation with HRM. Their review of union responses concludes with suggestions for effective trade union strategies. They argue that at the individual level one possible way forward is for unions 'to grasp the nettle of individualism within HRM and separate out those aspects which are acceptable for unions and beneficial for members. One solution to this is via a legal programme of rights on the substantive issues of employment' (1996, p 70), something which the TUC has recently proposed. At the collective level, they argue that:

> Where partnership models of industrial relations have been developed, this has eased one of the difficulties of collective action for the unions. If a shared objective can be developed between management and unions, then the tendency for workers to identify their interests as identical to those of capital is less of a challenge for the unions. There is a strong possibility that employees could display dual commitment to both the union and the company (1996, pp 71–2).

Here, the outline of a form of HR which respects the British context and is appropriate to the public sector, where the shared goal of public service is at the heart of the public sector ethos, can be discerned. In reaching it, unions arguably have an integral role. Exhibit 8.4 summarises management perceptions of the benefits and disadvantages of trade unions.

Exhibit 8.4

Reasons why management might resent trade unions

1 Trade unions seek to represent the collective interests of the workforce; managers may see this as a threat.
2 Trade unions may seek to formalise procedures; managers may require flexibility.
3 Trade unions sometimes use sanctions to pursue their claims.
4 Trade unions may be viewed as a third party that gets in the way of good relations between the employer and the employee.
5 Since the early 1970s trade unions have been out of favour and a hostile political climate has meant that unions have been seen as anachronistic.

Reasons why management might welcome trade unions

1 Unions can act as an agency for employees so that management does not have to deal with individual cases.
2 Trade unions act as the voice of employees and can bring problems to the attention of management before they become too serious.
3 Trade unions can manage discontent through the use of agreed procedures for settling disputes (*see* Freeman and Medoff, 1984).

Unions and the future

The third area where unions engage with HR is in coping with the consequences of changing workplace relations by defining their own strategic positioning.

There is some evidence that not only are unions compatible with workplace innovations but they can positively add value. Allen (1995) cites recent research from the USA which found more innovation in terms of team-based production, productivity, gain sharing and 'quality of working life' initiatives in unionised that in non-union firms. The reasons, he suggests, are that in union organisations employees enjoy (*inter alia*) individual employment rights, job security and some group cohesiveness – and these are the factors which make the productivity different.

Employers, then, may need unions. Unions certainly need employers. Willman *et al.* (1993) pointed out that unions operate in two markets – a member market and an employer market – that have to be reconciled. In the membership market they provide representation and membership and other services, seeking to maximise membership to guarantee revenue and bargaining power – often in competition with other unions. They also compete in the employer market to become bargaining agents. They need recognition; with that, and the facilities that usually come with it, they can shift some of the costs of organisation on to the employer. The two markets are, they say, related since, without recognition, membership is difficult to maintain and, without membership, recognition can be difficult to secure. A successful union has to be successful in both markets.

To market themselves both to employees and to employers, then, unions will have to show that they can 'add value' for both, through, for example, smoothing the employer's path in such areas as changing payment systems, disciplinary procedures or demonstrating expertise in areas such as health and safety, pensions, training and legal rights at work.

That employers and employees have a mutual interest in the future of the public service is axiomatic. If the way forward is to accept the responsibility jointly for securing that future, that would be added value indeed.

CONCLUSIONS

The management of human resources takes place within the context of changing technology, political and social ideas, the economy and all the other factors we discussed in Part 1 of this book. They will undoubtedly have an impact upon HRM. Thus, for example, as the change to non-standard forms of employment gather pace – with more flexible contracts, part-time working, temporary employment and so on – this will have an impact upon the nature of the psychological contract between the employee and the employer. At the same time as organisations recognise that they must utilise human resources and 'intellectual capital', employees are encouraged to take control of their own careers and become more employable by developing a portfolio of skills which each individual constantly updates and refreshes. Fears that the development of short-term contracts and local pay agreements will undermine the concept of a unified career civil service, leading to a decline in the public service ethos, have been expressed. We explore this further in Chapter 15.

REFERENCES

Ackerman, L (1985) 'Leadership vs Management', *Leadership and Organization Development Journal*, 6(2), pp 17–19.

Adair, J (1983) *Effective Leadership*. London: Gower.

Adams, T S (1965) 'Injustice in social exchange' in Berkowitz, L (ed.) *Advances in Social Psychology*. London: Academic Press.

Allen, M (1995) 'Modernising the workplace', *Renewal*, 3(2), pp 58–67.

Audit Commission (1989) *More Equal than Others: The Chief Executive in Local Government*. London: Audit Commission.

Bacon, N and Storey, J (1996) 'Individualism and collectivism' in Ackers, P, Smith, C and Smith, P (eds) *The New Workplace and Trade Unionism*. London: Routledge.

Bains Committee (1972) *The New Local Authorities, Management and Structure*. London: Department of the Environment.

Beer, M and Spector, B (1985) 'Corporate-wide transformations in HRM' in Walton, R E and Lawrence, P R (eds) *HRM: Trends and Challenges*. Boston: Harvard Business School Press.

Buck, M and May, T (1996) 'Does money talk? HRM in a social work setting'. Paper presented to the conference 'HRM – The Inside Story', organised by the Open University Business School, Milton Keynes, 1–2 April.

Chapman, R A (1984) *Leadership in the British Civil Service*. Beckenham: Croom Helm.

Clark, G (1996) 'PRP and employee values'. Paper presented to the conference 'HRM – The Inside Story', organised by the Open University Business School, Milton Keynes, 1–2 April.

Claydon, T (1994) 'HRM and the USA' in Beardwell, I and Holden, L (eds) *HRM : A Contemporary Perspective*. London: Financial Times Pitman Publishing.

Evans, R and Russell, P (1989) *The Creative Manager*. London: Unwin.

Fiedler, F E A (1967) *A Theory of Leadership Effectiveness*. New York: McGraw-Hill.

Fowler, A (1988) 'New directions in performance pay', *Personnel Management*, 20(11), pp 30–4.

Freeman, R B and Medoff, J L (1984) *What do Umons Do?* New York: Basic Books.

Guest, D (1990) 'HRM and the American Dream', *Journal of Management Studies*, 27(4), pp 377–97.

Hersey, P and Blanchard, K H (1977) *Management of Organisational Behaviour: Utilising Human Resources*. Englewood Cliffs, NJ: Prentice-Hall.

Herzberg, F (1966) *Work and the Nature of Man*. Cleveland: World Publishing.

Keen, L and Vickerstaffe, S (1996) 'From personnel management to HRM in local government: opportunities and constraints from the middle management perspective'. Paper presented to the conference, 'HRM – The Inside Story', organised by the Open University, Milton Keynes, 1–2 April.

Keep, E (1989) 'Corporate training strategies: the vital component' in Storey, J (ed.) *New Perspectives on HRM*. London: Routledge.

Kinnie, N and Lowe, D (1990) 'Performance-related pay on the shop floor', *Personnel Management*, 22(11), pp 45–9.

Kochan, T A and Cappelli, P (1984) 'The transformation of the IR and personnel function' in Osterman P (ed.) *Internal Labor Markets*. Cambridge, MA: MIT Press.

Kohn, A (1993) 'Why incentive plans cannot work', *Harvard Business Review*, Sept/Oct, 71, pp 54–63.

Kossen, S (1983) *The Human Side of Organisations*. New York: Harper & Row.

Legge, K (1989) 'HRM a critical analysis' in Storey, J (ed.) *New Perspectives on HRM*. London: Routledge.

Likert, R (1961) *New Patterns of Management*. New York: McGraw-Hill.

Livingstone, H and Wilkie, R (1981) 'Motivation and performance among civil service managers', *Public Administration*, 59(2), pp 151–72.

Local Government Training Board (1987) *The Leadership Audit*. Luton: LGTB.

McGregor, D (1960) 'The Human Side of Enterprise'. New York: McGraw-Hill.

Maslow, A H (1943) 'A theory of human motivation', *Psychological Review*, 50, pp 370–96.

Mayo, E (1971) 'Hawthorne and the Western Electric Company', in Pugh, D S (ed.) *Organisation Theory*, Harmondsworth: Penguin.

Peters, T J and Waterman, R H (1982) *In Search of Excellence*. New York: Prentice-Hall.

Randell, G (1991) 'The concept of motivation: What really motivates people in their work?'. Paper presented to the Institute for International Research, July.

Richardson, R and Marsden, D (1992) 'Does performance pay motivate? A study of Inland Revenue staff'. London: LSE.

Skinner, B F (1980) *Notebooks*. Upper Saddle River: Prentice-Hall.

Storey, J (1992) *Management of Human Resources*. Oxford: Blackwell.

Storey, J, Bacon, N, Edmonds, J and Wyatt, P (1993) 'The "New Agenda" and HRM: a round table discussion with John Edmonds', *Human Resource Management Journal*, 4(1), pp 63–70.

Tannenbaum, R and Schmidt, W H (1973) 'How to choose a leadership pattern', *Harvard Business Review*, May/June, 51, pp 162–80.

Tyson, S and Jackson, A P (1992) *The Essence of Organizational Behavior*. New York: Prentice-Hall.

Vroom, V (1964) *Work and Motivation*. New York: Wiley.

Warr, P (1987) 'Job characteristics and mental health' in Warr, P (ed.) *Psychology at Work*. Harmondsworth: Penguin.

White, R and Lippitt, R (1953) 'Leader behaviour and member reaction in three social climates' in Cartwright, D and Zander, A (eds) *Group Dynamics*. London: Tavistock.

Widdicombe, D (1986) Committee of Inquiry into the Conduct of Local Authority Business. London: HMSO (Cmnd 9797).

Willman, P, Morris, T and Aston, B (1993) *Union Business*. Cambridge: Cambridge University Press.

QUESTIONS AND DISCUSSION TOPICS

1 Do trade unions have a role to play in the relationship between the employer and the employee?

2 What are the contradictions involved in HRM?

3 What are the main motivators for public service employees?

9 Financial management

Sandra Nutley

AIMS

This chapter will:

- outline the financial context in which public services managers work;
- describe the cycle of activities involved in ensuring effective financial management;
- enable the reader to understand the main components of a budget and the process by which budgets are constructed;
- describe the format of a typical budget monitoring statement and explain how it should be used in controlling income and expenditure;
- identify the key issues involved in planning, controlling and accounting for the use of resources;
- critically discuss different methods of resource allocation;
- present an analysis of the devolution of financial management responsibilities;
- outline the key points of difference between financial management in the public and private sectors;
- describe the role of financial reports and external audit bodies in ensuring value for money.

INTRODUCTION

Before discussing the processes of financial management within public service organisations, it is helpful to have an understanding of the wider financial context within which these services operate. The slogan for public sector financial management in the 1990s is 'more for less'; that is, more public services for less public spending. Exhibit 9.1 illustrates this by outlining the resourcing of the probation service.

Whereas public expenditure on the probation service kept pace broadly with the increasing levels of community supervision orders during the 1980s and early 1990s, from the mid-1990s onwards there have been, in real terms, cuts in funding. The demands on the service have continued to increase. This scenario will be familiar to much of the public sector although, in many ways, the reality of 'more for less' did not affect the criminal justice services until much later than many other public services.

Exhibit 9.1

Probation service finance

The reduction in resources is a relatively new phenomenon for the probation service. They have, to date, fared much better than many local government services in the public expenditure allocation process. During the 1980s and early 1990s there was a substantial growth in the workload of the service, but there was also a growth in the level of resources available. For example, in the case of one probation service area, the revenue budget grew from £5.5 million in 1985/86 to £11.7 million in 1993/94 (a real terms increase of approximately 50 per cent). From the early 1990s it was predicted that this growth in resources would not continue and that the service would have to come to terms with doing more for less. Up to 1992/93 the service was funded on a volume of service basis, but this basis changed in that year with the introduction of cash limits. These cash limits and the relative reduction in the level of funding had its first major impact on the service with the 1995/96 budget settlement. At the national level, the funding for probation services was reduced by 1 per cent in cash terms in 1995/96. The effect of this cash settlement on individual probation service areas varied. For the probation area referred to above, the effect was a 6 per cent real terms reduction in their revenue budget. Further details of both the funding and workload levels for this probation service during the 1990s is provided in Table 9.1.

Table 9.1 Workload levels and revenue expenditure for a probation service area

	1992/93	1993/94	1994/95	1995/96
Number of community sentence commencement orders	3 250*	3 962	4 290	3 993
Community sentence case load for year	3 330	3 758	3 996	3 900
Custodial sentence case load for year (through-care)	1 956	1 891	2 074	1 935*
Number of probation service reports	6 898	8 151	8 424	7 767
Number of family court welfare reports	1 388	950	1 242	1 190
Staff numbers (full-time equivalents)	495.75[a]	511.25[b]	515.25[c]	475.5[d]
Revenue expenditure	£11 921 350	£12 945 275	£14 047 723	£13 933 868

* Estimates (precise figures not provided in *Annual Reports*).

Notes: a As at 31 December 1992.

b As at 31 March 1994.

c As at 31 March 1995.

d As at 31 March 1996.

Source: Probation Service, *Annual Reports and Accounts*, 1992 to 1995/96.

It is not easy to measure just how much more for exactly how much less. The measurement of public spending is not straightforward. There are many different definitions of what constitutes public expenditure, the figures are disputed and the definitions and terms used are controversial (Corry and Gray, 1997). Figure 9.1 (*see* p 166) uses one definition of public spending, general government expenditure (GGE) to plot public spending in real terms over the last thirty or so years.

What is noticeable in Fig. 9.1 is that, in real terms, there has been an inexorable rise in expenditure, with the exception of a temporary downturn in the mid-1970s. The real level of growth throughout the 1980s may be somewhat surprising given that the Conservative Government talked constantly about 'rolling back the frontiers of the state', controlling public spending and reducing taxation. There are many reasons for the divergence between political rhetoric and public spending reality. For example, Corry and Gray (1997, p 66)

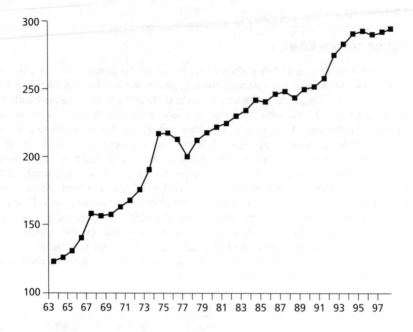

Fig. 9.1 Growth in public spending in real terms (£bn/financial year)
Source: Public Expenditure Statistical Analyses (PESA) (HMT, 1996), Table 1.1.

argue that 'In practice, spending is driven by enormous demographic and social forces that are largely beyond the control of government'. The real-terms growth in public spending slowed down in the first half of the 1990s. This pattern may continue throughout the 1990s as the Labour Government made an election pledge to adopt the same spending targets as the previous Conservative Government up to the year 2000. However, as was evident in the 1980s, a political will to control public spending may not be sufficient to achieve this target.

In the 1990s then there is likely to be little or no real-terms growth in spending by many government departments and bodies. The solution to the tensions between this and the demands for more and improved public services is seen as tighter financial controls and the search for greater efficiencies in the delivery of services. In this context public service managers are required carefully to plan and monitor their use of resources. This places ever-increasing demands on their financial and managerial skills. Good financial management is no longer seen as the responsibility of accountants alone.

The emergence of a managerial culture in public services, in contrast to the former administrative culture, has been discussed in earlier chapters. Not only have new managerial posts been introduced, but there have also been changes in the behaviour expected of senior practitioners. The delivery of public services has been restructured with the delegation of significant financial and other responsibilities to decentralised units. Some of these units have been required to operate somewhat commercially as part of a quasi-market. The devolution of budget holding down hierarchies to, for example, clinicians and head teachers places increased demands on their financial management skills. Such managers require accurate, timely and relevant information and the knowledge and skills to interpret this information and take action. This has not proved easy. As Coombs and Jenkins (1994, p ix) point out, 'Managers are often asked to exercise such skills whilst relying on financial information systems that were designed to produce financial accounts rather than managerial information'. The world of finance is full of jargon and it is worth pausing for a moment to check your understanding of this jargon. The glossary of terms provided at the end of this chapter provides brief definitions of each of these concepts. This chapter will explore many of them in more detail.

The focus of this chapter is mainly on the process by which staff in public service organisations manage and make best use of the limited funds available to them. Financial management can be envisaged as consisting of a cycle of activities as shown in Fig. 9.2. The aim of this cycle of activities is to ensure that resources are allocated and monitored in such a way that they have the greatest beneficial impact on overall service objectives.

This chapter is structured around the series of activities outlined in Fig. 9.2. The sections which follow provide:

- Consideration of the planning and budget-setting process.
- A detailed examination of the main approaches to resource allocation.

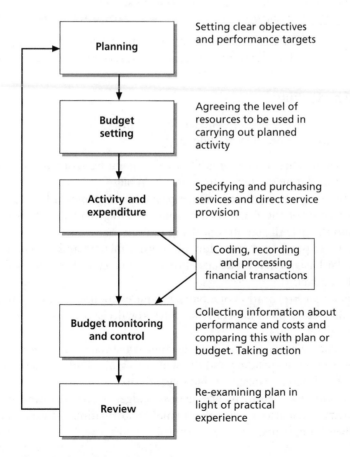

Fig. 9.2 Financial management

- A discussion of the monitoring of activity and expenditure and the use of budgetary information in exercising control.
- Consideration of the process of devolving budgets and the benefits and costs of delegating financial management responsibilities.
- A comparison of financial management practice in the public sector with that in the private sector.
- An overview of the ways in which the work of various audit bodies contributes towards ensuring improved value for money in public service organisations.

PLANNING AND BUDGET SETTING

Budget definition

A budget is a plan of activity expressed in financial terms; such plans are often short term, typically covering a period of one year. The Chartered Institute of Public Finance and Accountancy defines a budget as:

> A plan quantified in monetary terms, prepared and approved prior to a defined period of time, usually showing planned income to be generated and/or expenditure to be incurred during that period and the capital to be employed to attain a given objective (CIPFA, 1996, p 249).

Increasingly, however, the trend in local government is to opt for a longer-term budget plan, such as three years, in order to match resources to service planning and strategy.

The purpose of budgeting

Budget setting is a key activity in all public service organisations. Its importance is related to the different purposes or benefits of budgeting:

- *Planning* – budgeting fits into the middle of the planning structure; it provides the framework for translating strategy into operational plans.
- *Co-ordination* – an overall or master budget provides the framework for co-ordinating the various activities of the organisation, thus enabling managers to see how their activities fit into the overall activities of the organisation.
- *Control* – a budget provides a basis for monitoring income and expenditure against plans on a regular basis so that remedial action can be taken if there are significant deviations from the budget.
- *Communication* – the preparation of a budget requires communication throughout the organisation. Budgetary planning communicates key decisions in relation to medium- and short-term plans.
- *Authorisation and delegation* – the budget approval process generally provides the required authorisation of spending and the structuring of a budget makes it clear who is accountable for different aspects of that expenditure.
- *Measuring performance* – performance against budget is one performance indicator; budgetary systems often also provide the financial information required in developing other performance indicators.

The different purposes or benefits of budgeting closely match the definition of management provided by the classical management school. For example, Fayol (1949) defined the five functions of management as: planning, organising, commanding, co-ordinating and controlling. A classical management approach to the problem of management control likens the organisation to a machine (Morgan, 1997). This mechanistic perspective emphasises the functionality of the organisational components and the need for technical controls. Problems can arise because organisations, unlike machines, are not closed and highly predictable systems. Little wonder, then, that budget setting is a source of tension in public service organisations. Lapsley (1992, p 56) points out that 'the annual budget becomes the dominant management tool for planning, co-ordinating, organising and controlling activities'. This multifaceted role is a difficult one to fulfil and the implementation of the budget in public sector organisations is often a source of controversy.

The structure of budgets

The structure of budgets, the way in which a budget is subdivided, varies across organisations. The traditional budget structure has functional subdivisions, leading to budgets being produced for each of the main functions within an organisation. For example, within a local authority a functional division of the overall budget leads to separate budgets for each of the main departments (such as education, social services, housing, leisure and recreation, environmental health and central services). Within each of these functions, budgets are further subdivided into appropriate budget centres, each with a responsible manager. For example, a personnel department budget may be subdivided into the following budget centres:

Budget centre	Responsible manager
Employment service	Employment services manager
Training and development	Head of training and development
Health and safety	Health and safety manager

Structuring an organisational budget by function is not the only form of subdivision that is used. Alternatives include structuring a budget on the basis of:

- *physical location* – for example, to an area office;
- *programmes of care or client groups* – for example, children under five years of age or pregnant mothers;
- *specialities* – for example, in hospitals, groups of like diseases or treatment types, such as neurology or oncology.

Within each budget centre the budget is likely to be structured according to subjective cost headings, which emphasise the nature of the income or expenditure, sometimes known as line item budgeting. Alternatively, the budget may be itemised according to the purpose of the expenditure, known as programme budgeting. An example of a training budget analysed first by subjective headings and then by programme headings is shown in Table 9.2.

Table 9.2 Training unit budget 200X/200X

By subjective headings	
Expenditure	£
Salaries	78 430
Travel	1 250
Supplies and services	
Hire of training venues	15 000
Outside trainer fees	10 000
Stationery (inc. copying and postage)	7 500
Central services costs	6 500
Total expenditure	*118 680*
Income	
Course attendance fees	120 000
By programme headings	
Expenditure	£
Induction programme	5 400
Management development programme	55 240
Other training programmes	
Staff selection	10 300
Performance appraisal	15 520
IT skills	12 600
Customer care	8 300
Health and safety	11 320
Total expenditure	*118 680*
Income	
Induction programme	5 200
Management development programme	60 500
Other training	54 300
Total income	*120 000*

The most appropriate budget structure will depend upon how the organisation is organised to deliver services and the categories it uses in planning these services.

Types of budget

In many public service organisations a distinction is made between two types of expenditure, which may form two separate budgets:

- *revenue budgets* – these budgets are concerned with revenue expenditure and its financing; that is, expenditure on day-to-day running costs (such as salaries, heating and stationery).
- *capital budgets* – these budgets are concerned with capital expenditure and its financing; that is, expenditure on things of lasting value (such as land, buildings and major items of equipment).

In 1998 central government announced that it was abandoning its long-standing convention where capital and revenue items were amalgamated in the annual budgeting process.

Instead the items are now to be differentiated in a three-year planning cycle. Within other parts of the public sector, revenue budgeting has traditionally been distinguished from capital budgeting. Public service organisations are also likely to produce other types of budgets that feed into their revenue and capital budgets. These may include staffing budgets and cash-flow budgets. The preparation of capital budgets is beyond the scope of the chapter. The discussion of budgeting in this chapter relates solely to revenue budgets.

Budget setting

Setting a budget is as much an exercise in politics as a technical task. The budget-setting process requires decisions to be made about the allocation of scarce resources. The various stakeholders in public service organisations are likely to have different views about how best to allocate resources. Their differing and potentially divergent interests cannot be resolved by technical means alone; they need to be addressed within the political arena. (For example, Colville, 1989, provides a case study of budgeting in police authorities.) This subsection considers the various technical approaches to setting a budget; the next section reflects on the politics of the process.

The budget-setting process consists of a number of stages:

1 Agreeing key budget policies in the light of the organisation's strategic plans and the context within which it is operating.
2 Agreeing how the budget should be subdivided and identification of the main budget centres and responsible managers.
3 Appointing a budget committee to oversee the process and make the key decisions required.
4 Agreeing the format for the presentation of budgets, the timetable for their production and any standard rates to be used in the preparation of budgets (such as inflation rates).
5 Preparation of individual budgets according to the agreed subdivisions and the collation of these into a master budget for the whole organisation.
6 Approval of individual and master budgets and communication to all relevant managers.

A key decision taken in stage 1 is whether the budget figures use a fixed price base or whether they reflect the cash to be expended during the planning period. Fixed-price budgeting is also known as volume budgeting. Under such an approach, budgetary estimates are produced in terms of constant prices (the prices operative at a single date, say, November prices). Budget holders are allocated budgets based upon these fixed prices and subsequent pay and price increases are funded by the provision of additional monies (supplementary estimates). In effect, fixed-price budgeting means that the organisation is undertaking to fund a given volume of service regardless of future changes in pay and prices.

Producing budgets in cash terms is also known as cash-limited budgeting. Estimates of future changes in pay and prices are included in the budget figures, so that the budget is a statement of the cash that can be expended during a budget period. There is no subsequent adjustment to reflect any underfunding or overfunding of pay and price inflation. Increasingly, public service organisations operate cash-limited budgetary systems.

The above outline of the six main stages of budget setting belies the often fraught and complex nature of the budget-setting process. The precise method used to prepare budget estimates in stage 5 will vary across organisations. Three main methods for producing these estimates are incremental budgeting, zero-based budgeting and programme budgeting. Each of these is discussed in the next section. A fourth method of budgetary allocation, formula-based budgeting, is discussed later in this chapter. Where areas of public service are subject to a competitive environment, the budgetary process is likely to become more like that in the private sector. Here the focus is on estimating sales, budgeting costs and planning for the achievement of break-even or rate of return targets.

APPROACHES TO RESOURCE ALLOCATION

Incremental budgeting

Many organisations adopt an incremental budgeting method to produce budget estimates. Figure 9.3 outlines this method.

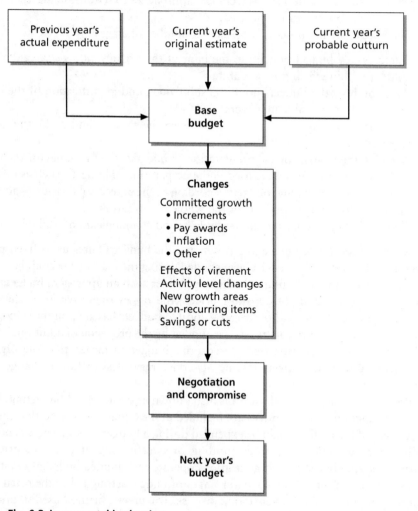

Fig. 9.3 Incremental budgeting

Incremental budgeting takes as its starting point the current year's budget and arrives at next year's budget by a series of adjustments to this. The adjustment process is sometimes referred to as rolling forward an existing budget.

There are a number of advantages arising from the use of an incremental budgeting method. It is a relatively straightforward process; only marginal changes to the existing budget need to be understood and agreed, thereby minimising the amount of time that needs to be spent on budget preparation. Hence it is a relatively inexpensive method of estimating a budget. Many of the services and activities of public service organisations are mandatory or are seen as fundamental to achieving their aims. Thus focusing upon what it will cost to continue to provide existing patterns of service can be interpreted as a sensible use of time. Incremental budgeting is well suited to doing just this. Over time, incremental budgeting can lead to changes in the pattern of service delivery, but such changes are by definition gradual or incremental in nature. Change is thus achieved in small steps and some (e.g. Lindblom, 1959; Schultze, 1968) would argue that this is sensible as it avoids the potential for serious mistakes and unforeseen consequences which might arise if a more radical approach to change is adopted. You may recall the discussion in Chapter 7 concerning strategy as a plan and strategy as a process. Incremental budgeting would tend to support an emergent strategy. Another major benefit of incremental budgeting is that it has proved to be organisationally and politically acceptable. There are no large winners and losers in such a process and this facilitates the identification of compromise solutions to budgetary problems.

The main disadvantages of incremental budgeting are linked to some of the advantages outlined above. This form of resource allocation does not clearly link budgeting and planning, particularly for changes in service delivery; the emphasis is on monetary inputs rather than the objectives that those inputs are intended to achieve. Because the budget for next year is based upon a budget that has been rolled forward from previous years, the resulting allocation of resources is more likely to reflect past priorities than current or future priorities. It is argued that too little attention is given to justifying the need for the base budget (Jones and Pendlebury, 1992). Another concern is the behavioural impact of incremental budgeting; it may encourage budget managers to spend up to the limit of their current budget in order to maximise next year's budget, to 'rush for the line' at the end of the year. The rationale for this is that underspending on an existing budget could be seen as a reason for reducing the base budget that is rolled forward. Finally, where cuts in budget need to be achieved, an incremental budgeting process tends to result in arbitrary cuts (for example a 3 per cent cut across every budget), rather than reductions to budgets in a way that protects priorities.

Although the drawbacks of incremental budgeting are readily recognised, it has proved difficult to find workable alternatives to it. The two main alternatives that have been tried are zero-based budgeting and programme (or output) budgeting. Each of these is now discussed.

Zero-based budgeting

In simple terms zero-based budgeting (ZBB) means just what is implied, building up a budget anew, that is, from a zero base. The term ZBB gained popularity in the 1960s, particularly in the United States where the Department of Agriculture first adopted it in 1962. There is nothing particularly new or revolutionary about the idea of building a budget from zero; every organisation has had to do this at some point in its history. The novelty of ZBB resides in its message that each year an organisation should begin its budgetary process with a clean sheet of paper. The main stages in a ZBB approach are outlined in Fig. 9.4.

In zero-based budgeting it is individual cost centre managers who are asked to estimate the cost of providing various levels or packages of service. These costed packages are then ranked by cost centre managers and passed up the organisational hierarchy. At each level in the hierarchy, managers are asked to decide upon the order of the decision packages as a way of ensuring that spending is linked to priorities.

One of the main advantages of ZBB is that there is a specific link between budget and activity. The budget process involves specifying objectives and considering cost-effective ways of achieving these objectives. Decision packages are prepared at the local cost centre level and involvement in the budgetary process should lead to better ownership of the resulting budgetary plan. Where it proves necessary to make adjustments to a budget during the year, say to achieve a higher level of savings, it should be possible to make informed decisions because the budget format should provide information about the cost and benefits of different levels of activity.

There are, however, distinct disadvantages of ZBB. One of the main problems is the amount of time it takes to construct a budget from zero each year. The information

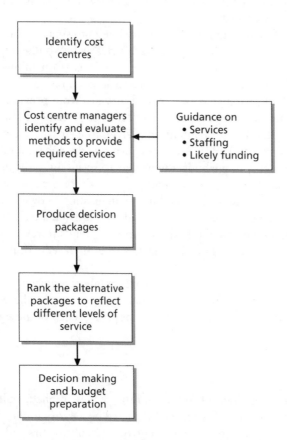

Fig. 9.4 Zero-based budgeting

requirements for ZBB are demanding and there is a danger that an organisation could spend most of its time on budgetary planning rather than delivering services. Wildavsky and Hammond argue that such an approach to budgeting 'vastly overestimates man's ability to calculate' (quoted in Jones and Pendlebury, 1992, p 90). In an analysis of budgeting in the United States, Anthony (1977, p 9) points out that 'In Georgia, there were 11,000 of them [decision packages]. If the Governor set aside four hours every day for two months he could spend about a minute on each decision package, not enough time to read it, let alone make an analysis of the merits.' This can be seen as wasted effort if the services provided by an organisation remain basically the same from year to year. There is also concern about any organisation's ability to cope with major changes in resource allocation from one year to the next. Therefore, ZBB is unlikely to be conducive to long-range planning and may lead to lack of certainty and potentially harmful discontinuity. Lapsley (1992) argues that considerable time and effort are required to make ZBB work and, at best, it might be regarded as a technique which might be used on a three-year cycle, rather than be an annual event.

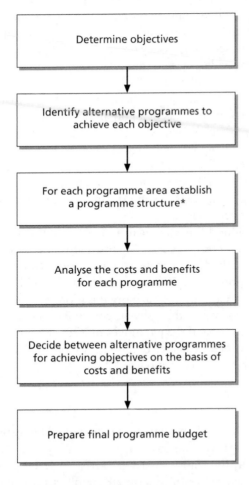

Fig. 9.5 Programme budgeting

*Identify the resources and activities required to achieve objectives – this may involve subdivision of the programme into programme categories and programme elements.

Programme budgeting

Programme budgeting is a generic title for an approach to budgeting rather than a specific budgetary method or process. The key stages in a programme budgeting approach are outlined in Fig. 9.5.

A specific form of programme budgeting is PPBS (planning, programming and budgeting systems). In order to overcome some of the problems of incremental budgeting, the United States introduced PPBS into the federal government in the 1960s. It was popular in the USA throughout the 1960s and early 1970s, but by the mid-1970s the euphoria had disappeared and it was abandoned (Caulfield and Schultz, 1989; Lapsley, 1992). As the name implies, the three main features of PPBS are planning, programming and budgeting. The emphasis is upon a programmatic approach to both planning and budgeting. For example, within a local authority, care for older persons might be a programme area and as such would encompass services provided by social services, housing, education, leisure and recreation departments. In this way PPBS, as a planning and budgeting system, cuts across the functional organisational structure in order that appropriate inputs can be drawn together to produce the required programme outputs. The programmes of activity are analysed in terms of costs and benefits so that budget choices are informed by knowledge of the impact of spending or not spending money on an activity. PPBS is an approach to budgeting which is intended to provide a system that relates expenditure at each stage of the budget to the purposes of that expenditure.

One of the main advantages of a programmatic approach to budgeting is that it exposes activities undertaken by different functional areas of an organisation that are overlapping or contradictory in nature. The approach provides information on the extent to which existing and alternative programmes of activity will impact upon objectives and the associated costs of these programmes. Therefore, PPBS enables resource allocation choices to be made on the basis of cost–benefit relationships. A further advantage is that programme budgeting, unlike incremental budgeting, looks beyond the immediate future and is concerned with the long-term effects of activities.

The disadvantages of PPBS include both technical and organisational difficulties. Technically, PPBS requires information on costs and benefits that is not readily available and, like ZBB, it is a time-consuming budgetary methodology. Organisationally, PPBS is a top-down and highly centralised approach to budgeting, which clashes with the structure and culture of many public service organisations. Such organisations are more federal in structure, with multiple power bases rather than strong corporate control. Wildavsky (1974, p 207) points out that this was one of the paradoxes of PPBS. Planning, programming and budgeting systems are intended to change organisations, but such organisations must first undergo change before they can accommodate PPBS.

Resource allocation in practice

Although the implementation of formalised and rational planning and budgeting systems has proved difficult, public service organisations have sought to improve the way in which they allocate resources. Although neither fully fledged zero-based nor programme budgeting systems have been implemented successfully in the UK, public service organisations continue to experiment with budget methods that link spending plans to service priorities (*see* Griffiths, 1987; Packwood *et al.*, 1991).

Despite the fact that there are technical problems with implementing budgetary methods such as ZBB or PPBS, commentators (such as Jones and Pendlebury, 1992) have suggested that the main reason for the failure of these budgeting systems has more to do with politics and organisational behaviour:

> PPBS is meant to introduce a highly formalised and rational approach to long-run decision making and planning, and yet it is argued that such an approach ignores the political and organisational realities of complex human organisations. When faced with loosely defined social objectives and future uncertainties political processes form an important part of decision making (Jones and Pendlebury, 1992, p 76).

BUDGETARY CONTROL

Budgetary control mechanisms form an important part of the management control systems of public service organisations. Indeed Perrin (1989, p 31) argues that 'In public services, where financial resources typically are cash-limited but the demand for service outputs often seem limitless, management by budgetary control against planned workload targets may be the most important single tool of successful management accounting and financial control'.

CASE STUDY 9.1

Since the late 1970s, one of the ways in which public spending has been controlled is through the use of cash limits. This article examines the tension that exists between local cash limits and traditionally demand-led services.

HEALTH AUTHORITIES URGE LOCAL BUDGET CAPS ON GP'S

By Nicholas Timmins

Family doctor services should be subjected to local cash limits, health authorities said in a report yesterday.

Creating such a cap on spending by GPs in each financial year is a long-held ambition of the Treasury. It was repeatedly considered but not pursued by the former Conservative Government.

The British Medical Association has argued that: 'It is a demand-led service. GPs cannot control their workload and tell patients to come back in two months' time, just by increasing waiting lists in the way that the hospital service can.

'It is the safety valve of the NHS, and any attempt to provide a total cap on its spending would be against the interests of patients.'

Other family doctor services are not subject to formal cash limits, a position which sometimes leads to overspends but which the BMA says allows the general medical services to act as a safety valve for the service, particularly in times of 'flu epidemics or other unforeseen emergencies.

The NHS Confederation says the change to a single budget, with a cash limit as the price being paid for that, was needed because at present the NHS could move money from the hospital side of the service to buy GP services but not the other way about.

An element of flexibility – probably in the form of a reserve – would still be needed in spending on general medical services, the confederation said. But merging of the budgets would also allow a tight rein to be kept on the management of prescribing and GP overspending in that local area.

The Confederation argues in its paper that separate commissioning and provision of health care must remain as the internal market is abolished, but the system needs to become more co-operative, with complete financial transparency between health authorities, trusts and commissioning groups to discourage one part of the system seeking a short-term advantage over another.

It also calls for much clearer national guidance about what the NHS is expected to provide and what it is not.

'Services are already being rationed as a short-term measure to balance the books,' the Confederation's consultation document warns.

'Unless the NHS receives annual funding increases of at least 3 per cent above inflation each year, more will follow.'

Source: Financial Times, 28 August 1997. Reprinted with permission.

Questions on the case study

1 To what extent does the imposition of local cash limits undermine the principle of healthcare free at the point of delivery?

2 What are the management implications for GPs?

Budgetary control in practice

Budgetary control involves the monitoring of actual income and expenditure against planned income and expenditure on a regular basis, identifying variances, investigating the reasons for significant variances and taking corrective action to ensure a balanced budget at the end of the year. Budget monitoring takes place for each of the subdivisions of an organisation's budget. In practice budgetary control is never quite as simple as this brief description might imply; an example will illustrate some of the problems involved. Case study 9.1 presents a case study example of a hostel for mentally disordered offenders, which receives monthly budget monitoring statements.

The monitoring statement included as part of the case provides information on the half-year budget position and you are asked to interpret this statement. The format of the budgetary control statement is fairly typical and provides information on: the annual budget estimates; the estimated budget allocation for the period to date; actual income and expenditure to date; and the variance between the budgeted and actual figures.

Reasons for variance

On first impressions the hostel which features in Case study 9.2 appears to face two main problem areas: it is overspending against its salary budget and it is under-performing against its income targets. Having identified variances you should then investigate the reasons for these variances. There are a number of possibilities that should be explored:

1 *Inadequate planning assumptions were made in drawing up the original budget.* The salary budget is overspent because staff were appointed on a higher grade than was originally estimated; maybe the original estimate was unrealistic for the quality and experience of staff required. Similarly, the budgeted income is based upon 100 per cent occupancy levels for the hostel throughout the year; this is unlikely to be realistic.

2 *The budget estimates have been inappropriately profiled over the year.* Do the figures in the second column (budget to date) make realistic assumptions about the proportion of the budget that should have been expended or the income that should have been received by the half-year point? A quick check of the figures in the second column reveals that the assumption is that income and expenditure will be evenly spread

| CASE STUDY 9.2 | **BUDGET MONITORING** |

A voluntary organisation runs a hostel for mentally disordered offenders. The warden for this hostel is responsible for monitoring and controlling the delegated budget. She receives monthly budget monitoring statements. At the half-year position the warden draws together a group of people to review the position. You are a member of that group. Unfortunately on the day of the meeting the Warden reports in sick, but requests that the group go ahead and review the situation and make recommendations to her. The budget monitoring statement for the six-month period is attached (see Table 9.3).

Notes
The telephone message from the warden included some additional information.

1 Several of the assistant wardens were appointed on a higher point on the pay scale than estimated in the original budget.

2 Due to a period of illness there was a need to pay for some part-time domestic assistance and to pay over-time rates.

3 The running costs budget (i.e. for premises-related, supplies and services and transport expenditure) is cash limited, but the employees budget is uplifted during the year to reflect the effect of pay awards. The reason for the difference between budgeted costs and actual costs for salaries is not due to a pay award (this being not due until January).

4 No overspending of the running costs budget at the year-end will be funded. It may be possible to carry forward some overspend, but this requires the approval of a senior manager in the voluntary organisation's headquarters.

5 The income from residents has been budgeted at the level of £51.87 per week for each of the 14 beds.

Table 9.3 Cost centre: Hostel for mentally disordered offenders: Budget monitoring report for September 200X

Heads of account	Annual budget	Budget to date	Expenditure/ Income to date	Variance
	£	£	£	£
Employees				
Salaries	113 550	56 775	60 330	−3 555
Wages	12 350	6 175	7 025	−850
Premises-related expenditure				
Heating and lighting	7 140	3 570	2 356	1 214
Cleaning	1 520	760	638	122
Supplies and services				
Food	8 500	4 250	3 986	354
Other supplies	2 200	1 100	1 670	−570
Equipment	4 000	2 000	1 645	355
Telephones	1 000	500	478	22
Transport	2 000	1 000	876	124
Total expenditure	152 260	76 130	78 914	−2 784
Income				
From residents	37 762	18 881	14 200	−4 681
From probation service	91 000	45 500	40 000	−5 500
Total income	128 762	64 381	54 200	−10 181

▶

Table 9.3 *cont.*

Heads of account	Annual budget	Budget to date	Expenditure/ Income to date	Variance
	£	£	£	£
Other expenditure outside the control of the cost centre manager				
Mortgage payments/rent	10 500	5 250	4 950	300
Council tax/rates	6 000	3 000	3 200	−200
Central services of voluntary organisation	4 500	2 250	2 300	−50

Question on the case study

What picture emerges from this report and what recommendations would you make to the Warden?

throughout the year; so that, at the half-year point half the budget should have been spent. Whereas the assumption of an evenly spread pattern of expenditure may be sensible in relation to salaries (provided there is not a pay-rise part-way through the year), it is not appropriate when estimating expenditure on heating and lighting, which varies with the seasons. Similarly, income may be received in regular payments throughout the year or in distinct blocks at certain points throughout the year. For these reasons some organisations draw up budgets on the basis of past income and expenditure patterns rather than simply dividing the total budget by the number of accounting periods.

3 *Inaccurate or late posting of income and expenditure.* Many budget holders complain that they do not believe the figures that appear in the expenditure to date column of their statements. Much time is spent checking on whether things have been correctly coded to a particular budget heading or cost centre. The more remote the coding and entry of information from the service area incurring this expenditure, the more likely it is that errors will occur. For this reason many new financial systems have been designed to allow for data entry at the cost centre level. Good budgetary control systems need to be able to provide timely, accurate and relevant information for budget managers.

4 *The status of the income and expenditure figures entered on monitoring statements is unclear.* In managing a budget it is important to know at what point income and expenditure are recorded on the accounting system. There are basically three points at which this can occur and these are outlined in Fig. 9.6. These relate to three different types of accounting system as shown in the figure: commitment accounting, accruals accounting and cash accounting. Most public service organisations operate accruals accounting systems, although some also record commitment information. The need for commitment information is particularly important where a budget manager purchases large volumes of supplies.

5 *Increases in the volume of service beyond the planning assumptions.* A common complaint made by budget managers is that the budgeted figures are insufficient for the level of service that is likely to be provided and it is difficult to limit service provision to the volumes estimated. For example, the Disabled Persons Act can lead to assessments of need that a local authority is then required to meet, regardless of whether sufficient resources

(a) Recording expenditure

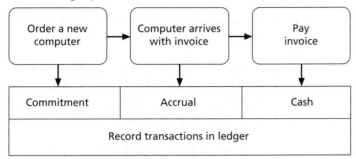

(b) Recording income

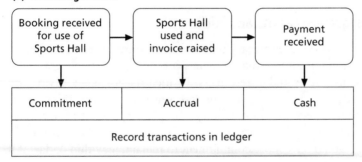

Fig. 9.6 Approaches to accounting

are available. It is clear then that, at the very least, good budgetary control mechanisms need some measure of workload built into the budget-setting and control process.

6 *Increase in inflation beyond the planning assumptions.* As discussed earlier in the chapter, most budgets are cash limited and are expressed in outturn prices. This involves the prior estimation of future inflation and the potential for underestimating inflation. The estimates of future inflation incorporated into central government spending plans are likely to be as much an expression of the desired levels of inflation as forecasts of actual inflation. If inflation is higher than planned, then those managing cash-limited budgets need to look for savings by cutting the quantity of resource inputs (e.g., staff hours or supplies).

7 *Poor management of resources.* There are examples of poor resource management in public service organisations, particularly in areas where budget management responsibilities have only recently been devolved. There is, however, a constant pressure on managers to review their use and management of resources. For example, resource allocation mechanisms within the NHS require the identification of efficiency savings that can be made within budgets. The work of internal and external audit bodies is, in part, focused upon the identification of more cost-effective ways of achieving organisational objectives.

The key lessons to be learned are, therefore, that there may be many possible explanations of variances from budgeted targets. In order to manage a budget effectively these reasons must be identified and the appropriate action taken. Such action may include: re-profiling the budget, limiting expenditure under certain headings for the remainder of the year, viring (transferring) budget allocation from one heading to another, trying to negotiate a revised budget allocation for the year.

Many budget allocations within public service organisations are fixed. That is, the level of the budget is decided before the beginning of the budget period and it is not varied during that period to reflect any fluctuations in the levels of service provided. The alternative to fixed budgets is flexible budgets. Flexible budgets are based upon establishing a level of funding for a planned level of service. Such a budget may be expressed in terms of a unit of resource for a given unit of service. The budgetary control process for flexible budgets monitors both the level of service and the level of spending. The budget allocation is then adjusted, or 'flexed', to reflect the current level of service.

Budget management carrots and sticks

One of the objectives of a budgetary planning and control system is to establish a framework of management control that provides incentives for managers and other staff to make the best use of available resources, to identify efficiency savings and to remain within budgeted totals. Designing systems and controls to achieve this objective is not easy. The link between budgets and motivation is complex. The work of researchers on the link between participation and performance (e.g. Coch and French, 1948) might suggest that budget holders would have more commitment to remaining within budget if they have participated in the budget-setting process.

On the other hand, public choice theorists (*see* Cullis and Jones, 1992) emphasise that we should be more sceptical about the motives of budget holders and assume that they will seek to maximise their budget allocations. As we saw in Chapter 8, motivation is a complex issue. However, if budgetary control systems are to provide any form of motivational framework, they need to clarify the implications for budget holders of not remaining within budget allocations. To be effective these consequences need to be sufficient to get people to modify their behaviour. There are a number of issues that need to be considered.

First, there is the question of the extent to which the pattern of spending in the current year should affect the budget allocation for the following year (*see* the earlier discussion on incremental budgeting). Where there is a direct and positive relationship between the level of current spending and future budget allocation, there may be few incentives to spend less than the current budget allocation.

Second, and more specifically, there is the issue of whether an under- or overspend will be carried forward into the following financial year. Although it might seem appropriate for any overspending to be carried forward (thus reducing the allocation for the following year), there is the problem that this potentially penalises future service users. However, if overspending is not carried forward then the organisation needs to draw upon a contingency fund to balance the overall budget of the organisation. If overspending is funded from a central source, this may have the adverse effect of encouraging overspending. The carry-forward of any underspends (which has the effect of increasing next year's budget allocation) might appear more straightforward. However, some organisations limit the overall level or percentage of underspend that can be carried forward. There is a good case for arguing that underspending resulting from management efficiency savings should be carried forward. There is less of a case for carrying forward underspending arising from a reduction in the level of service provided.

Third, there is the question of the extent to which budget holders should be given the freedom to transfer (vire) budget allocations from one heading (such as travel) into their budget for another heading (such as stationery). Budget holders may be given fairly wide-ranging powers of virement, except where this may result in a longer-term financial commitment. For example, it is often not possible to vire money from non-pay budget items into the staffing budget.

Flynn's (1987) study of delegated budgeting in social services departments found four basic approaches to introducing sanctions:

1 *Moral pressure* – for example, the publication of variances from budgets with comments from the finance officer directed towards the transgressors.
2 *Punishing or rewarding a group of clients* – that is, the carry-forward of over- and underspends into the following year.
3 *Disciplinary action* – for example, treating adverse variances as a disciplinary matter.
4 *No action at all.*

It was clear from Case study 9.2 on budgetary control that there are many possible reasons for reported variances. Some of these reasons are not within the control of the local budget manager. To be effective, any system of sanctions needs to be based on accurate and timely information and to distinguish between controllable and non-controllable items. Any system that does not achieve this is likely to be perceived as demotivating.

In summary, it is clear that establishing an appropriate motivational framework that helps ensure good budgetary control within public service organisations is not easy. It might be assumed that greater delegation of budgets to local managers would lead to a more responsible attitude to the use of resources. This is discussed in the next section.

DEVOLVING BUDGETS AND DELEGATING FINANCIAL MANAGEMENT RESPONSIBILITIES

In the introduction to this chapter the trend towards the devolved management of public services was discussed. Under devolved systems of management, managers not only have responsibility for delivering quality services within an overall framework, but they also allocate and manage the resources to be used in providing those services. The devolution of financial responsibilities aims to align management and financial responsibilities so that the staff who make service decisions are also responsible for the financial implications of these decisions. There are many examples of the introduction of delegated budgets:

● In central government, the 'Financial Management Initiative' and its successors have pushed financial responsibilities down the civil service hierarchy and beyond.
● In hospitals, budgets have been devolved to clinical directorates.
● In primary health care, the concept of GP fundholders was introduced in the 1990s, although these have now evolved into Primary Care Groups under the new Labour Government.
● In education, the budgets for individual schools have been delegated to head teachers.

● In social services, budgets have been delegated to a variety of local managers, such as the heads of residential establishments.

Designing devolved financial management systems

In devising a system of devolved financial management there are a series of questions that need to be addressed. These questions are set out below:

1 What items of expenditure and/or income should be devolved and down to what level?
2 What items should be retained centrally, and what should be the financial relationship between the centre and the devolved units?
3 On what basis should budget allocations be made to devolved budget holders?
4 Should budget holders be given lump-sum (bottom-line) budgets or should the amount of money available under different spending heads be detailed for them (line-item budgets)?
5 What powers of virement should be given to devolved budget holders?
6 On what basis should devolved budget holders be monitored and held to account?
7 What penalties, if any, should be incurred for overspending, and what rewards, if any, for identifying cost savings?

The issues raised in seeking answers to each of these questions are considered in the sub-sections that follow.

Delegated control verses central control

The first two questions in the above list are fundamental to the design of a devolved bud-getary system. There are no right and wrong answers to these questions, but there should be a rationale for whatever decisions are made. Figure 9.7 shows the pattern of budgetary devolution within a further education (FE) college.

The rationale for the decisions made in the FE college is that all the items of expenditure retained under central control are negotiated by the Principal and her management team. They commit the expenditure and should therefore be accountable for its control. Expenditure on those items devolved to departmental heads is directly controllable by these heads. A possible exception is salaries for lecturing staff; the rationale for devolving these is that staff costs are controllable in the long run as departmental heads are respon-sible for bidding for extra staff and they also determine their part-time staff requirements.

One of the main examples of devolved financial management within public service organisations is the local management of schools (LMS). Exhibit 9.2 (*see* p 186) provides an illustration of the decision making involved in the establishment of LMS in one educa-tion authority.

The more organisations move towards devolved financial management, the greater the need to address the financial relationship between central services and local budget man-agers. Traditionally, central services (such as personnel and payroll) have been funded by either top-slicing direct service provision budgets or by recharging central service costs to frontline services on some pro rata basis (such as the number of employees). In both situ-ations, local budget managers have no control over what is deducted from their budgets to pay for central services, and their lack of control leads to tensions between the centre and localities. As the autonomy and responsibilities of local budget managers have increased,

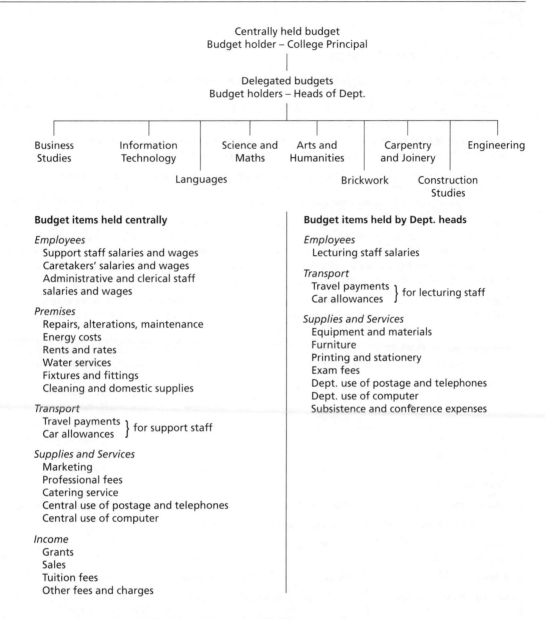

Fig. 9.7 Budgeting structure within a further education college

Source: Nutley and Osborne (1994) p 149. Reproduced with permission.

there have been demands for a clearer relationship between the charges made for central services and the level of service provided. Budget managers who have to competitively tender to provide frontline services (such as the heads of Direct Service Organisations and Direct Labour Organisations in local government) have been particularly keen to control the costs of central services.

The result of the above has been a trend towards establishing service level agreements between frontline services and central services. Such agreements set out the level of service

Exhibit 9.2

Local management of schools

The Education Reform Act 1988 changed the way education services are funded. The major change was in the funding and management of schools. Local management gave schools more control over their own affairs. It provided schools with a budget that would meet most of their costs. This budget is calculated by a formula which is based largely on the number of pupils at a school. The governing bodies of schools have local control over how they spend the budget.

Following the 1988 Act, Birmingham City Council published a consultation document on its proposals for the local management of schools. The objective of the scheme for Birmingham was described as:

> To create a flexible environment in which there is maximum delegation of financial and management powers and responsibilities to governing bodies, combined with continued access to support and guidance from the LEA which would not otherwise be readily available from resources within an individual school.

Under the 1988 Act the Local Education Authority (LEA) was required to produce a 'General Schools Budget' (GSB) which includes all the expenditure associated with the provision of education for pupils in primary and secondary schools and units. The GSB includes not only the direct costs of running the schools, such as employees and premises, but also the indirect costs of services used by the schools such as transport and the advisory service. The LEA was required to calculate the GSB before the beginning of the financial year and not alter it during the year except in the case of major emergencies.

Birmingham City Council's consultation document set out its proposals on what items of expenditure were to be delegated and the formula for calculating the level of the budget. These proposals are summarised in Table 9.4 to provide an example of the issues that need to be considered in delegating budgets.

It was proposed that some 69 per cent of the schools budget would be delegated in the first instance but that this would be increased over time. Governing bodies were to become responsible for the areas of expenditure set out in Table 9.4.

Table 9.4 Areas of expenditure delegated to schools

Employees	Supplies and services	Premises	Transport
Teachers (full-time, part-time and supply)	Books	Energy	To/from playing fields, baths etc.
Nursery nurses Classroom assistants	Equipment	Water	Car allowances
Midday supervisors	Examination fees	Sewerage	Travel and subsistence
Administrative and clerical staff	Printing and stationery	Rates	
Technicians (including laboratory)	Telephones	Non-structural repairs and maintenance	
Building services staff	Postage	Cleaning	
Employer's national insurance	Other goods and services	Security	
Employer's superannuation	Hired and contracted services	Grounds maintenance Building services staff accommodation	

The LEA was required to keep some items of the GSB centrally. These were known as 'mandatory exceptions' and comprised:

- specific government grant-aided expenditure;
- centrally provided services such as those supplied by the City Treasurer or the City Solicitor;
- administration and advisers;
- home to school transport;
- capital expenditure including interest repayments.

Exhibit 9.2 *cont.*

There were other items known as 'discretionary exceptions'. These were items that could be held centrally at the LEA's discretion. The original list of discretionary exceptions was seen as a temporary position, the plan being to delegate several of these items in the future. The list of discretionary exceptions included:

- psychological service;
- remedial teaching centres;
- insurance;
- education social work service;
- peripatetic teachers (e.g. musicians, home-teaching service);
- school library service.

The LEA was required to allocate that part of the GSB which was not retained centrally by way of a formula based on an assessment of schools' objective needs rather than on past spending patterns. The aim was to create a formula which was simple, clear and predictable in its impact. Legislation required the LEA to allocate at least 75 per cent of the schools budget on the basis of numbers of pupils weighted by age. Birmingham City Council's consultation document proposed that 80 per cent of the resources be allocated on the basis of pupil numbers and 20 per cent on other factors. The Council proposed to incorporate the elements set out in Table 9.5 into its formula.

Table 9.5 Proposed components of formula

Age-weighted pupil numbers

- To be used to allocate teaching staff, including supply cover, support staff, midday supervision, administration and clerical staff, all supplies and services including capitation and examination fees.

Age	2/3/4	5/7/8/9	6/10	11/12/13	14	15	16/17/18/19
Weight	1.11	1.0	1.20	1.39	1.50	1.51	2.20

Small schools

- Lump-sum allowance for all schools.

Social deprivation

- Free school meal entitlement to be used as an interim measure.

Split sites

- Planned expenditure to be allocated to those schools identified as split site.

Premises

- Non-structural repairs and maintenance (R&M) to be allocated via a pupil R&M points formula which takes account of the size, condition and type of building, as well as the number of pupils. Energy, water, sewerage and drainage, building services staff and other premises costs to be allocated initially on an average cost per square metre. Rates to be allocated on the basis on actual cost.

Physical education and entitlement

- The budgets for grounds and maintenance, transport to fields and baths, hire of pitches, entrance fees and purchase, repair and maintenance of physical education and playing field equipment to be allocated on age-weighted pupil units which will give a pupil PE score for school.

Age	2/3/4	5/6	7/8/9/10	11	12/13/14	15	16/17/18/19
Weight	0.50	0.98	1.00	2.43	2.06	1.58	0.97

Safety nets were planned to apply for four years to cushion the effect of the changes from historic spending levels to the formula-based budget. It was also intended that the formula would be refined over time.

to be provided for a negotiated charge. Although such agreements may serve to give more control to local budget holders and to make central services more aware that they have internal customers, there are concerns that they lead to increased administrative costs. The more the public sector moves towards establishing internal and external contractual relationships between the providers of various services, the greater the time spent on negotiating and monitoring contracts (*see* Flynn, 1993, on transaction cost analysis).

Resource allocation – formula-based budgeting

We have already considered three main approaches to budget setting (incremental budgeting, ZBB and PPBS). Any of these methods may be employed in allocating budgets to local managers. Increasingly, however, local managers are not given detailed (line-item) budgets, but overall (bottom-line) budgets. Another trend has been the use of resource-allocation formulae to determine the overall level of these bottom-line budgets. Exhibit 9.2 (on LMS) provides an example of the formula used to allocate the overall schools budget to individual schools. Although resource-allocation formulae have the advantage of endeavouring to tie the level of budget with an objective assessment of need, it is very difficult to devise such formulae. The first step is to decide what factors indicate budgetary need and then to determine the weighting of these factors. The result should be relatively simple, robust, clearly understood by budget holders and reasonably predictable in its impact. This is a tall order, and is difficult to achieve in practice.

The advantages and disadvantages of devolved budgets

The potential advantages of budgetary devolution are:

- quicker and/or improved decision making;
- increased flexibility at the local level;
- increased commitment at the local level; and
- a better use of resources.

The possible disadvantages are:

- discretion at the local level may distort the policies and practices of the service as a whole;
- financial management responsibilities may reduce the time available for service delivery; and
- there may be a reduction in the flexibility for switching resources at the organisational level.

One concern that many organisations have about devolving financial management responsibilities is the need to ensure that budget holders have the financial competence to match their responsibilities. The first stage in addressing this issue is to define the financial management competences required. Exhibit 9.3 sets out a framework of financial management competency requirements for middle managers concerned with negotiating and agreeing budgets and monitoring activities against these budgets.

Exhibit 9.3

Suggested core financial competences for budget managers

Competence area 1: Negotiate and agree budgets

Performance criteria

- Information relating to budget setting is offered to appropriate people in time to be used.
- Recommendations take account of possible future variation in levels of activity, whether related to growth or decline in need.
- The bases of calculations are understood and applied.
- Agreements reached balance the overall needs of the organisation with the demands of the manager's area of responsibility.
- All valid, relevant information and alternative courses of action are evaluated before allocations are made.
- All relevant people are informed of budget decisions in a manner and at a time which is likely to ensure their co-operation and confidence.

Competence area 2: Monitor and control activities against budgets

Performance criteria

- Expenditure is within agreed limits, does not compromise future spending requirements and conforms to the organisation's policy and procedures.
- Requests for expenditure outside the manager's responsibility are referred promptly to the appropriate people.
- Actual income and expenditure is checked against agreed budgets at regular, appropriate intervals.
- Where a budget under- or overspend is likely to occur, the appropriate action is taken with minimal delay.
- Prompt, corrective action is taken, where necessary, in response to actual or potential significant deviations from budget.
- Any necessary authority for changes in allocation between budget heads is obtained in advance of requirement.

THE DISTINCTIVE FEATURES OF FINANCIAL MANAGEMENT IN PUBLIC SERVICE ORGANISATIONS – MANAGEMENT ACCOUNTING

A common distinction drawn in accountancy is between financial and management accounting. Financial accounting is concerned with serving the needs of external users of financial information. Financial accounting and reporting practices should ensure that a true and fair picture of an organisation's financial position is provided. Management accounting is concerned with providing managers with the accounting information they need to carry out their planning and control functions. So far this chapter has been concerned with management accounting and, in particular, the role of the budget. This section takes the consideration of management accounting further by making comparisons with private sector practice. The next section considers financial accounting.

A discussion of all aspects of management accounting is beyond the scope of this chapter. Table 9.6 summarises the key points of difference between management accounting in the public and private sectors.

Table 9.6 A comparison of management accounting in the public and private sectors

	Public sector	Private sector
Budget structured around	Cost centres	Profit centres
Key budget factor or limiting factor	Public expenditure limits	Sales
Predominant costing methodology	Absorption costing	Standard costing and marginal costing as important as absorption costing
Methods of investment appraisal	Benefits arising from investments are not usually measured in monetary terms. Discounted cash-flow techniques may be used to identify least-cost options. Occasionally full cost–benefit analysis is undertaken.	Financial returns expected from investments. Investments appraised using pay-back, rate of return and discounted cash-flow methods.

Earlier sections of this chapter have discussed the structuring of budgets around cost centres and have also set the context by making it clear that the limiting factor is the public expenditure plans. This chapter does not consider investment appraisal and those interested in learning more about the contrasts summarised in Table 9.6 should refer to the sources listed in the References section at the end of this chapter. An important aspect of management accounting is the provision of cost information. The remainder of this section provides a brief overview of costing in the public sector.

The split between purchasers and providers in many public service organisations, together with the creation of markets for services, has increased the need for cost information. In general, costing techniques are not well developed in public service organisations. Cost information serves three main purposes, which are addressed by three costing techniques:

- *Planning* – as discussed earlier in this chapter, the key management accounting tool in the public sector is the budget. Costing for planning purposes tends to be the main form of costing, and the predominant technique is absorption (or full) costing. Absorption costing seeks to estimate the full cost of a unit of service. It does this by allocating direct costs and apportioning all indirect costs.
- *Decision making* – marginal costing techniques provide accounting information for decision making. Marginal cost analysis considers the way in which costs vary with the level of activity. Such an analysis is not widely used in the public sector. The predominance of absorption costing is in part due to central government policies. For example, under the 'Working for patients' reforms in the NHS the pricing of services had to be based on absorption-costing techniques, so that the prices charged reflected the full cost of the service. Marginal costing (and pricing) was only permitted where there was unexpected spare capacity.
- *Controlling* – as discussed earlier in this chapter, financial control in the public sector is exercised by comparing budget plans with outturn figures. The techniques of standard costing, which analyse variance in terms of the relative impacts of price and volume changes, tend not to be used.

Costing techniques are used to assist in the monitoring and management of performance. Absorption-costing techniques are employed to calculate the unit costs of services (e.g., cost per pupil, cost per tonne of waste disposed, cost per swimming pool visit). Such unit costs are compared over time and across different service providers to give an indication of performance. (*See* Chapter 12 for a fuller consideration of performance measurement and management.)

The fact that public service organisations tend not to use sophisticated management accounting techniques in planning and controlling resource use is not necessarily a cause for concern. Hofstede (1981) highlights the importance of context in deciding what management control techniques are appropriate for public service organisations. Hofstede identifies four aspects of organisational activity that affect the appropriateness of different management control techniques:

- the ambiguity of objectives;
- the ability to measure outputs;
- whether the effects of managerial intervention will be known;
- whether activities are repetitive.

The alternative management control processes are categorised as: routine, expert, trial and error, intuitive, judgemental, and political. Table 9.7 indicates the circumstances under which each management control process may be appropriate. For example, if objectives are ambiguous (as they often are in the public sector), the appropriate control process is political. Management accounting practices in the public sector need to be understood within this political context.

Table 9.7 Hofstede's model of the circumstances under which different management control processes are appropriate

Characteristics of situation	Type of management control information/process					
	Routine	Expert	Trial & error	Intuitive	Judgemental	Political
Objectives unambiguous	yes	yes	yes	yes	yes	no
Outputs measurable	yes	yes	yes	yes	no	—
Effect of intervention known	yes	yes	no	no	—	—
Activities repetitive	yes	no	yes	no	—	—

Note: The situations in which each type of management control information/process is appropriate are denoted in the columns; so 'trial and error' is appropriate when objectives are unambiguous, outputs are measurable and activities are repetitive, but where the effects of intervention are not known.
Source: Adapted from Lapsley (1992, p 46, Figure 3.1). Reproduced with permission.

THE DISTINCTIVE FEATURES OF FINANCIAL MANAGEMENT IN PUBLIC SERVICE ORGANISATIONS – FINANCIAL ACCOUNTING AND REPORTING

To reiterate, financial accounting is concerned with serving the needs of external users of financial information. Table 9.8 summarises the key points of difference between financial accounting in the public and private sectors.

This section first outlines the audience for financial reports, then discusses the features of good financial reports and, finally, considers the financial accounting systems employed.

Table 9.8 A comparison of financial accounting in the public and private sectors

	Public sector	Private sector
Capital structure	Taxation Borrowing	Equity Borrowing
Focus of accounting	Fund accounting	Entity accounting
Type of accounting system	Traditionally cash accounting, increasingly accruals accounting	Accruals accounting
Focus of financial reports	Financial and political	Financial
Performance measurement	Financial and non-financial	Financial
Audience for annual reports	Heterogeneous	Shareholders and lenders

Financial accounting practice in the private sector is designed to serve the needs of external providers of finance. Rutherford (1990) argues that this is a relatively homogenous group and that the accounting practice required to meet their needs is relatively easy to define. The users of public sector financial reports are much more heterogeneous and include:

- elected members;
- the public as voters and taxpayers;
- service users and their representatives;
- employees;
- customers and suppliers;
- other government organisations;
- competitors;
- regulators and auditors;
- lenders;
- pressure groups.

The diverse needs of this list of potential users have led to much debate about the form and content of public sector financial reports and the accounting techniques that underlie them. It is not easy to communicate complex financial information in a way that is suitable for all audiences. Many local authorities have worked hard to improve this aspect of their reports. Exhibit 9.4 reproduces an example of the way in which Birmingham City Council communicated information on the financial performance of its leisure services in 1996/97.

Likierman (1992) comments that a good annual report and accounts should provide readers with sufficient information to enable them to identify:

- current levels of activity, recent changes and prospects for the future;
- all sources of income;
- the amount of expenditure on each of the main activities of the organisation;
- whether the organisation is maintaining its asset base;
- variances from budgets or targets;
- the link between financial and other objectives;
- trends;
- comparisons with other bodies or services;
- indebtedness;
- solvency.

Exhibit 9.4

Focus on committees

Leisure services

Leisure Services Committee is committed to providing facilities and services both to enrich the quality of life of Birmingham's multi-cultural community and to benefit visitors to the city. Facilities include museums and arts, venues, libraries, adult learning centres, sport, youth, community and play centres and parks, playing fields and open space.

- *New consultation programme with young people aged 11–25 – giving an early result of an extra £600 000 allocated to the Youth Service.*

- *Sponsorship helped popular activities, e.g. Youth Festival and Monster Creepy Crawlies Show.*

- *Successful lottery bids for refurbishing Alexander Stadium, a new synthetic turf pitch at Wyndley Leisure Centre and refurbished galleries at the Museum Art Gallery.*

- *Sutton Park awarded National Nature Reserve Status*

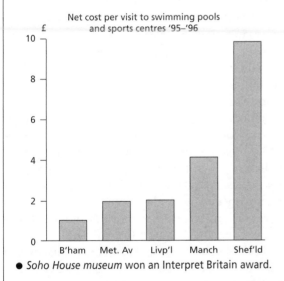

Net cost per visit to swimming pools and sports centres '95–'96

- *Soho House museum won an Interpret Britain award.*

- *Over 2 million visits to Council Libraries.*

Performance comparisons

1995–96	B'ham	Met Av.	Leeds	Liver-pool	Man-chstr	Shef-fld
Leisure services						
Recreation, parks & swimming pools – net cost per citizen (£)	21.94	24.91	12.53	37.56	35.86	55.3
Libraries – net cost per citizen (£)	13.65	12.11	9.48	16.33	23.33	9.5
The amount spent per head on books & other library materials (£)	1.97	2.32	1.62	2.16	4.76	1.23

Service costs *(£m)*

	Actual 96–97	Estimated outturn 96–97	Actual 95–96
Leisure services			
Museums and arts	8.2	8.1	8.7
Sport, youth, community and play	23.3	23.6	24.8
Parks and nature conservation	15.0	15.1	15.6
Libraries and adult learning	18.7	18.6	18.4
Total	65.2	65.4	67.5

Service statistics *(£m)*

	96–97	95–96
Leisure services		
Net cost per citizen	£63.87	£66.35
FTE employees per 1,000 popn	1.6	1.7
Museum attendances	1 104 574	930 357
Number of users		
● leisure centres & swim pools	6.8m	6.6m
● golf courses	368 497	378 354
No. of youth and community centres	41	41
Total no. of books at 31st March	3.0m	3.0m
No. of borrowings of books	6.9m	6.5m
No. of library service points (incl. mobile libraries)	43	43
Area maintained parks and playing fields (in hectares)	3432	3682

Source: Birmingham City Council, *Financial Review 1996–97*, p 18. Reproduced with permission.

A trend highlighted by Rutherford (1990) and CIPFA (1994) is an increasing convergence of public and private sector reports around the private sector standard. In particular, there has been a move from cash accounting to full accruals accounting in much of the public sector. There is less agreement about whether this is a good thing. Accruals accounting is concerned with revenues and expenses and not just with cash inflows and outflows (refer back to Fig. 9.6). Accruals accounting adopts the principle of matching expenses with revenues and ensuring that these expenses include the cost of the capital assets consumed during the accounting period (depreciation). The move to accruals accounting reflects:

- the need for greater accountability for the use of resources;
- the greater focus on performance and the need to measure outputs;
- the need for comparability with private sector providers as a result of market testing and the contracting out of services.

The concerns about the adoption of accruals accounting in the public sector include:

- the problems of developing appropriately valued capital assets registers;
- the introduction of more subjectivity into accounts in terms of how some items are treated (e.g. depreciation);
- the increase in administrative and accounting costs;
- the increased difficulty in ensuring central financial control, for example, the difficulty of ensuring that expenditure remains within spending limits when it is managers and suppliers who decide when invoices are issued, whereas it is accountants who decide when cash is paid.

ENSURING VALUE FOR MONEY – THE ROLE OF AUDIT

The introduction to this chapter highlighted the increased importance of ensuring that limited resources are deployed in ways that have the greatest beneficial impact on overall service objectives. That is, public service organisations must ensure, and demonstrate to others, that they provide good value for money. Financial reporting is a key element in the accountability of public service bodies. In addition to having access to the annual report and accounts, members of the public may consult a wide array of financial and other information on public service organisations. However, on its own, this is not a sufficient basis for ensuring accountability and value for money. The general public are likely to experience some difficulties in interpreting this array of information and there are only limited opportunities for them to hold public service organisations to account. For the most part, the public needs to rely upon the strengthened role of external audit bodies in ensuring value for money. The main external audit bodies in England and Wales are: the National Audit Office for all central government departments; the Audit Commission, for English and Welsh local authorities, police and fire authorities, health authorities and health service trusts (the sister audit body for Scotland being the Accounts Commission).

Historically, the role of the auditor has been to provide assurance on the regularity and lawfulness of published accounts. This role was initially expanded to include an assessment of any loss due to the lack of economy and efficiency. Since the Local Government Finance Act 1982, the audit of local government has also been concerned with effectiveness. In auditing effectiveness, the auditors should concern themselves with whether the organisation has made proper arrangements for securing effectiveness in the use of resources. The role of external auditors is in part reactive, particularly their annual audit of accounts and performance. They also have a proactive role in promoting and undertaking national and local studies of value for money.

For example, the Accounts Commission for Scotland has a role in relation to value for money that is set out in statute. It covers three major areas:

It has to carry out studies to identify opportunities for audited bodies to improve their value for money; it has to support external auditors in their review of the management arrangements which audited bodies have in place for achieving value for money; and, for local authorities, it has to publish directions which specify the performance information which councils have to publish (Accounts Commission, 1996, p 10).

In Scotland, each audited body has 20 per cent of its audit time allocated for value for money work. Such audit work has to incorporate local applications of national studies or reports, local projects, verifying data for the Citizen's Charter and the audit of management arrangements (Accounts Commission, 1996, p 12).

The auditor's role has been enlarged, but there is no cause for complacency. Bowerman (1996) highlights a number of deficiencies in the current arrangements for the external audit of public services. For example, there is a lack of clarity about whether the role of the auditor is to help management or to blame them. There is also confusion about who is the client for the audit and whether the public should have access to audit reports. As was discussed in Chapter 5 of this book, there has been a growth of quasi-governmental bodies during the 1980s and 1990s, and the auditing regime has struggled to keep pace with the increasingly fragmented structure of government. Bowerman argues that the precise role of audit in the changing public sector is far from clear. At the same time increasing emphasis is being placed upon audit as a means of delivering accountability.

CONCLUSIONS

This chapter has highlighted the increasing importance of financial management skills as budgets are devolved and local managers are asked to demonstrate that their limited resources are deployed to best effect. It has focused mainly on the financial management approaches, concepts and skills relating to budgetary planning and control. The chapter then outlined the distinctive features of financial management in public service organisations and the means of ensuring that they provide value for money.

The main conclusions to be drawn from this chapter are:

1 Public service organisations operate within a political environment and provide many intangible services, which limit the ability to measure outputs and outcomes. Both the political environment and the limited ability to measure the service provided have shaped the distinctive financial practices found in public service organisations.
2 The budget is the dominant management tool for planning, co-ordinating and controlling activities. This places a strain on budgetary processes and many organisations have struggled to develop budgetary systems that are capable of meeting such wide-ranging demands. A modified form of incremental budgeting still remains the predominant budgetary approach in many public service organisations. However, some organisations are developing resource allocation formulae to guide the allocation of funds to delegated budget holders.
3 Designing budgetary systems and controls that address the issue of motivation is a complex task. Any incentives for saving money or any sanctions for overspending need to avoid penalising present or future service users.
4 There is an assumption in the new managerial culture of the public sector that it is beneficial to delegate financial management responsibilities, so that the staff who make

service decisions are responsible for the financial implications of these decisions. Although devolved budgets do provide advantages, these need to be balanced against potential disadvantages.

5 The financial reporting practices of public and private sector organisations are tending to converge around the private sector standard. The move towards accruals accounting sharpens the focus on performance, but increases accounting costs, introduces more subjectivity into the accounts and potentially weakens central budgetary control.

6 Ensuring that the limited resources available to the public sector are deployed in ways that have the greatest beneficial impact on overall service objectives is not easy. The various external audit bodies play an important role as the watchdog of public service provision. Their role has expanded in recent years, but there continue to be concerns about who they should report to, whether they are judges or helpers and which public service organisations should fall within their remit.

REFERENCES

Accounts Commission (1996) *Strategy 1996–99*. Edinburgh: The Accounts Commission for Scotland.

Anthony, R N (1977) 'ZBB – a useful fraud', *Government Accountants Journal*, Summer, 11(2), pp 7–10.

Bowerman, M (1996) 'Public audit – Have we got the framework right?' in Public Finance Foundation (ed.) *Adding Value? Audit and Accountability in the Public Services*, pp 7–12. London: Chartered Institute of Public Finance and Accountancy.

Caulfield, I and Schultz, J (1989) *Planning for Change: Strategic Planning in Local Government*. London: Longman.

CIPFA (1994) *Setting Public Sector Standards*. London: Chartered Institute of Public Finance and Accountancy.

CIPFA (1996) *Management Accounting*. Foundation Open Learning Materials. London: Chartered Institute of Public Finance and Accountancy.

Coch, L and French, J R P (1948) 'Overcoming resistance to change', *Human Relations*, 1(4), pp 512–32.

Colville, I (1989) 'Scenes from a budget: helping the police with their accounting enquiries', *Financial Accountability and Management*, 5(2), pp 89–105.

Coombs, H and Jenkins, D (1994) *Public Sector Financial Management*. London: Chapman & Hall.

Corry, D and Gray, S (1997) 'Recent history of public spending' in Cory, D (ed.) *Public Expenditure – Effective Management and Control*, pp 62–89. London: Dryden Press.

Cullis, J and Jones, P (1992) *Public Finance and Public Choice – Analytical Perspectives*. London: McGraw-Hill.

Fayol, H (1949) *General and Industrial Management*. London: Pitman.

Flynn, N (1987) 'Delegating financial responsibility and policy-making within social services departments', *Public Money*, 6(4) pp 41–4.

Flynn, N (1993) *Public Sector Management*. Hemel Hempstead: Harvester Wheatsheaf.

Griffiths, P (1987) 'Mid-Glamorgan County Council', in Elcock, H and Jordan, G (eds) *Learning from Local Authority Budgeting*. Aldershot: Avebury.

Health, Department of (1997) *The New NHS, Modern, Dependable*. London: Department of Health.

Hofstede, G (1981) 'Management control of public and not-for-profit activities', *Accounting Organizations and Society*, 6(3), pp 193–211.

Jones, R and Pendlebury, M (1992) *Public Sector Accounting*. London: Pitman Publishing.

Lapsley, I (1992) 'Management accounting in the public sector' in Henley, D, Likierman, A, Perrin, J, Evans, M, Lapsley, I and Whiteoak J (eds) *Public Sector Accounting and Financial Control*, pp 43–64. London: Chapman & Hall.

Likierman, A (1992) 'Financial reporting in the public sector' in Henley, D, Likierman, A, Perrin, J, Evans, M, Lapsley, I and Whiteoak J (eds) *Public Sector Accounting and Financial Control*, pp 10–42. London: Chapman & Hall.

Lindblom, C (1959) 'The science of muddling through', *Public Administration Review*, 19, pp 79–88.

Morgan, G (1997) *Images of Organisation*. London: Sage.

Nutley, S and Osborne, S (1994) *The Public Sector Management Handbook*. Harlow: Longman.

Packwood, T, Keen, J and Buxton, M (1991) *Hospitals in Transition: The Resource Management Experiment.* Milton Keynes: Open University Press.

Perrin, J (1989) 'Management accounting' in Henley, D, Holtham, C, Likierman, A and Perrin, J (eds) *Public Sector Accounting and Financial Control*, pp 31–55. London: Van Nostrand Reinhold.

Rutherford, B (1990) 'Towards a conceptual framework for public sector financial reporting', *Public Money and Management*, 10(2), pp 11–15.

Schultze, C L (1968) *The Politics and Economics of Public Spending.* Washington, DC: Brookings Institute.

Wildavsky, A (1974) *The Politics and the Budgetary Process.* Boston: Little Brown.

QUESTIONS AND DISCUSSION TOPICS

1 What are the advantages and disadvantages of incremental budgeting?

2 Compare and contrast incremental budgeting and zero-based budgeting.

3 Why is the annual budget the dominant management tool for planning, co-ordinating, organising and controlling activities?

4 What features of the design of budgetary systems need to be addressed in order to provide an appropriate motivational framework for those with budget responsibilities?

5 Compare and contrast financial management in the public and private sectors.

6 How can greater accountability be ensured for the use of resources?

GLOSSARY OF TERMS

Audit   An independent examination of an organisation's activities, either by internal audit or the organisation's external auditor.

Base budget   The cost of existing policies, before growth or reductions, expressed at a specific price base. A base budget might be set as last year's original budget or last year's revised estimated budget, or some other base figure.

Budget   An amount of expenditure or income that is estimated or allocated for a financial period. A budget should be linked to the aims and objectives of a unit and is often defined as a plan of action expressed in financial terms.

Budget head   Each section of the budget for which estimates are produced and control exercised.

Budget profiling   The division of an annual budget into an amount for a financial period such as a month.

Budgetary control   The control of expenditure and income during the financial year against the budget.

Budgeting   The preparation of estimates of expenditure and income to form the budget.

Capital expenditure   Expenditure on significant assets, including land, buildings and equipment which will be of use or benefit in providing services beyond the financial year.

Carry forward   The balance of the budget (positive or negative) carried forward from one financial period to the next.

Cash limit   A method of expenditure control which restricts the amount available for spending to a specified cash amount, regardless of the effects of inflation.

Commitments   An expenditure commitment is made when goods or services are ordered. A commitments system records expenditure at the time orders are placed.

Contingency provision/fund   A sum set aside to provide for foreseen but unquantifiable future commitments or for the unforeseen expenditure which may become necessary during the year.

Cost centre   The definition of a unit within an organisation for which expenditure and income information is aggregated and reported.

Creditor   An amount owed by an organisation for work done, goods received or services rendered to the organisation within the accounting period but for which payment has not been made.

Debtor   An amount owed to the organisation for work done, goods received or services rendered to the organisation within the accounting period but for which payment has not been made.

Delegated budget   The budget share which has been delegated to a local unit for it to control and manage.

Direct costs   Costs that are directly traceable to the unit of service or product being costed.

Fixed costs   Fixed costs do not vary (in the medium term at least) with the level of activity.

Formula funding   The method by which an overall budget is distributed to agencies or units. Formulae consist of weighted factors, which when combined indicate the percentage of the overall budget that should be allocated to constituent units.

Incremental budgeting   The allocation of resources by adjusting last year's budget or expenditure to take account of pay and price inflation, new growth and expected savings.

Indirect costs/overheads   The terms indirect costs and overheads are often (but not always) used interchangeably. These are costs which cannot be directly attributed to a service or product and so have to be apportioned on some equitable basis.

Journal entry/transfer   The central debiting of one account and the crediting of another account. Journal entries may be used to correct errors or to transfer money between cost centres under an internal recharge.

Non-recurring items of income or expenditure   One-off items of income or expenditure.

Outturn   Actual expenditure and income for the whole financial year.

Outturn prices   The average price of items purchased during the financial year. A budget set at outturn prices represents the cash that was estimated to be required. It takes account of estimated inflation (see also price base).

Price base   The rates of pay and prices of goods or services at a specified date (most commonly, November).

Resource allocation   The process of distributing funds to cost centres.

Revenue expenditure   Expenditure on day-to-day running costs (such as salaries, heating and lighting).

Revised estimates   The approved estimates for the current year as updated.

Unit costs   The cost of a particular service related to one or more non-financial measurements of the service, e.g. cost per pupil, cost per passenger mile.

Value for money   An expression describing the benefit obtained (not just in financial terms) for a given input of cash.

Variance   The difference between planned and actual expenditure and income for a period of time.

Variable costs   Variable costs vary in direct proportion to changes in the level of activity.

Virement   The transfer of budget provision from one expenditure heading to another.

10 Marketing for the public services

David Chapman

AIMS

This chapter will:

- explain the nature of marketing;
- demonstrate the relevance of marketing for public services;
- illustrate how marketing tools can be used by public services organisations.

INTRODUCTION

The concept of marketing

In many ways the concept of marketing public services is quite new. The language of satisfying customer demand reflects the belief, from the early 1980s onwards, in increasing consumer choice and introducing public services markets – as we saw in Part 1. This chapter examines the concept of marketing and the nature of public services markets.

We can define marketing as:

The means by which an organisation achieves a match between what the customer expects, wants and needs and what the organisation is able and/or willing to provide.

Marketing is or should be based on knowledge of who the customers are. The use of the word customer may not sit happily in the vocabulary of many of those with an interest in public services. This chapter (and Chapter 16) provide us with an opportunity to debate the appropriateness of this terminology. Traditionally customers can be defined as 'end-users' but end-users might be only a part of the 'customer group' that a local authority manager, for example, is seeking to satisfy. This is part of the complexity of the public services, as discussed in Part 1; managing in the public services is about managing a multiplicity of stakeholders (*see* Chapter 11). A stakeholder map might identify other 'customers' – including decision makers, funders, users, professionals acting on behalf of users, customers, citizens, local communities and so on. We explore these complexities below. To return to the concept of marketing itself, the perception of marketing is often distorted. It can be argued that distortions of our perceptions of marketing can be represented by the 'five Ms' of marketing:

- misinterpreted;
- misunderstood;
- manipulative;
- misused;
- miscast.

Only the first three of the 'five Ms' are discussed below. The other two, misused and miscast, are not relevant to the present discussion.

For example, marketing is still *misinterpreted* as 'selling'. Selling in some cultures is still viewed with suspicion because it is associated with aggressive sales tactics, competition between the seller and the potential purchaser and with imbalances of power between the parties involved. In the recent past 'overselling' of products, such as pensions, has left the financial services sector and governments seriously compromised because of a basic misunderstanding of marketing concepts. Similarly, 'market forces' are now often associated with the reasons given for cutbacks and redundancies in organisations. However, good marketing is not about cutting costs, but about adding value to the product or service.

At the same time, marketing, particularly for the public services, can be *misunderstood*. British Rail for example, in the process of attempting to establish a customer orientation, frequently failed to recognise the specific needs of particular customers and customer groups. There was a failure to understand the real needs of its user groups.

There has also been a belief that marketing is about *manipulation*. Those who criticise marketing on these grounds assume that marketers have some Svengali-like characteristics which enable them to induce consumers to behave exactly as they wish. One may recall Abraham Lincoln's comment that you can fool all of the people some of the time, some of the people all of the time, but not all of the people all of the time. Where suppliers try to fool customers they ultimately fail. In devising a marketing strategy, businesses need to have a vast knowledge of the behaviour characteristics of those markets to which their products are being channelled so that supply fits demand rather than vice versa.

THE PUBLIC SERVICES ENVIRONMENT

As discussed in Chapters 1 and 2, the public services environment has been exposed to a more competitive environment, resulting from government action and driven by considerable changes in the expectations of the general population. The exposure to a competitive environment does not mean, however, that organisations will become more market oriented. The consequences of changes in the operational environment can be seen in Fig. 10.1.

In the course of a few years the public services have moved from a situation characterised by stable resources and stable markets, where administrative efficiency is the key requirement, to one characterised by changing markets and changing resources where marketing management is a key requirement. The paradox in relation to this change is that many of the reforms of the public sector in the 1980s were introduced to improve efficiency and productivity at a time when it was assumed that markets would remain stable. Many of these reforms led to decreasing levels of user satisfaction because the public services had not taken account of marketing issues. However, the growth of the welfare state from its earliest years relied on the growth of bureaucracy and was producer led. In marketing terms, there was an emphasis on 'the production concept' approach to the market

	Stable markets	Changing markets
Changing resources	Increase productivity by better production **Investment management action**	The need to forecast and anticipate the changes and take risk on the basis of a reading of the market **Marketing action**
Stable resources	Managing stability **Administrative style**	Probability of existing product becoming obsolete **Ostrich-style management**

Fig. 10.1 A matrix of managerial attitudes in different combinations of states of change

(*see* Kotler, 1994, pp 12–13). The production orientation leads to an emphasis on the uniqueness of the product or service and its ability to satisfy customer need.

Over the same period, there has been a cultural mistrust of marketing as a concept in the public services. The welfare state originally developed on the premise that the 'state knows best', expressed through professional control of service delivery. The state assumed a social responsibility in a spirit of benevolent paternalism – the impact of this being to force the public to have what it may not actually want. Thus the final user of the benefits or services provided had little market influence over the form of that provision. At the same time, the state effectively assumed a monopoly position, in which there was usually no alternative supply of benefits and services and therefore no real choice for the user.

This is partly as a result of public services being funded through general taxation rather than payment at the point of delivery and the fact that public services have traditionally been designed to meet needs (often defined by politicians or professionals) rather than wants. The concept of 'free at the point of delivery' means that increased use does not mean increased revenue for the provider, but greater demand for often scarce resources.

The history and nature of the public services means that the marketing of them has to be understood in terms of a framework which is both different from and more complex than that required for commercial marketing. These differences are as follows.

1 The legislative context involves statutory responsibilities to provide minimum levels of support to service users.
2 Resources are usually limited and their availability depends upon political choice.
3 User choice is often limited by the nature of the supply.
4 There is a tendency to focus on basic needs rather than on non-essential wants.
5 Public sector markets remain intimately connected to changes in society in political, social and economic terms.

STRATEGY AND MARKETING

Those whom an organisation regards as its customers will be determined by the answers to questions such as, 'Who or what are we and why are we here?' Organisations often set out their view of their role in mission statements and conduct the kinds of investigation concerning strategy that we identified in Chapter 7. The point of a mission statement is to reflect in broad terms what the organisation is trying to achieve and for whom. It enables an organisation to prioritise activities, to determine what is really important. The organisation can then seek to codify what it wants to achieve through the goals that it sets. If strategy is concerned with a broad portfolio of activities intended to bring about valued outcomes over a period of, say, three to five years then marketing can assist at various stages in the strategic process. In assessing customer needs, values, wants and expectations, organisations use market or customer research. Such research may involve a number of activities including customer surveys using postal questionnaires, street interviews or telephone surveys, and focus groups. Exhibit 10.1 presents a selection of the techniques involved.

Exhibit 10.1

Listening to the voice of the customer

In their text on entrepreneurial approaches to public services, Osborne and Gaebler offer 17 examples of how public services can implement a customer-driven approach. They include:

- customer contact reports where feedback is given directly to the employee;
- electronic mail where the public can e-mail government departments and expect a response within 24 hours;
- test marketing of new facilities such as credit cards;
- quality guarantees where colleges guarantee the skills of their graduates and offer retraining if necessary;
- telephone hotlines to report cases of bureaucratic bungling.

Source: Adapted from Osborne and Gaebler, 1993, pp 177–9.

Customers may be thought of as individuals or as groups. A group of customers who may be expected to react in the same way to the same set of marketing stimuli is termed a 'market segment'. (We discuss market segmentation towards the end of this chapter.) We can choose to divide the population served by an organisation into various segments defined in terms of age, gender, economic or social status, position in the life cycle, ethnic origin, particular need, geographic location, lifestyle and so on. An organisation can then decide which segments to target and the most appropriate way to approach each segment. This analysis will often identify a range of potential customers and a wide range of activities that could be provided for them.

How is an organisation to select the segments to target, and the most appropriate means to do so? One tool that was developed by the Boston Consulting Group in the

1970s is the Growth/Share Matrix. This 2×2 matrix identified relative market share and market growth rate. Products and services are identified as:

1 *Cash cows*, which have large market share but low growth. Products typically generate more cash than is required to keep the product in the market.
2 *Stars* are generally in high growth areas and have a large market share. Stars can generate a large cash inflow, but this is often matched by a large outflow of cash to maintain market share.
3 *Problem children* are products with low market share but in a high growth market. These products can consume large amounts of cash when the organisation tries to increase market share.
4 *Dogs* are products with low market share and low growth. They generate little revenue and what is generated tends to be used to maintain existing sales.

In terms of an organisation's approach to its market, the ideal is to maintain a balanced portfolio of products and services. We can imagine a further education college, like the one we saw in Chapter 7, using the growth/share matrix approach to determine the mix of courses that it offers, ranging from Business Studies (which could be a cash cow) to Computer Studies (which might be a problem child).

Many critics have argued that the Boston Matrix is an oversimplification in that it concentrates on two variables and it assumes that higher rates of market share generate higher profits. However, it is a useful tool that can be used to supplement a manager's judgement.

Having determined its strategy in broad terms (who it will serve, how it intends to serve them and what it hopes to bring about) an organisation needs to consider specific aspects of implementing this strategy, that is, the tactics. In marketing terms the tactics are often defined in terms of the 'four Ps'. Before we investigate the specifics and the tactics of marketing, however, we need to return to objectives and strategy.

In terms of implementing an organisation's strategy, the task is to translate broad goals into clear statements. Accordingly, marketeers have suggested that it is necessary to create 'smart' objectives, namely those that are:

● specific;
● measurable;
● achievable/agreed;
● relevant;
● time bounded.

An organisation needs to think about what it wants to achieve by a specific time, its 'desired state'. It also needs to translate strategic objectives into marketing objectives. In the private sector these include market share, sales volume, brand recognition, customer retention etc.

The marketing objectives for a local government marketing plan would need also to take into consideration the body's organisational capability and resources to deliver the marketing plan. For example there is no point in a college seeking to develop a Business Studies qualification because it is a lucrative market if it does not have the staff expertise to deliver the course. We have already examined, in Chapter 7, STEP as a tool that may be used to scan the environment. We might also add the two Cs – Competitors and

Customers – as part of that environment. Thus an organisation might conduct research on competitors' strategies, product research on their services and products, market research on customer needs and output research on the organisation's products and the reaction to them by customers. A SWOT analysis (which we also examined in Chapter 7) allows the organisation to see if its internal or current state of affairs has the capability to deliver the external and future needs.

PUBLIC SERVICES MARKETS

Public services markets are complicated by a number of factors which either do not apply to markets for private organisations, or which are of less relevance to the latter:

1 Measurement of performance is rarely based on profit or solely on financial criteria (an issue which is examined in detail in Chapter 12).
2 Income is usually derived from allocated resources rather than directly from transactions with users at the point of delivery. Indeed an increased level of activity in a public services organisation could well result in a financial deficit, whereas in a private organisation it can, and normally does, improve the revenue of the organisation. For this reason, managers in public services organisations tend to focus on the management of cost rather than the management of user satisfaction.
3 These markets are less sensitive to market needs because they are subject to a much higher level of statutory responsibility and regulatory control.

The market for public services consists of a number of different markets in each of which there are specific exchange relationships between different parties:

- industrial or organisational markets, in which the exchange is between people acting on behalf of an organisation rather than for themselves;
- government markets, in which the exchange is with a government department;
- consumer markets, in which the exchange is with an individual acting on his or her own behalf or sometimes, for example, professionals acting on behalf of customers or clients (an example is GPs acting on behalf of their patients);
- social markets, in which marketing is aimed at society as a whole, as for example, in public health campaigns.

In order to address these markets three questions need to be answered.

1 Who are the clients or customers?
2 How can they be responded to?
3 How can activities be resourced?

The public services also involve multiple markets. Theodossin (1986) for example, identifies at least four markets, each of which has its own particular needs and all of which may have an impact on a particular transaction. The needs of the different markets may be in conflict and in many cases may reduce the satisfaction of the primary market. These markets are:

1 The *user or primary market*, consisting of the actual users or direct beneficiaries of the service. The language of the private sector has been introduced to public services as users become customers rather than, say, passengers.

2 The *facilitator or secondary market*, consisting of those who can influence the choice of the transaction, e.g. the patient's doctor, the employee's manager and so on.

3 The *resource market*, involving those who are responsible for allocating the resources which are necessary to provide the service, e.g. government departments.

4 The *legitimiser market*, consisting of those individuals and bodies which exist to ensure that the service is provided in the approved manner subject to the approved quality standards, e.g. the British Medical Association.

The complexity of the market frequently means that, for any one transaction, an organisation may be working in a combination of different markets. Each of the four markets may have more than one constituent and a customer may be in more than one market, as demonstrated in Exhibit 10.2.

Exhibit 10.2

Multiple markets in business education

A university business school provides qualifications to managers through short courses in accountancy, the costs of which are partially met by Training and Enterprise Council (TEC) funding.

The primary market is the manager who receives the training even though this person may not have sought out the course. The secondary market is the employer, and most of the promotional effort may be targeted at this market. The employer facilitates the student attending and is an organisational market. Furthermore, the employer may also be part of the funder market.

The TEC is a government agency and is part of the governmental market at the same time as part of the funder market.

If the course is one which leads to a professional or vocational qualification, it will have to comply with the conditions of the organisation that validates the qualification. This could be an internal university department or an external organisation such as the Chartered Institute of Marketing.

Similarly, in the context of health provision, health service managers may identify their primary market as the general practitioner (GP) rather than the patient. In fact, the patient is the primary market and the GP is the facilitator. However, the satisfaction of the GP will be determined by the satisfaction of the patient. Much of the dissatisfaction with the health service stems from the failure of the service to identify its primary customer. Furthermore, the relationships between the different needs of the different constituents of the market have to be understood. This leads to an understanding of the behaviour of buyers and users. We return to behavioural considerations below.

Figure 10.2 presents an initial approach to the constituents, components, relationships within and segmentation of markets. The notion of different constituencies is further complicated when it is linked to the objectives of the organisation. Public services are often characterised by multiple and sometimes competing objectives, as illustrated in Exhibit 10.3.

Constituency of market	Components of market	User/provider relationships	Segmentation
Primary Secondary Facilitator Legitimiser	Need to consider the 'players' in each part of the market.	What is the state of the relationship between each competitor or supplier?	Is this relationship influenced by segment variables?

Fig. 10.2 An initial approach to market constituencies

Source: Chapman and Cowdell (1998, p 68). Reproduced with permission.

Exhibit 10.3

Marketing and museums

The UK Museums Association defines a museum as an 'institution which collects, documents, preserves, exhibits and interprets material evidence and associated information for the public benefit'. The UK system of support for the arts makes a distinction between private museums and those funded by the state. The latter are either national institutions funded from national taxation or those supported by local authorities. Increasingly, museums are expected to raise funds from other sources such as commercial sponsorship. Museums are adopting marketing techniques, both to increase perceptions of their accountability to the public and to attract funding. Research indicates that museums and galleries reach more of the country's population (between 31 and 39 per cent) than any other arts activities.

In terms of a multiple-market model, the museum markets can be defined as follows:

● the primary market: visitors and users;
● the secondary market: social and cultural structures and institutions;
● the legitimiser market: statutory provision, control and political decisions;
● the resourcer market: state, local authority and Arts Council funding, income generation and sponsorship.

However, conflict has emerged between museum staff. Some see their work as collection related, concentrating on the objects themselves, on research and scholarship, whereas others see their objectives as primarily user related, that is, concerned with the display and interpretation of artefacts and marketing them for the benefit of users.

THE MARKETING MIX

Marketing strategies can be seen as the means by which marketing objectives are achieved. How this is done is determined by the marketing mix, which consists of four variables: Product, Price, Promotion and Place (the 'four Ps'). The four variables are now often extended to cover intangible elements, such as those associated with People and their role in the process, the Process experienced by the customer and the Physical evidence (where issues of environment or ambience are considered important).

The product

The product element includes making the products or services, developing new products or services, ensuring that specific products and services have a clear identity (branding) and designing appropriate packaging or presentation of the finished product or service to users. Marketing practitioners take a wide view of products and include in this element not only services but also the perceptions that customers may have of the products and services. This wider definition is of particular importance for public services where the product is often a service, in the form of the understanding nature of the teacher or the listening skills of the social worker. These aspects are much more intangible than physical products. Here the People element is crucial in the provision of a high-quality service. In addition to the professional qualities of staff, in terms of their knowledge and competence, the politeness, approachability and general helpfulness of individual members of staff can often make a significant difference to organisational success.

CASE STUDY 10.1

Branding is all about giving a clear identity to services or products. Dobson's initiative is, arguably, an attempt to re-assert a public service ethos through the use of marketing techniques.

DOBSON TO REVAMP IMAGE OF NHS

By George Parker

Frank Dobson, Health Secretary, has ordered a major 'rebranding' of the National Health Service, in an attempt to redress a process of fragmentation in the past decade.

Mr Dobson is concerned that the Conservative health reforms of the 1980s diluted the impression of a truly national service, by creating scores of semi-independent NHS trusts.

In future Mr Dobson wants all health service organisations and facilities to include the NHS logo, against a blue background, on signs and stationery. The 'rebranding' exercise will coincide with government plans for a nationwide celebration of the 50th anniversary of the formation of the NHS next July.

The recreation of a national identity for the health service marks a shift in thinking from the Tory era, when ministers set about breaking up the monolithic service.

But Mr Dobson believes the system has now become too fragmented, with some NHS trusts offering no suggestion that they are part of a national service.

'We want to make people more aware of the NHS family of hospitals, health centres, clinics and so on,' said one senior health official. 'We don't want to start removing the identity of individual hospitals, but we want to reinforce a national element – the wider use of the logo will contribute to that.'

The blue NHS 'lozenge' will begin appearing on signs and letterheads when they need replacing, and will not be introduced immediately.

'We are aware of the issue of costs that might be involved in this, so this process will happen over a period of time,' said the official.

The government is intending to mark the NHS 50th anniversary on July 5 with a series of events, drawing attention to the fact a Labour administration set up the service in 1948.

However, the celebrations could be marred by a growing waiting list crisis, which is expected to reach its peak this winter.

Waiting lists are at record levels and Mr Dobson will not receive any extra cash from the Treasury to tackle the problem until next April.

Today he will issue guidance to all health trusts and authorities on measures to prepare for the winter.

Source: Financial Times, 28 August 1997. Reprinted with permission.

Pricing

For public service organisations, pricing may be irrelevant where services are provided free of charge. However, charges may be used to 'top up' public funding or to restrict demand for a service. Charges may also be made for those services that are considered to be non-essential, for example, a local authority's leisure facilities.

At the same time, it is worth recognising that the decision whether or not to charge may be made on political grounds rather than being driven by market forces. The prices of products and services offered need to be determined, perhaps with incentives being offered to purchasers and with appropriate contracts being provided. The basis of charging may vary. For example contracts in the NHS may involve block pricing, where contractors are paid for a block of work irrespective of how long it takes them to do it. Another form of contract is the spot contract, where one-off services are bought in to meet a specific need at a specific time, for example spot contracts for health care. In setting a price level the following options could be followed:

- *profit oriented* – to maximise the surplus of revenue over costs;
- *cost oriented* – to recover as much as possible of the actual costs of providing the service;
- *demand oriented* – to use price to stimulate or depress demand in certain identified groups;
- *image oriented* – to use price as part of the means of creating an image of the organisation, product or service.

Whatever pricing regime is followed, there must be good information on costs, both fixed and variable, and on usage, in terms of both volume and patterns. For example, compulsory competitive tendering in local government has led to greater clarity of information.

Place

Place is concerned with managing the ways in which products and services are organised and given added value, providing good customer/user care and service and organising the delivery of products and services to customers and users. It involves arranging access to products and services and their distribution. This process will be familiar to public services managers who provide services through one-stop shops, or who work in neighbourhood offices. By means of the place variable, services can be made more responsive to their customers by, for example, improving access by locating them closer to the point of delivery or offering opening times that reflect people's work patterns. In simple terms, if the product or service is not available to the customer when and where he or she wants it, then, at least in the private sector, it will fail in the market. This is a lesson with which the NHS is still grappling.

Promotion

Promotion involves the advertising and promotion of products and services, public relations and communications and 'relationship' marketing. The first task of promotion is to create awareness of the product and the organisation. The second task is to create interest and the third task is to promote desire. The fourth task is to persuade customers that they should take some action to acquire or use the product or service. Customers seek to acquire a bundle of benefits. In planning promotion an organisation needs to identify the customer that it is addressing, what benefits this customer is seeking, how this customer will evaluate the benefit and which features of the organisation's service provision enhance the receipt of that benefit. Under the heading of promotion we may argue that the customer is asking two questions:

- Why do I need this service?
- Why should I choose you as the provider?

Promotions can be captured by obtaining answers to the following questions:

1 Who am I talking to?
2 What do I want to happen as a result?
3 What is that action worth to me?
4 What message will make it happen?
5 What medium will get the message to the audience?
6 How will I know if it has worked?

Effective communication and promotion are vital parts of any coherent marketing strategy. Conversely, many organisations have found to their cost that unless the rest of the marketing mix is good and well thought through, promotion alone will not achieve the desired results.

An element which exists in public services promotion, but which is largely absent from promotion in the private sector, is attitude changing. Examples of areas in which attitudes may have to be changed are drug abuse and health education. The sorts of campaigns that are mounted in relation to these issues are rarely used by private sector organisations, although there are some notable exceptions. Social marketing is concerned with trying to influence people's habits in health care or safety issues (*see* Exhibit 10.4).

In public services promotion there is inevitably a political dimension, in that a political message must be put across in terms of 'the public interest'. It must also be recognised that the products or services which are the subject of a promotional campaign may not be wanted by the user and may be seen as intrusive. In some promotions, use and consumption are discouraged, for example in relation to road use or drug abuse. The process involved in such promotions may be termed 'demarketing'.

BEHAVIOURAL ASPECTS OF PUBLIC SERVICES MARKETS

During the 1990s the marketing profession has moved away from the mass marketing of volume-produced goods towards what Kotler (1994) described as the 'new marketing'.

Exhibit 10.4

Promoting police services

Historically, police campaigns targeted at the public tried to pass on a warning (e.g. the danger of car theft in a particular area) or invited the public to come forward with information. Modern campaigns seek more subtly to change public perception and behaviour. They often go beyond simple reliance on the media to pass on the message to the public. Assessing the effectiveness of such campaigns is difficult. It is reasonably straightforward to review the effect of a new policy on crime statistics; less easy to evaluate the effect of a campaign on public behaviour and attitudes. This reflects the difference between output and outcome, as we indicate in Chapter 13.

Who is the target audience for the police? Burglars known to be active in a particular patch, the owners of high performance cars? Do the police want to send a message to the general public or to criminals? What messages are sent internally to police officers?

Techniques may include direct marketing, aimed at those who, say, have been burgled more than once in the past five years; mail, telephone or face-to-face communication. It may also be appropriate for the police to engage in a joint marketing operation with a local hardware store on home security; or to undertake a joint approach with Neighbourhood Watch. The use of private security firms by groups of residents means that there is competition for the police and that the police have to promote their services in the same way as any other organisation does. On the other hand, the existence of alternative security services might give the police an opportunity to withdraw to concentrate on other areas of police work.

This enables buyers to express choice, and to obtain goods and services that most closely fit their particular requirements. Indeed, with modern technology, mass-produced products that are custom-made with variations to suit individual customer needs are likely to become a reality. This change in marketing focus has been brought about by the change in behaviour of consumers. Those who failed to recognise the need to respond to customer needs went out of business. Thus the study of the behaviour of consumers, buyers and customers has become a fundamental part of effective marketing.

The behaviour of people in public services markets is affected by the fact that these markets are much more complex than those of the private sector and have many constituencies with conflicting interests. Furthermore, the nature of the relationship between user and provider is affected by the nature of the transaction. Given the strong production orientation that prevailed in the traditional public sector one of the first philosophical changes that has to be made is to develop an understanding that:

● marketing is about markets;
● markets are about people, not products or services; and
● marketing is about understanding how people react to the provision of products and services and taking action on that information.

Individuals rarely make buying decisions in isolation and are frequently influenced by those around them. For example, in relation to the provision of housing, in the 1950s and 1960s people were concerned simply with having their housing and security needs met. Public sector housing was considered appropriate for meeting these needs. Since then, housing has become linked to concepts of image and status and people's attitudes to social housing have changed.

Provider–user relationships

Provider–user relationships are influenced by the freedom of the purchaser to make a decision to buy or not to buy. Many public services exchanges are necessarily 'distress purchases', in that individuals may need a benefit or a service because they have no alternative. For example, an injured pedestrian may have little or no choice how or where emergency medical treatment is received once a road traffic accident has taken place.

Because of the near-monopoly status in which many public services organisations operate, public services exchanges do not normally provide a degree of choice that is the same as, or even one that is similar to that usually offered in the private sector. Only certain services offer the customer a chance to change the nature or increase the standard of service provided, and then the only available alternative may well be to pay more by 'going private', by opting out of the public services market altogether. Moreover, because of financial and legislative constraints discussed earlier in this chapter, the providers themselves are likely to be limited in their ability to respond to demand. The nature of the buyer–seller relationship will therefore differ, in line with the willingness or unwillingness of the user to use the product or service and the ability of the supplier to provide the service. The various combinations are elaborated in the matrix in Fig. 10.3.

In the private sector the 'reluctant/restricted' dimension in Fig. 10.3 is rarely present and where it is, it frequently means that to supply the goods in question is against the law. The supply of drugs is an example. Figure 10.3 calls attention to the fact that, especially in public services markets, provider–user relationships are complex. In public services markets, the ability and the desire to provide services and to benefit from them are likely to be

		Provider		
		Active	*Inactive*	*Reluctant/Restricted*
User	*Active*	**Private sector** Opt out of the public sector	**Political demand** Lobby groups Social pressure	**Rights** As provider's duty; as user's privilege
	Inactive	**Societal marketing** 'It's good for you'	**No transaction**	**Resignation** User must accept Provider cuts costs
	Reluctant/ Restricted	**'We know best'** Legislation makes it work	**Distress purchase** Dire necessity	**Hostility** Mutual distress

Fig. 10.3 Public Services markets provider–user relationships

Source: Chapman and Cowdell (1998, p 42). Reproduced with permission.

more restricted, in various ways, than in the private sector. Users of public services, as has already been noted, may rarely enjoy the same freedom of choice as they would in a typically commercial transaction. The providers, on the other hand, are likely to be restricted by limits to the available funding, or by legal obligations with which they must comply. In fact, given the nature of the factors likely to influence the users' decisions, users may find that the best way to ensure that their expressed needs are satisfied may be to 'opt out' of the public services market altogether, into private sector provision. Many of those seeking what they perceive as high-quality education for their children do just that. However, such an option is often simply not possible, especially when a user is constrained by economic factors. The majority of people cannot afford to pay the fees of a private school without the benefit of scholarships or charitable grants. In other words, there are barriers to entry.

Many public services organisations may also find themselves working in a series of different relationships, for example in the police service, as discussed above. At Christmas time the police have, for some years, mounted anti drink-drive campaigns. In this case, the police are the active providers and the motorist who is stopped (the primary user in this instance), guilty or not, is a reluctant user. However, if the same motorist arrives home and finds the house has been burgled, then the motorist becomes immediately an active seeker of police services and any delay in response caused by a limitation of service due to budgetary constraints will cause pressure for a diversion of resources. In both instances there is the potential for aggrieved feelings by the primary market. In reality, public services organisations operate in areas where the user is reluctant and frequently in areas where the provider is restricted. The consequences for the development of effective marketing policies are considerable.

The marketing of services and the tangible/intangible element

One consequence of using the marketing mix model in public services marketing is that products and services need to become synonymous. There is considerable debate about the issue of services marketing (*see* Cowell, 1984 and, for the public sector, Chapman and Cowdell, 1998). In whatever terms a product or service is described, the demand for it is determined by a drive on the part of a consumer to satisfy a need or a want. Moreover, public services often take the form of 'intangible' benefits, benefits that cannot be stored or even easily quantified (Cowell, 1984). The quality of nursing care is notoriously difficult to measure, although the quantity of care can be measured in terms of working hours, staff–patient ratios, etc. The quality of such services, and thereby their perceived value, are often inseparable from the attitudes and qualities of the people who provide them. They usually serve a social need, an issue which is explored in Chapter 12.

The issue of services marketing and the tangibility/intangibility relationship has been the subject of considerable debate in the marketing profession for some time. In any transaction, the benefit of any product or service includes a mixture of tangible and intangible elements which may be classified as falling within three dimensions:

1 The first is the *perceived benefit* of the product or service, the factor which creates the demand in the first place. This factor is often ignored but if buyers see no benefit in a particular product or service, they will not use it. It is the failure to recognise that there is no benefit that causes products and services to fail.

2 The second dimension is that of *tangibility*. Tangibility refers to factors about the transaction which have physical form, which can be seen and touched, which have dimension and some measurable quality.

3 The third dimension is *service*. This relates to issues involved in the transaction itself. It concerns psychological elements and what may be described as the 'halo effect'. However, in services marketing one has to differentiate between the core benefit service sought by the customer and the transactional service given in the course of delivering the core service.

As an example consider the case of an elderly person who makes use of the home help service. The three dimensions of the service can be analysed as shown in Fig. 10.4.

In the situation represented in Fig. 10.4, a number of issues are involved. First, the elderly person is very active in seeking home help because of the need to satisfy the basic needs of life, food and security. The supplier is often restricted because of budgetary constraints. Therefore there is potential for conflict in the relationship and rationing is likely. The user feels that there is a right of supply although the supplier cannot supply. Furthermore, the supplier can exert considerable power. In these circumstances the quality of provision (tangibility) can be poor and the psychological aspects of the transaction can also be poor, even though the user of the service may not openly express dissatisfaction. In this case the benefit dimension takes precedence over the other dimensions but at the same time, user satisfaction is low. Good marketing would mean that the supply organisation would attempt to ensure that both the tangibility and psychological dimensions were of high quality to overcome many of the potential causes of dissatisfaction present in this transaction.

Benefit

- Physical and psychological benefits of the core product or service
- The drive for purchase in the first place
- Relates to the core needs of food and security
- Help with food preparation, house cleaning and day-to-day care

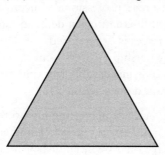

**Tangible factors of
the transaction**

- Quality of food
- Quality of cleaning
- Appearance of helper
- Punctuality of arrival
- Availability of helpers

**Psychological factors
in the transaction
('the halo effect')**

- Attitude of managers
- Attitude of home help
- Avoidance of conflict

Fig. 10.4 The three dimensions of 'service'

The analysis above relates to just one element of public provision, but it behoves anyone active in public services marketing to evaluate a particular product or service in relation to the buyer group being served. However the analysis does identify what are termed the marketing 'hygiene factors' and the marketing motivators. The hygiene factors are those aspects of a transaction that are the normal expectations of the buyer or user which, if not met, will lead to dissatisfaction. For example, if a person has a hospital appointment for 10.30 am, the normal expectation of that individual would be seen at 10.30. If the doctor sees the person at 11.30 then there will be dissatisfaction. Where an organisation is seeking efficiency, a queue will ensure that there are no gaps in the doctor's schedule, but there will be gaps in the patient's level of satisfaction. The marketing motivators are factors which are involved where more is given than expected. Identifying those factors is invariably specific to the product/user combination concerned.

The other issue identified in the above analysis is the fact that in services marketing, satisfaction is hard to measure and achieve. The following five factors have a bearing on this.

1 The *intangibility* of services. It is usually impossible to experience a service before it is actually bought.
2 The *inseparability* of the service from its delivery. It is rarely possible to separate the service provided from the person or people who provide it.
3 *Heterogeneity*, or lack of uniformity. It is virtually impossible to achieve a standardised level of service provision. As each individual is different, so each provider of a similar service is different.
4 *Perishability*. A service cannot readily be stored 'on the shelf' in the same way as goods. One crucial difference between goods marketing and service marketing involves the difficulties of synchronising supply and demand in service provision. It is usually more difficult, if not impossible, for a service to meet peaks of demand unless there is over-capacity. Recent drives for efficiency within the UK NHS have reduced spare capacity in the interests of controlling costs, but in such situations there will remain some doubt about the ability of a service to respond effectively if a major emergency arises. In the late 1990s there was widespread professional concern about the capacity of the health service to meet even normal fluctuations in demand especially during the winter, when peak demand for many services is experienced.
5 *Ownership*. The idea of ownership by users is much more difficult to apply to a service than to a product. If service is inseparable from the people that provide it, then questions of user capture are raised once again.

For these reasons, a growing body of marketing literature has been spelling out the message that services marketing has its own distinct characteristics and problems. Moreover, different service industries have their own, 'industry-specific' issues.

THE MOVE TO CUSTOMER ORIENTATION

The previous paragraphs point out that a shift to customer orientation requires an understanding of customer behaviour, which makes a key contribution to the design of innovative marketing plans and strategies. As a result, customer satisfaction becomes an important measure of quality performance.

In reality, the widespread use of the generic term 'customer' is not indicative of customer or indeed marketing orientation. What it does demonstrate is an unthinking application of a currently fashionable management concept that actually reduces customer satisfaction. For example, in the dash for privatisation, the railway companies became 'customer oriented'. Announcements took the form of, for example, 'We apologise to customers for the late arrival of their train'. Calling passengers 'customers' caused some real resentment, as was revealed in the considerable comment from both the media and the travelling public. Traditionally, railway customers were called 'passengers', that is, customers with particular needs that are determined by the benefit derived from using transport. All passengers are customers, but not all customers are passengers.

So-called customer orientation can also lead to the wrong group being identified as the primary customer, particularly in complex markets. A recent profile of a head teacher said that she 'called the parents customers'. Implicit in the identification of parents as primary customers is the view that the pupils are not 'customers', but are merely the raw material for processing, the outputs of the process being measured by school league tables. As discussed earlier, parents facilitate, and in some cases pay for, the education of the child, but the levels of satisfaction of the real primary customer, that is, the pupil, will also be revealed by many other indicators such as truancy levels. All pupils are customers but not all customers are pupils.

This lack of understanding of who are the customers and what consumer sovereignty means can be seen in the example of the Citizen's Charters in Exhibit 10.5.

MARKET SEGMENTATION

In the twentieth century, the idea of a mass society and a mass culture has often been associated with the idea of a homogenised, egalitarian and capitalist consumer society. When he was prime minister, John Major referred to his mission to create a 'classless society'.

Indeed many aspects of marketing in the past were concerned with mass markets for mass production. Herbert Marcuse (1964) argued that people in a capitalist society had become powerless within a system of false consumer needs, within a 'mass culture'. Conversely, Swingewood (1977) was highly critical of the myth which represents 'the masses' as a majority demanding uniform products and popular culture simply because some people believe that they have homogeneous patterns of consumption and 'low standards'.

One of the major tenets of public services provision is equality, whether of opportunity or outcome. Considerations of equality influence the managing of demand, as discussed earlier. Conversely, one of the major tenets of marketing is that all people are different and have different needs and that success in ensuring satisfied customers will be achieved by dividing up a homogeneous mass of people into groups which have similar needs.

This technique is called segmentation and it is in the application of this concept that

Exhibit 10.5

Citizen's Charters and consultation

The Citizen's Charter (1991) and the subsequent charters produced for a range of public services industries were intended to move organisations from a production orientation to a market orientation. The public services were to be more responsive to the wishes of their users. However, the Charters did not distinguish between different markets with different users having different needs.

The Patient's Charter issued by many hospitals gave patients the right to receive a full written response to a complaint within a specified time. The only respect in which such charters can only be regarded as good marketing practice is that they are likely to improve hospitals' understanding of their patients' behaviours, wants and needs. However, they can do little to improve the choices available to NHS patients, who are only able to choose an alternative medical service if they can afford to 'buy private health care'. The Patient's Charters can do little or nothing to improve the level of resources which the hospitals can afford to deploy, although they may help to improve the manner in which they do so. 'Rights', in this context, may be interpreted as procedures to deal with complaints, rather than as rights to choose treatment.

The best value regime in local government requires local authorities to consult their local community and to give local citizens a voice in determining the quality and type of service that they use. Consultation is taken to involve a full range of activities – listening to, talking to and acting on the public's wishes. It includes collecting opinions and views through market research and engaging with individuals and groups through more direct dialogue. Local authorities are 'learning to listen' and through that listening to be more responsible to the citizen's voice.

there is the greatest potential for resistance to marketing of public services. Despite the fact that only with effective segmentation will effective targeting be achieved, the idea of trying to satisfy all the needs of a population may remain attractive to the public services. Frequently, representatives of public services state that their mission is to provide services which satisfy as many people as possible. Even organisations which experience a 'natural' match between provision and demand try to broaden their scope of provision in order to attract more users. Resistance to segmentation from users arises from a public perception that the application of segmentation to public services may lead to the rationing of provision, whereas the same people will happily accept high levels of segmentation in their day-to-day transactions with commercial organisations.

The political dimension

Public services marketing cannot be separated from politics, and of all the factors influencing marketing policy, politics often has the greatest impact. Often this can mean that organisations become inward looking and upward looking and their managerial focus is on managing the political dimension at the expense of the needs of the primary user of the organisation or department. In private sector organisations such activities are often described derogatorily as 'politicking'.

In private sector organisations marketing has to work in an environment shaped by external and internal considerations. There is, first, a legislative framework relating to, for example health and safety and consumer protection. Some of the constraints imposed on organisations by legislation may often seem ludicrous but in many instances they are there to regulate unscrupulous (non-marketing-oriented) traders. Second, directors and managers of companies have corporate visions and missions which influence the direction of the organisation and hence the focus of its marketing.

In public services organisations these visions and missions are essentially political. Their influence on the direction of public services bodies is such that a change of political philosophy may lead to a complete change in marketing policy overnight. Two major factors have contributed, in recent years, to an increased political emphasis upon marketing principles.

First, there is obvious political capital to be made out of any initiative which pays at least lip-service to increasing the power of the individual, and the individual's influence upon exchanges. Hence most politicians are eager to be seen to be making public services more responsive to the wishes of their users, 'the people'. As a rallying cry 'the people', full of emotional resonance despite its vague, catch-all nature, is a very useful term for politicians trying to unite their followers, blur differences and attract as many votes as possible. The term has, therefore, overtones of populism (*see* Canovan, 1981), the political potential for representing the interests of 'the ordinary people'. As a marketing term, however, 'the people' has only a limited usefulness, as the above discussion of segmentation has illustrated.

The second factor is the connection between rising costs and a rise in prices. This connection is well established in the private sector. It is also entrenched in the public services market, largely as a consequence of service providers' aim to ensure fairness and to avoid cross-subsidy from one service to another.

In reality cost often bears little relationship to the perceived value of the good or service on offer and as a consequence pricing has become one of the most vexed questions in marketing. In the public services market the issue of price is further complicated by the facts that much of public services is publicly funded from taxation and that many services are free at the point of delivery. These are very significant issues, which differentiate public services marketing from private sector marketing.

To be successful, pricing must be market led rather than cost driven. The extent to which increases in an organisation's costs may be passed on to the consumer depends on the degree of competition, as reflected in the price elasticity of demand for its product. If buyer behaviour is price sensitive, cost-induced price increases will lead to a decline in revenue – unless they are counteracted by a change in the pattern of buyer preferences in favour of the product. Such change may reflect buyers' willingness to purchase larger volume, caused by, for example, an increase in disposable income, a relative increase in the price of competing products or a change in advertising/promotion. Price, as an element of an organisation's competitive strategy, is the one that competitors can most easily replicate. The use of non-price elements can therefore save organisations from the profit attrition resulting from overt price wars, particularly in oligopolistic markets where there is recognised interdependency between competitors. In such markets, the mutual interest of the competing parties lies in their differentiating their products, via promotion. Where they are able to create, among users, a perception of differentiated products, this can act as a barrier to competitive market entry.

CONCLUSIONS

More and more public services organisations are becoming aware of the need to employ marketing techniques as they seek to engage with their stakeholders on a long-term basis. We can summarise the key stages in the process of marketing as discussed in this chapter.

1 It is important that managers understand their own organisation's goals and objectives, underlying values and culture. These goals need to be translated into specific objectives and targets for individual units. At the same time managers need to understand how their freedom to select strategies to achieve those targets may be constrained by corporate objectives and/or corporate culture.

2 Managers need to develop a business strategy to achieve those targets, developed through a business plan which includes a marketing plan. The role of the marketing plan is to define the activities to be undertaken in order to manage the organisation–customer interface.

3 Marketing planning requires the defining of target customers, their specific needs, wants and expectations, and determining the viability of meeting those needs. Marketing planning identifies competitors and their strategies as well as the general marketing environment. This planning requires an understanding of how customers in the target groups choose between competing ways of meeting their needs.

4 The next step is designing a product or service which can be made and delivered at a cost which will enable customers to be charged a price at which they will 'buy' it in sufficient quantities to generate an acceptable payback to the organisation. The manager needs to:

   ● devise a way of making that product available to target customers which enhances its value in their eyes;
   ● employ a promotional strategy which informs customers of the product's existence and persuades them of the product's benefits;
   ● persuade customers that there are additional benefits to be gained from acquiring the product from his or her organisation rather than elsewhere.

5 The pay-off from marketing only occurs when the customer buys the product, uses the service, takes the desired action or accepts the promoted viewpoint. It is important to know who is in charge of selling and what the term means in this context.

6 Marketing does not end with the sale. What is promised must be delivered, and customers must be satisfied. To find out if this aim has been achieved requires market research.

Organisational competitive advantage is obtained by a continual review, at a number of levels, of the environment in which the organisation is working. Such a review must provide a complete picture of the needs, wants and expectations of the organisation's target customer groups. This involves not just market research and the setting up of control systems for planning purposes, but also the acquisition of information reflecting all aspects of the organisation's relationships with its various constituencies.

REFERENCES

Canovan, M (1981) *Populism*. London: Junction Books.

Chapman, D and Cowdell, T (1998) *New Public Sector Marketing*. London: Financial Times Pitman Publishing.

The Citizen's Charter: Raising the Standard (1991), Cm 1599. London: HMSO.

Cowell, D (1984) *The Marketing of Services*. London: Heinemann.

Kotler, P (1994) *Marketing Management: Analysis, Planning, Implementation and Control*. Englewood Cliffs, NJ: Prentice-Hall.

Marcuse, H (1964) *One-Dimensional Man*. London: Routledge & Kegan Paul.

Osborne, D and Gaebler, T (1993) *Reinventing Government: How the Entrepreneurial Spirit is Transforming the Public Sector*. Harmondsworth: Plume.

Swingewood, A (1977) *The Myth of Mass Culture*. London: Macmillan.

Theodossin, E (1986) *In Search of the Responsive College*. Bristol: Further Education Staff College.

QUESTIONS AND DISCUSSION TOPICS

1 What is the difference between a citizen and a customer, and how should this affect a marketing strategy for the public services?

2 Does the marketing of public services advantage the informed consumer over and above the inactive citizen?

11 Managing networks

Alan Lawton

AIMS

This chapter will:

- identify the nature of network relationships;
- investigate the challenges of managing across organisational boundaries;
- evaluate the significance of interorganisational management for public services management;
- identify the different forms that such relationships will take.

INTRODUCTION

This chapter examines the relationships that take place between the organisations that are involved in the formulation, delivery and monitoring of public services. These relationships are conducted through individuals and take many forms, which include:

- informal, personal, one-to-one relationships;
- partnerships between organisations such as that between a local authority and a voluntary organisation jointly managing a community centre;
- contractual relationships involving, for example, a hospital and a private cleaning firm;
- joint working forums involving multi-disciplinary teams in, for example, the preparation and delivery of community care plans.

Such relationships involve co-operation and collaboration and will take place between organisations of different standings and from different sectors. These relationships may be formal or informal, economic, legal or social in character. They may be continuous or intermittent, flexible or fixed.

Within the public services the analysis of organisational interactions becomes more complex when the delivery of services is carried out by voluntary or private sector organisations. The enabling role of local authorities, for example, encourages managers to look to other organisations to deliver services. At the same time, as managers are encouraged to refocus their activities towards the client, customer, citizen or consumer, new relationships also develop with a range of other public sector organisations, the voluntary sector and the private sector.

Public services are now delivered through a range of public, private and voluntary sector organisations either acting alone or as partners in a network of delivery agencies. The concept of, for example, the omnipotent local authority delivering a wide range of statutory services to a well-defined locality and clientele has become outdated. The UK local authority has lost control of further and higher education, has a more distant relationship with grant-maintained and locally managed schools, has little formal representation on local health authorities and is required by legislation to work with voluntary and private sector organisations in the delivery of many of the services it used to provide as a monopoly. In urban regeneration, economic development, health or welfare, the disaggregation of a single-organisation approach to public service delivery affords increased scope for innovative approaches to, for example, meeting community needs.

In a recent pamphlet, the prime minister outlined his vision for local government in the UK. This vision sees local government fulfilling a community leadership role, acting in partnership with a host of other organisations. He argues that:

> If local people are to enjoy a sound economy and a better quality of life and if communities are to deal with difficult cross-cutting issues like youth justice, drug abuse and social exclusion, we have to harness the contribution of businesses, public agencies, voluntary organisations and community groups and get them working to a common agenda (Blair, 1998, p 10).

However, this model of service delivery is not new, nor confined to one political party as the Single Regeneration Budget, described in Exhibit 11.1 indicates.

Exhibit 11.1

The single regeneration budget (SRB)

Successive UK governments have been keen to encourage economic regeneration and development and industrial competitiveness. The Conservative government of John Major sought to do this through fostering relationships between the statutory sector and the private and voluntary public sectors and local communities. To achieve this two linked measures came into effect from April 1994.

The first was a single network of government offices for the regions, replacing the regional offices of the Departments of Employment, the Environment (now DETR), Trade and Industry and Transport. The second measure was the creation of a single budget for regeneration.

The SRB requires that a variety of skills and energies are brought to bear to tackle local problems and exploit opportunities. The Budget supports action through partnerships. Local Authorities and Training and Enterprise Councils (TECs) will normally be key players in partnerships, as they are at the centre of regeneration and economic development activity in most areas. The aim is to support integrated partnerships bids in each area, which will break down the barriers between sectional interests, rather than a plethora of isolated projects. Successful bids have to demonstrate that a wide range of different organisations will work together in partnership.

The SRB is just one of the many activities in which the statutory sector is enjoined to work in partnership with other organisations. We investigate another example, that of community care, in some detail later in this chapter. The partnership approach has assumed increasing importance. Public sector organisations have always had to collaborate to deal with the 'messy' problems of, for example, crime or poverty. At the same time, the academic literature on networks has a long pedigree, going back to the 1970s (*see* Boje and

Whetten, 1981). However, a concern with partnerships and networks has achieved greater prominence in more recent years. One reason is undoubtedly political; successive Conservative governments were keen to reduce the size of the public sector and to stimulate alternatives to local authority provision. According to Ferlie and Pettigrew (1996), other reasons include:

- the greater emphasis on innovation and flexibility; opening up access to more sources of information;
- reducing market uncertainty through repeated transactions and the development of long-term relationships;
- adding value through joint projects;
- the growth in multinational organisations that cut across international boundaries.

Ferlie and Pettigrew argue that crude bargaining has been replaced by the building of co-operative relations, which might involve a social exchange of trust (*see* Chapter 15).

In other words, it is argued that hierarchy or markets are now supplemented by networks as a defining feature of public service structures; hierarchies are too rigid and markets are too brutal!

However, the challenge that managers face is how to manage these interactions through negotiation, bargaining, co-operation and control. Such a task is not easy. Policy issues rarely take heed of organisational, professional or geographical boundaries. Problems of co-ordination increase as different organisations pursue different goals and have different structures and cultures. As government departments are restructured into decentralised units, into cost centres, into agencies, into providers and purchasers, then the challenges of managing interactions increases.

We can distinguish between interorganisational relationships and intra-organisational relationships but such a distinction is becoming increasingly blurred as organisational boundaries become less clear. It may well be that the mode of the relationship is more important than where the agency is located. We are interested, then, in the nature of the Service Level Agreement (SLA) between the different departments or units within a local authority; the Framework Agreement between the civil service agency and its parent department; the quasi-contract between the purchaser and the provider of health care. The medium of exchange is important, as well as how it is managed.

According to Metcalfe and Richards (1990, p 220), 'Public management is getting things done through other organisations'. Metcalfe and Richards refer primarily to central government, but their words can be applied to other parts of the public services. In policy areas such as community care the voluntary sector is involved in providing a meals-on-wheels service or day care; the private sector is involved in the provision of homes for the elderly. One of the challenges for managers in local authority social services departments following the enactment of the National Health Service and Community Care Act 1990 has been to draw up contracts, specify targets and monitor the provision of services by organisations other than the local authority itself. Local authorities have been encouraged by central government to promote a mixed welfare provision. The relationships that local authorities have with different bodies vary. They may perhaps have close working relationships with a local health authority in the field of community care or information exchanges may characterise their relationship with European organisations. The local authority may be at the centre of a web of certain sets of relationships but at the periphery of others. For some local authorities, the scope of the web is ever widening. Benington and Harvey (1994, pp 27–8) describe the extent of local authority involvement in European networks and argue that:

> The emerging patterns of European policy-making often seem to involve a pluralistic melting pot of public, private, voluntary and community organisations and interest groups, drawn together in issue based rather than institution based policy arenas. Unfamiliar coalitions are merging, whereby a common interest is forged around a specific policy issue, between actors and organisations which traditionally have negotiated separately or even in opposition to each other.

They go on to argue that policy is now made through interlocking spheres as well as through the vertical tiers that characterise traditional central–local government relations built on a hierarchical model.

However, many of the key issues raised by hierarchical models of government still need to be addressed:

- Where is power and influence located?
- How is effective implementation assured?
- What is the role of the centre?
- Will all stakeholders have equal access?
- Where is accountability located?

We turn now to a discussion of the characteristics of these network relationships.

NETWORKS AND PARTNERSHIPS

The concept of a network of relationships, both personal and organisational, reflects interdependencies and also illustrates the complexity of such interdependencies. The concept of networks may therefore capture the complexity and uncertainty of management in the public services. Simple explanations of two-way relationships between, say, central and local government fail to capture this complexity. The traditional study of intergovernmental relations, which has tended to centre upon concepts of hierarchy and authority, has, according to Sharpe (1985, p 380), been replaced by:

> a more problematical model, derived from inter-organizational theory which sees the centre-to-periphery system as a network of actors, each with its own autonomy derived from different sources, through which the final outcomes is unlikely to correspond to legislative intention. Reciprocity and bargaining rather than hierarchy thus describe the way the service delivery system functions.

Network relations are more complex than a two-way flow of information or consultation. As described above, a network is a set of relationships that exist at different levels within and across organisations and involves both formal and informal channels. These relationships may be between individuals or groups and will change over time. A general definition is provided by Rhodes:

> The term 'network' describes the several interdependent actors involved in delivering services. These networks are made up of organizations which need to exchange resources (for example, money, authority, information, expertise) to achieve their objectives, to maximise their influence over outcomes, and to avoid becoming dependent on other players in the game (1997, p xii).

Participants in such networks will expect to gain some advantages from belonging to the network. Thus in the context of central–local government relations, central governments may wish to ensure stability and continuity in an uncertain world by engaging in a dialogue with local government. At the same time local authorities will expect to have their interests taken into account when policy is formulated or resources allocated. Such a relationship will also add legitimacy to the interests of local government, though such exchanges may not be equal. Indeed, one of the strengths of the power-dependency model of central–local government is the stress upon resources and their non-substitutability. Rhodes (1981) describes how relations between central and local government in the UK are characterised by bargaining over relevant resources. These resources include constitutional and legal, hierarchical, financial, political and information resources. According to Rhodes, central government has control over legislation, provides local authorities with finance, sets standards for and inspects some services and has a national electoral mandate. Local government in turn employs staff, has local knowledge and expertise, controls the implementation of policy, has the power to raise some finances and has a local electoral mandate. Central and local government manoeuvre for advantage, deploying their resources in such a way that dependence on the other 'player' is reduced. Although published in 1981, this analytical framework is still relevant.

Networks recognise the interests of different stakeholders. Networks exist within a context so that, for example, relationships between central government and subnational units of governance may be a preferred style of 'doing business'. According to Richardson and Jordan (1983) such a policy style can be characterised as 'bureaucratic accommodation', where bargaining and compromise are the tools of exchange. Such a style is consensus seeking; it enhances stability, it will continue over time and will be characterised by mutual adjustment rather than radical change.

The advantage of this approach over traditional centre–local relationships, according to Rhodes (1988), is that it illustrates the multiple, complex, dynamic and continuous character of centre–local relations. According to Rhodes, networks or communities can exist in a range of areas and may be bounded by policy, territory, issues, professions, intergovernmental associations or producer groups. For Rhodes, policy communities are based upon functional areas and are characterised by stable and continuous relationships between a restricted membership, vertical integration and interdependence and insulation from other networks – including the public.

Klijn (1997) understands policy communities as tightly integrated networks with 'dense' interactions between participants. Most authors emphasise the relatively closed nature of policy communities or subsystems. New actors can only enter this kind of network at a high cost to themselves. These costs are related to the investments required in order to learn the language and rules, establish patterns of relationships and offer advantages for one or more actors in the network.

The territorial community is similar to the policy community but is based upon a particular geographical location. Other networks differ in that they are less well integrated, with less interdependence, and movement between them is more fluid.

In his more recent work, Rhodes argues that, in the UK, local government has been transformed into a system of local governance embracing a range of different organisations involved in complex relations. Governance is about managing the networks through which these relationships take place. Rhodes (1996, p 663) argues that:

Interdependence, fragmentation, the limits to central authority, agency autonomy and attenuated accountability are all features of governance. Governance is relevant to British Government because self-organizing interorganizational networks are already part of the landscape of British Government.

Rhodes argues that this is all part of the 'hollowing out' of the state. Two strands can be identified; the first strand is that which sees public services cutting across organisational boundaries driven by legislation (as with the SRB), and which recognises that public policy cuts across organisational, professional or geographical boundaries. The second strand has been developed in the strategic management literature and is concerned with the benefits of strategic alliances.

In the private sector, networks are considered to be an ever-growing aspect of the business environment. Snow *et al.* (1992) argue that since the mid-1980s an organisational revolution has taken place whereby multi-level, vertically integrated hierarchies have given way to clusters of downsized, focused business units co-ordinated by market mechanisms. Strategic alliances allow access to new technologies or markets and encourage economies of scale through, for example, joint research, sharing risks or tapping into sources of know-how located outside the organisation (*see* Ring and Van de Ven, 1992). According to Snow *et al.* the move towards the business network is being driven by globalisation and technological change, by deregulation, by workforce demographics, and by advances in communications and computer technologies. They identify three different types of network.

1 *The internal network* is created to obtain market benefits without engaging in out-sourcing. It is characterised by a central unit establishing clear performance measures for each division so performance can legitimately be compared with that of outside suppliers. Each division has expertise in one particular area and co-operates with other divisions where appropriate. Some public sector organisations have established such networks, as, for example, in the creation of business units in the Next Steps agencies.

2 *The stable network* exists where assets are owned by several firms but all are dedicated to a particular business. A stable network may be dominated by one large core firm. A stable network spreads asset ownership and risk across independent firms. However, in bad times the core firm may have to protect the health of weaker members of the network. The benefits of stability are the dependability of supply or distribution as well as close co-operation on scheduling and quality requirements. The costs of stability are mutual dependence and some loss of flexibility.

3 *The dynamic network* is characterised by a small team of brokers at the centre which links together a host of specialist firms. Such networks run the risk of quality variation across firms, of needed expertise being temporarily unavailable and of possible exploitation of the network by those with control over knowledge or technology. The dynamic network works best in competitive situations where there are many players, each guided by market pressures to be reliable and to stay at the leading edge of its speciality.

THE COMMUNITY FOCUS

The concept of a network is a descriptive term covering a multiplicity of organisational linkages. Increasingly, public services managers are being encouraged to look outward to customers or clients or citizens and to engage in activities with the support of their local community. Whereas a network may not have a specific locality, many public services managers have responsibility for the delivery of services to a particular locality. The community focus is thus more bounded than a network would be and, because of this closeness, its characteristics may be different from those of a network.

The concept of community has a long pedigree in the social science literature. We are all familiar with concepts such as community care, community policing or the local business community. How is community defined? From the perspective of community studies we learn that the community may refer to interpersonal ties that exist outside the household; residence in a common locality; activities and sentiments expressing some sense of solidarity. There is a sense of social linkages binding people together. The focus is on the individual and on groups of individuals and the relationship between them. These relationships will hinge upon shared feelings of:

- a sense of belonging;
- a sense of solidarity;
- a sense of continuity over time;
- a sense that the community is one into which it is difficult for the outsider to enter.

A community may not have specific goals and may exist in and for its own sake rather than to serve particular purposes. There may also exist different communities within the same geographical location based around race or religion. What incentives are there for individuals to channel their special interests towards the common good? Supporters of community government argue, according to Hill (1994, p 3) that 'some concept of the community as the shared experience of place provides the justification of the locality as the arena for the exercise of citizenship'.

From this perspective, advocates and partnerships argue that membership provides opportunities to enhance participative democracy.

In contrast to the members of the private sector networks described by Snow *et al.*, the public services manager will not have a choice of entering or leaving the community in the same way that a private sector firm can enter or leave a particular market. An example of a public sector network is the community development programme, which has a long history in the UK, with local authorities engaging in support for community action, neighbourhood work, consultation exercises and, increasingly, Citizens' Panels.

CASE STUDY 11.1

Stakeholding as a concept has been used in strategic business analysis. It is particularly useful in a public services context, given the wide range of groups with interests, financial or otherwise, in those services.

THE PUBLIC SECTOR CAN OFFER COMPANIES LESSONS ON STAKEHOLDING

By Greg Parston

Stakeholding is not an academic theory or a political philosophy. Nor is it the limp thinking of some well-meaning executives. It is a social reality which managers cannot avoid.

Executives might have lessons to learn from an unexpected quarter: the public sector, where managers have had to respond to similar social change. John Plender's account of the phenomenon, A Stake in the Future, ascribes the rise of stakeholding to the uncertainties and inequalities of our age.

People no longer enjoy the security of employment that they once did. At the same time, economic growth has not had the beneficial trickle-down effects which many on the political right promised. The consequence is a demand from a growing population of unempowered workers for a greater stake in our prosperity and in their future.

But it would be wrong to see this simply as a rise in employee dissatisfaction. Paradoxically, in conditions of uncertainty and inequality, a relatively wealthier and better-informed public is placing other demands on business. Corporate decisions are more exposed than ever to wider public review and debate. Public perception that business has a responsibility to do more than just make money and minimise the darker side-effects of production is growing.

This is not just about directors' pay or employee empowerment, or even environmental sustainability. 'What is business doing for our community? For our schools? For our hospitals and elderly?' are questions more frequently asked of managers who in the past focused only on shareholders.

The consequence is a shift in managerial accountability. Shareholder value and customer service are no longer enough. Today's bottom line includes social as well as financial results, and these are not optional.

Public managers have faced similar change, but the other way round. Long held to account for producing goods for collective consumption, such as housing and healthcare, managers of public services have also had to take account of the demands of individuals. Monolithic public provision has proved inadequate. This focus on the consumer – as an addition to, not a substitute for, public good – lies at the heart of much public-sector reform.

How have public managers responded to these demands? Sometimes they have skewed the balance between customer satisfaction and public good, substituting the former for the latter and failing to deliver both. But at other times, more creatively, they have found new ways to involve stakeholders and to balance their often competing claims.

One example is in Milton Keynes, where police have forged a new partnership with local retailers, local authorities and other justice agencies to take on young shoplifters. The programme helps first-time offenders to address the reasons for and consequences of crime through informal meetings involving parents, shop managers, police officers and professionals from local agencies. The results have been impressive, with sharp reductions in re-offending.

Public-sector managers are having to balance accountability to individuals and to society – the real challenge of stakeholding. This is being done by building organisational understanding of the new complexities and then developing the capabilities to deliver. In Milton Keynes this has entailed an effort by the entire police force to strengthen the problem-solving capabilities of beat officers, as well as a performance management regime which makes community policing as important as arrest rates.

Successes in the public sector have also entailed working with others over whom one has little control. How do health managers hit targets for reduction of road traffic deaths? Not by building faster ambulances. Rather, by joining education, police and health promotion officials to design collaborative programmes focused on preventing road accidents in the first place.

Each organisation's performance is important, but often the results demanded by stakeholders require more than any one organisation can deliver. There is also a lesson in the continuing engagement in the public sector with all those making demands of services – politicians, the Treasury, citizens and customers. Some call this building social capital. But it is really a recognition that managing down in the organisation is insufficient; managing out and up are also essential. Stakeholders, too, must understand that there are demands other than their own; the management's job is to listen and to educate.

These lessons can help business leaders as they face their own accountabilities and search for new ways of managing.

Stakeholding is a recognition that in a society of globalisation and instant information, every one's business is every one's business. With this level of connectedness, we need to learn from everyone, too.

Source: Financial Times, 14 May 1997. Reprinted with permission.

Questions on the case study

1 What are the reasons for the rise in the 'stakeholder society'?

2 What does it mean for the public services manager?

3 How can the private sector learn from the public sector in this respect?

NETWORK CHARACTERISTICS

Let us now examine how the character of a network, including its location, access and resources, can affect the relationship between the various organisations in the network. We need to address a number of questions.

1 Why enter into relationships?
2 What resources are available?
3 What position is held in the network?
4 How easy is access?
5 How do members view each other?
6 What is to be gained by joining a network?

Why enter into relationships?

The impetus to enter networks may come from a number of different sources. In the first instance the organisation may have no choice. Central government agencies have to provide a Framework Document, agreed with the Minister, in order to be granted agency status; social services departments have to provide for a mixed type of welfare provision as stipulated in the National Health Service and Community Care Act 1990. The political impetus for this Act came from a belief in extending choices for the consumer or user. As well as being influenced by the political impetus, which may be expressed through legislation, organisations may wish to enter into relationships and arrangements with other organisations because they form part of a wider policy network. The police are, for example, part of a legal system that includes the courts, the Home Office and the prison and probation services, so that actions by one agency will impact upon the rest of the system. Thus the increased use of cautions for certain types of offenders by the police may result in a different balance of cases being heard in the magistrates' courts, a different pattern of referral to higher courts and variations in the processing time of courts which in turn will affect the prison population – since approximately 20 per cent of the prison population are on remand.

It may be necessary to enter into relationships with others if one organisation does not possess the necessary resources of finance, skill or information to deliver a service itself. An organisation may decide that its goals are best achieved with the assistance of other organisations. This will be easier to achieve if other organisations share a common set of values and purposes. An advocate of community policing, former Chief Constable John Alderson, assumed that individuals would acknowledge some sense of shared community values and that the key to effective policing is the consent of the community, leading to public support and co-operation (*see* Alderson, 1984).

However, voluntary organisations may seek some safeguards that will protect their freedom to act and to retain their independence. A voluntary organisation may believe that it can play a larger role in the community if it enters into an agreement with a social services department to provide care in the community. This may, however, compromise its traditional role of advocacy and its ability to involve those people whom statutory agencies fail to reach. The voluntary sector's capacity for innovation, diversity and responsiveness may be curtailed if it enters into close agreements with the statutory sector.

What resources are available?

Resources include expertise and information, human resources and time, as well as financial resources. One group may come to dominate a network because of a concentration of information and expertise. At the same time, reciprocity is easier if such resources are evenly spread. An organisational asset that is much undervalued is that of time. The time that an individual or group can devote to participating in the network and building relationships will determine what can be contributed to, and what can be gained from, network participation. An organisation must invest scarce resources and energy when, often, the potential returns are not always easy to determine.

What position is held in the network?

The more central the position in the network the more important the member of the network. One key factor is control over resources. A position of centrality may allow greater control over other members of the network. The central actor may also be performing a different role from that of other members in the network. Public services in the UK have been encouraged to separate the strategy-making core from the service-delivery periphery. Next Steps agencies are an example of this, in which the parent department is identified as the strategic decision maker and the agency its implementer.

How easy is access?

Does each member in the network have access to other members or are internal communications screened through the centre? Information is a key network currency. Another network currency is trust, that is, are the members open in their dealings with each other?

We might also wish to know how easy it is for other groups to break into the network. The tighter the network in terms of size, geography or policy area, the more the network will come to have the characteristics of a community, as discussed above.

How do members view each other?

Perceptions of who is important, how the different groups and individuals view each other, and the extent of the perceived importance are crucial. Central actors may be perceived to have greater potential for mobilising resources controlled by others. At the same time respect for, and an appreciation of, other members' qualities will enhance co-operation.

Different members of the network may also have different perceptions of the purposes of the network or the problems that networks are set up to resolve. Indeed, there may be different perceptions concerning what problems exist, let alone their solutions (*see* Termeer and Koppenjan, 1997).

What is to be gained by joining a network?

Presumably, groups and individuals enter networks to gain some benefits either in the short or long term. What does a group give up in order to benefit from network participation? It may mean giving up some autonomy but perceived long-term advantages may outweigh short-term considerations. Oliver (1991, p 945) found that 'The propensity for organizations to enter into relationships with one another was shown to be unrelated to the degree of commitment or loss of autonomy required by these relationships'. Organisational legitimacy or the reduction of uncertainty, say over future funding, may offset any perceived loss of autonomy.

MANAGING INTERORGANISATIONAL RELATIONSHIPS

The delivery of public services through networks poses new challenges for the manager. Management activities are directed towards improving and sustaining interaction between the different actors involved and uniting the goals and approaches of the various actors. Kickert and Koppenjan (1997, p 44) define network management as 'promoting the mutual adjustment of the behaviour of actors with diverse objectives and ambitions with regard to tackling problems within a given framework of interorganisational relationships'.

Managing across jurisdictions

Chapter 1 sets out the broad context of public services management including the legal and constitutional aspects of managing in the public services and Chapter 5 examines accountability. Organisations have legitimate interests and expect to have their autonomy respected. Different definitions of the proper remit of public service activities are held by different agencies. Management under such circumstances requires the ability to balance both the goals of the individual organisation and those of the network as a whole. The manager needs to recognise that members of a network in the public services may represent separate and distinct legal entities with different systems of accountability.

Managing different stakeholders

Public services management has a distinctive political component. This entails recognising the political nature of the enterprise and involving politicians as well as officials. Managers in local government, for example, have to balance their legal duties to the council as a whole with the political reality of their relations with the majority party. The different concerns of the different stakeholders have to be recognised, as well as the managers' legitimate fear of losing autonomy. We can identify the different stakeholder interests as shown in Fig. 11.1. Thus, where a key stakeholder is antagonistic to a particular issue – located in the top right-hand section of the figure – then that stakeholder will have to be won over.

Common interests need to be identified and perceived as being more important than conflicting interests. Managing stakeholder interests means enforcing commitments across organisational boundaries.

Managing implementation

The operational component of management involves overcoming the problems associated with organisation, planning and services delivery, for example, bringing together different specialists and specialisms to create a base of common information, standards, monitoring and so on, and to overcome differences in organisational design and structure. At the same

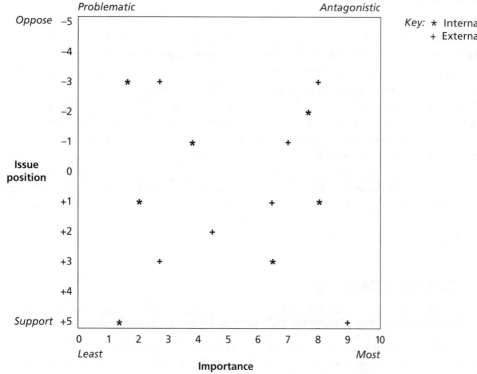

Fig. 11.1 Classifying stakeholders

Source: Based on Backoff and Nutt (1989).

time, mechanisms for joint planning or provision cannot be created without agreed objectives and the will to carry them out.

Managing the exchanges

Problem solving across organisations involves identifying perceptions of similarities and common concerns, relatively open exchange of information, and searching for and selecting alternatives that benefit the largest number of parties. It means respecting confidences and building trust. In the first instance, if trust and goodwill do not exist joint venture agreements specifying the rights and obligations of the different parties may have to be signed.

Managing incrementally

Management within traditional bureaucracies is defined by systems of hierarchy and authority, by the specification of tasks and control processes, all bounded by rules. Managing across organisations is concerned with bargaining and negotiation in which different parties seek to maximise their gains through negotiation and mutual accommodation and to avoid mutually damaging behaviour.

Managing negotiations

Successful negotiation depends upon trust, openness, mutual respect, an ability to take the longer-term view. Clarity is required in terms of who should do what, in what order and by when, and procedures for representation, reporting back, and decision making.

Negotiation requires the parties involved to find out who they are dealing with, what kinds of behaviour to expect, what customs, traditions and values apply. Agreement must be sought in relation to targets and points of likely resistance, the roles of the participants, for example, spokesperson, recorder, information supplier, how these roles will be played, participants' expectations and approach. Negotiators need to consider as wide a range of potential outcomes as possible, and to seek areas where agreement may be achieved.

A skilled negotiator plans a strategy; is clear about the process; uses resources – people, information and environment; tries to see the process through the eyes of the other party; flags intentions and is open about motives; listens more than talks, and asks questions; seeks clarification and understanding; summarises; has a long-term vision which allows for both parties to reach a mutually acceptable agreement.

CASE STUDY 11.2

COMMUNITY CARE

The Griffiths Report, *Community Care: Agenda for Action* (1988) paved the way for the National Health Service and Community Care Act 1990. The main recommendations of the Griffiths Report included:

- Primary responsibility for community care should lie with local authorities.
- Collaboration between local authorities and the health service should precede the presentation of plans to the minister for community care.
- Local authority social service departments should be reoriented towards the design and co-ordination of packages of care largely provided by others.

The report suggested that a mixed type of provision should be encouraged in which agencies from the private and voluntary sectors actually provide the service. The local authority was to act as an enabling authority with a remit to set local priorities, design individual packages of care, arrange delivery and make maximum use of other agencies. The principles of the Griffiths Report were endorsed by the Conservative government in so far as it believed that such an approach would encourage consumer choice and flexibility, stimulate competition and improve efficiency and effectiveness in service delivery.

However, the concept of community care is open to interpretation. Different groups may have different perceptions, so that we might find a definition of health care that is in competition with social care. Where are the boundaries between them? A further problem is that the concept of community care assumes that there is something called the community. It may well be that some areas or neighbourhoods are more sympathetic to, say, the disabled than others. This is an important consideration if the aim of community care is to integrate individuals into the community.

Not all local authorities support the idea of an enabling authority. For political or ideological reasons some authorities do not see their role in this way. Similarly, what happens if there is no agency in the private or voluntary sector willing to undertake the work? The assumption is that there are a host of agencies that are able and willing to provide the service. However, the voluntary sector may cherish its advocacy role and may be unwilling to become involved in large-scale service delivery. At the same time, the private sector may find providing residential care for the elderly attractive but be less interested in providing services for highly dependent people.

The proposals also required a profound shift from services-led delivery to needs-led delivery, needs which are notoriously difficult to define. However, to implement community care local authorities have had to:

- stimulate a mixed delivery of care;
- introduce competitive tendering and contracting out;
- introduce cost-centre management and devolved budgeting;
- introduce resource management systems;
- separate the purchase from the supply of services;
- establish key indictors and performance measurement.

Community care also has an impact on the roles of professionals in so far as new skills need to be developed: new skills of management by the medical profession, new skills of contract management by local authority officers and new skills of collaboration by all concerned. At the same time, service users and informal carers need to be articulate in their demands to ensure full use is made of consultation.

Joint planning and action is crucial. Does it exist already, is there a tradition of working together? At what stage should the voluntary sector be involved? At the very least we should expect there to be agreement on common goals, on defining needs, on priorities and on the implementation of a common strategy. Success depends upon the interorganisational production of community care plans and the interprofessional production of individual care packages. It is necessary to ask how local authorities and health authorities collect, share and agree upon basic information such as demography, dependency characteristics and the scale and scope of needs within geographical areas, particularly if there is no tradition of interagency collaboration. The vehicle that drives the partnership approach must include trust, commitment and common goals.

The underlying philosophy which local authorities have adopted in their community care strategies include the principles of:

- giving individuals the maximum possible independence and quality of life;
- enabling people to achieve their full potential;
- giving individuals a greater choice and a greater say in the services they need;
- recognising the role taken by carers;
- increasing access for all groups with no discrimination.

These principles may be reflected by an approach whereby provision is planned in consultation with users, carers and providers on the basis of clear evidence of assessed need. People may be encouraged to live in their own homes, reducing the need for long-term hospital or residential care.

Community care requires interagency collaboration. Roles and responsibilities need to be clarified, there must be agreement on needs, unnecessary duplication must be avoided and there may be a clear separation between purchaser and provider.

The independent sector is often tied in to agency agreements and to contract specifications with appropriate quality standards. Service-level agreements are used with in-house service providers. The relationship with the health authorities may be more problematic but jointly agreed criteria for access to health and social care services are being developed. Joint information systems will be needed. In some cases agreements between local authorities and health authorities are statements of intent. In other cases local authorities have good working relationships with the health authority and joint arrangements are in place and working.

The onus is upon the local authority to encourage choice in pursuing a mixed economy of care. A major issue is how this is to be achieved. The voluntary sector may not wish to enter into contract agreements; the private sector may need incentives to provide other than residential care. Some local authorities give financial support to national voluntary organisations which are active locally. Other local authorities provide 'seed corn' funding to encourage voluntary sector provision and provide information to, and advocacy for, groups; others continue providing support to voluntary organisations which provide holiday schemes and evening and weekend leisure facilities.

The challenge for managers

Managing through networks or partnerships is different from managing through traditional hierarchies and requires managers to develop new skills. Managers will have to find ways of dealing with the following issues:

1 Reconciling competing values and definitions. Not only will different stakeholders have different sets of values but they may define community care in different ways.

2 Finding agreements on common values, principles and responsibilities. The user needs to know who is providing what.

3 Recognising competing jurisdictions, both organisational and professional. Professionals are notoriously territorial and it will not be easy for some to give up responsibility for the delivery of services, and the definition of needs, to others.

4 Compensating for loss of autonomy. Voluntary organisations may be unwilling to enter into formal contractual arrangements with the local authority which they may see as constraints upon the advocacy role of the voluntary sector.

5 Creating commitment to a common policy through co-operation, trust and openness. This may not be easy if previous relationships between different organisations have not been harmonious.

6 Developing competences for managing across organisational boundaries. Managers will need to develop skills in negotiation, bargaining and communication, as well as skills in drafting contracts and monitoring them.

7 Solving the operational problems. Appropriate structures will need to be put in place such as joint working groups. However, putting in place new structures will not be sufficient; there will need to be commitment by all the parties involved to making them work.

The challenges of joint working

Wistow (1992) argues that joint working of all kinds had been a major disappointment in community care. He puts forward seven learning points:

1 *Structure* – there has been an over-emphasis upon structure at the expense of processes and results. Structures are not ends in themselves but serve ends.

2 *Planning orientation* – planning processes have tended to be dominated by resource inputs and intermediate outputs rather than achieving specified outcomes for users.

3 *Scope* – project-based working has been more successful than comprehensive planning.

4 *Skill base* – networking and interpersonal skills are important. At the same time, hard-nosed bargaining and negotiation skills may be more important than 'idealistic' commitments to joint working.

5 *Multidisciplinary working* – professionals have often worked alongside rather than with each other. Integrated assessment and care packages have been slow to develop.

6 *Financial incentives* – joint finance can bring agencies together, but financial mechanisms will be most powerful where rewards are provided only for demonstrable performance.

7 *Involving the voluntary sector* – the formal involvement of the voluntary sector in joint planning has had mixed results. Voluntary sector contributions need to be supported and resourced.

However, Wistow considers the most important considerations to be concerned with *accountability* and *resources*. There must be mechanisms in place that hold to account the principal actors in joint planning. There must also be in place a resource regime which combines resource adequacy with transition/bridging funds and incentives geared to policy objectives for users and carers. According to Wistow, the way forward is to develop early a clear agenda of realistic and achievable targets and to disseminate existing examples of joint working and establish pilot projects in areas where experience is limited. The building blocks of multi-agency working, through the joint determination of values, principles and service objectives, will need to be put in place. Wistow also argues that managers will need to think through the implications of purchaser/provider splits and examine possibilities of joint purchasing and to recognise that community care needs to be seen as a core and not a marginal activity.

Questions on the case study

1 What appear to be the major problems in implementing community care?

2 How can the demands of different stakeholders be reconciled?

Many of the lessons that Wistow points to are valuable for any organisations involved in the joint delivery of services or products. Finally, Kernaghan (1993, p 61) links partnerships to empowerment: 'the broad working definition of a partnership used here is a relationship involving *the sharing of power, work, support and/or information* with others for the achievement of joint goals and/or mutual benefits'. Government officials cannot simply give up power to outsiders; they must ensure that they have the authority to do so and that there is adequate accountability for results.

Kernaghan puts forward a number of propositions concerning the requirements for successful partnerships;

1 A partnership must include all stakeholders whose contribution is necessary for achieving the partnerships goals.
2 The greater the degree of mutual dependence between/among the partners, the greater the probability that the partnership will be effective and enduring.
3 The greater the degree to which the individuals, groups and organisations are empowered by a partnership, the greater the probability that it will be effective and enduring.
4 The pooling of resources in a partnership will have a synergistic effect in that the combined impact will be greater than the sum of the efforts of each partner acting alone.
5 A partnership with limited objectives is easier to develop and maintain than one with broad objectives.
6 The more formalised a partnership is, the more likely it is to be maintained.

CONCLUSIONS

For alliances to be successful they require more than formal systems. They also require interpersonal connections and internal infrastructures that facilitate learning. According to Kanter (1994) collaboration is about creating new value together, rather than mere exchange – which is about getting something back for what you put in. Kanter uses the metaphor of the marriage and argues that relationships between companies begin, grow and develop or fail, much like a marriage. To pursue the marriage metaphor, many people enter into marriage knowing that the chances of success are low. Successful partnerships require a commitment on the part of talented managers to make them work. Kanter provides a framework for success (*see* Exhibit 11.2).

However, problems are often best solved at the level at which they are most salient. In the community care example it may well be that there are excellent relationships at the point of delivery between the social worker and the health visitor. It may be that any problems that arise in working together arise higher up the organisation where senior managers and professionals may be protective of budgets or professional territories.

Waddock (1991, p 507) argues that:

> If a narrow and technically oriented problem is attacked by a group of high-level executives (institutional managers), it will become extremely difficult to sustain partners' interest in the problem. Such executives may have neither the expertise in solving the problem that is needed nor the time or interest to deal with it because other concerns more related to their job focus their attention elsewhere. In contrast, if technical-level managers attempt to resolve a broad-based societal problem, they may not be able to muster the necessary organizational resources to make decisions needed to actually deal with the problem. They will not have the necessary power to commit their organizations to action. As a result, they will be ineffectual in their efforts to bring about changes because they will lack an adequate power base.

Exhibit 11.2

Eight 'I's that create successful 'We's

1 *Individual Excellence* – both partners are strong and have something to contribute.
2 *Importance* – partners enter into the relationship in order to fulfil long-term strategic goals.
3 *Interdependence* – the partners need each other to accomplish what they cannot accomplish alone.
4 *Investment* – the partners are prepared to invest resources, including finance, to demonstrate commitment to the relationship.
5 *Information* – communication is open and information is shared.
6 *Integration* – linkages are developed at different levels within the organisation.
7 *Institutionalisation* – the relationship has a formal status, including role responsibilities and clear decision processes.
8 *Integrity* – mutual trust is generated as partners behave towards each other with integrity.

Source: Kanter (1994).

In recognising the attractiveness of partnerships and networks as a solution for problems and policies that cut across organisational boundaries, we should not underestimate the challenges involved in making such partnerships or networks work.

REFERENCES

Alderson, J (1984) *Law and Disorder*. London: Hamish Hamilton.

Backoff, R W and Nutt, P C (1989) 'A process for strategic management with specific application for the non-profit organisation' in Bryson, J M and Einsweiler, R C (eds) *Strategic Planning*. Chicago: Planners Press.

Benington, J and Harvey, J (1994) 'Spheres or Tiers? The significance of transnational local authority networks', *Local Government Policy Making*, 20(5), pp 21–30.

Blair, T (1998) *Leading the Way: a new vision for local government*. London: Institute for Public Policy Research.

Boje, D M and Whetten, D A (1981) 'Effects of organizational strategies and contextual constraints on centrality and attributions of influence in interorganizational networks', *Administrative Science Quarterly*, 26, pp 378–95.

Ferlie, E and Pettigrew, A (1996) 'Managing through networks: some issues and implications for the NHS', *British Journal of Management*, 7 (Special Issue, March), pp S81–S99 .

Griffiths, Sir Roy (1988) *Community Care: Agenda for Action; A Report to the Secretary of State for Social Services*. London: HMSO.

Hill, D M (1994) *Citizens and Cities: Urban Policy in the 1990s*. Hemel Hempstead, Herts: Harvester Wheatsheaf.

Kanter, RM (1994) 'Collaborative advantage: The art of alliances', *Harvard Business Review*, July–August, pp 96–108.

Kernaghan, K (1993) 'Partnership and public administration: conceptual and practical considerations', *Canadian Public Administration*, 36(1), pp 57–76.

Kickert, W J M and Koppenjan, J F M (1997) 'Public management and network management: An overview' in Kickert, W J M, Klijn, E-H and Koppenjan, JFM (eds) *Managing Complex Networks: Strategies for the Public Sector*. London: Sage.

Klijn, E-H (1997) 'Policy networks: An overview' in Kickert, W J M *et al*. (1997).

Metcalfe, L and Richards, S (1990) *Improved Public Management*, revised edn. London: Sage.

Oliver, C (1991) 'Network relations and loss of organisational autonomy', *Human Relations*, 44(9), pp 943–61.

Rhodes, R A W (1981) *Control and Power in Central–Local Relations*. Aldershot: Gower.

Rhodes, R A W (1988) *Beyond Westminster and Whitehall*. London: Unwin Hyman.

Rhodes, R A W (1996) 'The new governance: governing without government', *Political Studies*, 44, pp 652–67.

Rhodes, R A W (1997) 'Foreword' to Kickert, W J M *et al*. (1997).

Richardson, J J and Jordan, A G (1983) 'Overcrowded policy-making: Some British and European reflections', *Policy Sciences,* 15, pp 247–68.

Ring, P S and Van de Ven A H (1992) 'Structuring cooperative relationships between organizations', *Strategic Management Journal,* 13, pp 483–98.

Sharpe, L J (1985) 'Central co-ordination and the policy network', *Political Studies,* 33, pp 361–81.

Snow, C C, Miles, R E and Coleman, H J (1992) 'Managing 21st-century organizations', *Organizational Dynamics,* Winter.

Termeer, C J A M and Koppenjan, J F M (1997) 'Managing perceptions in networks' in Kickert, W J M *et al.* (1997).

Waddock, S A (1991) 'A typology of social partnership organizations', *Administration and Society,* 22(4), pp 480–515.

Wistow, G (1992) 'Working together in a new policy concept', *Health Services Management,* February, pp 25–8.

QUESTIONS AND DISCUSSION TOPICS

1 What other examples can you give of public services being delivered through partnerships?

2 What are the advantages of delivering services through partnerships?

12 Managing performance

Jacky Holloway

AIMS

This chapter will:

- introduce the reader to the increasing importance of performance management in public services, in terms of both generic and more distinctive aspects;
- demonstrate the need for both qualitative and quantitative forms of assessment in performance management on a range of dimensions;
- take a closer look at some management practices which enable managers to meet stakeholder needs;
- make links between the performance of the whole organisation and of suborganisational levels such as departments, and relate these to the wider context.

INTRODUCTION

The first section of this chapter presents current thinking about the design of 'good' performance indicators, set in the context of the growth of performance management from the early 1980s. The next section traces the development of a simple model in which performance indicators and measures contribute to an everyday process of service delivery. The final section raises a few of the more challenging issues which have to be addressed by managers when they seek to change performance (usually for the better) in complex situations where they cannot always assume that all stakeholders agree on priorities and the impact of taking controlling action cannot always be predicted.

There are perhaps two overriding themes to Chapter 12. First, public service bodies are like all other organisations in that they are complex systems existing in environments which often exert unpredictable influences on the system. So performance management systems generally need to be flexible and robust, and in public services they also need to be tailored to the distinctive characteristics of those services. Second, the activities which managers of public services undertake to measure and manage performance have a great deal in common with the activities of their private services peers, and both can learn from each other. Performance management today is an essential part of 'normal' management.

WHY WORRY ABOUT MANAGING PERFORMANCE?

During the late 1980s and 1990s, 'performance management' has grown in importance to become the subject of countless seminars and courses, books and articles in both the popular and more academic management literature. Perhaps unusually for a management trend, this one appears to have reached the public sector at the same time as its rise to prominence in commercial organisations (although it has impinged on most voluntary and charitable organisations somewhat later). This 'wave of performance assessment' in public services (Pollitt, 1986) has washed over many European countries and beyond, providing opportunities for managers to compare experiences and commiserate over what some may perceive as a diversion of their efforts from their 'real' work, for uncertain benefits. Yet surely managing performance is what managers do all the time anyway, by allocating resources, participating in decision processes, planning and controlling. It could be asked why 'performance management' should be selected for special attention.

There are many examples of service improvements which would probably not have occurred without this shift in emphasis, but there have also been some negative effects. Later in this chapter we will explore the potential for poorly designed performance management systems to have negative impacts at the organisational level and to be of little or no benefit to 'customers', but it is worth noting here some of the effects on managers themselves. Naturally it has been stressful for managers to introduce new working practices to measure performance and be more responsive to customers (internal as well as external), despite generally receiving no additional resources to facilitate implementation (McKevitt and Lawton, 1996). However the negative impact on middle and junior managers in particular has been compounded by a tendency in many public services organisations to impose performance measurement systems from top management down, with the apparent aim of increasing their control (often in conjunction with politicians). Where commitment to such systems is not fully shared by those who have to implement them, because managers have not participated in their design, they are unlikely to work effectively.

The emphasis in the late 1990s is particularly on comparisons: within and between industrial sectors, and within and between countries. The practice of comparing can lead to shared learning, or, conversely, to the attribution of blame. Although we would generally acknowledge that external political, social and economic factors can affect organisational performance regardless of how hard the employees work and how skilfully they are managed, today attention often turns to management practice. The focus of this chapter will therefore be mainly on how managers in complex organisational settings can work with colleagues and other stakeholders to measure and improve performance, while retaining some control over the process. Exhibit 12.1 illustrates the widespread adoption of performance management in continental Europe.

SOME DEFINITIONS

We have suggested above that efforts to improve performance at the level of professional and functional specialisms have not necessarily led to organisational success. If they had been fully effective, government departments would not still be increasing the levels of inspection and reporting for health services and schools, and publishing league tables to

Exhibit 12.1

Performance management in Europe

The changing context in which public services managers work is to be found far beyond the United Kingdom. Flynn and Strehl (1996) examined the ways in which the managerialism flowing from the 'new public management' style of reforms (Hood, 1995) had been implemented in Germany, Austria, Switzerland, the Netherlands, the United Kingdom, Sweden and France. Although there were some strong differences, reflecting for example national cultures and legal and government structures, Flynn and Strehl (1996, p 12) observed a common strand:

> In all the states we examined there have been attempts to redirect managerial effort from conformance to performance. This necessitates several changes in the way in which organizations work. There needs to be a process in which the purposes of the organizations are agreed and their activities and products are defined and measured. Once this has been achieved, there have to be ways of ensuring that they achieve an agreed level of output. This implies that people managing units of the organization are able to organize themselves to make an efficient use of resources, will be committed to the targets and will have a reason for achieving results. This is a different managerial task from complying with laws, legal norms and calculable rules.

Their study identified a variety of ways in which the sample countries were attempting to define and agree the expected performances, reflecting their varied administrative structures. It also revealed problems – in defining objectives clearly enough to enable their achievement to be measured, in developing rewards and sanctions which would encourage the attainment of targets, in turning the 'rhetoric of output orientation' (p 13) into reality in the face of financial constraints, for example. In spite of the ethos of greater public accountability and customer orientation, targets were still set 'without reference to the citizens or customers of the services' (*ibid.*). However, from their detailed case studies Flynn and Strehl concluded that they had observed some significant types of changes.

> Whatever the difficulties, real efforts are being made to guide or steer public sector organizations, rather than simply make them conform to legal norms and rules of behaviour. (*ibid.*)

The notion of using performance management to steer public services organisations is an underlying theme in this chapter.

bring 'poor performers' to public attention. Instead organisations would be trusted to monitor and control the adequacy of their performance, and their 'market share' would reflect the quality of their services, the value for money they offer and the extent to which they meet customers' needs.

Clearly the introduction of quasi-markets in public services has not brought an end to unacceptable variations in performance. Maybe there are not only performance problems, but performance measurement problems, indicating that the measurement and management of organisational performance needs to be examined in its own right.

First, we should be clear about what we mean by performance management. At its broadest, performance management can be defined as the managerial work needed to ensure that the organisation's top-level aims (sometimes expressed as 'Vision' and 'Mission' statements) and objectives are attained. Usually this will require realistic time periods for their attainment, and the identification of sub-objectives and tasks which in turn have to be attained in a controlled way, contributing in a tangible way to top-level objectives.

Whether we focus on attainment of strategic or shorter-term objectives, we need to assess performance on a number of dimensions, or aspects, of performance. Of key concern is the effectiveness of the organisation and its activities: the dimension of performance referring to the relationship between the final results of the organisation's activities, and its objectives. Are people at all levels in the organisation 'doing the right things', so that desirable short- and long-term outcomes occur? As we will see later, effectiveness can be hard to assess or measure but many people feel that it is the most important dimension of organisational performance.

Performance management requires performance measurement, but these are not the same thing! Measurement is part of a control process leading to actions in the light of the findings. (We will return to the subject of control later.) As well as measuring whether objectives are being attained through the right things being done, we may be concerned with how well activities are being performed. Are people 'doing things right', particularly in terms of efficiency? This dimension of performance – defined in a technical sense as the ratio of inputs to outputs – has sometimes been regarded as synonymous with performance, particularly in public services. Pressure to measure and improve efficiency tended to dominate UK public policy in the 1980s, for instance through the 'Rayner scrutinies' of central government departments and 'value for money' studies in a number of public services. Metcalfe and Richards (1990) provide a full discussion of these policies. Although performance measurement can be a 'neutral' management activity leading to benefits for all of the organisation's stakeholders, this emphasis on efficiency at the expense of other important dimensions has contributed to the negative connotations which performance measurement sometimes holds.

You may have seen references to the 'three Es' of performance measurement. Generally this triumvirate comprises effectiveness, efficiency and economy. The last of these basically involves minimising inputs, doing things as cheaply as possible. Fortunately today this is rarely seen as an adequate basis on which to judge organisational performance, although an awareness of costs of inputs is clearly needed for effective decision making.

In the context of public management, a fourth 'E', equity, is often added to the dimensions of performance which deserve explicit attention. The principle of providing equal access to services of appropriate quality, for all people with equal needs, is enshrined in most public and charitable services. A public service which was inequitable would be unlikely to be achieving its objectives, of course, so to a large extent addressing effectiveness should also ensure equity. However, the fundamental importance of this principle, cases combined with the challenges of measuring and improving equity have led to its treatment as a separate dimension. We examine these issues in Exhibit 12.2.

We are now able to start to build a picture of some of the factors which the designers of performance management systems need to be aware of. Most of these factors are generic, relevant to all sorts of organisations with diverse sets of stakeholders. The multidimensional nature of organisational performance needs to be addressed, so that measures and indicators related to all important dimensions or aspects of performance – efficiency, effectiveness and so on – are incorporated. We will consider the use and measurement of various dimensions of performance in public service performance management in more detail below.

WHAT MAKES A *GOOD* PERFORMANCE INDICATOR?

This chapter is concerned with performance management, and we would counsel against equating this with performance indicators (PIs) which, as noted above, have been the focus of effort in some public services since the 1980s. On the other hand, properly designed PIs

Exhibit 12.2

Crossways Arts Centre

Crossways Arts Centre is an inner city theatre and art gallery owned by the local authority and run by a manager and small number of staff, assisted by volunteers. It provides a venue for repertory theatre companies, comedy acts, concerts and exhibitions of painting, photography and sculpture often by local artists. Among its objectives are to increase access to the arts for people who have not traditionally been theatre-goers or visitors to art galleries, particularly young people and those from ethnic minority groups.

Under increasing pressure to reduce the subsidy needed by the Arts Centre each year, or at least to be able to justify it to the local taxpayers and auditors, the local authority has asked the manager to provide a business plan and set of performance indicators for the coming season. The Director of Arts and Leisure suggests that a key indicator could be staff salary costs – which should preferably be lower than this season, through the greater use of volunteers.

Naturally the manager and staff are not happy with this emphasis on economy! They suggest that the set of indicators should give equal emphasis to the other three Es, for example:

● ratio of fixed to variable costs (an efficiency measure, which could also reflect on the efficiency of the local authority as the owners of the building);
● percentage of users from 'target' groups – people under 21, and people with ethnic minority origins (a measure of effectiveness);
● level of subsidy per seat sold, which should be comparable to subsidies for seats in venues in similar locations elsewhere, and to subsidies for other venues run by the local authority (a measure of equity).

The Director of Arts and Leisure accepts these proposals provided that the data will not cost the staff additional money to collect, and that some further efficiency measures are included together with explicit targets for improvement. The Director also requests the manager to draw up appropriate Customer Satisfaction forms for visitors, for people who hire the venue for shows and exhibitions, and for people who live near the Arts Centre and may be inconvenienced by any changes. Finally the Director asks the manager to undertake a programme of market research to find out 'what users really want' and to develop a marketing plan with clear targets for the coming three years. The manager and staff agree to these requirements, with some trepidation and concern that they are going to be distracted from the real business of running an arts centre.

---

are essential components of a performance management system. Therefore, before we move on to consider the relationship between performance measurement and management in more depth, it is worth considering the purposes of PIs and noting some ground rules which can increase their value as a management tool. We refer to 'indicators', as this term embraces both direct measures and indirect or proxy measures of variables which can be meaningfully linked to aspects of performance which interest us.

Although we may most readily think of PIs as providing information for management control, the picture is not as simple as this association may suggest. Mayston (1985) studied non-profit performance indicators in the UK and the USA in the mid-1980s, from the perspective of public sector economics. He attributed the under-use of available indicators at that time both to a lack of clearly identified roles for PIs in decision making, and to the need for reliable and decision-relevant indicators within an effective control framework. Mayston identified nine roles or objectives for non-profit PIs which address the preferences of all key stakeholder groups:

1 To clarify the organisation's objectives.

2 In the evaluation of the final outcomes resulting from the organisation's activities.

3 As an input into managerial incentive schemes.

4 To enable consumers to make informed choices.

5 To indicate performance standards in the licensing or contracting of privatised services, and to monitor the fulfilment of these terms.

6 To indicate the effectiveness with which different service activities in a given policy area contribute to each of the dimensions of achievement relevant to the policy area.

7 As a trigger for further investigation and possible remedial action to improve the quality of inputs and outputs.

8 To assist in determining the most cost-effective set of service levels to attain a given target in each direction of achievement.

9 To indicate areas of potential cost saving in attaining a given set of intermediate outputs.

Pollitt (1987, p 89) presents a very similar list of roles, with the important addition of 'To provide staff with feedback designed to enable them to develop and improve their practice'. No single set of indicators or performance assessment scheme is likely to perform all these roles, not least because the costs of data collection and analysis are likely to place competing claims on limited budgets. However, the use of PIs has continued to spread in relation to the non-profit services – for example in the UK, education, police and local government authority services are being scrutinised. You may also agree that organisations which provide commercial services have needs for management information very similar to these. Before we move on to consider the place of PIs in performance management systems, we should note a set of characteristics which, if given due consideration, may enhance their value (*see* Exhibit 12.3).

Exhibit 12.4 provides a salutary reminder of what might happen if insufficient attention is paid to key criteria of relevance, directness, clarity and cost-effectiveness. Not only does the measure induce obviously inappropriate behaviour, but it could also cause resistance to the development of sensible PIs.

To summarise, so far we have noted that where performance management is concerned, there are both important similarities and important differences between the public services and the commercial services today:

1 Managers of both need to develop and use a range of performance measures to satisfy key stakeholder groups and avoid unintended (or uncontrollable) knock-on effects.

2 Public services managers may need to make particular efforts to measure qualitative, longer-term and more complex aspects of performance, so that explicit policy objectives relating to equity, user satisfaction and economic impact can be attained.

3 Managers of public services may face more significant conflicts of interest between stakeholder groups when it comes to the pursuit of particular objectives.

4 Public services may have structural and cultural characteristics which can generate resistance to the import of technically useful approaches from the private sector.

A conclusion we can draw from these similarities and differences is that effective use of performance measurement and evaluation involves not just the correct technical application of measurement techniques, but also appropriate choices of approach to performance improvement. What works well in one organisation or in relation to one service may not be feasible or accepted in another since contingency factors come into play.

Exhibit 12.3

What makes a good performance indicator?

- *Timeliness* – the immediacy and frequency with which data become available as information. To exercise effective control, data need to be collected at appropriate time intervals (to detect trends or cycles) and analysed rapidly enough for action to be taken which will have the desired effect. Where an effect takes a long time to become evident (such as impacts on the physical environment of airborne industrial outputs), intermediate indicators such as the monitoring of levels of gases like carbon dioxide in the air may be required.

- *Directness* – the capacity to measure direction and pace of change reasonably directly, indicated by the level or state of key variables measured after the elapse of appropriate intervals of time and compared with intermediate targets or a desired trend. The return of fish to previously polluted rivers, and the growth rate of their populations, would enable us to monitor a positive trend in pollution control.

- *Sensitivity* – assessed in terms of the intervals at which data are collected and the calibration of any measures. Are they small enough to detect the levels of change we want to observe? The risk of missing a change, or dismissing it as an error, artefact or due to chance, must be minimised.

- *Specificity* – this is problematic in many areas of performance evaluation. With how much certainty can we say that A, or a particular aspect of A, causes B? How far can we progress beyond noting correlations? Organisational performance assessment can rarely take the form of controlled experiments, so assumptions need to be made explicit and open to challenge. How far does the presence of a 'failing' teacher in a school account – wholly or in part – for its position in the latest league table, for instance? Why might that be so? One might remove that teacher and see performance improve, but to prove that this was solely due to the staff change would be difficult without being able to control other variables.

- *Validity* – how confident are we that we are measuring what we want to measure in order to assess, say, progress towards a medium-term objective? A familiar example is examination results. Suppose a school wants to ensure that the quality of its teaching is improving year by year. It therefore monitors the average number of examination passes per student. Does an increase in the average per capita examination passes necessarily tell the school's managers (and local parents) that teaching is getting better? Perhaps the students this year are simply better at examinations, or have chosen subjects about which they are more confident rather than 'risky' ones, or the school has not entered students considered likely to fail. So the examination results may give us little information about improvements in teaching quality.

- *Reliability* – the extent to which a measurement procedure or instrument will produce the same result when used by different people (or the same person on another occasion), other things being equal. It is relatively easy to test reliability of measuring equipment used by a public health inspector to monitor pollution or to check food samples, for instance (indeed such equipment has to be carefully calibrated to be of any use at all). Social research instruments such as surveys to measure public awareness of a service can also be carefully tested until they produce reliable results when used by a large number of interviewers or by the same interviewer on different occasions. Tools for measuring subjective features such as racial discrimination or client perceptions of the attitudes of professionals can be hard to 'calibrate', and in qualitative investigations the notion of reliability may need to be exchanged for the concept of usefulness.

- *Ambiguity* – this can seriously damage the confidence placed in a measure, and can be one factor affecting the accuracy of data collection or recording. This can be a particular problem with scaled or subjective measures, less so for frequency counts. Perhaps you have experienced being asked to indicate, on a five-point Likert-type scale from 'very' to 'not at all', your response to questions like 'How satisfied are you with the services at this leisure centre?' If you are very happy about the entry fee, quite satisfied with the condition of the squash court but not at all satisfied with the showers, where would you mark on the scale? If you put your mark in the middle this does not tell the management much about what would make you recommend the centre to your friends!

- The *accuracy* with which measurements are made and data are recorded is not simply a function of the carefulness of the individuals involved. Normal motivational factors such as the clarity of instructions, explanation and understanding of the significance and purpose of data collection, the convenience and complexity of collection procedures and the presence of distractions can all contribute to the quality of raw data. Staff who handle data

Exhibit 12.3 *cont.*

need to have the necessary skills for any coding or manipulation, as well as an interest in their tasks that is conducive to accuracy.

● Can *artefact effects* be eliminated – for example the 'Hawthorne effect'? (That is, the subject of investigation being changed unintentionally by the process of investigation; see Roethlisberger and Dickson, 1939.) Perhaps we can change the way we look at and classify things, or adjust our expectations of what it is worth looking for during the evaluation? People who are keen to be discharged from hospital after a hip replacement may manage to climb stairs particularly well when they are being assessed, but find it harder in private; perhaps the 'assessment' should be based on routine observations over several days.

● *Feasibility* – can targets be set, if appropriate, and are the targets based on realistic expectations? For example, the UK government's *Health of the Nation* policy included a target to reduce the percentage of men and women aged 16–64 who are obese (defined as having a body mass index of over 30) by at least a quarter for men and at least a third for women between 1986/7 and 2005. However by 1994 the percentages had increased rather than declined. Perhaps the target was just unrealistic; or perhaps because obesity reflects a wide range of lifestyle factors operating over a person's lifetime it was not really appropriate to focus on this target.

● *Relevance* – does the indicator still tell you something of interest? If the objectives or environment have changed significantly, or the aspect of performance is no longer problematic, it may no longer be necessary to continue to monitor a particular characteristic. For example, when the UK National Health Service Patient's Charter was launched in 1991 it included a target for health authorities to allocate patients to a general practitioner (GP) within two working days. By 1996 this had been fully achieved throughout the NHS for two years, so central monitoring of this indicator was dropped.

● *Availability* and *cost-effectiveness* (which are often related) deserve some consideration; the costs of data collection, analysis, storage and retrieval can be considerable. Performance monitoring often uses data collected for other purposes, and therefore does not incur much additional cost, but you must judge its value for your needs in terms of the factors outlined above. The costs of obtaining 'bespoke' data (assuming that doing so is feasible), compared with the anticipated benefits, may preclude their collection. The 80:20 'Pareto principle' often applies to performance measurement – the costs of obtaining that final 20 per cent response rate from a survey may be out of all proportion to the additional information obtained!

Source: Adapted from Lewis and Holloway (1996, pp 26–7). Reprinted with permission.

Exhibit 12.4

Social work or bell ringing?

A social services department wanted to gather information on its own effectiveness in alleviating distress in its area. Among other initiatives, it decided to instigate a performance measure for its social workers.

The aim was to see how effective the group was at solving – or at least coping with – the major social problems in the area. Of course, measuring something as qualitative as 'reduction in distress' was not straightforward, and would probably be very complex and expensive to administer.

The department therefore settled on a proxy that was simple and cheap to implement: number of visits made per social worker. The logic was that there should be a reasonably strong link between calls made and provision of social services to the client population.

Unfortunately the system had a major flaw. Ringing the doorbell of a client's house or flat counted as a 'visit'. A social worker could therefore achieve a much better rating by 'visiting' many empty homes in the same length of time it would take to deal with a case where someone had the temerity to be at home when the doorbell rang.

Source: Wheatcroft (1994, pp 17–18). Reprinted with permission.

WHAT DOES PERFORMANCE MANAGEMENT INVOLVE?

Some working assumptions

In order to concentrate on models and examples of performance management in practice, in this section we will make the following assumptions:

1 Clear strategic goals have been translated into shorter-term objectives and tasks for managers and their staff, with desired outputs and outcomes reflecting the level in the organisation and any functional specialism.
2 Many organisational processes will be parts of chains leading to an external customer, so the satisfaction of internal customers along the chain is important if the final customers are to be satisfied fully.
3 Performance management embraces processes of routine and *ad hoc* quantitative measurement, qualitative evaluation and the instigation of action to improve performance towards defined objectives.
4 It can be useful to think of performance management in terms of the operation of a feedback control loop whereby the outputs of a process are measured and compared with a target, and the inputs are adjusted if a change is needed.

These assumptions are of course highly rational, and we have already noted the need for approaches to performance management to be compatible with organisational cultures and political factors which may be rather less rational. In fact many management texts do assume that the rational model is sufficiently realistic to allow the writers to make firm prescriptions about how performance management (and other management roles) should be undertaken (*see*, for example, Hogwood and Gunn, 1985). We will be rather more circumspect, treating the above points as working hypotheses, and we will return to consider the impact of limits to the rational model in the final section.

To start with, we will develop the simple control model in a context that may be familiar to you, in order to introduce some generic 'technical' elements of good practice in performance measurement. Later we will consider measurement and evaluation in other circumstances which illustrate some of the complexities involved.

Performance management as control

Figure 12.1, the feedback control loop, is probably familiar from earlier studies; indeed many everyday activities in which we all take part involve responding to feedback and adjusting the inputs to some sort of process. In the diagram presented in Fig. 12.1, inputs to a process are being controlled by the actuator – a person, or equipment such as a valve in an automated system. The inputs will be adjusted if information about outputs from the process indicates a need for change; and such a need is identified by sampling the outputs at appropriate intervals and comparing relevant properties with some form of reference levels or standards. The comparison is made, unsurprisingly, by a comparator. Again this may be a person, checking dimensions of a product against a quality control chart or comparing levels of customer satisfaction with previous survey findings, for instance; or the comparison process may be automated, involving computers or machine settings.

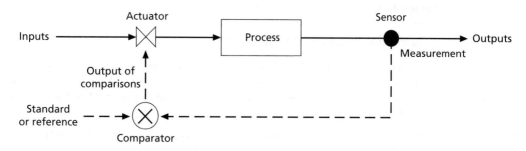

Fig. 12.1 Single-loop feedback control

A basic feedback control loop may appear a crude way of describing a key part of managerial work, but it does potentially encapsulate all the main ingredients needed to ensure that operational targets are achieved. Note the word 'potentially' – we have already assumed that public service life may not be perfectly rational, and as we review what each part of the control model involves it will be seen that there are some fairly complex considerations involved in designing an effective control system for managerial work.

For present purposes, however, we will assume that there is a reasonably clear objective to be attained, and that part of the job of a manager involves ensuring that the right inputs are transformed into the correct outputs which contribute to that objective. This is a major part of what 'performance management' involves, even if some of the inputs and outputs may be 'soft', difficult-to-quantify ones such as attitudes and client satisfaction.

We will illustrate this control process (*see* Exhibit 12.5) by following a college lecturer who is putting the finishing touches to a module which will be running for the first time in the semester just about to start. Many of this professional's experiences will have direct parallels to those of public services managers. Increasingly, 'management' is part of the lecturer's job, so you should not regard this as a specialised example but more a working illustration. Most managers are also likely to have participated in such a system, which has its equivalents in many countries, so the Exhibit is interspersed with prompts to assist in the application of the model.

We noted some quite detailed technical characteristics of 'good' performance indicators above, but what makes the suggestions in Exhibit 12.5 'useful' data? There are a few key features we should note in the context of operational control in particular.

First, the measures need to be relevant to the target or standard against which they will be compared (and thus relevant to the lecturer's objective to which the standard directly relates). In this case, we could assume, for instance, that the standards for the lecturer's current semester are: all the syllabus to be covered to the depth described in the course specification; presentation style ratings of 'good' or 'excellent' from at least 85 per cent of students; assignment grades fitting a normal distribution around a mean of (say) 55 per cent; examination pass rate to be within 5 per cent of previous years' results and/or other modules on the same qualification programme, with mean and standard deviation at levels acceptable to the examination board and external examiner. So far, the approaches to measurement that we have proposed should provide data in a form relevant to these standards.

Exhibit 12.5

Managing teaching performance

The situation facing the college lecturer is that enough students have registered for the new module, teaching rooms and equipment have been booked, reading lists and lecture notes have been prepared, and audio-visual aids are ready. Among the operational objectives for the lecturer in running the course over the following months are:

- to retain enough students so that an acceptable proportion complete the course;
- to conduct lectures and classes so that the syllabus is covered;
- to answer enquiries from individual students to assist their progress;
- to mark assignments and return them to students;
- to set the examination paper, prepare marking notes, and ensure that marking arrangements are made according to college rules.

How can the control loop model assist the lecturer in achieving these objectives? Bear in mind that, like the students, the lecturer is probably going to be assessed on this course. Performance as a lecturer will be monitored by students, colleagues, including their line manager, and possibly students' parents or employers.

We will look first at the transformation process – the 'black box' in which inputs are transformed into outputs. If we could see into the 'black box' which is the whole of the teaching process in operation, we would find a large number of complex activities taking place. So, to make the discussion simpler, we will focus on the lecture and class processes (leaving on one side for now the exams, assignments, administration and so on). We would see *inputs* such as course handouts, the lecturer's words and the ideas they convey, and students with their prior knowledge and views. The intellectual inputs will be manipulated in students' brains and through discussions, and even the students as 'bodies' may undergo change, as *transformations* take place. *Outputs* from this part of the *process* would include students' written work, changes to their ideas, perhaps improved skills and capabilities. But are they the 'right' outputs? How can they be defined so that we can check that the 'right' outputs are emerging?

Let us look first at the objective of 'to conduct lectures and classes so that the syllabus is covered', and see if the outputs indicate that this is being achieved. A useful objective is one that is specific, measurable, achievable, relevant and time related (or SMART). We know that the focus of this objective is on lectures, classes and the syllabus – relatively specific, although when we come to measure its attainment, we will need different measures for each aspect. Lectures may cover some parts of the syllabus, classes other parts and in different ways. We have 'the syllabus' as a useful measurement device though, as it has probably been agreed by the college and perhaps an external examiner, and written in precise terms. If this objective is not achievable at least under normal circumstances, the college and its staff would appear to be failing in their core business!

Is the objective relevant, and to what or to whom? Clearly it is relevant to a lecturer, whose job even today still involves such traditional activities as lectures and classes; it should also be relevant to students provided that they have chosen an appropriate course (a factor over which the lecturer may have no control). Finally, the objective itself implies when it should be attained, as it relates to a module running for a semester with a fixed start and end. We can look at all the key objectives for

Exhibit 12.5 *cont.*

the lecturer in turn, and check that they seem to add up to a blueprint for doing an appropriate job in the current context of the college and its student and course profile. We will consider later the implications if the context changes.

What we cannot ascertain, just by checking that the lecturer has a good, clear objective, is whether the lecturer will do things the right way so that desirable outputs are produced! This is where the loop part of the model comes in. Continuing with our focus on the lectures, classes and syllabus, we can identify some simple measures against which the lecturer's performance in delivering the course can be compared. For example:

- accuracy of information conveyed to students (factual correctness);
- coverage of the syllabus;
- clarity of presentation;
- grades attained by students in assignments;
- pass rates of students in examinations.

You may like to compare these five measures with the 'good PI' criteria in Exhibit 12.3 and assess their value as a set of indicators for assessing the lecturer's performance in the lecture theatre. Would any single one of them be adequate on its own to ensure a satisfactory learning experience for the students?

Clearly there will be a limit to how far the lecturer's teaching can be responsible for the output in terms of the students' learning – some students may be less able to assimilate the ideas because of a lack of relevant prior knowledge or innate ability, others may not attend all the lectures or concentrate very hard when they are there. But provided these variations are taken into account when deciding on any future action, there is some merit in monitoring the lecturer's performance by undertaking some measurements of the outputs of the lecturing and class process, as suggested above. The lecturer's performance can then be compared with targets or standards which have been identified as necessary to achieve in order that the lecturer's (and ultimately the organisation's) objectives will be met.

So how might the measurement process be put into practice? Some common ways of obtaining useful data about these sorts of aspects of performance are:

1 A colleague looks at samples of students' work in assignments or examination papers to check for any signs that the lecturer has not conveyed factual information correctly, or has missed parts of the syllabus.
2 Students provide feedback on a questionnaire about the lecturer's presentation skills (whether they could hear and see well enough what was being said, whether the lecture was delivered at an appropriate pace, whether requests for clarification were always acceded to, etc.).

Other data will be generated through processes undertaken elsewhere in the college, for instance: quantitative data, collected through record keeping and formal academic administrative processes, about assignment grades and examination pass rates, probably compared with previous years of the same (or a similar) module and maybe with standards expected for a course at this level; attendance rates collated from class registers; and so on.

The measures also need to be direct: as we will note next, there is little point in collecting a large quantity of performance data without being able to relate it directly to the process and any necessary action. The measures we have proposed should at least help the lecturer, and his or her colleagues if necessary, to decide on some sorts of action to improve performance if it is needed.

The measures should also be clear, as probably the easiest way to discredit performance measures is through ambiguity. To ensure clarity it may be necessary to measure in a less sophisticated way than some people may desire, so that it is transparent to all involved what the performance data reveal. Some provisos may still be needed in interpretation – we noted above that the inputs in the form of students' abilities and efforts will affect the outputs of the process, for instance – but as far as possible performance measures should reflect known causal links or at least clear correlations.

Finally, and this applies equally to all sectors, measures need to be cost-effective. If it costs more to collect some particular item of data than will ever be saved by improving performance, it is probably not worth collecting. This constraint may not be relevant to situations where there are many changing factors and data are needed in order to begin to understand what is going on, but in routine operational monitoring it is safe to say that performance measurement needs to pay its way.

It may appear that we have started at the back end of the control loop, but the aim has been to demonstrate how the nature of inputs to a process may need to change in response to performance measurement and targets or standards. If we were unable to measure the impact of processes, perhaps because they took so long to have an effect (in preventive health care for instance), we might set up the inputs once, on the basis of the best available evidence at the time and then concentrate on monitoring factors in which we could intervene to more immediate effect. In the single loop feedback control model, while the lecturer is delivering the course during the semester, he or she will be looking ahead to see how his or her performance may need to improve for the benefit of students, the college and his or her own career prospects. If the course becomes unpopular with students or receives critical examiners' reports, considerable resources may have been wasted and there will be knock-on effects throughout the programme of study; the college could even lose accreditation for the course and considerable revenue with it. The lecturer, and managers in their daily work, are the actuators in control systems: they make things happen by changing the inputs. If there is no intention to change any of the inputs, there is little point in measuring the outputs.

Closing the loop

Finally, before we leave the example of the college lecturer, we should look at the implications for action once measurement has taken place. Here we will concentrate on the two measurement areas relating to syllabus coverage and presentation style. Obviously we have jumped ahead now – the lecturer has been running the course, and it is time to take stock. Consider Exhibit 12.6.

All of the measurement processes considered in the example of the lecturer can be put into place at the start of the course so that when it finishes, or at appropriate points during the semester, any changes the lecturer needs to make can be implemented. It is usually far easier and more effective to incorporate measurement processes at the start of implementing a new activity or system, than to bolt them on later. In an ideal world we would

Exhibit 12.6

Improving teaching performance

First, suppose that it appears that, after samples of assignments and examination papers have been reviewed by experienced colleagues, a topic at the end of the syllabus seems to have been covered in inadequate detail. None of the students whose work has been examined has been able to use a particular concept correctly in assignments or the examination. Before the lecturer is able to make adjustments to the teaching it is important to find out what type of problem has occurred: perhaps the lecturer misunderstood the concept, or did not prepare the class very well, or assumed that students already understood the concept from a previous course. In discussion with colleagues, it transpires that the lecturer had a great deal of material to cover during the final class of the course, including items which had been postponed from a previous class, so the lecturer simply handed out some notes on the concept concerned. There was no opportunity for students to discuss the concept, as it was the end of the course, and they were not advised clearly enough about its importance so that they did not pay sufficient attention to it in completing their coursework or in revising for the examination.

What sorts of actions may be taken to improve the situation for the future, particularly in terms of adjustments to the inputs to the system which may lead to more desirable outputs?

In this example, the following sorts of actions can be taken for the next semester: the lecturer can improve time management to increase the prospect of covering important concepts in good time, and if he or she does get behind, it should be possible to ensure that students are made fully aware of any material to which they should pay extra attention outside the class. The lecturer can also provide some additional written notes for such topics and ensure that students have opportunities to raise any queries about these topics. So, by changing the inputs of timetable, student support and course notes, it is possible to adapt the process of syllabus delivery to improve the outputs.

Fortunately, the lecturer did gain ratings of 'good' or 'excellent' from 85 per cent of the students for presentation style! However, as we will see in the next section, this should not give grounds for complacency. The chosen target is just that – chosen. Targets in management control systems rarely have an intrinsic validity of their own, unless they are critical control systems in relation to safety, where the lowest acceptable risk is sought. Even if the targets or standards reflect the 'best in class', the highest standard to which such a process can currently aspire, they are still human activity systems and as such involve choices and values which may change.

undertake most of our monitoring during the operation of a process, look at 'interim' outputs and be able to adjust the inputs to the process as it goes along so that the student's experience improves during the semester. Such ongoing monitoring often characterises customer satisfaction programmes – which are increasingly common in the public sector.

However in the normal world, particularly when service procedures may be relatively short or interim outputs hard to interpret, we often have to operate in a 'quality control' mode and detect poor service after it has happened. It is only then that we can move towards quality assurance and prevent a recurrence of the poor services, by adjusting the inputs appropriately. Where services can be specified to reflect 'best practice' (which is itself subject to constant review), we can move towards a total quality or continuous improvement approach to performance. But for the time being we will concentrate on implementing control effectively, as a way of increasing the likelihood that agreed objectives are met.

We have gone into considerable detail because at face value the control loop model is a highly simplified tool which could easily be used in a mechanistic way just to explore the flows of things which are easy to quantify. However, it also provides a framework for organising performance management so that the measurement aspects are not taken out of context.

CHANGING PERFORMANCE

In the last section, we concentrated on a situation which is actually rather unrealistic in public services: one in which the goalposts were not moved during the game! The hypothetical college lecturer knew what standards were expected in relation to clear objectives, and it was possible to measure performance to see if those standards were being attained. In turn it was also quite straightforward for the lecturer to identify adjustments to make to inputs to the system to improve performance.

We now consider two characteristics of public services which make more sophisticated models necessary for performance management. The first is the tendency for standards and targets to change, and the second is the desirability of measuring longer-term or wider impacts of public services activities. These are both major topics in their own right but coverage here is necessarily brief.

Let us recall that at least in theory, in a rational organisational context, managers' objectives and targets reflect what the organisation needs the managers to achieve in order that higher level organisational objectives can be attained. (Others have provided some important models for appreciating and working within the limits to rationality but they are beyond the scope of this chapter.) In the previous discussion we looked in some detail at how the attainment of objectives can be put into operation, and the contribution of the measurement and improvement of the performance of the individual manager or professional employee to ensuring that important organisational services and products are delivered to the satisfaction of a range of stakeholders. We focused there on a lecturer, but made the point that much of the lecturer's role involved management activities. In public services management, although the nature of 'management' has changed radically over the past decade or so, it is important to recognise that management is undertaken by professional and technical staff as well as full-time general or functional managers. In some organisations such as the NHS professional staff drive the commitment of resources, and encouraging them to recognise the contribution which their actions make to 'management' is essential. So in this chapter we have not confined our attention to performance management by people in 'pure' management roles.

In reality, the predictability and stability which makes a single feedback loop an adequate tool for controlling the performance of relatively routine operational activities is rarely present for long. Disturbances from the environment – elsewhere in the organisation, the political context in which it operates, the market even – mean that targets and the objectives of our 'actuators' (people who ensure the right inputs are fed into processes) need to be kept under constant review. It is difficult to measure environmental turbulence, but experience in the public sector tells us that at least the political environment has a major and often direct impact on all levels in public services, probably stronger and less predictable than its impact on most of the private sector. So a more complex control model is likely to be needed in order to ensure that objectives and targets are revised when

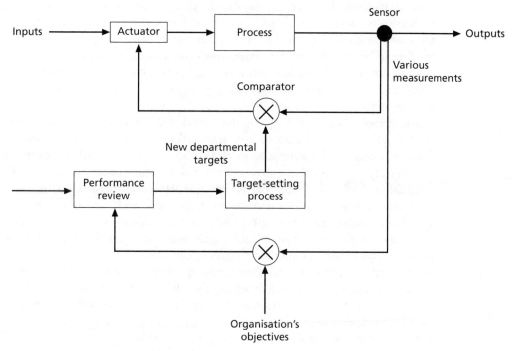

Fig. 12.2 Double-loop feedback control

necessary, as well as to ensure that individual processes make appropriate contributions to the achievement of objectives. The double-loop feedback control model (Fig. 12.2) satisfies these requirements.

In the example of the college lecturer, for instance, student feedback was contributing to efforts to bring all teaching staff up to a reasonable standard of presentation style, which was regarded as a proxy indicator that lectures were meeting students' learning needs. However, rather than simply trying to ensure that at least minimum levels of student satisfaction are met, the college may feel that if some lecturers can consistently obtain a 95 per cent satisfaction rating, with sufficient training all staff ought to be able to meet this target. 'New departmental targets' on Fig. 12.2 indicates this change. It may mean higher expenditure on training, but if market research has indicated that presentation style is a key factor in shaping the reputation of colleges and their attractiveness to new students, department heads may need to plan for this investment in the near future. Otherwise student numbers may fall and courses may have to be cancelled.

In addition to this sort of continuous improvement through raising targets, senior managers in the college are likely to be undertaking more strategic reviews of the college's objectives in the light of external factors such as education policy and market forces, and adjusting the mix of programmes, courses and teaching methods. From time to time it will be necessary to review even the college's fundamental aims, as some may simply no longer be relevant to the community or attainable within available resources in the foreseeable future. Such fundamental reviews can be painful, but if they are conducted with the participation of all key stakeholder groups they can ensure the survival and success of institutions in rapidly changing environments.

In exploring the role for feedback control loops in managing organisational performance, we have tended to focus on outputs of processes, rather than their longer-term or eventual outcomes. In higher education, some simple outcome indicators are starting to be used to compare institutions, such as the percentage of former students in employment after six months. However, it is tempting to say that the fundamental outcomes and purposes of education are being neglected in favour of things which are relatively easy to measure.

The school and college league tables introduced in the UK in the early 1990s provide a clear example of this situation. You may well be aware of debates surrounding the production of league tables for schools and colleges based primarily on examination results and truancy rates. Local newspapers are quick to report both 'success' and 'failure' of the hospitals and schools in their catchment area. However there are many problems associated with such league tables. For example, they tend to focus on features which are easy to measure, either inputs or outputs but rarely processes or longer-term outcomes. They are often based on unadjusted data which does not allow for differences in the human inputs to the systems. 'Good' performance of a school may reflect benefits in terms of a more healthy or affluent local community; 'poor' performance may be due to a high proportion of people with social disadvantages. It has also been suggested that schools are ceasing to enter for public examinations pupils who are unlikely to gain high grades, to avoid the risk that their grades will pull down the school's average, and thus its place in the league table (*see* Goldstein and Spiegelhalter, 1996).

The problems of measuring the true benefits and comparative performance of public service institutions could be said to be even more acute in situations where all the outcomes or effects of a process may take many years to become evident – such as the effect on individuals of medical treatments, or the impact of current lifestyles on the physical environment.

Turning to the UK National Health Service, we all know of scandals arising from medical interventions where the longer-term outcomes were not properly understood – the use of thalidomide to control sickness during pregnancy but which also produced a high number of serious birth defects, for example. During the 1990s the NHS has included in its strategic goals to 'Invest an increasing proportion of resources in interventions which are known to be effective and where outcomes can be systematically monitored, and reduce investment in interventions shown to be less effective' (NHS Executive 1995, p 21). Achieving this goal is known to require a complex combination of: increased research and development, improved targeting of information about the results, an expectation of participation in continuing professional development (CPD), removal of resource barriers to the take-up of CPD and a willingness to address the ethical and political debates which tend to arise when patients are refused treatment on grounds of expected efficacy.

Few people like to feel that they are receiving medical treatment the clinical effectiveness of which is unproven, which causes problems in later life or which is known to be a waste of money. So it is conceivable that with careful management a shift towards 'evidence-based medicine' will eventually occur, provided that medical education and public awareness are mobilised in the same direction. Case study 12.1 identifies some of the complex issues involved in implementing such a change.

Although the measurement of performance can be traced back to the early years of the welfare state, it has yet to achieve the status of an exact science. This article illustrates some of the problems that managers encounter.

STATISTICS THAT GIVE THE NHS A HEADACHE

by Mark Suzman

As with managers in most other areas of the public sector, National Health Service executives are no longer strangers to terms such as benchmarking or to having to measure themselves against clearly specified performance targets.

By and large, these techniques have proved successful in boosting productivity: hospital trusts are increasingly managing to meet tough financial efficiency targets while steadily improving performance on other quantitative measures such as reducing waiting lists, or improving response time in accident and emergency wards.

Increasingly, however, many people involved in the NHS believe that such statistics tell only half the story.

Financial data and information about waiting lists give managers useful information about inputs and throughput – how many patients there are, how much it costs to deal with them and how quickly they are discharged – but are far less useful in understanding outcomes.

They tell us little about whether patients recover fully, which treatments are most successful in achieving this, and why.

Such evidence as exists, moreover, suggests that statistics about the efficiency of individual treatments disguise some serious problems about their efficacy.

In the UK, part of the problem is that measuring such outcomes is a goal that has traditionally not been required of hospitals by their 'purchasers' – the health authorities and GP fundholders who contract with trusts for patient treatment.

To help change this, the government has over the past five years significantly expanded the use of clinical audits within hospitals and set up a national advisory group to examine the subject. It is also currently promoting greater use of evidence-based medicine – ensuring that doctors and hospitals use only treatments that are clinically effective.

There is some evidence that this has had some impact. A survey published in June by the National Association of Health Authorities and Trusts* found that almost a third of health authorities now claim to be using clinical effectiveness as the leading determinant in their purchasing decisions, an increase of 50 per cent in just two years.

According to Sharon Redmayne, the author of the report, this is being based on extensive consultation with clinicians, with some even looking at how specific procedures are being carried out. 'If the guidelines indicate that a patient would benefit, then the procedure will be performed,' she says.

Even so, such changes remain relatively small-scale, and while the advent of evidence-based medicine has been enthusiastically received in principle, it is not yet well developed in practice.

One of the few people looking seriously at the issue of how to improve systematically the management of clinical outcomes in the health service is Harry Burns, director of public health at the Greater Glasgow Health Board.

He is convinced that much more could and should be done.

'Despite all the resource and effort that has gone into clinical audit over the past few years the public remains convinced that we run a service in which serious clinical accidents can occur without control or sanction,' he wrote in a recent study.

'As the health service is organised at present, improving clinical outcomes is well nigh impossible.' Even so, Burns is making an effort to do so by analysing differences in outcomes more closely. For example, he discovered that the number of haemorrhoidectomies carried out in Scotland's 50 or so local districts diverge widely, with a few showing a rate several times above the norm.

'There seems no reason other than surgical preference and habit for these variations,' he notes. 'The patient may get a wonderful operation but if he doesn't need it, he is hardly likely to benefit from surgery.' For Burns the way to start cutting down on such unnecessary – and expensive – over-treatment is for hospitals to stop gauging success by 'efficiency episodes' – the number of hospital inpatient treatments. Instead, he feels they should start actively measuring clinical outcomes and using that information to predict and manage the outcomes of further treatments.

But he remains gloomy about the scope for real improvement until there are structural changes in the NHS that actively encourage health authorities to require such data and hospitals to incorporate it in their management decisions.

'If clinical work is to be used to the benefit of patients we have to think of the health service as a complete system,' he argues. 'Part of that system must be a range of controls and incentives to use outcomes data effectively.

Outcomes will not matter until the system makes them matter.' It is a challenge the NHS has not yet managed to meet.

* NAHAT (1996) *Making Outcomes Matter* (NAHAT, Birmingham Research Park, Vincent Drive, Birmingham B15 2SQ).

Source: *Financial Times*, 3 July 1996, p 7. Reprinted with permission.

Questions on the case study

1 From the point of view of performance management, what would the health service as a 'complete system' consist of?

2 What would the outcomes of a health system look like and how might we measure them?

PUTTING PERFORMANCE MANAGEMENT TO WORK

In this chapter we have been urging the adoption of a systemic or holistic approach to performance management, noting that public services have a diverse set of stakeholders and that their managers need to link operational with strategic performance. We have also noted that many public services are particularly vulnerable to the impact of external changes, often with political origins, which reduce the capacity of local managers to control the definition and pursuit of objectives. How and why then should they resist the temptation just to measure those things which are easy to quantify, to pursue only those targets governed by statutory or regulatory obligations, and to focus on the short-term budgetary or electoral cycle rather than the long-term impact of their organisations' actions?

We need not dwell here on 'why', as (quite apart from one's own beliefs about the responsibilities of public services) the formal objectives of many public services embrace an obligation to be responsive to a wider range of stakeholders than simply those paying for the service today. Changes in political control are unlikely to endorse a more parochial approach in future. In addition experience from the private sector (*see*, for example, the work of Eccles, 1991, and Kaplan and Norton, 1992) reminds us that a wide range of performance indicators is essential to survival even in the relatively short term. A major challenge for managers is how to manage the 'difficult-to-measure' aspects of their services, while not losing sight of the needs of the whole service. The examples from the NHS in the previous section may be relatively extreme, but in any organisation there will be some processes or policies which are very hard to evaluate with any degree of confidence or consensus.

As well as issues relating to environmental performance or quality of life, among other 'difficult-to-measure' areas we could include factors such as ethical problems which arise in the process of acting on performance measurement information – choosing whom to offer medical treatment to when balancing costs and evidence about treatment effectiveness, for instance; and problems in evaluating the impact of policies, particularly when these policies are not the only changes being implemented at any one time. The ethical issues surrounding the provision of services in the face of constrained resources are too large to consider here; suffice it to say that as we gain better management information about costs, and research information about benefits, choices may become more explicit. This can make them more controversial; but it could be argued that at present such choices are made in comparative ignorance and the gathering of performance data is at least enabling more informed choices to be made.

It is certainly the case that whereas evaluation at the micro level, for instance of medical interventions or local social projects, is gradually becoming more common, evaluation of large-scale changes in public policy is still unusual (*see*, for example, Flynn and Strehl, 1996, and Robinson and Le Grand, 1994). This partly reflects technical difficulties: it is hard to organise a 'control' group when a policy intrinsically affects a whole community, for instance. We rarely have the foresight to collect data about current policy impacts that will enable us to do 'pre' and 'post' change comparisons. And several policy changes often come together, such as the reduction in junior doctors' hours in the UK NHS, and changes in the nurse and specialist medical education systems. The comparative rarity of large-scale evaluations of policies also tends to reflect national political traditions.

CONCLUSIONS

The examples given above have illustrated some of the features of public services which it is very important to take into account when adopting management approaches from the private or commercial sector. We may summarise these as follows:

- Evaluating the long-term impact of the service may be very difficult and may require special attention, as long-term effects may be central to the objectives of the service concerned.
- The accountabilities of the public services, and the ethical responsibilities involved, are often different from those of commercial organisations.
- Professional staff are frequently major participants in public service provision, and have to address the requirements or standards of their own professional bodies as well as local and personal standards.
- There is a need to be responsive to users who may have limited choice and power and therefore may not be adequately served by a wholly 'market-driven' service, but who deserve high-quality services even from monopoly suppliers.
- There is a relative lack of 'protection' from political changes at short notice, and potentially higher levels of regulation than operate in the private sector.

To be worth having, performance management systems need to reflect and address these challenging characteristics, rather than deny their significance or concentrate on the 'easy but unimportant' aspects of performance.

To end this chapter, it is worth reiterating that in spite of important contextual differences, the practical management skills needed for the sorts of performance measurement and management activities which have been described above are largely generic. Different professional groups and types of organisation (public and private) have an enormous amount in common when it comes to facing the challenges of identifying what to measure, how to measure it, and how to tackle important aspects of a service which do not, perhaps should not, lend themselves to ready quantification. The public and private sectors are also growing increasingly close as privatisation and the Charter movement is being followed by a shared awareness of the need for environmental management. Appreciating how actions taken to control performance can have an effect on the wider organisation or environment is an important part of developing sets of performance indicators and performance measurement systems that meet the requirements for accountability which still characterise public services.

REFERENCES

Eccles, R G (1991) 'The performance measurement manifesto', *Harvard Business Review*, Jan–Feb., pp 131–7.

Flynn, N and Strehl, F (1996) *Public Sector Management in Europe*. Hemel Hempstead: Prentice-Hall Europe.

Goldstein, H and Spiegelhalter, D J (1996) 'League tables and their limitations: statistical issues in comparisons of institutional performance', *Journal of the Royal Statistical Society A*, 159(3), pp 385–443.

Hogwood, B and Gunn, L (1985) *Policy Analysis for the Real World*. Oxford: Oxford University Press.

Hood, C (1995) 'The "New Public Management" in the 1980s: variations on a theme', *Accounting, Organizations and Society*, 20(2/3), pp 93–109.

Kaplan, R S and Norton, D P (1992) 'The balanced scorecard: Measures that drive performance', *Harvard Business Review*, Jan.–Feb., pp 71–9.

Lewis, J M and Holloway, J A (1996) *Performance indicators and management control*, Unit 1 of Open University course B889 Performance measurement and evaluation, 3rd edn, pp 26–7. Milton Keynes: Open University.

McKevitt, D and Lawton, A (1996) 'The manager, the citizen, the politician and performance measures', *Public Money and Management*, July–Sept., pp 49–54.

Mayston, D J (1985) 'Non-profit performance indicators in the public sector', *Financial Accountability and Management*, 1(1), Summer, pp 51–74.

Metcalfe, L and Richards, S (1990) *Improving Public Management* (2nd edn). London: Sage.

NHS Executive (1995) *Annual Report 1994/95*. Leeds: NHS Executive.

Pollitt, C (1986) 'Beyond the managerial model: the case for broadening performance assessment in government and the public services', *Financial Accountability and Management*, 2(3), Autumn, pp 155–70.

Pollitt, C (1987) 'The politics of performance assessment: lessons for higher education?', *Studies in Higher Education*, 12, pp 87–98.

Robinson, R and Le Grand, J (eds) (1994) *Evaluating the NHS Reforms*. London: Kings Fund Institute.

Roethlisberger, F J and Dickson, W J (1939) *Management and the Worker*. Cambridge, MA: Harvard University Press.

Wheatcroft, R (1994) *Evaluating financial and economic performance*, Open University course B889 Performance measurement and evaluation, Unit 6, pp 17–18. Milton Keynes: Open University.

QUESTIONS AND DISCUSSION TOPICS

1 Thinking of an organisation with which you are familiar, identify four measures which would tell a public services manager something about how well that manager's organisation is performing on the dimensions of effectiveness, efficiency, economy and equity. Which of the organisation's other main stakeholder groups would be interested in each measure?

2 Take several of the criteria for good performance indicators (PIs) in Exhibit 12.3, and identify examples from your own experience or studies to illustrate where these criteria were met. Also identify examples of PIs which appear not to have met these criteria, and suggest reasons why this situation may have arisen.

3 What is your view about the value of publishing league tables for schools and hospitals, based on selected performance indicators? Compare the benefits and limitations of public service league tables with those traditionally used in the context of sports such as football. What sort of case might you make for developing league tables for a wider range of private sector businesses?

4 For a sector or organisation with which you are familiar, identify a key aspect of performance which you regard as 'difficult to measure'. What characterises the difficulties? Consider the implications for the main stakeholder groups if such difficulties are not resolved.

13 Managing change

Alan Lawton

AIMS

This chapter will:

- investigate the pressures for change on public services organisations;
- describe the tools that are available to managers to manage organisational change;
- examine the form that change in the public services takes;
- discuss the criteria for effective implementation of change.

INTRODUCTION

Part 1 of this book examined the context within which public services are delivered and illustrated some of the changes that have taken place in the environment for public policies. We have also examined some of the responses that organisations have made in their internal structures, processes and human resources to these changes in their external environments. Some of the responses have been described under the umbrella term New Public Management which we have discussed in previous chapters (*see* Chapters 3 and 5). You will also recall the STEP factors which can be used to map changes in the external environment. This chapter will look at the concept of change in more detail and analyse the tools available to managers for handling change. The importance of change for public services managers is captured in the following quotation from the Local Government Management Board (LGMB):

> Change is the only permanent feature of our world. The pace of change may be fast now but it will become faster. Unless local authorities remain cohesive, they could be thrown off the spinning wheel of survival as if by centrifugal forces. Whether in the public or private sector, we live in a world where courage, creativity, confidence and competence provide the path not only to being at the leading edge, but to survival itself. **Nobody manages change; what we must do is manage people to adapt to change.** (1996, p 61.)

Given the title of this chapter, the last sentence in the quotation begs many questions. We shall investigate the validity of that last sentence in this chapter.

Before proceeding further, however, we need to clear up the language concerning the concept of change. Change is often presented as a good thing and is attractive to politicians; in his Redcliffe-Maud Memorial Lecture at the Royal Institute of Public

Administration (RIPA) (1989), Kenneth Baker, then Secretary of State for Education and Science entitled his lecture 'Change is our ally'. Justifying changes in the local management of schools and college, Baker argued that over-centralised systems do not cope well with change. Responsibility should be given, he argued, to those closest to the outcomes and thus most committed to their success. We shall discuss below whether 'over-centralised' systems hinder or aid change, but for the moment let us concentrate on the concept of change itself. Change can be either for good or for bad; when something changes it moves from one state to another. This may not necessarily constitute progress. If we consider change in terms of progress then reform is a more appropriate term to use. Brunsson and Olsen (1993) identify four basic attributes of administrative reforms:

1 Simplicity and clarity: the reforms proposed simplify and clarify existing organisational practices.
2 Reforms are normative: they represent attempts to bring order out of chaos.
3 Reforms are one-sided: they reflect a single view of the world in contrast to organisational practices which often reflect different and inconsistent values.
4 Reforms are future oriented: reforms are not immediate actions but promise future benefits.

Change, as a descriptive term, belongs to a family of concepts which involve moving from one state to another. Is this movement linear or spontaneous? Quirk (1997, p 571), a senior manager in local government, for example, uses the metaphor of 'change as fire':

> Fires consume things, they don't just change them. Things which once burnt can never be unburnt. And fires change the state of things in quite unpredictable ways. Moreover, fires are all process and no substance. Is this not the essence of the changes we witness? Change as process with no pre-figured end-state; change as irreversible force.

Our view of what change is, and how it occurs, will influence our views on whether, or how, we feel change can be managed. Another view is expressed by Nutt and Backoff (1997, p 235):

> A transformation creates a sustainable metamorphosis from a vision that produces radical changes in an organisation's products/services, consumers/clients, market channels, skills, sources of margin, competitive advantage, and persona, integrating these changes with core competencies.

According to Nutt and Backoff, to create and implement transformational change, organisational leaders must abandon past practices and seek new ones. Change must be revolutionary and must seek a new paradigm of practices and values that alters the rules of the game and changes the basic make-up of the organisation in terms of its core processes, cultural commitments, products and/or services, markets and strategic alliances. In the view of Nutt and Backoff (p 241), many old practices are no longer relevant for the new paradigm.

The popular usage of the term 'paradigm' stems from the work of Thomas Kuhn (1962) on scientific change. He argued that, contrary to popular opinion, advances in science came about not always because of new discoveries or revolutions but through piecemeal progress. Kuhn said that scientific paradigms provide a broad framework that defines what the interesting questions are and then provides answers to those questions. A consensus develops and a period of 'normal science' follows that requires routine investigations of detailed problems within the paradigm. However, anomalies or fundamental novelties are suppressed for a time because they do not easily fit the existing paradigm. The paradigm will eventually come to question its own failure to explain the puzzles thrown up by these anomalies. If a new paradigm is generated which can amount for these puzzles, then a revolution has occurred and a period of normal science sets in again. However, our concern is with the paradigm that seeks to explain the workings of public services organisations. Thus, for example, a bureaucratic paradigm is associated with a set of beliefs, values, perceptions; in short, a way of seeing the world. It may not be stated explicitly, it may be taken for granted, it is a way of seeing reality, a mindset. A paradigm shift occurs when a theory no longer explains phenomena associated with that reality.

Brooks and Bate (1994, pp 184–5) capture the strength of the prevailing paradigm in their research on change within central government agencies:

> Agency members were governed by the continual desire to worship the status quo. They saw change as a culturally deviant activity. It made them feel vulnerable and consequently they went to great lengths to 'protect' themselves against it. We found there was a dedication to tried and tested modes of reason and action. Old remedies were continually applied to new problems and situations, while the perennial problems frequently alluded to by organisational members, such as ineffective communication, lack of attention to quality of service and risk aversion, remained largely unaddressed and unsolved. Energy was channelled into solving the manifestation of the problems rather than their underlying cause. To attack the root cause would have been to create upheaval and to run counter to the constraining schema.

Brooks and Bate argue that if a new paradigm, such as that expressed through the Next Steps Agencies, is to take hold, it needs to be legitimised through what they term the 'politics of acceptance'. They found that this issue was not addressed, as the need to reduce the anxiety caused by change was not dealt with; furthermore, the change was imposed from above.

MODELS OF CHANGE

One model of change is offered by Pettigrew (1988) who has examined the dynamics of the relationship between the environment (the outer context) and the organisation's inner context in terms of its culture, structure and management. The outer context consists of the economic, political and social structures which affect organisations. Pettigrew sees the process of change in terms of the interaction of the stakeholders involved with the content of change, which refers to the particular area of the organisation undergoing change. Pettigrew argues that the 'why' of change is derived from an analysis of the inner and outer context, the 'what' of change is captured under the label of content and the 'how' of change is derived from the analysis of process, the actions and reactions of the various stakeholders as they seek to move the organisation from its present to its future state. The 'why', the 'what' and the 'how' of change are crucial questions and we address each of these in turn in the next three sections.

Why change occurs

We have examined some of the reasons for change in Part 1 of this book. Let us explore these a little further. Change is driven by a number of imperatives both external and internal to organisations. We use the term imperative to illustrate the force of these drivers for change. In the public services, there are key pressures from the external environment which have a major impact. These include:

CASE STUDY
13.1

The London Borough of Hackney's deep-seated political and management problems resulted in consistently poor performance, as testified by the Audit Commission performance indicators. This article looks at one attempt to reform the borough.

HACKNEY'S NEW BROOM

By Alan Pike

Hackney's credits are grim: Britain's first failing school to be closed by the government; the country's longest delays in reletting vacant council homes; a bitter split within the ruling Labour group, with 17 members expelled and neither faction left in control of the council.

Indeed, things have been so bad that the London council is to be abolished on 31 December – and started all over again with an entirely new organisational structure the next day.

Tony Elliston, the chief executive, believes Hackney's restructuring programme is the most extensive ever attempted in a single public-sector organisation.

Elliston makes the case for the reorganisation in terms that even the council's strongest external critics might avoid.

'Hackney charges one of London's highest council tax rates for some of its worst services. We have a number of excellent, leading-edge services but many others are just not good enough. Externally, our image is very poor, and internally the organisation runs on a basis of departmental baronies, feudalism and piracy. We are not close enough to our customers. There are too many excuses. The only thing that ever gets delegated is blame.'

In fairness to Hackney, the Audit Commission's latest performance indicators this month showed the council had made progress in a number of areas during 1995–96. But Elliston quickly stifled any tendency towards self-congratulation among his colleagues. 'We have to get away from the idea that incremental improvements are adequate,' he told them. 'Ours is a culture of mediocrity, and incremental improvements will not lift us out of it.'

The proposed senior management structure builds on a model pioneered by Kirklees council, West Yorkshire. Chief officer roles such as director of housing or education will disappear. They will be replaced by four executive directors responsible for cross-boundary issues of significance for the council as a whole – such as regeneration and partnership, or service quality and performance improvement. Executive directors will have no direct management responsibilities for running services but will form a policy board, with Elliston and leading elected members at the heart of the council.

Services for the public will be devolved, with separation of responsibilities between the staff charged with commissioning and providing them. Internal activities – such as legal services, transport, payroll, civil engineering, catering, cleaning and training – will operate as trading units. Each will become a separate financial entity, surviving on its skill at selling its services within the council.

The council is showing a new willingness to embrace the private sector, and is talking to seven companies about outsourcing its £9m-a-year benefits and council tax administration services.

Hackney councillors, now divided between official and unofficial Labour groups, Liberal Democrats, Conservatives and an independent, have approved Elliston's reorganisation plans in principle, although some senior and middle managers are opposed to them.

Elliston acknowledges this problem and has presented a report to the council emphasising that, although existing chief officers would be invited to apply for the new executive-director posts, 'it does not follow that internal appointments would be made'. The intention to transform Hackney seems serious.

Source: Financial Times, 27 March 1997. Reprinted with permission.

Questions on the case study

1 Why do you think that Hackney has chosen such a radical approach to change?

2 How will restructuring help?

- the *efficiency* imperative, which requires that public services organisations spend tax-payers' money as efficiently as possible;
- the *economy* imperative, which requires that costs are kept to a minimum;
- the *environmental* imperative, which requires that public policy, increasingly, takes account of the impact on the environment, on the quality of life and so on;
- the *effectiveness* imperative, which requires that the impact of public policies must be positive;
- the *evaluation* imperative, which requires that those charged with the delivery of public services should be held accountable for performance;
- the *ethics* imperative, which reflects a concern with standards of conduct in public life;
- the *market* imperative, which characterises citizens as customers and requires that public services organisations respond to them.

All of these imperatives result from changes in political, social and economic ideas that are expressed through legislation.

As an example of the change in ideas, Al Gore (1994) the vice-president of the USA identifies a perceived decline in trust in government as a key mover in the demands for change citing the fact that in 1993 only 20 per cent of the American people trusted the federal government to do the right thing most of the time, compared with 76 per cent in 1963. Gore (1994) argues that two recent developments shifted the premises upon which public and private sector management has been based:

- a shift in the understanding of human capacity;
- the new role of information technology (IT) in transforming the manager's job.

We now have different ideas from those held in previous generations about human capacity and we are more ready to push power down the organisation. Similarly IT encourages decentralisation. At the same time, however, the impact of external change factors depend upon the receptiveness of organisations to change. Commenting upon change in UK local authorities, Lowndes (1997, p 85) argues that 'While external triggers to management change are important, the susceptibility of individual authorities to change, and the direction of that change, is related to internal power relations and to local sensibilities and circumstances'.

According to Lowndes, change occurs to ensure greater managerial control and efficiency as a result of the introduction of quasi-markets and the development of user-led approaches to service delivery. The latter two are examples of change and reflect more fundamental changes concerning the belief in market forces. It is important to separate the reasons for change from the vehicle through which change is carried out and to ask, 'How much has really changed?'

Lowndes confirmed that there is variability in the embeddedness of change and that this depends on institutional frameworks, which include levels of technology, degrees of professionalisation, legal and regulatory frameworks, resource demands and, finally, the nature of relationships with the public.

Again we have to separate change from the factors that will effect its implementation. This we do in more detail below.

Hartley, Benington and Binns (1997) identify five variables that will affect change in local authorities:

1 External pressures such as budget cuts or local government reorganisation.
2 Changing political control.
3 Relations between councillors and managers.
4 Values underpinning change (e.g., the role of professionals and the extent to which change is initiated by management).
5 Relations with departments (i.e. where the power bases are).

These variables impact upon the role of the change agent which we examine below.

What has changed?

Despite the rhetoric of change in the public services, as described in our opening quotation, what is the evidence that change has taken place? Young in LGMB (1996) examines changes in local government from 1992 to 1994 and found that, for example, there was little change in the adoption of Performance Related Pay (PRP) during this period and that the tide of restructuring was slowing down. Here the net effect of changes has been to reduce the number of departments. Young also found a concentration of decision-making powers in small groups outside the formal arenas and identified new ways of working together through the use of joint member/officer working groups. Among his other findings were that the adoption of service level agreements and the creation of trading accounts had increased and that councillors were beginning to come to terms with change. When longitudinal change of this nature is examined, a key issue is what time period is taken and from when. By 1994, according to Young, local authorities were coming to terms with change.

The second part of Young's research argued that local government has in the past been reactive to change and has rarely been proactive and voluntarily innovative. The reasons given include:

- uncertainty;
- legislation which has caused unforeseen difficulties and unintended consequences;
- local government review and white collar compulsory competitive tendering (CCT) have invariably been distractions;
- inherent organisational inertia;
- social change among the communities themselves;
- a weakening of the capacity of local government to cope with change as a result of the transfer of services away from local authorities; examples of services which have been transferred include further education, and the removal of LA representatives from health authorities etc.;
- tensions caused by having to balance the requirements of key stakeholders.

The respondents in Young's survey seemed to believe that the review of local government and CCT had been distractions; they did not accept them as a normal part of organisational life. Increasingly, such 'distractions' may be met on a daily basis. In practice, many of the changes that have taken place in the public services in recent years have proved to be a mixed blessing. In Exhibit 13.1 we examine in detail the impact of CCT which has been described by Rao and Young (1995, p 45) as 'without doubt, the most dramatic set of changes in the history of British local government'.

Exhibit 13.1

The impact of compulsory competitive tendering: change in practice

The history

In the 1980s compulsory competitive tendering (CCT) for local authority services was introduced as a result of the Local Government, Planning and Land Act 1980 and the Local Government Act 1988. Initially the services covered were building construction and maintenance and highways maintenance work, the latter Act extending the services to include building cleaning, grounds maintenance, schools and welfare catering, street cleaning, vehicle maintenance and refuse collection. Professional and technical activities were later included, following on from the Local Government Act 1992. Among the reasons for the introduction of CCT were: a belief on the part of members of the Conservative government that the public sector is inherently inefficient and that CCT would reduce costs; a belief in competition and privatisation; a desire to see better value for money and greater accountability for public spending. The reasons need not detain us here. What we need to examine is the nature of the real changes as opposed to the espoused changes. We need to ascertain whether the stated intentions were met in practice.

The political make-up of individual local authorities had a marked effect on each authority's initial responses to competition, with Conservative-led councils being the most likely to embrace the changes. The response was hampered by the ambiguity of the legislation, which could be interpreted in ways to suit the views of individual authorities. Those who were committed to retaining services in-house were uncertain of the extent to which they could take into account factors such as redundancy costs, pensions provision and the financial background of the contractor when seeking to justify maintaining the status quo. One interpretation of the implementation of CCT might be that legislation cannot cover every contingency and is an imperfect policy instrument, used by those who seek to avoid compliance.

There was also the unexpected impact of European legislation on the implementation of CCT. In 1981, the Transfer of Undertakings (Protection of Employment) Regulations (TUPE) were enacted to comply with the European Commission's Acquired Rights Directive (1977), the purpose of which was to provide protection in law for the jobs and working conditions of employees when the organisation for which they worked was transferred from one employer to another. Where such a transfer took place, the new employer had to take over the contracts of employment of the employees on the existing terms and conditions. Although it was not clear initially that this Directive applied when employment was transferred from the public to the private sector, the European Commission ruled that it did. Among the implications of this ruling were the need for councils to define redundancy; and for private sector organisations to clarify whether they could employ former local authority personnel and reduce their wages.

The experience of local authorities in relation to CCT has been conditioned by a number of factors, including:

● their initial approach to competition;
● their pre-existing competitiveness in terms of service costs, labour practices and management capability;
● the intensity of competition from private companies for contracts.

The results

1 Competition has resulted in tangible cost savings although the extent of savings has varied widely.
2 The majority of contracts have been retained in house, with reduced staff levels and lower conditions of service.

Where local authorities have achieved productivity gains, depressed pay levels and trimmed back on benefits, they have competed with success. Restrictive practices have been relinquished because they have been found to have an impact on work practices.

Local factors have had a tremendous impact on the implementation of CCT. Therefore the pace and extent of change are bound to vary from place to place. The impact of CCT on public service values and good employment practices must also be considered. One effect of CCT has been to discourage and disengage councillors from direct involvement in the services provided by private contractors. This has had unintended consequences for roles and relationships! It also begs the question of how far an authority can contract out services before it risks losing control over strategic direction.

Another impact of CCT is that on managers, who now have to grapple with financial management, negotiations, contract management and other matters which were not previously part of their role. Competition has introduced new disciplines into management practice. The gains have been: in terms of responsibility, greater clarity; in terms of the purchasing and provision of services, heightened awareness of performance on the part of clients, greater precision in the measurement of performance and the identification of hidden costs. Whether these changes would have come about without compulsion is a moot point.

By 1994, CCT-driven change was being re-evaluated. According to the LGMB survey (LGMB 1996), morale has declined as a result of CCT and the change has failed to propel elected members into taking a longer-term view. Thus the impact on organisation processes is not particularly favourable. The impact on service delivery is quite marked, however: quality, customer satisfaction and standards have all improved.

The lessons that have been learned from CCT may be summarised as follows.

1 The impact of CCT can be variable in terms of both benefits and costs.
2 There is no causal link between stated policy objectives and policy outcomes.
3 The impact of CCT depends upon the existence of conditions that favour, or are receptive to, change.
4 CCT affects stakeholders in different ways, depending on their interests.
5 Political affiliation is important.
6 Local conditions are important.

We return to reconsider CCT in Case study 16.2.

How to change

Change requires a response, both in the short term and in the long term. In the short term organisational survival may require a different response from that which might lead to longer-term reform. At the same time, there may be a political agenda which is short term. Slatter (1984) studied firms which were attempting to recover from change. Not all of the firms survived. Although the research is based on private sector firms it contains lessons for public service organisations, particularly those that control their own budgets and those that are in competitive markets such as hospital trusts or direct service organisations. Slatter identified eight steps for survival, which are presented in Exhibit 13.2 in the order in which they should be taken; several may need to be taken at the same time.

Exhibit 13.2

Slatter's eight-step recovery strategy

1 *Gain management control.* Slatter argues that, in the first instance, control over the organisation – in terms of cash, expenditure, stock etc. – is crucial. Apart from the immediate impact in these areas, this action will also demonstrate to employees that the organisation is back under control.

2 *Establish credibility with stakeholders and maintain communication with them.* Key stakeholders including banks, suppliers, trade unions, customers, clients and employees need to be assured that the planned turnaround is taking place. The most important stakeholder in the public services may be the politician.

3 *Assess existing managers and replace if necessary.* This step is sometimes difficult to implement in the public services. However, it is proposed that, in the case of schools and local authorities which are deemed to be in crisis, or to be underperforming, a Task Force headed by a manager from the private sector be sent in. This solution to the problem, which is encouraged by OFSTED (the Office for Standards in Education) and the Department for Education and Employment (DfEE) fulfils this condition.

4 *Evaluate the business.* The diagnosis of the causes and the identification of the issues critical to survival are crucial.

5 *Action planning.* A framework for implementation needs to be drawn up, concentrating, in the first instance, on the issues which will produce the greatest immediate benefit. Management must be seen to be doing something.

6 *Implement organisation change if appropriate.*

7 *Motivate management and employees.* At all times and in all places, the changes have to be communicated to staff and the expected benefits clearly explained.

8 *Install or improve budgetary systems.* This will aid the need for management control identified in Step 1.

In the longer term, organisational development (OD) is essentially a long-term strategy which takes a systemic approach. It assumes that reactions and resistance to change are a normal part of life. A major part of this strategy is linked to change and is designed to deal with change. The emphasis is on empowering people in order to change the system.

Organisational development is presented as a cycle:

1 Confrontation with environmental problems, change opportunities, recognising the issues that confront the organisation.
2 Identification of implications for organisation.
3 Education to obtain understanding of implications for organisation.
4 Obtaining involvement in project of key stakeholders.
5 Identification of targets and specific goals for change.
6 Change and development activities.
7 Evaluation of project and programme in current environment and reinforcement.
8 Return to stage 1.

Organisational development recognises the importance of groups and is concerned to build effectiveness through team building. For OD to be successful it requires a learning organisation where communication is valued and where skills development is encouraged. Graham (1989) indicates some of the techniques that have been used in the public sector:

- customer care training;
- the encouragement of personal responsibility through:
  - career planning;
  - appraisal systems;
  - human resource strategy;
- self-managed training;
- joint training of managers and politicians in local government;
- networking;
- coaching;
- mentoring.

THE LEARNING ORGANISATION AND CHANGE

In order to change, organisations may need to develop a learning capacity. Morgan points to a number of barriers to organisational learning which are particularly common in bureaucratic organisations. First, fragmented organisational structures lead to poor flows of information and knowledge, and people in those organisations take departmental views. Second, systems of bureaucratic accountability tend to reward success and punish failure. This encourages a defensive culture in the organisation where issues are obscured and problems are hidden (*see* Morgan, 1986, p 90). This capacity to learn may be affected by the power and dominance of professional groups. As Stewart (1985, p 52) observes, a number of factors in local government mitigate against the organisation's capacity to learn:

> Organisational tendencies to restrict learning are reinforced in the traditional management of local government. Professionalism is a powerful force restricting learning to established professional patterns. Local authorities do not hear easily of, or accept, information or knowledge that challenges accepted professional knowledge or practice.

We are concerned with what changes: superficially in terms of structures or people or more fundamentally in terms of the 'mindset' or paradigm. This is where organisational learning comes into play. Morgan makes the distinction between the process *of* learning and the process of learning *to* learn. Learning to learn involves systems which 'are often able to detect and correct errors in operating norms and thus influence the standards that guide their detailed operations. It is this kind of self-questioning ability that underpins the activities of systems that are able to learn to learn and self-organise' (1986, p 87).

Morgan suggests the following guidelines for the development of a learning-oriented approach. Following this approach, organisations should be open and reflective, and accept that uncertainties are inevitable features of a complex and turbulent environment. Problem-solving approaches should recognise the importance of exploring different approaches. Decision makers should avoid the imposition of predetermined goals and objectives on organisations (*see* Morgan, 1986, p 92).

Argyris and Schön (1976) makes the distinction between single-loop learning and double-loop learning. Single-loop learning involves solving problems that currently face the organisation. For example, an organisation may detect that it has a high error rate in payments made to the public. Once this becomes apparent, the organisation takes corrective action in order to reduce the error rate. You will recall the discussion of single-loop and double-loop learning in Chapter 12.

Double-loop learning requires the ability to question operating norms. Such questioning may reveal contextual constraints such as policies, culture and attitudes which lead to errors or unintended consequences. Only when such fundamental weaknesses are corrected can the organisation expect lasting improvement in performance. According to Handy (1990, p 199), 'Organisations which encourage the wheel of learning, which relish curiosity, questions and ideas, which allow space for experiment and reflection, which forgive mistakes and promote self-confidence, these are learning organisations, and theirs is a competitive advantage which no-one can steal from them'.

All of these development-type approaches recognise that how change is brought about is just as important as what changes. The process of change is crucial.

In moving from one stage to another, Lewin (1947) argues that the process will go through various stages:

Steady state → Unfreezing → Movement → Refreezing (new steady state)

To move from a steady state to unfreezing involves recognising that the organisation is not performing as well as it should and that this needs to be communicated to staff. As with any change process, individuals need to be reassured about how change will affect them and senior managers will support them in the transition from one stage to the next. Unfreezing the present patterns of behaviour may be through promotion, termination of employment or changing structures.

To begin to move towards a new state can be painful. Movement can only begin when the readiness for change is there. Staff will need to recognise the need for change, that they would have a part to play, that the changes provide opportunities rather than threats and that a new culture will be internalised. Trust, openness and participation will be key ingredients in this stage.

Refreezing is a new equilibrium, where what needs to be frozen is recognition that change is a challenge, that changes need to be institutionalised within the culture of the organisation – that is, permanent revolution. The new behaviour becomes the operating norm.

CASE STUDY
13.2

The case of the Prison Service shows how change in public services links to themes discussed elsewhere in this book. Thus, in concluding this part of the book, the Case study urges a reconsideration of accountability, the use of market mechanisms, performance management and financial management.

STIRRED PORRIDGE

By Mark Suzman

Chinese communism may be out of fashion in its home country, but the 38 000 staff of the Prison Service could be forgiven for thinking one of Chairman Mao's best-known doctrines – permanent revolution – has been the mantra of their employer for four years.

During that time, the service has been in near continual reorganisation, prompted in part by unprecedented growth in the prison population and deep budget cuts.

More recently it has had to weather scandals over escapes, deaths in prison and the shackling of prisoners, which have sparked outrage and caused severe political embarrassment.

At the heart of the problems are two questions: first, what is the most suitable structure to run such a large, politically sensitive organisation, and second, how best to improve the efficiency of individual prisons?

In 1993 the government was convinced it had found the answer to the first question, when it decided to transform the Prison Service into a Next Steps Agency. That meant effectively turning it into an independent organisation mimicking a private company.

Management decisions are made by the 'chief executive' – the director-general – while the Home Secretary is expected to be the 'owner', setting the broad policy framework but staying out of day-to-day operations. While the formula has met with some success in other public sector bodies, the Prison Service's experience has been mixed – symbolised by the sacking in 1995 of Derek Lewis, the former television executive brought from the private sector to oversee the shift to agency status in 1993.

The immediate cause for Lewis's dismissal was the Learmont report into a prison breakout that criticised his management changes for generating paperwork while diverting governors from their most important task – maintaining security of the prisoners.

Nevertheless, during his tenure, Lewis largely succeeded in changing the psychology and the structure of the Prison Service. In trying to institutionalise a business-type culture of benchmarks and performance indicators he caused initial resentment but managed to win over suspicious governors and officers.

In doing so he met most of his targets – a particularly impressive feat given that the adjustment to life as an agency coincided with a tougher law and order policy which has seen the prison population soar from just over 42 000 in 1992 to a record 60 000 today.

But the summary nature of Lewis's departure over an issue that many observers thought breached the tenuous division between 'operations' and 'policy' meant no outsider was willing to take the job. His eventual replacement was Richard Tilt, a career Prison Service manager who had served as Lewis's deputy.

Despite stressing that his first priority was to provide 'stability, continuity and balance' for the shell-shocked service, Tilt has found all three qualities elusive. A series of new problems last year culminated in a fiasco when a misinterpretation of sentencing guidelines by senior officials resulted in the early release of hundreds of prisoners.

That incident led to yet another bout of reorganisation, prompting a number of changes at director level and the strengthening of the director-general's secretariat. Tilt has launched a full-scale review of the management and structure of the service, due to be completed by the end of the year. Tilt insists the new culture of performance management and accountability accompanying the shift to agency status has been beneficial.

'I think (using performance indicators) has been extremely effective, especially in directing people's attention to some key issues,' he says. 'But they are very crude measures individually. What we need to be concerned about is the broad movement over the couple of years.'

That movement has so far been quite positive, but with money increasingly scarce, if progress is to continue the service will need to generate substantial efficiency gains to offset the steady tightening of its £1.3bn budget.

For inspiration in that drive, governors are increasingly turning to the infant private prison sector. Despite some teething problems, several recent studies have confirmed that the country's four privately-run prisons – several more are being built – tend to be 10 per cent to 20 per cent cheaper to run than their public sector equivalents, with no significant differences in quality.

The introduction of the private sector has 'acted as a spur to the public sector and been a powerful force for change,' says Tilt.

Nevertheless, Jack Straw, the shadow Home Secretary, has said that a Labour government would not only stop the building of private prisons but consider scrapping the service's agency status, bringing back the direct control of the Home Office.

In a recent book Lewis says the agency concept is unsuitable for the Prison Service. It encourages 'ministers imposing half-baked policies' while the director-general has 'responsibility without power'.

He would like to see the service spun off completely from the government, with an independent board to act as its 'owner' rather than the Home Secretary.

Given the current debate, the new review and the forthcoming election, Mao's dictum seems likely to be the Prison Service's credo for a little longer.

Source: Financial Times, 14 March 1997. Reprinted with permission.

Questions on the case study

1 Would you describe the Prison Service as a learning organisation? If not, what obstacles need to be removed for a learning organisation to develop?

2 Is changing the status of the Prison Service, say from public to private, sufficient to guarantee success?

3 What has been the Labour Government's approach to managing prisons?

MANAGING CHANGE

To return to the question we posed at the beginning of this chapter, to what extent can the change process be managed? Nadler (1980, p 97) examines the nature of change management. The implications of managing the process, and the actions to be taken, are set out in Table 13.1.

The lessons for managing change successfully include:

1 Work hard at establishing the need for change.
2 Don't think out the change, think through it – that is, what will the change mean for all the stakeholders involved?
3 Initiate change through informal discussion to get feedback and participation.
4 Positively encourage those concerned to give their objections.
5 Be prepared to change yourself.
6 Monitor the change and reinforce it (*see* Pugh, 1978).

What is the status of this kind of treatment? It takes the form of a 'Can do' list or a checklist. A checklist is all about action; we need to do more than just understand change, we need to know how to deal with it, how to respond to it, how to implement it and so on.

Table 13.1 Managing change

Implication	Action steps
Need to shape the political dynamics of change	1 Assure the support of key stakeholders. 2 Use leader behaviour to generate energy in support of change. 3 Use symbols and language to stress the importance of change. 4 Build in stability to reduce uncertainty and anxiety.
Need to motivate change	5 Surface dissatisfaction with the present state to demonstrate the need for change. 6 Participation in change, to build ownership. 7 Rewards for behaviour in support of change. 8 Make time and opportunity to disengage from the present state.
Need to manage the transition	9 Develop and communicate a clear vision of the future. 10 Use multiple and consistent leverage points; change must be organisation-wide. 11 Develop organisational arrangements for the transition. 12 Build in feedback mechanisms.

Source: Based on Nadler, 1980.

A change management strategy may take the view that change can best be understood as a sequence. All you then have to do is to recognise where you are and act accordingly. This contrasts with the notion that change is messy and that all the change management skills reside in the individual. Is it the distinction between judgement and merely applying a timetable or checklist approach? The assumption with all of these is that change can be managed. How realistic is this?

Resistance to change

If change involves challenging existing power arrangements, resistance to change is almost inevitable. Obstacles to change may include:

- the self-interest of individuals and groups who fear that change may encroach on their territory and challenge existing power bases and practices;
- the fear, insecurity, and resentment of individuals who may perceive change as a threat. For example, the introduction of a new computer system may mean that existing skills become redundant or structural reorganisation may threaten job security;
- the lack of trust that may follow if change is imposed from above and without consultation, with the consequence that individuals may question the motives behind change.

Of course, there are costs to change. Lawton and McKevitt (1995, p 53) quote one chief executive in a local authority that had undergone change:

> In fact, in retrospect, I think it was too intensive; we expected them to take on too many things too quickly. Not only convince them that the future with the organisation lay in the 'Way Ahead' as we called it, but we had to give them the basic skills of manpower and financial responsibility in a very short space of time. I think that what we did was to overload one or two of them, but the ones that could take it on board were the ones that actually succeeded.

Dealing with resistance to change can take a number of forms. Kotter and Schlesinger (1979) offer a continuum of techniques:

- *Education and communication*, which has the advantage of getting people on board but can be time consuming.
- *Participation and involvement*, where key stakeholders have the power to disrupt implementation but this can also be time consuming and there are no guarantees of success.
- *Facilitation and support*, used when individuals are having adjustment problems, but can be time consuming.
- *Negotiation and agreement*, used when powerful but reluctant stakeholders need to be brought on board. It may avoid major resistance but could prove expensive if other groups seek to negotiate.
- *Manipulation and co-option*, which may lead to quick solutions but may generate problems in the long term if individuals feel manipulated.
- *Explicit and implicit coercion*, which may be essential if time is at a premium but it could leave individuals feeling angry.

A useful tool to determine the likely resistance to change is Force Field analysis, first described by Lewin (1947) and based on the idea that any situation at any given time is not static but is subject to countervailing forces, either external or internal. One set of forces seeks to drive change, to move from a stable state; another set seeks to restrain change (*see* Fig. 13.1).

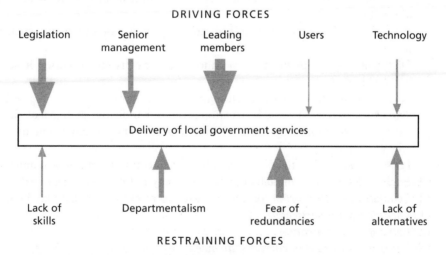

Fig. 13.1 Driving and restraining forces

The arrows can be drawn in at different widths to reflect the strength of the forces. The manager who wishes to move from the existing state of service delivery, to say, a partnership with a voluntary agency will need to consider how to overcome the restraining forces and how to support the driving forces. The means might include:

- restructuring with a view to breaking down entrenched positions expressed in traditional territorial disputes between departments;
- offering sceptical staff retraining in contract management;
- pump priming the voluntary sector to ensure that partners can be found;
- demonstrating how technology can be a tool for good;
- supporting user voice.

Use of these techniques should enable any manager to work out who is likely to oppose and who is likely to offer support.

IMPLEMENTING CHANGE

In implementing change, a change agent may be necessary to act as a catalyst. Apart from identifying supporters and opponents as described above, the change agent will need to 'sell' the change to key stakeholders, particularly politicians. The change agent will need to be open and responsive to the needs and concerns of others, be comfortable with ambiguity, be able to clarify complex problems, possess good communication skills, have the freedom to act quickly and possess the ability to be detached from the detail.

Even where there is a change agent, implementation may still not be straightforward. Drawing on the works of Alexander (1985), Hogwood and Gunn (1984) and Baier, March and Saetren (1986), we can identify a number of factors which will have an impact on the successful implementation of change:

1 *Time and sufficient resources* – implementation invariably takes more time than was originally allocated.
2 *Unidentified problems* – which surface during implementation and which had not been identified in advance.
3 *Co-ordination* – the implementation process may not be sufficiently creative or imaginative.
4 *Distractions* – competing activities and crises may distract attention from implementing the change.
5 *Lack of skills* – those charged with implementation may not have the necessary skills.
6 *Training* – the training and instruction given to handle the change may be insufficient.
7 *Turbulent environment* – uncontrollable factors in the environment will have an adverse impact.
8 *Lack of leadership* – there may be a lack of direction from senior managers.
9 *Lack of detail* – key implementation tasks may not have been clarified.
10 *Evaluation* – the information systems used to monitor progress may be inadequate.
11 *Lack of clear objectives.*
12 *Lack of communication.*
13 *Tasks not specified in correct sequence.*

Baier *et al.* (1986) identify two implementation problems. The first, which might be a technical problem, results from bureaucratic incompetence. The second set of problems are associated with conflicts of interests between policy makers and implementers; such problems arise from deficiencies in organisational control.

An interest in ensuring the support of stakeholders leads policy makers to be vigorous in enacting policies and lax in enforcing them. Some tasks are just not feasible. There may be goal incongruence between different parts of the organisation. There may also be multiple actors, and public services organisations are pressed to meet the inconsistent demands of a continually changing group of actors. Baier *et al.* (1986, p 212) argue that 'Any simple concept of implementation, with its implicit assumption of clear and stable policy intent, is likely to lead to a fundamental misunderstanding of the policy process and to disappointment with efforts to reform it'.

CONCLUSIONS

Change comes about through external factors such as legislation, or internal factors such as the appointment of a new chief executive. It is sometimes proactive but is often reactive, as public services organisations respond to a turbulent environment. A change agent in the public services has to manage both the political process and the managerial process. Change may involve a radical break with the past, and sometimes there are good reasons for fundamental change. Tinkering with a bureaucratic structure may not address problems of responsiveness; it may be better just to replace the structure with a different type of organisation altogether. Indeed, this was part of the rationale for involving the private sector in the delivery of public services. However, change can be carried out simply for the sake of change and organisations may suffer 'change fatigue'.

Brunsson (1989, p 226) argues that:

> Forgetfulness is also easily achieved: most organizations thrive happily on the fact that almost all reforms look better ex-ante rather than ex-post. Reforms are often launched as simple slogans which attract and inspire, while the actual work of reform tends to reveal the complications and the drawbacks. So it is easy to argue that the new reform now being proposed is better than the old one already tried, and a new attempt is always worthwhile.

According to Brooks and Bate (1994, p 189):

> As far as we can tell – and more importantly, as far as the participants themselves believe – there has as yet been no such 'paradigm failure' in the civil service. No one has been able to prove, to the members of one agency at least (and we suspect others), that the present situation does not work and that the new one would work much better.

Although their research is based on one agency only, given the challenges to managers in bringing about fundamental change it would not be surprising if their findings have application to other organisations.

REFERENCES

Alexander, L D (1985) 'Successfully implementing strategic decisions', *Long Range Planning*, 18(3), pp 91–7.

Argyris, C and Schön, D (1976) *Organizational Learning*. Reading, MA: Addison-Wesley.

Baier, V E, March, J G and Saetren, H (1986) 'Implementation and ambiguity', *Scandinavian Journal of Management*, May, pp 179–212.

Baker, K (1989) 'Change is our ally', Redcliffe-Maud Memorial Lecture. London: RIPA.

Brooks, I and Bate, P (1994) 'The problems of effecting change within the British Civil Service: a cultural perspective', *British Journal of Management*, 5(3), pp 177–90.

Brunsson, N (1989) *The Organization of Hypocrisy: Talk, Decisions and Actions in Organizations*. Chichester: John Wiley.

Brunsson, N and Olsen, J P (1993) *The Reforming Organization*. London and New York: Routledge.

Gore, A Jr (1994) 'The new job of the Federal Executive', *Public Administration Review*, 54(4), pp 317–21.

Graham, A (1989) 'Management development in the public sector', *Public Money & Management*, Autumn, pp 25–33.

Handy, C (1990) *Inside Organisations*. London: BBC Books.

Hartley, J, Benington, J and Binns, P (1997) 'Researching the roles of internal-change agents in the management of organizational change', *British Journal of Management*, 8, pp 61–73.

Hogwood, B W and Gunn, L (1984) *Policy Analysis for the Real World*. Oxford: Oxford University Press.

Kotter, J P and Schlesinger, L A (1979) 'Choosing strategies for change', *Harvard Business Review*, March/April, pp 106–14.

Kuhn, T S (1962) *The Structure of Scientific Revolutions*. Chicago: University of Chicago Press.

Lawton, A and McKevitt, D (1995) 'Strategic change in local government management: Comparative case studies', *Local Government Studies*, 21(1), pp 46–64.

Lewin, K (1947) 'Frontiers in group dynamics', *Human Relations*, 1, pp 5–41.

Local Government Management Board (1993) *Challenge and Change: Characteristics of Good Management in Local Government*. Luton: LGMB.

Local Government Management Board (1996) *Portrait of Change 1995*. Luton: LGMB.

Lowndes, V (1997) '"We are learning to accommodate mess": Four propositions about management change in local government', *Public Policy and Administration*, 12(2), pp 80–94.

Morgan, G (1986) *Images of Organizations*. Beverly Hills, CA: Sage.

Nadler, D A (1980) 'Concepts for the management of organizational change', in Mabey, C and Mayon-White, B (eds) *Managing Change* (2nd edn). London: Paul Chapman/Open University.

Nutt, P C and Backoff, R W (1997) 'Organizational transformation', *Journal of Management Inquiry*, 6(3), pp 235–54.

Pettigrew, A (ed) (1988) *The Management of Strategic Change*. Oxford: Blackwell.

Pugh, D (1978) 'Understanding and managing organisation change', *London Business School Journal*, 3(2), pp 29–34.

Quirk, B (1997) 'Accountable to everyone: postmodern pressures on public managers', *Public Administration*, 75, Autumn, pp 569–86.

Rao, N and Young, K (1995) *Competition, Contracts and Change: The Local Authority Experience of CCT*. London: Joseph Rowntree Foundation/LGC Communications.'

Slatter, S (1984) *Corporate Strategy*. Harmondsworth: Penguin.

Stewart, R (1985) *The Reality of Organisations*. London: Macmillan.

QUESTIONS AND DISCUSSION TOPICS

1 What do you think is the most difficult issue concerning change?

2 What are the criteria for the effective implementation of change?

3 Do you think that change can, in fact, be managed?

PART 3

The public services assessed

This part concludes the book by assessing modern public services. Public services in the United Kingdom may be at a turning-point. The General Election of 1997 saw the end of a Conservative administration determined to impose a radical change agenda on the public services. We have examined this agenda from a number of perspectives and in this part we continue to do this, paying particular attention to the perspectives of ethics and responsiveness.

New Labour brings new changes. It is clear that change will continue to dominate the agenda. The instruments of change and the direction of change may differ, though it is too early to draw any firm conclusions. However, early signals show that responsiveness will continue to be a key theme and the management mechanisms at the heart of public services will continue to be instruments of this theme. Reforms in health care, local government and central government show clearly that government will continue to use market mechanisms to deliver services, but not to the exclusion of other tools.

However, as Part 1 discussed, the nature and shape of public services are not determined by national politics alone. Technologies provides new tools which help to shape the nature of services. International experience continues to offer new agenda. We cannot be insular.

Chapter 14 examines public service culture. This offers a valuable opportunity to consolidate a number of themes raised in earlier chapters by looking at how organisational cultures have changed and developed and examining the issues involved in organisational culture.

The ethical dimension of public services management is discussed in Chapter 15. It provides a framework for discussing ethical issues and locates ethics at a number of levels. The chapter examines the nature of the public service ethos and explores concepts of trust, probity, accountability and integrity.

Chapter 16 considers the theme of responsiveness. In Part 1 we examined the environmental pressures that are being exerted on public services. Responsiveness as a theme is examined through a comparison of a number of new and revised public service reform initiatives including the Citizen's Charter and 'best value' in local government.

Chapter 17 examines the nature of comparative public services management both in terms of comparative methodology and in terms of approaches to public services management internationally. The chapter raises issues including 'why compare?' as well as 'what to compare'.

Chapter 18, which concludes Part 3, revisits themes from earlier chapters. It also is concerned with the nature of management and the relationship between theory and practice. The chapter also introduces some of the key themes that are emerging for managing public services in the new millennium.

14 Public service culture

Charles Edwards

AIMS

This chapter will:

- examine the meaning of the term 'culture';
- analyse the principal typologies of organisational culture and demonstrate their relevance to public services;
- show how public service organisational cultures have developed and changed;
- indicate the issues faced by public services managers when they try to influence organisational culture.

INTRODUCTION

> He was appalled at what he saw when he arrived at the Council [as Chief Executive] in July 1995: 'People wanted to be thanked for being mediocre . . . You could smell the culture when you walked into the building . . . *Transforming Hackney*'s aim is to introduce a culture of customer care, quality services and valued staff throughout the council' (Tony Elliston, Chief Executive Officer, London Borough of Hackney in *Local Government Chronicle*, 4 July 1997).

This quotation suggests, first, that different organisations have different cultures and second, that such cultures are relevant to the performance of public service organisations. In this chapter, we explore the roots and meaning of the term 'organisational culture' and see how this term is used in the management of public organisations. We pay particular attention to the attempts of public service managers such as Tony Elliston to change organisational cultures: why and how they do so and what issues they face.

WHAT IS MEANT BY ORGANISATIONAL CULTURE?

The term 'culture'

All the meanings of 'culture' are connected in some way with growth and cultivation, and with their resulting forms or patterns. This chapter is concerned with culture as a description of particular patterns of human behaviour and expressions which have grown or developed in particular settings. These settings can be geographical, as in Mediterranean or Highland cultures; or temporal, as in Restoration, Victorian or Viking cultures; or religious, as in Protestant or Jewish cultures; or social, as in upper middle or working class cultures. Although this chapter considers the cultures pertaining to a specific work sector or organisation, the meaning is similar. Sets of human behaviours, traits and expressions are being labelled and identified with a particular setting. This is usually done in order to understand, and often to caricature, what makes these cultures different.

It may be self-evident that people behave differently in Madrid and Manchester, or in a stock exchange trading floor and a probation service. It may be easy to notice examples of behaviour in these different settings and attribute them to their distinctive cultures. However, it is rarely easy to define in a few words what comprises different cultures; indeed, attempts are often inadequate, exaggerated, superficial or even insulting.

Culture has been described as being like the wind, obviously present and important but elusive to capture. Or like the coastline; it is crucial to the land mass, evolving slowly over time and adapting to the elements. Whatever the metaphor used, it is particularly difficult to isolate culture from or more accurately to relate it to, other variables such as climate, location, individual personality, etc.

This applies in the 'organisational cultures' with which we are concerned. It is a truism for people who have worked in different sectors or organisations to say that their cultures differ. Or even to go qualitatively further, and observe that people tend to be more content, positive and productive in some organisations than in others.

The proposition that organisations, like peoples, have their own cultures is not very helpful without some understanding of what organisational culture is in relation to other characteristics of organisational life. Some of the major texts on organisational cultures in the business world (e.g. Deal and Kennedy, 1982) talk of organisational culture as shared meanings in organisations which both influence and determine behaviour; or of 'the way things are done around here'.

The expression 'the way things are done' gives perhaps an undue action emphasis to organisational culture, undue because culture also incorporates the ways people think and communicate with each other. The idea that groups of people create their own beliefs and participate in distinctive rituals and functions by sharing meanings was developed through social anthropological observations and studies, often of discrete tribes and communities. From these roots, culture is now generally considered to cover much more than the specific actions which people undertake in their work. This anthropological bias is evident in the following definition:

> The basic values, ideologies and assumptions . . . which guide and fashion individual and business behaviour. These values are evident in more tangible factors such as stories, ritual, language, and jargon, office decoration and lay-out and prevailing modes of dress amongst the staff (Wilson and Rosenfeld, 1990).

It is because culture came to be seen in management studies as a variable of organisational performance that it has featured strongly in the discipline. The following definition captures the idea of purpose in organisational culture:

> the set of beliefs, norms and values which forms the basis of collaborative human behaviour and makes human actions to some extent predictable and directed towards a set of commonly held purposes or the maintenance of some commonly accepted state (Normann, 1984).

This begins to explain why so many managers and organisational leaders engage with organisational culture. If they can understand why groups of people think and behave as they do, there is the prospect that they may be able to influence thought and behaviour patterns in such a way that the organisations can perform better.

CULTURE IN ORGANISATION AND MANAGEMENT STUDIES

Interest in the cultures found in different organisations became an important aspect of management studies when it was suggested first that there was a causal link between national cultures and national economic performance and then, by extension, that there were such links between the culture and the performance of specific organisations.

Geert Hofstede has applied the idea of national characteristics to management, noting that management is conceived and practised differently in different countries (Hofstede, 1993). Hofstede traced historical, sociological, linguistic and other reasons to explain why, for instance, German management theories tend to concentrate on formal systems, why Dutch managers practice consensus and why American management theories tend to stress market processes, the individual and managers more than workers.

This interest in the links between culture and performance became central to many commentators on the relative performance of the Japanese and American economies in the 1970s and 1980s. Japanese culture, and more specifically Japan's way of doing business, was considered to be a major source of its then comparative advantage over the US economy. The strengths of networks, both within Japanese companies and also with their suppliers, banks and customers, were perceived to give Japanese companies clan-like strengths, superior to the rational, hierarchical characteristics of American business (Ouchi, 1981). American writers and consultants began to analyse their own business cultures. One of the most influential such studies was Peters and Waterman's account of the distinguishing characteristics of successful American companies in the early 1980s (Peters and Waterman, 1982). (*See* Exhibit 14.1.) Their argument was that the way employees thought and behaved, specifically towards customers, determined commercial success. This led to attempts to replicate or foster the customer orientation of apparently successful companies across commercial and public organisations in many Western countries.

Before asking whether programmes 'work', it is necessary to ask a more basic question: is there a cause and fathomable link between organisational culture and performance in the first place? One difficulty is that many of the champions of culture change, such as the chief executive quoted at the beginning of this chapter, have a vested interest in driving performance through culture change.

In a rare empirical study in the public services, Gerowitz *et al.* (1996) carried out research in 122 hospitals in the UK, Canada and the USA. They classified their cultures against four predefined main organisational cultural types and against a range of predefined measures of efficiency and effectiveness.

On one level their findings were unsurprising: that those hospitals whose cultures exhibited familial senses of care and cohesion performed best in performance measures relating to human relations and employee commitment. Hospitals with cultures that exhibited strong achievement-oriented and externally focused leadership performed best in performance measures relating to resource acquisition and 'competitiveness'. On another level the findings were interesting because they hint at an issue to which we will return later in

Exhibit 14.1

Culture and performance in the London Borough of Hounslow

In 1990, middle managers in the various Direct Services Organisations (DSOs) of the London Borough of Hounslow, responsible for the provision of schools meals, highway maintenance and refuse collection, were required to watch videos of Tom Peters extolling the successes of American non-profit and public organisations which had developed 'cultures of excellence'. This was part of a management training programme aimed at helping Hounslow's service departments survive and succeed in an era of significant environmental change.

Specifically, the DSOs were required by new legislation to compete with private sector firms for contracts to provide the services they traditionally performed. Hounslow's councillors and senior managers wanted the DSOs to win the contracts, but were not able to (and did not wish to) reduce the key cost differential between DSOs and private firms: wages. They hoped that if the DSOs' staff were more motivated, conscientious, trained and productive than those of their competitors, this would more than neutralise the wage cost differential. Management wished the 'organisational culture' of Hounslow's DSOs to become a principal form of competitive advantage. Showing the managers the Tom Peters video was one component of a programme of management training, quality improvement and employee communication aimed at cultural change.

this chapter: the self-perpetuating nature of organisational culture. If an organisation has the characteristics which mean that it performs well in an aspect of its operations, then it is more likely to attract and retain those people and practices that identify with this aspect of performance. Similarly, any attempts to change the culture risk challenging the organisation's strengths and the prevailing perceptions of what works. The issue of culture change programmes is developed later in the chapter, after we consider the principal characteristics of public service organisational cultures.

Thus far then, we have argued that there are different and distinguishing traits of human behaviour in different cultures and that key components of cultures are: the ways things are done in particular places, and peoples' shared meanings and consequent behaviour. The study of organisational culture has its roots in anthropological studies that described the behaviours and rituals of different societies. We have also suggested that the links between culture and performance have become an important part of management thought, both in national economic and in organisational studies. Culture has been promoted as a key variable of organisational performance and although there is some evidence to support this contention, it is complicated by the subjectivity of what constitutes culture and performance in public organisations.

MODELS FOR UNDERSTANDING ORGANISATIONAL CULTURE

Typologies

Many writers who have studied organisational cultures have tried to group them into a few main types or models, against which organisations can assess where they fit. Although such groupings are inherently oversimplified and contentious, describing them does provide an insight into the issues which define and differentiate organisational cultures.

Charles Handy's seminal work, *Understanding Organisations* (1978), was one of the more influential sources of labels for different organisational cultures. Although his four principal models have been challenged and adapted, they have influenced future attempts at categorisation and the four models presented below draw on his work.

Leadership or power culture

A leadership or power culture can be thought of as a spider's web, with power located in the leadership at the centre. The leadership's power permeates the organisation through both formal and informal lines of authority. Ways of thinking or behaving which are inconsistent with those of the leadership would soon lead to incongruence and/or conflict. The leadership's power may be based on respect or fear, or indeed both simultaneously. Features of such cultures include charismatic leadership, speed of decision making and the centrality of being in or out of favour with the leadership.

However, this first model can also be considered under the labels 'market' or 'rational', because it is identified with externally focused, driven organisations, wherein activity is made to conform (hence the rationality) with the clear vision and targets of the leadership.

Although often found in owner-managed businesses, a leadership culture can also develop in larger organisations and within sections in public services organisations. It would be a mistake to label such cultures as inherently unpleasant, unstable or problematic to work in; they can feature familial senses of loyalty, respect and care, as well as comforting degrees of certainty and clarity as to where the power is located.

Hierarchy culture

The second model can be thought of as a hierarchy culture; it is sometimes portrayed as a pillared temple, in which each pillar represents the distinct functions, or sections or departments, of the organisation. Power is less leader-centred than in leadership cultures, and the organisation has a timeless sense of continuity, whoever is in charge. It is characterised by rules and order and as such is seen as essentially bureaucratic and mechanistic.

Other labels for this model include 'role' or 'bureaucratic' cultures. Many public service organisations are characterised, often in a derogatory fashion, as examples of slow, risk-averse hierarchical cultures. In fact, bureaucratic hierarchies – especially if well run – can be considered to have some important inherent advantages in terms of the delivery of public services: transparency, accountability, stability and equity.

Task culture

The third model is a task culture, where power and behaviour are determined by the task in hand. This culture has also been labelled as 'open' or 'developmental', or as an 'adhocracy'. Features are entrepreneuralism, innovation, risk and loose boundaries. People are organised so as to meet the challenges of specific projects, with a culture that is more flexibly task oriented. Teams will use the knowledge, talents and resources of different parts of the organisation. Networks matter more than official vertical lines of managerial authority.

Perhaps because task cultures are often found in the assignment teams of consultancies, it is much advocated as a modern, consensual and results-oriented culture. However, in practice it can discomfort those who prefer working in known patterns. It is not always consistent with efficiency in organisational administration and resource allocation, which are key requirements of many public services.

Nevertheless, this type of culture is increasingly fostered and found in UK public organisations; an indication is the growth of 'task forces', and interdepartmental or interorganisational working parties and project management, to deal with particular or urgent issues.

Clan culture

The fourth model is the clan culture, also known as a 'support' culture. Based on familial notions of mutual care and support, it focuses on employee commitment and morale. Productivity arises because of the cohesiveness and sense of belonging of employees. A conservative culture, it is likely to be more internally focused than a leadership culture, although it may still be led by a strong, paternalistic manager.

Public services organisations which have been accused of being provider led and averse to change are sometimes labelled clan cultures. Professional cultures may be depicted as clan cultures. However their stability may more than compensate for any lack of external focus in the delivery of reliable, quality services.

The models described above are not the only ones, but they are amalgams of some of the best known and can usually be related to other typologies which may be proposed. One of the advantages of such modelling is that it enables surveys to be constructed, whereby managers can compare their own organisation's culture against the models. The answers to questions are computer analysed. A condensed version of such a questionnaire is presented in Exhibit 14.2 to provide a basic illustration, and to help readers to begin to position the culture of public organisations with which they are familiar against the models presented above.

The questions listed in Exhibit 14.2 are only samples of the types of issues raised when staff are asked questions to see which model of organisational culture best fits their organisation. The analysis can be complex and does not necessarily produce clear results. However, as may be apparent, the more you agreed with Statements 1 to 4, the more likely it is that you are analysing a *leadership/power* culture. The more you agreed with Statements 5 to 8, the more likely it is that you are analysing a *clan* culture. The more you agreed with Statements 9 to 12, the more likely it is that you are analysing a *task* culture. The more you agreed with Statements 13 to 15, the more that likely that you are analysing a *hierarchical* culture.

Limitations of typologies

A danger with such models is that they encourage pigeon-holing. Organisations can look for what they think they are meant to look for! Even if models are accepted as broad and oversimplified caricatures to help organisations understand themselves, it would be a mistake to see such models as fixed. They change and overlap in organisations according to a number of factors. Among these are:

- *size* – of either the overall organisation or the parts of it wherein different cultures can develop;
- *structure* – both its formal and informal structures of responsibility, accountability and power;
- *goals* – different organisations have different aims and priorities at different times;
- *history* – a unique mix of personalities, events and circumstances shapes each organisation;
- *environment* – what shifts are taking place in the society in which the organisation operates.

Exhibit 14.2

Organisational culture questionnaire

Answer the following 15 questions, circling:

5 if the statement applies absolutely to the organisation
4 if it generally applies
3 if it is as true as it is not
2 if it does not generally apply
1 if it certainly does not apply to the organisation

	Statement	*Response*
1	When I think of management, I picture one or two people who are strong leaders.	5 4 3 2 1
2	Mostly you are left to yourself in how you organise your own workload.	5 4 3 2 1
3	Excuses are not allowed for if you fail to produce the results.	5 4 3 2 1
4	People talk about developments in other similar organisations at lunch-time.	5 4 3 2 1
5	We usually organise something on people's birthdays.	5 4 3 2 1
6	Staff know and talk a lot about each other's personal life and problems.	5 4 3 2 1
7	All this government-imposed change to the organisation's work upsets people.	5 4 3 2 1
8	People prefer to be properly consulted about any change which may affect them.	5 4 3 2 1
9	There's often something new and challenging happening.	5 4 3 2 1
10	Many staff have done lots of different jobs with different people here.	5 4 3 2 1
11	Staff often use contacts outside the organisation when getting something done.	5 4 3 2 1
12	It doesn't matter how old you are or what you wear, as long as you pitch in.	5 4 3 2 1
13	People talk a lot about who has been, or might be, promoted.	5 4 3 2 1
14	At work, there are clear boundaries of acceptable and unacceptable behaviour.	5 4 3 2 1
15	When major changes happen, they take time and cause upheaval and some upset.	5 4 3 2 1

Pheysey (1993), for instance, has developed a complex succession of cultural typologies which may succeed one another as organisations go through different stages of growth or contraction in response to their operating environments. She sees these cultural models as inseparable from linked models of organisational structure and design. To further complicate the business of labelling the cultures of specific organisations, she argues that cultures change according to the balance in the permanent tension between central control and decentralised autonomy which is found in most organisations. Her suggestions below for what might be the optimum culture to prevail in different organisational circumstances should be considered with the qualification that in one organisation, different 'clusters' of subcultures can coexist simultaneously.

Pheysey suggests that clan and task cultures are compatible with self-managed groups, or with the informal egalitarian structures that befit entrepreneurial organisations which need to respond creatively and quickly to changing competitive circumstances. She suggests that leadership/power cultures are more compatible with large, centralised organisations where communication is essentially channelled vertically, whereas hierarchical cultures are compatible with classic bureaucracies where relationships are formal and governed by regulations.

The link between environment and culture is particularly significant here. Many of the anthropological studies of culture define it as the means by which people frame and structure their relationship with the environment in which they live: geography, climate, fertility, neighbouring communities and mysteries of good and bad fortune. Similarly, organisational culture can be considered to develop in response to the issues, opportunities and threats which face different organisations at different times.

Pheysey's suggestion that organisations can feature hybrid cultures, to cope with the complex range of internal and external pressures upon any organisation, is important to an understanding of the complexity of organisational culture in public services. Tradition, the demands of public accountability and the risk of media censure may result in a classic hierarchical culture prevailing in, for example, local authorities. It is precisely for this reason that managers in such organisations sometimes establish small task forces to tackle issues which demand radical thinking. They do not do so just because small groups can tackle issues more quickly than big groups. They do so because an innovative and risk-taking culture may have more chance of developing in such a group than if the same issue is addressed through formal committee mechanisms. However, such a culture may be inappropriate if the group is involved in a painstaking investigation of a procedure failure in a sensitive area of public service delivery.

CASE STUDY 14.1

The Labour Government has announced proposals for alternatives to the committee system in local government. This article shows how firmly this system is embedded in the culture of local government.

NO TIME FOR ANY OTHER BUSINESS

By Alan Pike

Of all love-hate relationships, the one between meetings and those who regularly attend them is probably among the most complex. Meetings are the place where issues are scrutinised and action determined, and time spent at them can usually be justified. But there are often grounds for suspicion that they can be a diversion from the real job.

In local government, committee meetings are a deeply entrenched part of what is still a largely late-Victorian model of decision-making. The Audit Commission, responsible for promoting efficiency in public service, expressed worries six years ago about the amount of time, energy and resources devoted by councillors to meetings in a report called *We Can't Go On Meeting Like This*. Most councils went on as though it had never been published. A minority trimmed their committees, but often replaced them with working parties.

Today the commission returns with a second document – *Representing the People: the Role of Councillors* – in a renewed attempt to persuade local authorities to review their meeting arrangements.

It includes the results of a survey of 1700 councillors that offers a classic illustration of the love-hate relationship. About 70 per cent saw representational work in the community as their most important role, while fewer than 30 per cent put committee meetings first. Yet committee meetings were by far the single most time-consuming activity of the councillors surveyed.

Paul Vevers, associate director of the commission, says it recognises the necessary part that committee meetings play in the democratic process – they ensure that decisions are taken openly and formally,

▶

help guarantee the accountability of officers and contractors, are an opportunity for the public to witness the proceedings and can be a valuable way for opposition members to raise issues. But, says Vevers, meetings are too often 'deluged with detail', with insufficient time spent following up the results of previous decisions or monitoring performance.

Councils could, he argues, release much more time for members to carry out other duties through quite modest adjustments to committees. Imagine a 60-member council that pruned its 25 committees to 23, cut each committee's meetings from 10 to eight a year, the number of members per committee from 25 to 20, and the length of meetings from four to three hours. The average meeting-time commitment of a councillor – or a manager in any other organisation that did the same – would come down from 417 to 184 hours a year.

A few councils have gone further than this hypothetical example. Members of Wycombe district council became concerned about a jump in the number of their committees from 11 in 1989 to 27 in 1995. Their solution has been to abandon the tradition of each council activity having its own committee, in favour of four committees, each focusing on one of the authority's core strategic objectives – creating a caring community, a thriving economy, a healthy environment and providing value for money.

Hartlepool unitary authority has tried to improve the quality of decision-making by setting up different committees to deal with policy, service delivery and monitoring.

Advocates of change have to find a way through another of the ingredients of the love-hate relationship – the traditional route to becoming leader of a council is through having successfully chaired its committees.

Source: Financial Times, 20 February 1997. Reprinted with permission.

Questions on the case study

1 What advantages might there be in an alternative to the committee system, such as a directly-elected mayor?

2 How might the committee system impact upon the culture of local authorities?

Problems with subcultures can arise if they expose, or even are deliberately set up to challenge, conflicting forms of power in an organisation. For instance, consultants in a hospital may be part of a professional culture developed over time and beyond the specific hospital where they work. They may feel threatened by an *ad hoc* task force if it comprises people not of the same professional culture, or if it reports to a point in the hospital where the consultants do not wield power. The very culture, or working approach, of the task force can itself become an issue.

In this section we have described the leadership/power culture model, featuring strong leadership and external goal orientation; a hierarchical culture, where roles and procedures tend to be defined and strong; a task culture, where structure and authority are contingent on the task in hand; a clan culture, where a cohesive family looks after its own members. Some of these types of culture are found in different parts of the public service (e.g. hierarchy cultures, where propriety, equity and transparency are key requirements of service). Environmental change can result in organisations having hybrid cultures; simultaneous cultures in the same organisation and culture can be determined by size, structure, goals and history. The next section considers in more detail developments in public service organisational cultures.

PUBLIC SERVICE CULTURES

Perceptions of the past

The roots of different national and institutional public service cultures are difficult to isolate and agree upon. The Napoleonic reforms in France, or the demands upon the civil service of political reform, industrialisation and empire in Victorian Britain, would feature in there somewhere. In Britain, the centralised planning involved in the Second World War, and the subsequent post-war consensus to build more and better welfare services, were also important influences on the organisational cultures in the UK civil service, health service and local government. It is important to recognise that at any one time there is a range of complex historical and environmental factors underlying prevailing public services organisational cultures. Some of these factors are so strongly rooted that change is not straightforward.

As discussed in other chapters, a prevailing global paradigm of the late twentieth century was that public services were contributing to rather than solving society's problems. Public services were perceived to have grown, to become ossified consumers of resources and sources of obstruction to reform. In this paradigm, public service cultures were seen as wrong, or as out of kilter with the requirements of society.

This view challenged many who worked in or who were believers in the existing public services. Their views had often been formed when the efficient and thorough bureaucratic organisational form had been a goal to strive for. Bureaucracy, once associated with modernity and the replacement of nepotistic or authoritarian sources of public power, had now become the problem. The battle lines were set in the 1980s and 1990s for a cultural conflict which challenged the shared meanings which gave identity and which determined process in many public services.

Characteristics of public service cultures

The essence of an organisational culture often only becomes apparent at the point at which it is under attack. Many accounts of public service cultures are given by those whose perspective is either that of an advocate of change or that of a resister of change.

Of the former, the Americans Osborne and Gaebler (1992) have been among the most influential. Their thesis was that public services had literally to reinvent what they did and how they did it or they faced losing the confidence of the taxpayers on whom they depended. This thesis was predicated on a description of the prevailing public service culture as one which was so obsessed with rules about preventing minor fraud that risk, innovation and change were stifled; and as so concerned with procedures for administering inputs that outcomes rarely featured in management's concerns.

Note that both of these examples of Osborne and Gaebler's critique are about the mindsets which lay behind the practices. It is *their* perception of the way public organisations think and behave. In creating their case that the crisis in American public services required the wholesale cultural change they advocated, Osborne and Gaebler needed to label the existing culture:

> Federal employees we know, describe colleagues who spend their days reading magazines, planning sailing trips, or buying and selling stocks . . . most estimated the number of useless personnel in their offices at 25% to 50% (Osborne and Gaebler, 1992, p 127).

This illustrates one of the key problems with organisational culture: what it is and whether it is good or bad in terms of organisational performance is a subjective issue, related to the standpoint of the person describing it. People look for and describe those anecdotes illustrating organisational cultures that are consonant with their view of the world.

Empirical attempts to characterise public service cultures are unable either to contradict or to support Osborne and Gaebler, in part for methodological reasons: anthropological studies which actually track behaviour over long enough time-frames are inherently rare, expensive and subjective. Those that exist tend only to reinforce the view that organisational cultures vary enormously within and between organisations and over time. It is thus difficult to support or reject a view that before or after a certain time public service cultures were like this or like that!

One of the most illuminating insights into a UK public service culture and its response to an overt process of cultural change can be found in Metcalfe and Richards' (1987) account of the then Conservative Government's attempts to reform the central civil service. They note that the businessman brought in to oversee the reforms, Derek (later Lord) Rayner, encountered 'the culture of Whitehall'. This was not an explicit culture, but a 'taken-for-granted' mixture of beliefs and values about the roles and responsibilities of civil servants. This featured certain characteristics: a high regard for professional expertise, a view of financial issues as administrative matters. However one of the most interesting characteristics of the culture was its attempt to resist, or at least not wholeheartedly welcome, change.

Metcalfe and Richards describe a culture which had developed an entrenched scepticism about the futility of all organisational change as mere tinkering, as bound to fail and as unrealistically loaded with jargon about long-term issues. The reality of civil servants' experience was that what matters to politicians (and therefore to civil servants) is the immediate crisis.

The account is an example of the cultural battle taking place in UK public services at the time. Professionalism, proper process and thoroughness featured in the defence of the prevailing culture. The prosecution presented a culture which was over-bureaucratic, administrative and provider led. What they advocated was a culture more responsive to the public.

A key element in the divergence of views was the role of the market. The then government took the position that it was market signals that demanded responsiveness to customers in private organisations. The view that public services had failed to generate their own signals was challenged by those who argued that the 'market' and 'customer orientation' were simply not transferable to public services, because they existed on and for a different basis (Flynn, 1988). People may not want public services (e.g. prisoners) and often have no right to choose whether to consume or not (e.g. defence).

Some prescribed a mimicking of market signals in order to generate a more responsive culture, and many of the structural reforms in public services were couched in the language of culture change.

Others stressed the need for public organisations to reorientate their thinking, procedures and practices to be more responsive to their publics. In what Michael Clarke and John Stewart (1987) called the Public Service Orientation, local authority managers were urged to:

- have the capacity to analyse service for the public
- be close to the customer
- open up the authority to the public
- make service for the public the guiding management criterion.

They specifically challenged staff who judged service quality by professional rather than customer standards or who did not involve customers in service decisions.

The idea of a 'professional culture' is important. Meek (1988), who studied cultural conflict in a university setting, contends that professional organisations such as are found in public services (e.g. education or health) are an obvious source of cultural conflict, because of the tensions between allegiance to the profession and to the organisation. The strength of a professional culture was also evident in Metcalfe and Richards' (1987) account of cultural change in the civil service, which we consider again more closely in Exhibit 14.3.

Exhibit 14.3

HM Government statistical service: professionalism under threat?

The review aimed to change attitudes in the government statistical service with the result that statisticians would become more cost conscious and would supervise data-processing staff more actively. Essentially the review team considered the statisticians to be providing on many occasions a level of statistics beyond that which was necessary for the purpose, therefore expending unnecessary costs and time. This contention was regarded as an affront to the professional integrity of the statisticians, who considered quality to be non-negotiable, and resource and staff management as administrative tasks ill-suited to self-respecting professional statisticians.

Both sides felt different pressures had greater priority in characterising the culture of the service. For the statisticians, a culture of public service was felt to demand the highest level of accuracy and professionalism. For the review team a culture of customer orientation was felt to demand that statisticians provide the statistics which were appropriate to the needs and resources of those who would be using them.

Meek argues that the tensions identified can be exacerbated by pressures for change from the external environment, leading to two competing interpretations, or stories, about what is happening to the organisation, why and what it means. This idea of hybridity, introduced earlier, is worth exploring further.

Many public organisations in the UK in the 1980s experienced hybridity of organisational culture: one group of people implementing and believing in a series of organisational reforms often predicated on market discourses and another resisting the same reforms utilising the discourse of their profession or of the 'public service ethos'.

Recall the earlier discussion of the London Borough of Hounslow's DSOs (*see* Exhibit 14.1). The Council's aim was to change the culture of that part of the Council which was being exposed to external threat. There developed increasingly different cultures operating in the same authority – hybridity again – and increasing conflict between these cultures. Managers of DSOs felt that central service departments were unresponsive, conservative and obsessed by rules. Central department managers felt that DSOs were becoming increasingly detached from the procedures and ethos which characterised being part of the Council.

Earlier, we suggested that culture is partly about how groups of people interpret the world and its events and frame their responses. It is perhaps inevitable that attempts to foster, resist or describe particular cultures in public service organisations in the UK of the 1980s and 1990s could not but be bound up in the wider political conflicts about the extent, nature and purpose of public services in society.

However, the roots of different public service cultures are steeped in their own histories and circumstances and the common view has developed in recent decades whereby the culture prevailing in public services was seen more as a problem than as an asset. This view was inherently subjective and ideologically laden and yet prescriptions for cultural change are predicated on the notion that it is because of their cultures that public services are not delivering. Increasingly, the notion of responsiveness has been offered as a prescription for public service cultures but there is a distinction between those who argue that market structures in public services foster a more responsive culture, and those who argue that a public service orientation can be fostered by training and best practice. One of the principal characteristics of the public service orientation is a shift from a professional focus to a customer focus.

TRYING TO CHANGE PUBLIC SERVICE CULTURE

Attitudes and behaviour

Underlying this chapter have been accounts of attempts to change the culture of public service organisations. Exhibit 14.4 presents a description by Colville and Packman (1996) of the results of an overt programme of bringing about cultural change in a part of the civil service in the early to middle 1990s.

The reported incongruence between attitude and behaviour described in Exhibit 14.4 goes to the heart of a managerial understanding of organisational culture in the public services. Behavioural change can be viewed as an indicator of management's success in changing organisational culture. However the case described in the Exhibit suggests that the claims of managers who report behavioural change as the result of overt programmes of cultural change need to be treated with caution.

This finding is borne out by a detailed study of a major top-down cultural change programme in a Scottish local authority in the mid-1990s (Martin, Beaumont and Staines, 1997). They report that the programme failed to change culture as desired by the Chief Executive behind it. It did not generate any common purpose within and between council departments, nor did it penetrate or last beyond a few senior managers. Indeed the programme apparently had a negative impact on the organisation's culture: increased resentment, cynicism and hostility among employees became evident.

This and other studies, in and beyond the public services, led in the late 1990s to a general reduction of the ambitions of culture change programmes, although they have remained important parts of wider programmes of organisational change.

A number of reasons can be suggested for the lack of enthusiasm with which the claims of success for cultural change programmes are viewed. First is the vested career interests of senior managers, or leaders, in exaggerating how much has changed for the better since and because of their arrival.

Second, changes in behaviour may be the result of specific changes of procedure or of resource availability and care should be taken in attributing them to cultural change.

Third, managers will behave to a certain extent in the way that their organisation officially encourages them to behave, for reasons of ambition, conformity and/or the desire for an easy life. This may not reflect an underlying shift in or rejection of prevailing culture and attitudes. The process is of course symbiotic: if what people do changes, for whatever reason, then that will inevitably influence to some degree the character of the future organisational culture.

Exhibit 14.4

Cultural change in Customs and Excise

An anti-smuggling unit in the Customs and Excise service was engaged in a search for drugs. Without reference to senior management, the staff decided to take a non-routine course of action and defrost a consignment of frozen fish about which they were suspicious. Nothing was found, nor were the soon smelling fish salvageable. Despite the consequences of a compensation claim and complaints about the slowing up of legitimate trade, the unit's line management supported the initiative shown by the staff.

The staff involved in this and similar incidents reported that this behaviour was an illustration of change in Customs and Excise, featuring more local initiative and teamworking. They also reported that the European regulatory environment often limited the scope for such initiative and that the critical factor was the personality of their particular managers rather than the departmental policy. This departmental policy featured an overt programme of cultural change, with the desired objectives of developing:

- greater freedom and accountability;
- financial and personnel delegation;
- local initiative;
- improved operational planning systems.

In practice, some staff were sceptical of higher management's tolerance of such local initiative taking. Most staff did feel, however, that communications both within units and between units and headquarters management – with 'guidelines' replacing 'instructions' – had become much more informal and two-way. Such change did not please all staff, especially longer-serving ones, and it had also led to some lack of clarity between units and headquarters over what had and had not been delegated. A more significant gap between actual and espoused behaviour was found in the 'people' aspects of the culture change programme, which deployed the currency of encouraging personal development and recognising the contribution of individuals.

Overall the evidence suggests that there was cultural change in the Customs and Excise service, but of a fragile nature which was reflected more in behavioural than in attitudinal changes. It may also not have been of the scale or permanence which changes in the operating environment, especially financial ones, required of Customs and Excise.

Source: Based on Colville and Packman (1996).

Consent and leadership

The notion of consent is important. When Westerners were observing tribes in Papua New Guinea, there was perhaps inevitably a tendency to see the cultures as the shared expressions of the individuals observed and thereby to lend culture the notion of 'collective will', or a consensus which was inherently unchallenged and unchangeable. This explains both why many leaders try to persuade all individuals to 'own' the desired new cultures and why such attempts are probably doomed to fail. The notion that a new tribal leader could both change the practices which had developed over centuries and get all to believe in the change, with its inherent jettisoning of the very factors which gave identity and meaning to the individuals' lives, is patently over-ambitious.

It can be argued that there is a contradiction between consent and leadership: if one of the key features of an organisation's culture is its shared meaning and beliefs, cultivated

Exhibit 14.5

Culture change at Hackney Council

The starting point of Elliston's progress is his analysis of the misfit between the prevailing culture and requirements of the environment. In his view, the environment demanded dramatic service improvements for the residents of the borough, who also wanted value for money and a more welcoming approach from the Council staff and buildings. He claimed he found:

- 'a blame culture which stifled innovation';
- a culture in which 'the concept of improving services seemed alien';
- 'no concept of the customer';
- staff who 'were more willing to achieve mediocrity than fall just short of excellence';
- 'deeply cynical and obstructive' senior officers.

This first stage featured a concept touched upon earlier in this chapter, an analysis that the organisation had reached crisis point and could only be saved by drastic and immediate action.

His second stage was to define the culture to which he aspired, which was essentially the opposite of what he claimed he found, 'a culture of customer care, quality services and valued staff throughout the Council'. Significant here is the force of the leader's vision. He did not develop a vision from a long process of consultation with citizens or staff; instead he canvassed support for a vision he put before them, although he obviously required support from key councillors and staff supporters to be in place for any progress to be made.

The third stage was to lead and implement the change from the present to the future culture. The methods he describes include:

- establishing systems which generated information about quality of services and track any changes thereto;
- high-profile publicity: 'staff have been deluged with leaflets, posters, booklets, videos and talks spelling out what *Transforming Hackney* means';
- getting rid of senior staff perceived as resisters: 'We have to change the culture of the organisation and that means changing some of the people';
- training, e.g. a 'quality leaders programme';
- restructuring: scrapping more than 400 posts and holding senior managers accountable for achieving results;
- proclaiming immediate achievements: in answering telephones, processing housing benefit claims, council tax collection and the repairing of potholes.

The fourth stage would be the embedding of the new culture, with Tony Elliston recognising that there are forces which are resisting and/or not showing the new 'culture' in their attitudes and work. He accepts that the changes have affected staff morale.

Tony Elliston concludes: 'There are some real service improvements coming through. We are going to get there. The pace of change is incredible. No one is going to doubt we mean business.'

Source: (1997) *Local Government Chronicle*, 4 July.

out of an unknowable blend of personalities, history and environment, then does that render it impervious to leaders who try to change it? One of the most important writers on organisational culture, Schein (1985), argued that 'organisational cultures are created by leaders, and one of the most decisive functions of leadership may well be the creation, the management, and – if and when that may become necessary – the destruction of culture.'

This brings us back to Hackney Council, with which the chapter started and which serves as an example of why and how managers try to change the cultures of public service organisations (*see* Exhibit 14.5). Tony Elliston, the then Chief Executive who could 'smell' the culture when he walked into the building, was not only observing the culture that existed (the anthropological interpretation of culture as what an organisation 'is'). He was also, as a leader, trying to prescribe and create the culture that he wanted to exist (culture being interpreted in accord with Schein as a variable within the changeable attributes that an organisation 'has').

Whether the culture did change in Hackney in Tony Elliston's four years as Chief Executive, which ended with his resignation in March 1999, (and for better or worse) is a subjective question and would in part depend on who was asked the question.

Pollitt (1993) criticises as crude, contradictory or ineffective the many British and American attempts to remould given public service cultures to order. Pollitt tends to see managers' pretensions to be able to change organisational cultures as symptomatic of the growth of managerial self-confidence and private sector management ideas in public services in recent decades.

CONCLUSIONS

The preceding discussion raises two levels of questions with which to conclude. The first is the desirability of overt culture change: are the individual and collective values, rituals and meanings of people at work the property of management to try and change? The values and actions of individuals are often regarded as resources for organisations to make use of. Can leaders impose on these resources to have all staff interpreting the environment and their actions in one way? The counter-argument is that, if culture is a variable of performance, then managers have a duty to try to engage with culture in order to deliver better performance to the publics which the organisation serves.

The second question returns to the issues raised at the start of the chapter: if culture is as intangible as the wind, is it possible for managers to change culture? Are they letting a genie out of a bottle, one over which they will have little control? This argument features strongly in the work of Pollitt and other social scientists, who see the source of organisational culture as exceedingly complex, with the actions of the present management in this analysis being but one, albeit important, ingredient of that culture. Is it possible for managers (a) to predict the results of their interventions and (b) to persuade others to frame the world in the same way in which they do?

The difficulty is that managers such as Tony Elliston can be very persuasive in reporting the benefits of their attempts to change from a culture few would defend to one for which dramatic results are being claimed. To rule culture 'out of bounds' for management may be not only inappropriate but impossible.

This last section has considered cultural change. You should now:

- be able to recognise that cultural change programmes have been widespread across UK public services in the 1980s and 1990s;
- know that, to differing extents, those responsible for such programmes encountered problems in changing culture both as extensively or as permanently as they claimed or hoped for;

- appreciate that even if behaviour related to service performance may change, underlying attitudes may not do so, and may react against the programmes;
- understand but question Schein's view that the creation and/or destruction of organisational cultures is one of the key functions of leaders;
- be able to describe some of the difficulties managers experience in this function: e.g. short-term horizons; confusing individual and collective identities; lack of control over end-result;
- be able to list the stages of a change programme as typified by Tony Elliston in Hackney: identify current culture as ill-fitted to environmental demands; envisage the new culture; implement many and symbolic changes (to systems, structures, personnel, language, training, etc.); embed and promote the achievements of the cultured change programme;
- be able to engage with the debate about the appropriateness of managers trying to change the way an organisation's staff think and behave.

REFERENCES

Clarke, M and Stewart, J (1987) 'The public service orientation: issues and dilemmas', *Public Administration*, Vol. 65, Summer, pp 161–77.

Colville, I and Packman, C (1996) 'Auditing cultural change', *Public Money and Management*, 16(3), July–September, pp 27–32.

Deal, T and Kennedy, A (1982) *Corporate Cultures*. Reading, MA: Addison-Wesley.

Flynn, N (1988) 'A consumer-oriented culture?', *Public Money and Management*, 8(2), Spring/Summer, pp 27–31.

Gerowitz, M B, Lemieux-Charles, L, Heginbotham, C and Johnson, B (1996) 'Top management culture and performance in Canadian, UK and US hospitals', *Health Services Management Research*, 9.

Handy, C (1978) *Understanding Organisations*. Harmondsworth: Penguin.

Hofstede, G (1993) 'Cultural constraints in management theories', *Academy of Management Executive*, 7(1), pp 81–95.

Martin, G, Beaumont, P B, Staines, H (1997) 'Changing corporate culture: paradoxes and tensions in a Scottish Local Authority' in Mabey, C, Skinner, D and Clark, T (eds) *HRM: The Inside Story*. London: Sage.

Meek, V L (1988) 'Organizational culture: origins and weaknesses', *Organization Studies*, 9(2), pp 453–73.

Metcalfe, L and Richards, S (1987) *Improving Public Management*. London: Sage.

Normann, R (1984) *Service Management: Strategy and Leadership in Service Business*. Chichester: Wiley.

Osborne, D and Gaebler, T (1992) *Re-inventing Government*. Reading, MA: Addison-Wesley.

Ouchi, W G (1981) *Theory, Z: How American Business can Meet the Japanese Challenge*. Reading, MA: Addison-Wesley.

Peters, T J and Waterman, R H (1982) *In Search of Excellence*. New York: Harper & Row.

Pheysey, D C (1993) *Organizational Cultures: Types and Transformations*. London: Routledge.

Pollitt, C (1993) *Managerialism and the Public Services*. Oxford: Blackwell.

Schein, E H (1985) *Organizational Culture and Leadership*. San Francisco; Jossey-Bass.

Wilson, D C and Rosenfeld, R H (1990) *Managing Organizations: Texts, Readings and Cases*. New York: McGraw-Hill.

QUESTIONS AND DISCUSSION TOPICS

1 What are the challenges involved in changing public service culture?

2 What are the key variables in seeking to change organisational culture?

15 Ethics and management

Alan Lawton

AIMS

This chapter will:

- illustrate the nature of ethical issues for public services managers;
- consider the role of ethical frameworks in understanding ethical issues;
- analyse the ethical implications of changes in the management of public services;
- examine the proposition that managing in the public services is an ethical activity and is driven by the public service ethos.

INTRODUCTION

In the UK the first report of the Nolan Committee (1995) resulted from the concerns of the then Prime Minister John Major, that 'sleaze' in government would not be tolerated. In a statement to the House of Commons on 25 October 1994 in response to 'public disquiet' about standards in public life, John Major argued for a committee:

> To examine current concerns about standards of conduct of all holders of public office, including arrangements relating to financial and commercial activities, and make recommendations as to any changes which might be required to ensure the highest standards of propriety in public life (*Hansard*, 25 October 1994, col. 758).

The wide-ranging terms of reference for the committee included the activities of ministers, civil servants, government advisers, MPs and Euro MPs, members of non-departmental bodies and the National Health Service (NHS), elected politicians and senior managers in local government, and members of quasi-governmental agencies. According to the Prime Minister:

> This country has an international reputation for the integrity and honour of its public institutions. The reputation must be maintained and be seen to be maintained (*Hansard*, 25 October 1994, col. 758).

Such a concern is not unique to the UK. The Organisation for Economic Co-operation and Development (OECD) (1996) examined the role of public officials in eight countries and argued that there is a growing convergence in what is seen as 'good and proper' behaviour.

More recently, in response to the Nolan Committee's report on local government, the Labour Government has sought to develop a new ethical framework for local government;

Accordingly, the Prime Minister committed the Government, working in partnership with local government, to establish a new ethical framework for the conduct of the more than 20,000 councillors and 2 million council staff in Great Britain. It is the Government's agenda to make the radical changes needed to put in place a new conduct regime which will build and secure the people's trust in those who serve them in their local councils. (DETR, 1998, para 1.6)

Ethical management in the public services is firmly on the agenda. The notion of 'the manager' in public services is not always clear-cut and we take it to include different categories of public service employees. Thus, teachers, nurses, doctors and a whole host of professionals in the public services are carrying out managerial responsibilities, particularly in terms of managing people or budgets. Our concern is therefore with:

- the impact on managers of managing in an increasingly complex and ambiguous environment where the management task is no longer a given and involves managing across organisational boundaries;
- the increasing demands for managers to take more responsibility but without necessarily having the appropriate authority;
- reconciling individual values with organisational values;
- the nature of the public service ethos;
- issues concerning the implementation of public policy so that it does not affect in an adverse way those that are charged with implementation and those that are the recipients or users of such services;
- the changing organisational context and the resulting pressures on staff;
- the relationship between politicians and managers and the location of accountability and responsibility;
- the motivation of those working in the public services and their perceptions of their duty to citizens as a whole;
- the ascription of responsibility to public services managers when it is often difficult to isolate the performance of individual managers;
- the pressures that are brought to bear on managers including peer pressure – 'This is the way we do things around here'; pressure from the law; organisational pressures to meet targets; rules and codes of conduct; pressure from an ever-demanding citizenry that is increasingly vocal in pursuit of its rights.

CASE STUDY 15.1

Managerial reform in the public services can have implications for the ethical base on which it rests. This article focuses on how delegation of responsibility has implications for accountability and safeguards.

CIVIL SERVICE OVERHAUL 'CREATES RISKS'

By Nicholas Timmins

The public management 'revolution' in Whitehall over the past decade has created risks and raised new anxieties which have still to be resolved, Sir Robin Butler, the cabinet secretary and head of the home civil service, warned yesterday.

Declaring himself 'a little demob happy' in the run-up to his retirement early next year, Sir Robin said the devolution of management responsibility to arm's-length agencies and open recruitment to top civil service posts had been 'inevitable and right'.

But he warned the government that many issues raised by the changes 'remain to be tackled' and that they had created 'new risks' over accountability, ethics and policymaking. He told an Economic and Social Research Council conference on the future of Whitehall: 'There . . . remain concerns that in our zeal to improve management we have neglected the policy process.' There was a risk of departments and agencies becoming so focused on delivering their own results that they pursued them at the cost of each other and 'of the larger objectives of the government'.

There remained concerns that delegation to chief executives 'obscures and blunts the democratic accountability of ministers'. In addition, delegation of powers needed 'to be accompanied by powerful auditing and transparency' and strong training so the public sector tradition of equity of process was preserved amid the demand to achieve results.

While the government had made clear the drive for efficiency and responsiveness would continue, Sir Robin said: 'It is to these areas that some of the emphasis will now switch as part of the process of building greater confidence between citizen and government.'

He added: 'The shortage of public resources to meet the ever-growing demand for high quality public services is as acute as ever.' Who's watching the watchdogs?

Source: Financial Times, 25 September 1997. Reprinted with permission.

Question on the case study

Which of the ten bullet points listed above the case study might be affected by the changes indicated in the article?

ETHICAL ISSUES

Our first concern is to identify ethical issues. There are certain issues which appear to be universal and enduring, whether the matter with which we are concerned relates to police corruption, fraud, bribing officials, the acceptance of gifts, the outside employment of officials, the misuse of contracts and so on. Whether such matters are becoming more widespread is a moot point. If they are on the increase is it because individual managers are becoming more corrupt or is it because organisational monitoring processes are breaking down or not being enforced? In its report on probity in the NHS, for example, the Audit Commission (1996, p 14) found instances of fraud, particularly in the area of prescription charges, but argued that:

> NHS trust and HA boards and senior managers must remain vigilant and ensure that a strong framework of effective internal controls is in place to prevent and detect fraud and corruption. The majority of fraud cases occur in areas of lax controls, poor segregation of duties and lack of regular monitoring. This fact reinforces the need for management to review constantly the effectiveness of their control mechanisms.

The eighth report of the Committee of Public Accounts (1994) came to similar conclusions in its investigations, finding that most problems arise because of the inadequacy of financial controls, failure to comply with existing rules, inadequate stewardship of public money and failure to provide value for money. The report concludes that it is not so much the immoral behaviour of individual managers that is of concern but the failure of existing procedures and rules. Nevertheless, individuals in organisations do act unethically and we cannot shift all the responsibility on to the failure of processes.

What counts as unethical behaviour is, however, difficult to decide. Try to complete the questionnaire presented in Exhibit 15.1.

Exhibit 15.1

Ethics at work

Please tick the appropriate column	Never	Sometimes	Often
Have you taken stationery or other items home from your workplace for personal use?	☐	☐	☐
Have you used the office telephone for personal calls without permission?	☐	☐	☐
Have you asked a colleague to cover for you when you are out?	☐	☐	☐
Have you told 'white lies' to customers or clients such as 'the cheque is in the post' when it is not?	☐	☐	☐
Have you blamed and criticised colleagues?	☐	☐	☐
Have you exaggerated your achievements?	☐	☐	☐
Have you revealed confidential information when not authorised to do so?	☐	☐	☐
Have you done what you believed to be wrong because everybody else does it?	☐	☐	☐
Have you tempered advice to politicians and senior managers to give them what they want to hear?	☐	☐	☐
Have you taken free lunches from clients or customers?	☐	☐	☐
Have you shifted blame to elsewhere in the organisation, e.g., 'It's the computer's fault'?	☐	☐	☐
Have you bent the rules to get things done?	☐	☐	☐
Have you carried out a task that you fundamentally disagreed with?	☐	☐	☐
Have you covered up for a colleague?	☐	☐	☐
Have you acted in favour of a contractor or client because of a bribe?	☐	☐	☐
Have you acted in favour of a client or contractor out of friendship	☐	☐	☐
Have you presented misleading information?	☐	☐	☐
Have you manipulated performance indicators so as to reach targets?	☐	☐	☐
Have you kept information back from clients concerning entitlements because of resource constraints?	☐	☐	☐

Did you answer 'Never' to all of the questions in Exhibit 15.1? The point of the exercise is not to demonstrate how 'squeaky clean' you are but to show the range of issues that we face in our organisational lives. All of the above questions seem to involve:

- our relationship with others, both inside and outside organisations;
- our relationship with the organisation as a whole;
- values;
- our personal behaviour;
- the relationship between means and ends;
- stealing;
- fraud;
- loyalty;
- impartiality.

How you respond will demonstrate how you perceive organisational behaviour. We are not here interested in indicating 'right' and 'wrong' behaviour but in illustrating where ethical considerations might come into play.

Should we be concerned just with the 'big' issues? In their research, Steinberg and Austen (1990) presented 1000 American government officials with a set of 14 ethical dilemmas. The following reasons were given to justify unethical behaviour.

1 Good intentions – managers expressed frustration with red tape and took short cuts to achieve what they believed to be desirable ends.
2 Ego power trip – where individuals saw opportunities to demonstrate their control.
3 Plain greed.
4 Ignorance of rules, laws, codes, policies and procedures.
5 Peer pressure which condones unethical behaviour.
6 Friendship.
7 Ideology and political values.
8 Personal or family gain.
9 Offering favours in order to secure future employment on leaving public service.
10 Financial problems and pressures.
11 Stupidity.
12 Exploiting the exploiters – a feeling of being hard done by.
13 Survival at all costs.
14 Following orders.

Sometimes people do immoral things for good reasons. However, commenting upon business ethics, MacLagan (1995, pp 161–2) makes the point that:

> The emphasis on decision-making in 'dramatic' cases which is so often assumed to be the essence of business ethics, deflects attention from the point that, since many ethical issues are much more pervasive than that, these may be overlooked. The everyday things – matters of discourse and conduct towards others . . . or the insidious way in which systemic factors such as culture, control mechanisms and 'taken-for-granted' culture in the organisation . . . can have ethical implications – need to be brought to peoples' attention.

This quotation encapsulates the position taken in this chapter: that ethics is as much concerned with the way we treat each other as individuals as with the 'dramatic' cases involving fraud, corruption, bribery and so on. Managers interact with a range of stakeholders both internal and external and hold positions of trust, power and privilege. How that trust is discharged in terms of fulfilling obligations, protecting the rights of others and so on is at the heart of ethics. Many of the issues are enduring, and organisational pressures to meet targets, manage with scarce resources or respond to a range of different stakeholders are not unique to the UK, nor are they unique to managers working in the public services.

THEORY AND PRINCIPLES

We are concerned with ethics as a practical guide rather than simply as a set of theories about human action. However, we do need a theoretical background. Ethics can be defined as a set of principles, often defined as a code or system that acts as a guide to conduct. These guides to conduct will be concerned with how individuals act, what are their intentions in so acting and a set of values defining what is to count as right or wrong action. These values will be morally significant; respect for human life is a value that is morally significant; preference for a particular type of car may be a value but it may not be morally significant. The relationship between values and ethics is not always clear-cut, particularly if we accept that different cultures and societies have different values. For example, managers in the UK may feel it unethical to hire staff on the basis of nepotism. The concept of appointment by merit is highly valued. In other parts of the world, however, family loyalty is of profound importance and it is expected to be of relevance in the appointment or promotion of staff.

The notions of good or bad are an essential part of the language of ethics although their meaning is sometimes obscure. Is the good manager the same as the good person? We can construct a list of qualities that we would expect the good manager to possess and these might include loyalty to the organisation, enthusiasm, commitment, efficiency, resourcefulness, having certain competences in people and financial management and so on. The notion of the good person might include notions of generosity, unselfishness, being loyal to family and friends, respecting the rights of others and so on. There is also the possibility that being a good manager may come into conflict with being a good person.

We can distinguish between morals and ethics. We take morals to be concerned with action and ethics with setting the boundaries or providing a framework for appropriate action. An individual may have a firm grasp of the principles at stake in a particular situation and still decide to act immorally. Morals define how a person lives up to the demands of what is perceived to be correct behaviour. Ethics defines the effort to systemise and define the reasons for our moral assessments. We do pass judgements on others from an ethical point of view. What are the kinds of decisions that can be made? Is making a moral decision similar to making any other kind of decision where we add up the pros and cons and proceed if the pros outweigh the cons? Why do people act the way that they do? Criteria might include:

- act in accordance with rules;
- act out of a sense of justice;
- act to secure the most beneficial consequences for most people;
- act out of a sense of duty;
- act in a way that satisfies conscience;
- act out of guilt;
- act in such a way because everybody else does;
- act in such a way because told to do so by friends, family, senior managers etc.

All of these criteria can be located within ethical traditions and we examine briefly the main tenets of these traditions.

ETHICAL THEORIES

Deontological theories

Deontological theories maintain that the right action to pursue is independent of the consequences of that action. The ends are less important than the means. The right action is to keep promises, repay debts, abide by contracts irrespective of what the consequences are. This view is most commonly associated with the work of the German philosopher Immanuel Kant whose famous categorical imperative argued that 'I ought never to act in such a way except that I can also will that my maxim should become a universal law'. In other words, do unto others as you would have them do to you. It is about treating people fairly and with respect. We can think of many relationships within the public services that are of this kind. The doctor has a duty of care towards the patient, the teacher towards the student. This is a characteristic of professional roles within the public services. However, it is often difficult to always keep promises or to always tell the truth irrespective of the consequences. Should the doctor always tell the patient that he or she has a terminal illness? We do consider the consequences.

Teleological theories

Teleological theories provide the second major guide to moral decisions, where actions are evaluated in terms of their consequences. Public policy goals, in terms of a better educated or healthier citizenry, might be examples of such consequences. Utilitarianism is the best-known teleological theory. Utilitarianism holds that an action is morally justifiable if it leads to the greatest happiness of the greatest number. The concept of measurement is a key feature of utilitarianism and a variation of utilitarianism can be found in cost–benefit analysis. For example, in the planning of a new airport, the costs and benefits of noise pollution, road congestion, threats to life and wildlife, threats to the quality of life, the benefits of different forms of transport and so on would be calculated in as comprehensive a manner as possible. Utilitarianism is concerned with the maximisation of good and the minimisation of harm. However, it may be difficult to put a figure on, for example, the quality of life, even though it has become commonplace when allocating medical resources to be required to do so. However, the problems with this approach are numerous:

1 In practice it is impossible to weigh up all the available options before acting.
2 We may never be able to account for all the consequences of an action.
3 Over what timescale are we to calculate costs and benefits?
4 It presupposes that we can put a numerical value on everything.

The virtues approach

A virtues approach looks to the qualities of individuals which allow them to be moral. This approach has a long history going back to Confucius and Aristotle and its modern equivalent can be found in those virtues that are said to characterise public officials. It is thus argued that public policies will be ethical because those managers involved in the formulation and implementation of policy possess integrity and probity, are impartial and honest and so on. This view is one that is shared by professionals in the public services, who see their professional ethos as virtuous.

The justice approach

Justice is concerned with issues of fairness, entitlement and desert. The formal principle of justice can be stated in terms of treating like cases alike and unlike cases differently. Justice can take two forms, distributive justice and procedural justice. The first is concerned with how goods and services are distributed in society. It is argued that the market is unjust since it discriminates against those who are poor, uneducated and unemployed. Within organisations, criteria for distributive justice might be applied, for example, when allocating an annual bonus and may take the form of:

- to each person an equal share, irrespective of individual contribution;
- to each person according to need, an approach which recognises individual needs;
- to each person according to individual rights, possibly as stipulated in a contract;
- to each according to individual merit, an approach which recognises the quality of individual contributions;
- to each according to effort.

Procedural justice is concerned to make sure that processes and procedures are fair and non-discriminatory. Arguments in favour of bureaucracy are often made from the point of view of procedural justice.

The rights-based approach

Individuals have rights. These include legal, political, employee and human rights. Rights are often seen as correlatives of duties. That is, employees may have certain rights such as the right to a healthy and safe working environment but at the same time they may have a duty to give 'a fair day's work for a fair day's pay'. At the time of writing the Labour Government is seeking to rewrite the Patient's Charter for the NHS which takes account of the fact that patients do have rights but also have duties, such as keeping appointment times and not abusing staff.

We have indicated the flavour of some of the best-known ethical theories which can inform the actions of public services managers. At the same time we need to recognise that:

> Making moral decisions usually involves finding a balance among different values that conflict. This kind of 'moral pluralism' is highly pragmatic and well suited to the type of value diversity that characterises modern democratic societies. In terms of consequences, a realistic public administrator cannot ignore any basic moral principle that is 'out there' and likely to influence the effectiveness of the agency's mission. Tolerance thus lies at the heart of the ethical responsibility of the administrator in a democratic society (Pops, 1994, p 165).

This will particularly be the case if we see the task of the public services manager as reconciling the interests of a multitude of different stakeholders.

In reality it is likely that managers will act as a result of group norms and values, sets of principles and traditional practices rather than consciously follow a consistent adoption of an ethical theory. There appears to be, at least, some agreement on what those principles might be. The Nolan report, which we introduced at the beginning of this chapter, identified seven principles of public life:

1 *Selflessness* – which is consistent with a wider concern with the public interest.
2 *Integrity* – which focuses on obligations and duties.
3 *Objectivity* – which is concerned with merit and principles of justice.
4 *Accountability* – which involves procedural justice.
5 *Openness* – which is linked to the wider public interest.
6 *Honesty* – which involves duties and conflicts of interests.
7 *Leadership* – which extols the virtues required by public services managers.

However, both ethical theorists and practitioners indicate that a range of principles should be taken together rather than rely on one principle, and that these principles reflect an ethical framework. Public services managers are as much concerned with *how* services are delivered as with *what* is delivered, with means as well as ends. Looking after client interests means treating them with care, attention and sensitivity, and indeed with respect.

Both the OECD and the UK government have recently identified key principles for public services (*see* Table 15.1).

Table 15.1 Principles of public service

OECD principles 1998	UK local government principles 1998
Ethical standards for public service should be clear	Community leadership, preserving public confidence in the council
Ethical standards should be reflected in the legal framework	Duty to uphold the law
Ethical guidance should be available to public servants	Constituency; recognising that there are general interests as well as constituents' interests
Public servants should know their rights and obligations when exposing wrongdoing	Selflessness, acting in the public interest
Political commitment to ethics should reinforce the ethical conduct of public servants	Integrity and propriety
The decision-making process should be transparent and open to scrutiny	Hospitality; refusing hospitality which might be intended to buy influence
There should be clear guidelines for interaction between the public and private sectors	Decisions should be the responsibility of the individual, but the influence of, for example, party groups should be recognised
Managers should demonstrate and promote ethical conduct	Objectivity in decision taking, decisions taken on merit
Management policies, procedures and practices should promote ethical conduct	Accountability
Public service conditions and management of human resources should promote ethical conduct	Openness
Adequate accountability mechanisms should be in place in the public service	Confidentiality is handled in accordance with law
Appropriate procedures and sanctions should exist to deal with misconduct	Stewardship of council resources
	Participation in council decisions
	Declarations of private interests
	Relations with officers, respecting the roles of officers

Sources: PUMA (1998); DETR (1998).

The local government principles presented in Table 15.1 are written as guidelines for politicians but they can, for the most part, be applied to managers.

THE PUBLIC SERVICE ETHOS

We have certain expectations of our public managers, and see the relationship between the citizens and their officials as a cornerstone of government:

> Effective democratic government – be it at central or local level – requires a bond of trust between the people and those in public life who serve them. To restore and maintain that trust at local level is at the heart of our agenda to modernise local government (DETR, 1998, p 5).

Many of the principles described in the above quotation are said to be part of the public service ethos and that those working in the public services are bound by, and subscribe to, this ethos. It is generally considered to be a 'good thing' and is said to consist of honesty, impartiality, integrity, probity, accountability, promotion on merit and so on. Public services managers bring all of these qualities to bear in promoting the public interest.

The public service ethos is said to consist of a set of values held in common by public services managers and expressed through the virtues described above. Pratchett and Wingfield (1994) in their work on local government describe a generic public service ethos comprising accountability, bureaucratic behaviour, a sense of community, motivation and loyalty. However, two main assumptions are made concerning this ethos:

1 There is something distinctive about managing in the public services. This view is contested, as we have argued in Part 1 of this book.
2 There is a common ethos that binds those who work in the public services.

Let us examine the second assumption. The concept of a unified and uniform public service may have little meaning given the differences between managing in local government, the civil service, health and any number of other bodies. If we examine the civil service alone, we find civil servants engaged in a number of different tasks which include the analysis of policy issues, the formation of policy under political direction, the implementation of policy, the delivery of services to the public, the management of resources, the regulation of outside bodies and so on. In the UK civil service, policy work is carried out by some 10 per cent of the total and yet the concerns of those who work in the 'Whitehall Village' have, to all intents and purposes, dominated the agenda.

In local government and in health services, the agenda has been dominated by a different set of stakeholders, notably professionals. Pratchett and Wingfield (1994, p 14) question the assumption of a generic public service ethos in local government:

> The public service ethos is a confused and ambiguous concept which is only given meaning by its organisational and functional situation, and may be subject to very different interpretations over both time and location.

They identify differences on the basis of:

- the role that the local authority plays – the minimalist local authority which seeks to encourage the delivery of services through other organisations, questions the importance of the public service ethos, in contrast to those who see themselves more readily engaging with the wider community;

- the diversity of professionals, with individuals tending to look to their own profession rather than to the organisation as a whole.

Increasingly it is also believed that the public service ethos is coming under threat from the management reforms that have taken place in recent years in many OECD countries (*see* Lawton, 1998a). There are fears that the new world of public services management, made up of risk-taking, innovative and entrepreneurial managers who engage in a range of relationships with the private sector, is in some way being corrupted. There is little evidence for this widespread belief and little evidence that managers in private sector organisations are in general any more corrupt. However, the fragmentation of service delivery may erode a sense of collegiality but it is difficult to ascertain how strong that sense was in the first place. Not only that, but group norms can act negatively as well as positively and 'don't inform on your mates' becomes an operating credo even though 'your mates' might be corrupt! It may be the case, as we discussed above, that some of the traditional controls of bureaucracy are being undermined by allowing managers 'the freedom to manage', with the result that accountability is being bypassed.

However, there appears to be little evidence that the public ethos service is being undermined, notwithstanding its elusiveness in the first place. Indeed, those who support management reforms and the introduction of more market-like conditions for the provision of public services argue that greater competition and transparency actually leads to less corrupt government.

There is also an assumption that the public service ethos is necessarily a good thing. One former senior civil servant has argued that the values of senior officials are a complex blend of, on the one hand, all the traditional virtues such as honesty, integrity, loyalty to colleagues and an enormous capacity for hard work. However, they also include traditional vices such as conservatism, caution, scepticism, elitism, a touch of arrogance and too often a deeply held belief that 'the business of government can be fully understood only by government professionals' (Plowden, 1994, p 74). Pratchett and Wingfield (1994) found that a quarter of their local authority survey believed in the existence of the public service ethos and characterised it as a negative concept which stifled initiative, was bound by red tape, providing little challenge or stimulation and occasionally corrupt.

There are those who look back to a 'golden age' of the public service ethos and regret its passing; we have questioned its existence in the first place and challenged the assumption that it is necessarily a good thing. However, a range of organisational and peer group pressures will have an impact on the individual manager, perhaps more readily than societal pressures.

THE ORGANISATIONAL DIMENSION

Individuals work in organisations and we should also be interested in the organisational pressure that individuals are placed under by their organisations. It is part of the rhetoric of Human Resource Development (HRD) that people are an organisation's greatest asset. Organisations are places where people interact with each other for a good deal of their lives and we are as much concerned with the way in which public service organisations treat their staff as with the impact of their policies in the wider community. Means are as important as ends. As Reiser (1994, p 28) argues:

> Yet organizations declare what really counts by their treatment of staff, the institutional goals they set, and how they handle controversy and conflicts. What they do tells us what they value.

How organisations treat their staff will be mediated through the structures that they adopt. You will recall the discussion of bureaucratic structures. Hummel (1987), for example, argues that bureaucracies require that individuals follow rules and conform to certain role expectations and that their activities are depersonalised. Bureaucrats are treated as means to an end and bureaucracy is oppressive to employees. The evidence for this tends to be rather weak, although strong on rhetoric. Indeed, Goodsell (1994) has argued that bureaucrats are pretty much like everybody else and that individuals do not become petty tyrants when they enter organisations. We may wonder at the extent to which the 'bureaucratic mentality' exists in individuals before they enter organisations. If it does not exist does it result from the bureaucratic culture? We have already considered the argument that the public service ethos is deemed to be a good thing which may be challenged by the confines of a bureaucratic ethos. However, as we have already indicated, the public services are characterised by diversity rather than homogeneity. There is a real diversity in the activities of public officials working in agencies and departments which perform a range of functions including regulation, delivery, policy advice, collecting taxation, trading and so on. In Chapter 14 we examined the notion of culture and subcultures in detail.

The relationship between the organisation and the individual is a complex one involving reciprocal rights and duties, as we discussed earlier. The nature of the individual's commitment will depend upon:

- the extent to which the individual has internalised the views of the organisation which in turn will depend upon how congruent individual and organisational values are;
- the extent to which organisational objectives reflect individual objectives;
- the extent of the involvement and psychological immersion in work;
- the extent to which individuals value the organisation as a place where they spend a large chunk of their waking lives.

Occasionally, the relationship is called into question when individual employees 'blow the whistle' and reveal information about an organisation and its activities that the organisation does not wish to have revealed. One well-known example of whistleblowing was the case of Clive Ponting, a senior civil servant in the Ministry of Defence, who leaked information to an Opposition MP concerning the sinking of the Argentine ship *Belgrano* during the Falklands War. Ponting argued that government ministers had lied to Parliament and that it was in the public interest that this information should be made public. Ponting contended that he had a duty to Parliament and the public interest over and above that of the government of the day. Ponting was put on trial and acquitted.

A key issue here is the loyalty of public servants. Chapter 5 examined this in the context of accountability. Critics argue that the act of whistleblowing may be justified in extreme circumstances and where the individual is not acting in bad faith; has reasonable grounds for believing the information to be accurate; is not making the disclosure primarily in order to make financial gain and has raised the matter internally first. Increasingly, whistleblowing is being sanctioned as a legitimate act (*see* DETR, 1998).

How an organisation treats its staff is crucial to a discussion of ethics for managing the public services. Our view is that it is no good focusing on lofty discussions of the public interest when employees are being pushed to work longer hours, take on more responsibility or have their contracts renegotiated. It is at the level of relationships between individuals that ethics is played out. Claims that an organisation is promoting the common welfare or the local community do not stand up if it treats its own staff appallingly. Not only would it be unethical but it would not, ultimately, be credible.

THE INDIVIDUAL: ROLES AND RELATIONSHIPS

The heart of ethics is about individuals acting and making decisions about a range of issues concerning other individuals and themselves. The public services manager engages in a range of relationships which will take different forms:

- with customers, which might involve an economic exchange dominated by purchasing power;
- with citizens generally, where rights and duties will be involved;
- with the client, which might be dominated by a professional exchange and depend upon power;
- with politicians, which will be hierarchical in nature and be determined by authority and accountability;
- with colleagues, which might be open-ended exchanges where equal status is shared.

Much of the evidence involving managerial work seems to indicate that managers spend much of their time engaged in establishing and maintaining relationships (*see* Hales, 1986 and Conway, 1993). The principles of public service, as described in the previous section, are expressed through individuals engaged in these relationships in terms of obligation, trust, loyalty and duty. It is in seemingly small acts that the public service ethos is revealed. The manager is at the centre of a web of relationships and with a network of loyalties. The manager gives expression to the ethos through dealing with people in terms of care, diligence, courtesy and integrity. It is the quality of these face-to-face relationships that is important.

Thus, the civil servant may be subject to a range of competing duties and obligations; to ministers, to the Crown as an employer, to colleagues, to a professional body, to citizens and to others in his or her capacity as a private individual. The location of duties and obligations will depend on the functions performed. For example, senior officials in policy areas are concerned with traditional accountability to the minister and with offering impartial advice; chief executives in agencies with a more commercial role might be concerned with 'more bang for the buck' to ensure that public money is not wasted.

However, officials may have extra responsibilities because of their public roles, but they do not leave aside their consciences at the office door. In requiring public officials to treat their clients with respect, integrity and courtesy, we are demanding more than we would demand of them as private citizens. As Jos and Hines (1993, p 382) argue:

> The public service presents employees with moral issues that require attributes often associated with private lives – sensitivity, compassion, trustworthiness – as well as those generally regarded as appropriate to our public and professional lives – impartiality and effective attainment of externally imposed goals. That is, the administrative domain is not solely public or private.

The importance of trust between parties is a key factor in sustaining relationships. It takes different forms, for example, between ministers and their officials, between professionals and their clients. Trust is thus at the heart of any of the relationships that abound in the public services. We now examine these in turn.

Minister–civil servant relations

Minister–civil servant relationships are, in theory, characterised by officials offering impartial advice to ministers in return for ministerial protection in front of, for example, Parliamentary committees. This trust appeared to break down in the 1980s as the civil service was blamed for problems suffered by the economy in the early 1980s. The then Prime Minister, Margaret Thatcher, disapproved of their lack of commitment and the tradition of neutrality sits uneasily alongside that. Evidence of the decline in the relationship can be found in civil servants leaking information, the attack on pay and conditions, the reduction in the number of civil servants, increased use of outsiders for advice and civil service strikes.

That the relationship between civil servants and ministers is in need of clarification is evident from our discussion of accountability in Chapter 5 where we saw that the creation of arm's-length agencies has created problems concerning the locus of accountability and responsibility. Trust appears to have declined, unspoken agreements appear to have been broken, hence the call for codes of conduct to clarify the relationship.

Professional–client relations

A second dimension involves professional–client relationships where we have to trust the professional because we do not have the expertise or the information possessed by him or her. In return, for the relationships are always two-way, the professional gains a high degree of control over the work he or she does, and high status. Discretion is exercised at all levels within the public services whether it be in terms of policing, social work or whatever. We have to trust professionals to do their job and not abuse their power.

There is a danger, as critics of professionalism argue, that they may have too much power and act in their own interest rather than that of their clients. Hence, the need for codes of conduct, and for the increased use of contracts to specify performance.

GUIDELINES FOR CONDUCT: RULES AND REGULATIONS

Individuals working in groups operate within systems of rules, both formal and informal, which perform a number of different functions.

1 Formal rules can ensure consistency, continuity, control and accountability.
2 Informal rules will aid in developing an organisational culture, in establishing customs and norms and in helping to develop harmonious relationships.

Sometimes, however, compliance with rules becomes of overriding importance, so that the existence of a rule becomes an excuse for suspending critical judgement. Employees can get worn down by too many rules which appear to erect barriers to achieving objectives. Staff may take short cuts.

One way of regulating behaviour in organisations is through codes of conduct. A code can function as a public statement of ethical principles and it informs others of what to expect. Codes can take various forms. Kernaghan (1975) identified codes as lying on a continuum, at one end of which is a 'Ten Commandments' approach which includes a general statement of broad ethical principles but which makes no provision for monitoring or enforcement. At the other extreme is what Kernaghan called the Justinian code, which represents a comprehensive and detailed coverage of both principles and administrative arrangements.

Codes can perform a number of general functions, which include:

- acting as a guide to conduct, promoting ethical behaviour;
- regulating behaviour, and deterring unethical behaviour;
- providing a set of standards of behaviour, a written benchmark;
- identifying a set of principles and values;
- providing clear guidelines, thus minimising ambiguity;
- providing a means to resolve disputes and dilemmas;
- providing sanctions in the case of unethical conduct.

Most codes that are applied to managing in the public services seem to include:

- specifying the legal environment;
- disclosure of information;
- relations between politicians, managers and the wider public;
- employment matters;
- outside commitments and conflicts of interest;
- hospitality and relations with outside contractors.

There are, however, a number of powerful criticisms of codes:

1 They can provide a false sense of security – 'We have a code, therefore we must be an ethical organisation'.
2 They cannot be comprehensive enough to cover all eventualities.
3 They may reflect the interests of those who draw them up. For example, in further and higher education there are key issues to be resolved between managers and lecturers in terms of new contracts, teaching hours, quality and so on and yet managers are keen to develop a code of conduct that focuses on the staff–student relationship.
4 They are often vague and generalised and do not offer enough specific advice for the hard-pressed manager.
5 They can act as a shield to hide behind and may protect the professions.
6 They may be ineffective in dealing with systemic corruption.

Written codes are an important but insufficient means of promoting public service ethics. How ethical issues are internalised is crucial. Professional socialisation can play an important role when it becomes second nature to put the interest of the client first. High-profile issues such as those involved in corruption are only a small part of the field.

CONCLUSIONS

A focus on ethics can take place at different levels: the individual, the organisational and the social. We might ask the following questions:

1 How can we make public services managers more ethical, assuming that we feel that they should be?
2 What are the pressures that organisations place individuals under and how can the ethical organisation become a reality?
3 Does society want its public services to be ethical and how does it define those ethics?

In response to the first question, we might have to accept that there will always be individuals in any organisation who are willing to act corruptly or in ways that are generally considered to be immoral. Dittenhofer (1995) identifies a number of syndromes that motivate people to act in undesirable ways:

- the injustice syndrome, which drives people to fraud because they believe that their remuneration is unfair;
- the rejection of control syndrome, where people fight against perceived control through perpetrating minor irregularities;
- the challenge syndrome, for whom beating the system is a challenge;
- the 'due me' syndrome, where individuals do not feel that they have received their due reward;
- the 'Robin Hood' syndrome, redistributing what are deemed by the perpetrators to be 'social assets';
- the borrowing syndrome, where the individual borrows small amounts which become increasingly difficult to pay back;
- the 'it will never be missed' syndrome, where stepping over the line is seen as no big deal;
- the need/temptation syndrome, which is the most frequent reason for fraud and embezzlement;
- the ego syndrome, which may lead a person to falsify targets or accounts to make performance appear better than it is;
- the dissatisfaction syndrome, where the individual believes that he or she has been victimised and wishes to take revenge.

There may be psychological explanations for corrupt behaviour. Research on the moral development of individuals is relevant here. Kohlberg (1976) offers the best-known approach and he argues that individuals pass through three basic levels in terms of their capacity to engage in independent moral reasoning, which takes place in six stages:

Level 1: Pre-conventional

- Stage 1, where individuals adopt reward-seeking and punishment-avoiding behaviour in an almost stimulus–response manner, and where rules are followed without question.
- Stage 2, where individuals seek to maximise personal gain and take an instrumental view of human relations. Obligations will be met, unless one can get away with not doing so.

Level 2: Conventional

- Stage 3, where individuals will seek to get along with peers and win approval from them.
- Stage 4, which is characterised by classical role conformity and where the importance of rules is paramount. It conforms to the classical depiction of the bureaucrat.

Level 3: Post-conventional

- Stage 5, which recognises a wider commitment to the public interest and to a rational view of social utility.
- Stage 6, which is concerned with principles or autonomous reasoning by individuals, committed to moral principles.

It is interesting to speculate where a whistleblower might fit into this!

A second focus on ethics relates to the role played by the organisation. We have already discussed codes of conduct and suggested that these may be necessary but not sufficient. Organisations may go a stage further and introduce ethical training as part of their HRD programmes. Such programmes could cover a range of topics including knowledge of ethical principles and use of case studies to explore their application; understanding of the role of public services in the wider community; understanding of traditional administrative principles of accountability, loyalty, integrity, probity etc.; recognising the location of power in organisations. Increasingly, organisational theorists are advocating the development of the learning organisation as the most appropriate vehicle for such training, as we discuss in Chapter 16.

Finally, such an approach may also need a societal dimension. This is the argument developed by Ranson and Stewart (1994), who argue for a public services as part of a learning society. Chapman (1995) takes this view and argues that there are two considerations to be taken into account to ensure that ethical standards are maintained. The first is concerned with education and training both for holders of public office and for the public at large. The other is:

> continuing public discussion and emphasis of the high standards that are expected. A society which fails to demand high standards in public life and which sneers and denigrates those who are doing their best in difficult circumstances, cannot expect that high standards will be achieved or maintained. This is not just the responsibility of a relatively few people in public life, but a social responsibility for everyone (1995, p 13).

Many of the issues raised in this chapter are explored more fully in Lawton (1998b).

REFERENCES

Audit Commission (1996) *Protecting the Public Purse: Ensuring Probity in the NHS*. Abingdon: Audit Commission Publications.

Chapman, R A (1995) 'The first report on standards in public life', *Teaching Public Administration*, 15(2), pp 1–14.

Committee of Public Accounts (1994) *Eighth Report: The Proper Conduct of Public Business*. London: The Stationery Office.

Conway, D (1993) 'The day of the manager', *Community Care*, 19 August, pp 20–1.

DETR (1998) *Modernising local government: A new ethical framework*. London: Department of the Environment, Transport and the Regions.

Dittenhofer, M A (1995) 'The behavioural aspects of fraud and embezzlement', *Public Money & Management*, January–March, pp 9–14.

Goodsell, C T (1994) *The Case for Bureaucracy: A Public Administration Polemic* (3rd edn). Chatham, NJ: Chatham House.

Hales, C P (1986) 'What do managers do? A critical review of the evidence', *Journal of Management Studies*, 23(1), pp 88–115.

Hummel, R.P. (1987) *The Bureaucratic Experience* (3rd edn). New York: St Martins Press.

Jos, P H and Hines, S M (1993) 'Care, justice and public administration', *Administration and Society*, 25(3), pp 373–92.

Kernaghan, K (1975) *Ethical Conduct: Guidelines for Government Employees*. Toronto: Institute of Public Administration.

Kohlberg, L (1976) 'Moral stages and moralization; the cognitive development approach' in Lickona, T (ed.) *Moral Development and Behaviour: Theory, Research and Social Issues*. New York: Holt, Rinehart and Winston.

Lawton, A (1998a) 'Business practices and the public service ethos' in Samphford, C, Preston, N and Bois, C.-A. (eds) *Public Sector Ethics: Finding and Implementing Values*. Sydney: Federation Press.

Lawton, A (1998b) *Ethical Management for the Public Services*. Buckingham: Open University Press.

MacLagan, P (1995) 'Ethical thinking in organizations: implications for management education', *Management Learning*, 26(2), pp 159–77.

Nolan Committee (1995) *Standards in Public Life*. London: The Stationery Office.

OECD (1996) *Ethics in the Public Service: Current Issues and Practices* (PUMA paper No. 14). Paris: OECD.

Plowden, W (1994) *Ministers and Mandarins*. London: Institute for Public Policy Research.

Pops, G M (1994) 'A teleological approach to administrative ethics' in Cooper, T L (ed.) *Handbook of Administrative Ethics*. New York: Marcel Dekker Inc.

Pratchett, L and Wingfield, M (1994) *The Public Service Ethos in Local Government: A research report*. London: CLD Ltd with ICSA.

PUMA (1998) *Principles for Managing Ethics in the Public Service* (Policy Brief No. 4). Paris: OECD.

Ranson, S and Stewart, J (1994) *Management for the Public Domain: Enabling the Learning Society*. Basingstoke: Macmillan.

Reiser, S J (1994) 'The ethical life of health care organisations', *Hastings Centre Report*, 24(6), pp 28–35.

Steinberg, S S and Austen, D T (1990) *Government Ethics and Managers: A Guide to Solving Ethical Dilemmas in the Public Sector*. Westport, CT: Quorum Books.

QUESTIONS AND DISCUSSION TOPICS

1 Has the public service ethos been undermined by recent changes in the practice of public service managers?

2 How can ethical theories help the practising manager?

3 In what ways can an organisation impact upon an individual's ethical actions?

16 Responsive public services

Aidan Rose

AIMS

This chapter will:

- highlight the coverage of responsiveness issues in previous chapters of this book;
- analyse what responsiveness consists of;
- illustrate tactics organisations have adopted in order to become more responsive;
- define the conditions which encourage responsiveness.

INTRODUCTION

The emerging theme of responsiveness

The term 'responsiveness' immediately raises a number of questions, for example, 'responsiveness to whom?' 'responsiveness by whom?' and 'responsiveness for what?' Taking the 'to whom' issue first, we can identify a number of reference points. Traditional public service organisations emphasised the bureaucratic chain of command, upward-reporting mechanisms and control whereas more recent perspectives have emphasised the need for outward-looking public services which encourage innovation and creativity. Looking outwards involves the identification of complex signals from a variety of sources. Citizens as members of civic society send signals to public services not only through votes in elections but also through demands articulated through interest groups. Those same individuals are also users of services who may define themselves as clients or customers. Elsewhere, looking upwards, policy signals urge services to move in a particular direction. New public management initiatives introduced markets in policy areas such as health care. Markets are mechanisms sending signals to encourage particular forms of responsiveness usually entailing a choice about cost and benefit (*see* Rose, 1989). As we saw in Chapter 4, public servants often act as agents of users when making allocative decisions.

This takes us to the 'by whom' question. In local government in the United Kingdom, traditional authority systems showed great deference to the culture of the professional. Departments were organised along professional lines with career progression determined by professionals. Policy development took place largely in professional circles with claims to expert knowledge working under 'delegated discretion' from elected members (Rowbottom, 1974). Thus professionals exercised control over an area of work and related

313

processes. Keen and Scase (1998, p 41) point to the conflict that professionals faced, with demands for loyalty both from the professional body with its nationally imposed standards and from their 'local' employing body. This self-regulated pattern of working has been criticised for its inward-looking culture and lack of responsiveness to users (Flynn, 1997).

Lipsky (1979) discusses what he termed 'street level bureaucrats' such as teachers and policemen and women who, because of the nature of their work, make decisions at the point of delivery and are able to exercise considerable personal initiative. New public management reforms tackled this question. As Mintzberg (1998, pp 335–6) points out, there is a tension between the need to create a division of labour in organisations and the desire for co-ordination through mutual adjustment, supervision or control. New public management sought to resolve this tension by placing greater authority in managers and the imposition of external control mechanisms. Thus, managers find themselves in the middle, bombarded with demands from politicians, professionals and the public in their many forms. Added to this are the signals sent by the proliferating evaluative bodies such as OFSTED and the Audit Commission (*see* Hood *et al.*, 1998). If organisations are to develop their capacity to learn then they need to create capabilities which will enable the capture of learning at the individual level and develop this into a competence which can inform organisational decision making.

The 'for what' question requires us to reflect on a number of issues which have been raised in Part 2 of this book, especially in Chapter 12 on Managing Performance. Efficiency considerations focus on a cluster of concepts revolving around the inputs, processes and outputs of organisations. However, as Peters points out, 'efficiency is not the only goal' (Peters, 1993, p 52). Equity issues revolve around both the fairness of the process in adhering to rules and distributional questions about outputs and outcomes. Analysis of performance measurement regimes often points to the emphasis that has been placed on inputs and processes rather then outputs and outcomes (Metcalfe and Richards, 1990, p 29).

All three of these questions reinforce the argument made in Chapter 11 in relation to managing stakeholders that one of the distinguishing features of public services management is the multiplicity of stakeholders who have an interest in the activities of public service organisations and the complex and often competing demands that they make. The public management task can therefore be described as one where choices have to be made about competing priorities and messages have to be reported as to the extent to which these priorities are met (*see* Peters, 1993).

Learning organisations

As we discussed in Chapter 13, organisations and individuals are required to adapt. To do this, Metcalfe and Richards argue (1990), government needs to develop the capacity to learn. This is not without its problems.

Morgan makes the distinction between the process *of* learning and the process of learning *to* learn. Learning to learn involves systems which 'are often able to detect and correct errors in operating norms and thus influence the standards that guide their detailed operations. It is this kind of self-questioning ability that underpins the activities of systems that are able to learn to learn and self-organise' (Morgan, 1986, p 87).

He suggests the following guidelines for the development of a learning-oriented approach. Organisations should be open and reflective, and should accept that uncertainty and errors are inevitable features in complex and turbulent environments. Problem-solving approaches should recognise the importance of exploring different approaches. Decision makers should avoid the imposition of predetermined goals and objectives on organisations (Morgan, 1986, p 92).

Whereas Morgan writes about the factors that inhibit learning in bureaucratic organisations generally, Willcocks and Harrow's (1992) research considers the problems that public services organisations in particular face in developing such a capacity. Among the factors they identify are:

- ambiguity over the common purpose of the organisation;
- lack of political support;
- poor communication structures to disseminate findings;
- management concerns about budgetary savings;
- organisations adopting a crisis management approach (Willcocks and Harrow, 1992, pp 72–3).

This, however, raises a fundamental question about the capacity of organisations to learn. First, it is not enough for organisations to face pressure for change; they need to perceive that pressure: 'Organisational change is stimulated not by *pressures* from the environment, resulting in a build-up of problems triggering an automatic response, but by the *perceptions* of that environment and those pressures held by key actors' (Kanter, 1983, p 281).

This implies a profound change in organisational culture which, as Handy (1990, p 199) argues, can generate ongoing benefits:

> Organisations which encourage the wheel of learning, which relish curiosity, questions and ideas, which allow space for experiment and for reflection, which forgive mistakes and promote self confidence, these are learning organisations, and theirs is a competitive advantage which no-one can steal from them.

The changing demands that the environment places on public service organisations offer opportunities for learning. The pressures to move away from bureaucratic structures to more responsive ones offer the possibility of a virtuous circle of improvement. However, the extent to which this opportunity is seized depends on the attitudes of people in those organisations. Willcocks and Harrow's (1992) research shows that people vary in their views about the capacity of public services organisations to learn from private sector practice. They identify (1992, p 74) four categories of response:

- resisters;
- doubters;
- inevitable acceptors;
- welcomers.

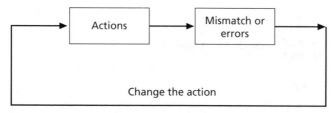

Fig. 16.1 Single-loop learning

Source: Overcoming Organizational Defenses: Facilitating Organizational Learning, p 92, by Argyris, Chris © 1990. Reprinted by permission of Prentice-Hall, Inc., Upper Saddle River, NJ.

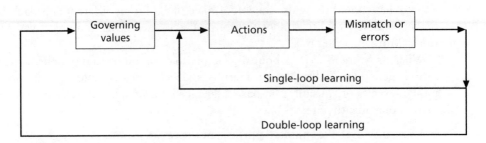

Fig. 16.2 Double-loop learning

Source: Overcoming Organizational Defenses: Facilitating Organizational Learning, p 94, by Argyris, Chris © 1990. Reprinted by permission of Prentice-Hall, Inc., Upper Saddle River, NJ.

ORGANISATIONS AND THEIR ENVIRONMENT

Part 1 of this book looked at the environment of the public services. This provided the reader with a contextual backdrop against which the detail of public service change can be examined.

As Fig. 16.3 illustrates, a number of factors make up the environment of public services. The precise identification of these factors is a matter for analysis, an exercise which is often adopted by businesses when engaging in the strategic planning process (*see*, for example, Johnson and Scholes, 1997). Some, as Bryson discusses (1995, pp 87–92) choose to add further factors such as education or law. Others such as Morgan (1986) may debate the extent to which environmental factors *determine* the context for public services and the extent to which public services can *influence* the make-up of its environment. As we saw in Chapter 7, Pettigrew (1988) makes the distinction between inner and outer contexts. The outer context is the broad environment in which organisations must operate – as set out in Fig. 16.3. By inner context he refers to organisational structure, organisational culture and politics.

However this debate is resolved, this conceptualisation offers the reader a framework with which to analyse how public services relate to the wider world. It is worth reiterating a point made in Chapter 4 – that there is a danger of over-generalisation and issues that may impinge closely on one public service may be of little relevance to another. All this adds to the theme of responsiveness and to the importance of making critical judgements about specific public services.

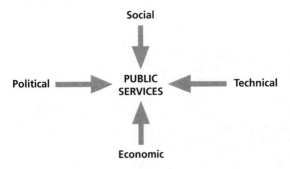

Fig. 16.3 Factors in the public service environment

Political factors

Chapter 1 examined the political context of public services. Perhaps one of the major trends in British politics has been the increasing focus on the management of public services. Governments have taken an increasing interest in public services management partly as a result of the concern to reduce the overall size of the public sector and the burden placed upon public services.

Table 16.1 Key milestones in civil service reform

Date	Initiative	Rationale
1970	Creation of Central Policy Review Staff (CPRS)	Co-ordination of policy within and between departments
1979	Rayner scrutinies	90–day scrutinies aimed at efficiency savings and lasting cultural change
1980	Management Information System for Ministers (MINIS)	Provision of information for ministers on the activities of departments
1982	Financial Management Initiative (FMI)	Delegation of resource responsibilities to managers
1988	Next Steps Agencies	Creation of quasi-independent agencies responsible for service delivery
1990	Competing for Quality	Introduction of greater competition in the public services
1991	Citizen's Charter	Umbrella for public service reform focusing on users and performance measures
1999	Modernising Government	Labour Government White Paper

In examining these initiatives, it is possible to identify two trends. First, there has been a shift in focus from policy making to the management of services. Initiatives such as the introduction of the Central Policy Review Staff (which was abolished in 1983) focused on the co-ordination of policy and the generation of alternatives to orthodox policy solutions generated by departments. With the election of the Thatcher administrations, the emphasis shifted to the implementation of policy, and there was a greater focus on the development of a management system which would assume greater responsibility for the control of limited resources. Second, the Major administration's flagship policy of the Citizen's Charter shifted the focus to the effective use of resources, with an emphasis on the users of services. The charter required of all public services that:

● precise standards of performance be laid down;
● these standards be transparent and open;
● where possible the consumer should have choice;
● the service should be consistent and responsive;
● there should be opportunities for the redress of grievances;
● services should provide value for money (Citizen's Charter, 1991).

The provision of information enables 'voice' (Hirschmann, 1970). Individuals now, in theory at least, have information to enable them to make a judgement of performance. They can then exercise their right to express 'voice', through grievance procedures and complaints mechanisms. The Charter has been the subject of a number of criticisms. One is that the information provided is inadequate and does not effectively measure performance (Boyne, 1997). Others have criticised its emphasis on the consumer, rather than the citizen (Bellamy and Greenaway, 1995). Hambleton and Hoggett (1993) also argue that in reality it will have little impact on citizens as they do not have the power to 'exit' from most services. However, whereas there is little choice available in most services, households could 'take their custom elsewhere' by moving between local authorities. This is known as the Tiebout model, which suggests that citizens can 'vote with their feet'. John *et al.* (1995) test this model and show that in London households move away from local authorities with high taxes and towards those with good services.

Alongside similar initiatives operating in local government and the National Health Service (NHS), increased emphasis was placed on service quality and service outputs and outcomes (Pollitt, 1993). The Blair administration has recognised some of the weaknesses of Conservative approaches by appointing a minister responsible for the co-ordination of government policy (known colloquially as the 'enforcer') and dealing with some of the, perhaps unintended, consequences of managerial approaches in its White Paper, *Modernising Government* (Prime Minister and Minister for the Cabinet Office, 1999).

Social factors

In Chapter 2 we examined the social and political context of public services. The discussion identified a number of key themes which have influenced the changing patterns and modes of public service delivery. Two points are worth highlighting here. The first relates to the changing demographic structure of society and the way in which this influences peoples' demands and needs. For example, the ageing population increased demand for particular types of health care. The changing balance between the working population and those dependent on them raises a number of questions for public policy and service management. For example, those over retirement age need to secure income usually from pensions, whether provided by the state or financed privately. Policy choices about the role of the state as a direct provider of pensions or whether the state wishes to encourage private provision need to be made. If the latter emerges as the policy choice then the maintenance of a viable private sector in which the public has long-term confidence emerges as an issue, as do equity considerations.

Second, public expectations about society in general and public services in particular have changed rapidly over recent years. As Osborne and Gaebler (1992, p 15) argue:

> We live in a knowledge based economy, in which educated workers bridle at commands and demand autonomy. We live in an age of niche markets, in which customers have become accustomed to high quality and extensive choice . . . Today's environment demands . . . institutions that are responsive to their customers, offering choices of nonstandardized services; that lead by persuasion rather than commands.

Economic factors

Economic factors include not only the overall performance of the economy, which is relevant in that the generation of tax income finances public services, but also the nature of specific parts of the economy and the sophistication of particular markets. If we take the issue of specific parts of the economy first, we may note that the 1980s and early 1990s saw substantial restructuring of the UK economy as the traditional heavy industries such as iron, steel and coal declined, with major repercussions for employment prospects in particular regions of the UK. New industries, including financial services, motor car assembly, computer manufacturing, fast food and tourism, have developed. As a result, traditional methods of education and training have, in many areas, become obsolete and new generations need to be prepared for new types of employment. Those made redundant from old industries often found themselves with skills that the labour market no longer required and local authorities and Training and Enterprise Councils (TECs) had to develop strategies. In particular, local authorities have given high priority to economic development as an essential part of their strategic plans along with mandatory service delivery.

Second, the reform of public services inspired by the Conservative administrations has involved a shift from largely in-house provision to a mixed economy of public service provision. The 1991 White Paper *Competing for Quality* (HM Treasury, 1991) rested on the propositions that public services would benefit from involving the private sector in the provision of services and that there was an active, vibrant private sector able to complete against in-house providers for work. In some cases the lessons from local government and health care show that internal markets with multiple providers able to compete effectively may be more a vision in policy makers' minds than a reality. Evidence about managed competition in the NHS shows that there was limited change and innovation because of weak incentives and strong constraints (Le Grand *et al.*, 1998).

Technological factors

The discussion about information and communications technology in Chapter 3 highlighted the massive impact that technology plays in the operation of government and the possibilities for new interfaces between our system of public administration and the public. It offers opportunities for speedier, more efficient and more remote interactions between individuals and government departments. However, there are the civil liberties dangers of centralised storage of large amounts of personal information and inequity since in many cases those who use public services are often those who are least likely to have access to the necessary resources.

Accountability and responsiveness

Case study 16.1 discusses the issues of accountability and responsiveness.

**CASE STUDY
16.1**

The traditional direction of accountability in the civil service was upwards through the Minister. Attempts at responsiveness have sometimes given individual civil servants a more public face.

ROAD MANAGERS FACE THE PUBLIC

By Charles Batchelor

Motorists with complaints about roadworks or the availability of lavatories on their journey will be able to complain to a road manager whose name, telephone number and even photograph will be on display along the route.

The plan to appoint several dozen managers – all civil servants employed by the Highways Agency, responsible for the government's trunk road programme – was announced as part of a programme to improve management of the 6750-mile network of motorways and trunk roads.

The news comes shortly after the government was criticised by the Conservative-dominated Commons transport select committee for failing to invest enough in maintaining bridges and roads.

Road manager details would be posted on road signs, lay-bys and service areas in an initiative reminiscent of the Department of Transport's ill-fated Cones Hot Line between 1992 and 1995. Nearly 20 000 motorists phoned the hot line but cones were removed in only five cases and the scheme was widely seen as an embarrassing failure for the government.

The road managers initiative forms part of a wider programme to make the network more customer-focused, said Mr John Watts, the roads minister.

This involves a review of roads to assess the quality of journeys, including ride quality, safety, congestion, reliability of journey times, availability of driver information and rest facilities.

Road management is currently carried out under different programmes of engineering work, covering areas such as new construction, maintenance and traffic control equipment. This approach does not always identify priorities efficiently or respond effectively to drivers' needs, said Mr Watts.

Road improvements identified under the programme would be funded from the government's budget for small schemes: those costing under £3m. This was cut this year to just £20m but is expected to increase to £50m next year.

The Highways Agency plans to begin implementing the new strategy on six routes shortly. The Automobile Association welcomed the initiative saying it would put an end to the problems on long distance routes caused by different counties having differing policies. But it required a commitment to long-term funding, it added.

The Freight Transport Association, representing hauliers and companies with goods to move, said: 'These schemes will amount to nothing if there is no spending on maintaining roads.'

Source: Financial Times, 14 February 1997. Reprinted with permission.

Question on the case study

This initiative raises the possibility of the management of roads being more accountable to users. Discuss the strengths and weaknesses of this approach.

Accountability is, as was discussed in Chapter 5, a multifaceted phenomenon. Many of the developments that come under the umbrella heading of 'new public management' are essentially changes in accountability regimes. Traditional 'public administration' emphasised accountability through traditional channels of ministerial and parliamentary accountability and the committee system in local government. Elections as a method of conferring legitimacy on public administration come into question when turnouts, at the local government level, often fall well below 30 per cent. Accountability reforms as a tool to elicit responsiveness has taken a number of dimensions.

1 Moves such as Financial Management Initiative (FMI) heralded an increasing emphasis on the control of human and financial resources in public service organisations. Motivated by a concern for efficiency, government sought greater control over resources. Other initiatives such as the Local Management of Schools (LMS) delegated responsibility for resources closer to the point of delivery while ensuring that those responsible for those resources were increasingly accountable upwards for the use of those resources. Broadly, we could term this *managerial responsiveness*.

2 More recently, a range of initiatives have sought to elicit greater accountability and therefore responsiveness to users of public services. Recognition of the inadequacy of traditional methods of accountability has led to interest in alternative methods of communicating with the public, especially in their role as service user as opposed to their role as citizen. Methods include user panels, surveys, and delegation of budgets to social service users through the Community Care (Direct Payments) Act 1996. We term this *user responsiveness*.

Building on the theme of user responsiveness, one of the major developments in the interface between service users and the system of public administration has been the extension of judicial review beyond being a mechanism for dispute resolution. As Radford (1997, p 42) argues, 'By extending the grounds for judicial review to include "irrationality" and "procedural impropriety" the courts have been concerned to structure the use of discretionary power and to shape the way in which public administration is conducted'.

In addition, there have been substantial developments in the use of alternatives to the courts, for example, complaints mechanisms to resolve disputes. Mulcahy and Allsop (1997) discuss the development of complaints mechanisms in the NHS and Boyle (1994) documents the growth of tribunals, inquiries and ombudsmen as alternatives to the courts for challenging executive action.

EMERGING DIMENSIONS OF RESPONSIVENESS

Three themes of responsiveness emerge from this analysis of the environmental context. Broadly speaking, responsiveness has three dimensions

- managerial responsiveness;
- market-led responsiveness;
- user responsiveness.

Reform rarely takes one of these dimensions alone and can change as priorities of policy makers and managers change. In order to examine this in further detail we shall examine the management of local government services. This follows the course from the early 1980s of Compulsory Competitive Tendering (CCT) through to the more recent Labour policy of Best Value.

FROM CCT TO BEST VALUE

Since 1980 the Conservative Government followed a policy of using competition as the primary lever to drive managerial change in local government. The major pieces of legislation were the Local Government (Planning and Land) Act 1980 and the Local Government Act 1988. These Acts required local authorities to subject an increasing range of services to compulsory competition. In the early years the focus was on selected manual services such as roads maintenance; a more comprehensive approach to the contracting of so-called blue collar or manual services was adopted in 1988. In the early 1990s the approach extended to white-collar support services such as legal services and information technology (IT) services.

Central to the implementation of these local government supply-side reforms was the creation of a distinction between the responsibility for commissioning services and that for the delivery of the service: a distinction between policy making and management. A major stimulus for this distinction comes from the New Right critique of public services, with its attack on bureaucratic growth, producer-dominated services with powerful professions and trade unions which were inefficient and failed to deliver services to users. The late Lord Ridley demonstrated the application of the New Right view in this area:

> The root cause of rotten local services lies in the grip which local government unions have over those services in many parts of the country . . . Our competitive tendering provisions will smash that grip once and for all. The consumer will get better quality services at lower costs (Ridley, 1989).

The implementation of compulsory competitive tendering (CCT) has been assessed by a number of researchers including Walsh (1995 and 1997). Walsh (1995, pp 123–6) points to the problems of contracting for services such as social care where it is more difficult to determine the relationship between price and quality than for manual services. Also, the shift from hierarchy to contract involves implementing a new set of institutional arrangements including marketing, contract specification and evaluation. Thus, efficiencies gained through improved service delivery may be outweighed by so-called transaction costs (Walsh, 1995, pp 136–7).

The Labour Government Green Paper on local government management recognised that the CCT regime forced local authorities to address difficult management issues. However, it also set out a number of key criticisms of the policy. They include:

- service quality was neglected;
- efficiency gains were uneven;
- in practice, arrangements were inflexible;
- high staff turnover;
- staff demoralisation;
- antagonism between local authorities and the private sector;
- competition becomes an end in itself rather than a means to an end (DETR, 1998a, pp 5–6).

The Labour Government marked a shift in policy when, in 1997, it announced that it would require local authorities to demonstrate that they are achieving Best Value. This policy is to be implemented over several years. It rests on the assumption that local authorities can use a variety of levers to raise performance which include but do not rely exclusively on competition. The White Paper states:

> A modern council – or authority – which puts people first will seek to provide services which bear comparison with the best. Not just with the best that other authorities provide but with the best that is on offer from both the public and private sectors. Continuous improvements in both the quality and cost of services will therefore be the hallmark of a modern council, and the test of best value (DETR, 1998b, para 7.1).

Since early announcements about Best Value, it became clear that the initiative is part of a much wider programme of reform of local government. Among the associated policy initiatives are:

- new democratic procedures concerned with how councils relate to their local communities (known as democratic renewal);
- new decision-making processes including the introduction of directly elected mayors and a clarification of the role of councillors;

- a new code of conduct for councillors and officers (known as the ethical framework);
- reform of the local government finance system (see IPPR, 1998; DETR, 1998a, p 5; DETR, 1998b).

Implementing Best Value

In England, the introduction of the Best Value regime began with a set of approximately 40 pilot sites selected by the Minister from the 150 authorities submitting applications for pilot status. Government commissioned an evaluation of the pilots to be conducted by the Local Government Centre at University of Warwick Business School.

Table 16.2 Timetable for Best Value

Date	Initiative
June 1997	Ministerial announcement, draft statement of principles of Best Value
October 1997	Deadline for local authority applications
December 1997	Government announces English pilot projects
March 1998	Publication of Green Paper, 'Modernising local government: improving local services through Best Value'
April 1998	Finalisation of service plans by local authorities. Best Value pilots commenced
May 1998	Green Paper consultation ended
Summer 1998	White Paper, 'Modern Local Government: In Touch with the People' published
Session 1998–99	Scheduled Best Value legislation
April 2000	Anticipated full implementation

Sources: Based on DETR, 1998a and DETR 1998b.

The criteria for the pilots sets out that the proposals should demonstrate:

- good consultation with service users and other members of the local community;
- use of measurable local performance indicators and targets to manage performance;
- a willingness to share information with other authorities;
- rigorous and transparent examination of the options for delivery (DETR, 1997, p 3).

The Government envisaged a four to five year programme of review of local services. This involves a number of stages which are set out in the White Paper. They can be summarised as:

1 Authority-wide objective setting.
2 Agreement of a fundamental performance review programme over four to five years.
3 Implementation of the programme.
4 Publication of local performance plans.
5 Independent audit/inspection and certification.
6 Problems referred to the Secretary of State (DETR, 1998b, Chapter 7).

The initiative requires the implementation of a new system of performance indicators for local authorities. These will be developed by Government in association with the Audit Commission and others in the local government community. The White Paper notes a shift in emphasis with 'indicators . . . designed to focus attention on what services have delivered (outcomes), rather than what resources have been devoted to them (inputs)' (DETR, 1998b, para 7.11).

Questions about the case study

1 What would you describe as the essential differences between the CCT and Best Value policies?

2 Does the policy change represent a change of view about the responsiveness of local authorities? If so, in what new directions?

SOCIAL ENTREPRENEURSHIP

The rise of social entrepreneurship is a recent phenomenon. It is, though, a response to a continuing theme of this book – that the organisations created to deliver welfare services in the post-war period are no longer appropriate in a world that is characterised by new sets of social problems. It is also offered as an alternative to the radical reforming agenda which emphasised economy in public spending and reduced entitlements to welfare.

Social entrepreneurship places a premium on social innovation to identify and deliver new forms of welfare. It recognises the need to mobilise existing resources which are currently under-utilised. Crucial to the need to invest in and derive benefits from social capital, leadership skills of individual social entrepreneurs are used to lever resources, and entrepreneurial organisations are flexible and creative with an 'open and porous approach to their environment' (Leadbeater, 1997, p 9).

Work on social entrepreneurship is in its early stages. Most published work is at an advocacy level and involves the presentation of a number of case studies of social entrepreneurs who work in areas of social care and community work. We can trace the intellectual roots of social entrepreneurship in organisation theory. Burns and Stalker's (1994) work on the microelectronics industry in Scotland in the late 1950s and Rosabeth Moss Kanter's work, *The Change Masters* (Kanter, 1983), both offer a typology of organisations which is set out in Table 16.3.

The second pamphlet published by Demos on this theme, *Civic Entrepreneurship* (Leadbeater and Goss, 1998), applies this thinking to public services organisations which, they argue, are in need of revival and revitalisation rather than restructuring and rationalisation (1998, p 13). Thus, new public services organisations need to be outward looking, focused on outcomes and with a capacity to learn. They recognise the distinctiveness of public services organisations in terms of their statutory responsibilities and stewardship of public monies. Hence they see civic entrepreneurship as characterised by:

- an emphasis on political renewal as well as managerial change;
- collaborative leadership encouraging working across boundaries rather than heroic leadership as is often found in the private sector;
- going beyond mere innovation by disseminating it and creating social value (1998, pp 16–17).

Thus civic entrepreneurship is defined as 'the renegotiation of the mandate and sense of a public organisation, which allows it to find new ways of combining resources and people, both public and private, to deliver better social outcomes, higher social value and more social capital' (*ibid.*).

You will have noticed that Leadbeater and Goss use the term social value. This can be related to a similar term that an American writer, Mark Moore, uses: public value (Moore, 1995). He argues that the aim of public management is to create public value using resources including money and the authority of the state in order to achieve public objectives and to show that value has been created in the pursuit of collective aspirations. In conceptualising the purpose of public management, he identifies a number of different standards. These are:

- achieving mandated objectives efficiently and effectively;
- politically neutral competence;

- analytical techniques for assessing public value;
- focusing on customer service and client satisfaction (Moore, 1995, Chapter 2).

Thus, he is arguing that there are a number of ways in which public managers can gauge the value of their organisations. Most recently, public managers have identified the public in their role as 'customers' of public services engaging in 'service encounters'. He also recognises the potential flaws if this model is applied without recall to the concept of citizenship and the role of representative government in making judgements about the values and delivery of public services.

Table 16.3 Inward- and outward-looking organisations

Inward-looking organisations	Outward-looking organisations
Hierarchical	Flatter structures
Rule bound	Flexible
Professional culture	User-led culture
Process driven	Results driven
One size fits all services	Consumer choice

CONCLUSIONS

Responsiveness provides a challenge to traditional methods of public administration. The failure of traditional methods such as the link between the elected member and the state has led to the development of a variety of mechanisms to enhance responsiveness. Market-led reforms may produce services that are more efficient but fail to deliver on other criteria such as effectiveness or equity. Mechanisms that focus on users may fall short if those with whom authorities consult are not representative of client groups as a whole.

Public management is faced with the challenge of devising new systems to regain the confidence and trust of the public in their roles as citizens in general and users in particular. Long-recognised imperatives for public services management, such as the balancing of conflicting demands, need to be combined with the development of new, more sophisticated techniques to gather information about needs and satisfaction of those needs. There is the danger that new mechanisms for improving public services can become new routines with the new means becoming the new ends, thus losing sight of the major challenges that the new public service environment poses.

REFERENCES

Bellamy, R and Greenaway, J (1995) 'The new right conception of citizenship and the Citizen's Charter', *Government and Opposition*, 30(4), pp 469–91.

Boyle, A E (1994) 'Sovereignty, accountability and the reform of administrative law' in Richardson, G and Genn, H (eds) *Administrative Law and Government Action: The Courts and Alternative Mechanisms of Review*. Oxford: Clarendon Press.

Boyne, G (1997) 'Comparing the performance of local authorities: an evaluation of the Audit Commission indicators', *Local Government Studies*, Winter, 23(4), pp 17–43.

Bryson, J M (1995) *Strategic Planning for Public and Nonprofit Organizations: A Guide to Strengthening and Sustaining Organizational Achievement* (rev. edn). San Francisco: Jossey-Bass.

Burns, T and Stalker, G M (1994) *The Management of Innovation* (rev. edn). Oxford: Oxford University Press.

DETR (1997) 'Successful Best Value pilot authorities announced', Press Release, 4 December.

DETR (1998a) 'Modernising local government: improving local services through Best Value', Green Paper. London: DETR.

DETR (1998b) 'Modern Local Government: In Touch with the People', White Paper. London: DETR.

Flynn, N (1997) *Public Sector Management*. Hemel Hempstead: Prentice Hall.

Hambelton, R and Hoggett, P (1993) 'Rethinking consumerism in public services', *Consumer Policy Review*, 3(2), pp 103–11.

Handy, C (1990) *Inside Organisations*. London: BBC Books.

Hirschmann, A (1970) *Exit, Voice and Loyalty*. Cambridge, MA: Harvard University Press.

HM Government (1991) *Citizen's Charter: Raising the Standard*. Cm 1599. London: HMSO.

HM Treasury (1991) *Competing for Quality*. London: HMSO.

Hood, C (1991) 'A public management for all seasons', *Public Administration*, Vol 69, Spring, pp 3–19.

Hood, C and Jones, G (1990) 'Progress in the Government's Next Steps Initiative', in HM Treasury and Civil Service Committee *Eighth Report: Progress in the Next Steps Initiative*. London: HMSO, Appendix 6, pp 78–83.

IPPR (1998) 'Local Government must thrive to change', Press Release, March.

John, P, Dowding, K and Biggs, P (1995) 'Residential mobility in London: a micro-level test of the behavioural aspects of the Tiebout Model', *British Journal of Political Studies*, 25(3), pp 379–97.

Johnson, G and Scholes, K (1997) *Exploring Corporate Strategy: Text and Cases*. London: Prentice-Hall.

Kanter, R M (1983) *The Change Masters: Corporate Entrepreneurs at Work*. London: Routledge.

Kanter, R M (1990) *When Giants Learn To Dance: Mastering the Challenges of Strategy, Management and Careers in the 1990s*. London: Unwin.

Keen, L and Scase, R (1998) *Local Government Management: The Rhetoric and Reality of Change*. Buckingham: Open University Press.

Le Grand, J, Mays, N and Mulligan, J-A (1998) *Learning from the NHS Internal Market*. London: King's Fund.

Leadbeater, C (1997) *The Rise of the Social Entrepreneur*. London: Demos.

Leadbeater, C and Goss, S (1998) *Civic Entrepreneurship*. London: Demos and The Public Management Foundation.

Lipsky, M (1979) *Street Level Bureaucracy*. New York: Russell Sage Foundation.

Local Government Association (1998) *Best Value: A Statement of Objectives*. London: LGA.

Metcalfe, L and Richards, S (1990) *Improving Public Management*. London: Sage.

Mintzberg, H (1998) 'The structuring of organisations' in Mintzberg, H, Quinn, J B and Ghoshal, S (eds) *The Strategy Process* (rev. European edn). London: Prentice-Hall, pp 332–53.

Moore, M (1995) *Creating Public Value: Strategic Management in Government*. Cambridge, MA: Harvard University Press.

Morgan, G (1986) *Images of Organisations*. Beverly Hills, CA: Sage.

Mulcahy, L and Allsop, J (1997) 'A Woolf in sheep's clothing: Shifts towards informal resolution of complaints in the health service' in Leyland, P and Woods, T (eds) *Administrative Law Facing the Future: Old Constraints and New Horizons*. London: Blackstone, pp 107–35.

Osborne, D and Gaebler, T (1992) *Reinventing Government: How the Entrepreneurial Spirit is Transforming the Public Sector*. Reading, MA: Addison-Wesley.

Peters, B G (1993) 'Managing the hollow state' in Eliassen, K A and Kooiman, J (eds) *Managing Public Organizations: Lessons from Contemporary European Experience*. London: Sage, pp 46–57.

Pettigrew, A (1988) 'Introduction: Researching strategic change', in Pettigrew, A, Ferlie, E and McKee, L (eds) *Shaping Strategic Change: Making Change in a Large Organisation – The Case of the National Health Service*. London: Sage.

Pollitt, C (1993) *Managerialism and the Public Services* (2nd edn). Oxford: Blackwell.

Prime Minister and Minister for the Cabinet Office (1999) *Modernising Government*, Cm 4310. London: The Stationery Office.

Radford, M (1997) 'Mitigating the democratic deficit? Judicial review and ministerial accountability' in Leyland, P and Woods, T (eds) *Administrative Law Facing the Future: Old Constraints and New Horizons*. London: Blackstone, pp 35–59.

Ridley, N (1989) 'Ridley roughs out quality plans', *Local Government Chronicle*, 14 April 1989.

Rose, R (1989) 'Charges as contested signals', *Journal of Public Policy*, 9(3), pp 261–86.

Rowbottom, R (1974) 'Professionals in health and social services organisations' in Billis, D, Bromley, G, Hey, A and Rowbottom, R (eds) *Organising Social Services Departments*. London: Heinemann.

Walsh, K (1995) *Public Services and Market Mechanisms: Competition, Contracting and the New Public Management*. London: Macmillan.

Walsh, K, Deakin, N, Smith, P, Spurgeon, P and Thomas, N (1997) *Contracting for Change: Contracts in Health Social Care, and Other Local Government Services*. Oxford: Oxford University Press.

Willcocks, L and Harrow, J (eds) (1992) *Rediscovering Public Services Management*. Maidenhead: McGraw-Hill.

QUESTIONS AND DISCUSSION TOPICS

1 To what extent have public management reforms empowered users? Give examples.

2 Does responsiveness undermine accountability?

3 What methods are used to hold the organisation to account and by whom?

17 Comparative public services management

Aidan Rose and Alan Lawton

AIMS

This chapter will:

- enable the reader to understand the comparative approach;
- describe the similarities and differences between public service management in different countries;
- explore the assumptions behind the generalisability and universal application of public sector management;
- examine the evidence presented for the convergence of public services management in different countries.

INTRODUCTION

We make comparisons all the time, whether in our private lives or in our organisational lives. We compare performance, in particular, in a number of different ways, through appraisals, audit, the production of league tables and so on. Indeed we have examined this aspect of comparison in Chapter 12. We are also used to comparing over time and space; we compare the past with the present as we, for example, look back to some 'golden age' where, in the context of, say, the civil service, wise and experienced civil servants provide a Rolls Royce service offering impartial policy advice to discerning politicians. Whether such a golden age ever existed is open to question. Hence, the longitudinal approach, comparing over time, is an established component of the comparative approach. We also compare in space, as it were, as we seek to compare countries or different parts of the same country. We seek to understand differences, or to plot regularities.

There are two key issues that we will address in this chapter. The first issue is concerned with *relevance*: why should we be interested in public services management in other countries? What relevance does, for the sake of argument, the way in which Hornsby Council (in Sydney, Australia) organise the delivery of its local services have for the local authority manager in a London borough, or in Bombay, Hong Kong or Kiev? Even more so, what relevance does Hornsby Council have for a senior civil servant working in Whitehall, Canberra or Washington? At one level the student of public services management may just find a description of how public services are delivered in different parts of the world interesting. At another level, the manager of a public service in, say, Australia, may find it quite useful to know how services are delivered in Canada. We will examine comparative methodology in the next two sections.

A second issue is concerned with *practice*: to what extent is there convergence in the delivery of public services across different countries? The head of the UK civil service, Sir Robin Butler, has indicated that: 'As I look around the world, the remarkable fact about public service reform is that there are great similarities, not only between governments but between different governments of quite different complexions' (1995, p 4).

Butler offers three reasons for his belief that this is the case:

1 The increase in citizen demands.
2 Greater stress on the individual citizen who is no longer prepared to accept a standard service.
3 The loss of confidence in command structures and hierarchies.

Therefore, public services organisations have to be more responsive to the citizen; this imperative is universal. We will examine claims such as these later in this chapter. Our focus in this chapter will therefore be on the international domain and we shall examine the extent to which claims that the delivery of public services is converging to conform to one model can be verified. However, we need first to examine the nature of comparative methodology.

COMPARATIVE METHODOLOGY

The comparative approach has a long history of respectability in the social sciences as a means to further understanding of the phenomenon under discussion. Castles (1992, p 9) argues that 'comparison is not merely a means of explanation or hypothesis testing, but also a mode of locating and exploring a phenomenon as yet insufficiently understood, and that the two functions can and should be iterative in character'.

Rose (1991, p 7) uses the concept of lesson-drawing to further explain the usefulness of the comparative approach: 'A lesson is seen as a short cut, utilizing available experience elsewhere to devise a programme that is new to the agency and attractive because of evidence that it has been effective elsewhere'.

There are good reasons for seeking information on how other agencies or organisations operate. We are interested in the question of 'Why compare?' A number of arguments can be presented which justify a comparative approach.

1 To illustrate examples of best practice. It is always useful to learn from successful organisations elsewhere.
2 To help the theorist in constructing models: the greater the extent of generalisability, the more robust the theory. The search for similarities may help the researcher to validate arguments. Throughout the book we have used case studies to illustrate key issues concerning the management of public services. However, it is impossible to generate plausible theories of public sector management from case studies alone. We need to take a much broader view. The comparative approach relies upon that broader view.
3 As organisations are increasingly working with each other to deliver public services, whether in community care or economic development, an understanding of different values, norms, processes, institutional arrangements, services provided, delivery mechanisms etc. is crucial.

4 The increasing importance of transnational and global institutions, such as the OECD or the European Commission, has meant an awareness of how public services are delivered in other countries.

5 The existence of common variables driving convergence. We examine this in more detail below when we examine the claims made on behalf of new public management (NPM).

6 Management is a practical activity and managers can learn from how similar problems are treated elsewhere, and indeed what is to count as a problem in the first place.

7 To see whether one way of doing things can be transferred from one culture to another.

8 The impact of globalisation and the arguments that the world is shrinking through the power of communications and the role of multinationals. This has been given greater momentum by the collapse of communism as a rival ideology to capitalism.

9 A common language is developing so that the public services manager in, say, Singapore uses the concepts of accountability, decentralised budgeting, devolved responsibility, integrity and probity and so on.

10 There appears to be greater interdependence and the growth of network government (which we discussed in Chapter 11).

11 The existence of a public sector management paradigm. In Chapter 15 we discuss the notion of a common public service ethos.

12 The existence of common problems, as indicated by the quote from Sir Robin Butler in the introduction to this chapter, such as an ever-demanding citizenry, common fiscal problems and common problems of large-scale bureaucracy.

13 If shared solutions are generated the risks and costs involved are minimised. Managers do not have to reinvent the wheel.

14 There is a shared agenda of change.

15 The concept of policy convergence which implies that countries and organisations are inextricably bound together and are either drifting closer together or being pushed in a certain direction.

Our interest in comparative methodology reflects, then, both a practical and a theoretical concern. However, we need to ask a number of questions concerning the nature of the comparisons that we make. We might agree that comparison itself is valid but we have to consider the following:

1 What issues are universal and what are local?

2 Can we identify the key variables and isolate them for the purposes of comparison?

3 Are we comparing like with like?

4 Is there agreement in the language and the concepts used?

5 Do functions perform the same role in different countries? For example, education is valued differently in different countries and we need to understand how this might impact on any comparison.

6 What issues are generic and what are specific?

7 How extensive is the study or is the researcher extrapolating from a limited research base?

You will recall that in Chapter 12 we touched on many of these issues, particularly when we discussed league tables. For example, what are the key variables in comparing schools with each other through the introduction of league tables? We can use the systems model introduced in that chapter and compare:

- *inputs* in the form of the social background or the entry qualifications of students, or the resources allocated to education;
- *throughputs* in terms of classroom sizes or teacher expertise;
- *outputs* in terms of examination results;
- *outcomes* in terms of a better-educated citizenry or a more highly skilled workforce.

The use of a comparative methodology is not just concerned with technical issues. It also raises cultural and ethical issues. For example, cultural imperialism results when aid is tied to reforming the public services in a way that satisfies the agenda of the donor. (For a discussion on cultural differences, *see* Schneider and Barsoux, 1997). In ethnocentric research, researchers look for similarities across different cultures for validating their theories. However, they have to be wary of assuming the character of their own group or race to be superior to that of other groups. The researchers themselves have to be wary of passing judgement on those that they are studying just because they happen to be different.

At the same time we need to be aware of our own values and how these will colour our perceptions. Many of us might, for example, consider it to be unethical for a local authority to appoint staff on the basis of nepotism or on bribery. In some countries this is considered to be appropriate behaviour, particularly, for example, where family ties and loyalty are strong and are of paramount importance. (These issues were also raised in Chapter 15 in relation to the ethics of governing principles and in Chapter 14 where differing cultural characteristics were discussed.) Comparative methodology can be located at any point on a spectrum, as set out in Fig. 17.1.

Fig. 17.1 A spectrum of comparative methodologies

COMPARATIVE METHODOLOGY IN PUBLIC SERVICES MANAGEMENT

From an academic perspective, the methodology employed for identifying the key issues for public services management appears to be fairly uniform. Take any standard text on public services management and in general terms it will be concerned with:

- the context within which public services are delivered, usually seen in terms of the political, social and economic factors operating at a macrolevel;
- the internal structures and processes of organisations in terms of the relationship between different layers of government and the decision-making processes that are adopted;
- the relationship between politicians and managers;
- the resources of the organisation in terms of people and finance;
- the location of responsibility and accountability;
- performance measurement.

In their book on public services management in Australia, for example, Wanna *et al.* (1992) examine:

- the structure of government and the nature of bureaucracy;
- the difficulty of reconciling competing objectives such as equity, efficiency and electability;
- the location of accountability, decentralisation and discretion;
- the role of managers in terms of co-ordination planning and organising;
- evaluating performance;
- economy, efficiency and effectiveness;
- professionalism;
- resourcing and corporate management and financial systems;
- the role of ethics.

A more recent work by Ferlie *et al.* (1996) which concentrates on public services management in the UK is similarly concerned with accountability, the role of professionals, structures, the use of markets, the role of the manager and so on.

Kingdom (1990) argues that the comparative approach allows student to acquire basic information about other countries; to gain an increased understanding of important concepts; and to develop greater insights into the role and nature of public bureaucracies elsewhere. Thus, in an examination of the civil service across eight countries, Kingdom offers a common framework for analysis which includes political setting, historical background, political executive, the structure, the bureaucrats, control and accountability, management and policy making.

The concern of academics to explore similarities is interesting enough but we might also want to build models to make more meaningful statements concerning public services management. Model building will take the form of:

- experience;
- observation and reflection;
- development of propositions;
- testing a set of propositions;
- building a theory.

Depending on the approach adopted, theory could be developed first and then tested through experience. However, whatever the approach we need to be aware of the following.

1 The bias of the researcher in terms of the researcher's choice of topic to investigate. For example, researchers may be drawing conclusions on public services management purely on the basis of an examination of civil service practice.

2 The assumptions and values that the researcher might bring to the topic to be researched. It might be assumed that the move towards a more market-like public services automatically brings advantages. The researcher might be seeking to have assumptions confirmed and ignore evidence to the contrary.

3 Access to key stakeholders and their availability. Researchers may only be given access to senior managers when they also need to canvass the views of frontline deliverers or clients.

4 The 'technical' problems of research in terms of the time available, the limits to the number of organisations that can be visited and the stakeholders interviewed and so on.

The management and delivery of public services is full of complexity and it is often difficult to isolate key variables or to determine the effect of one variable on another. Does the effectiveness of a local authority depend on its political make-up? If so, why do authorities with similar political configurations perform differently? Is the key factor size, location, organisational structure or the charisma of the chief executive? Is the size of public expenditure as a percentage of GDP the key variable? All of these, and more, have been examined by researchers and we examine their findings below.

COMPARATIVE PRACTICE AND NEW PUBLIC MANAGEMENT

As indicated above, public services managers will be interested in comparisons from a practical point of view and will be interested in what can be learned from best practice elsewhere. This implies that managers seek to improve their performance and that of their organisation. What improved performance means and how it is to be achieved will be open to question. In the first instance we would have to examine the extent to which there are common goals and criteria for judging achievements. This invariably will be concerned with issues such as:

- What is the appropriate role for the state?
- Do countries seek to increase or decrease public expenditure?
- How is welfare defined?

Just on the basis of the questions raised above we would need to allow for differences in political ideology and political values. Similarly, governments in different countries have different levels of public expenditure. Is it therefore appropriate to compare say the UK and Sweden, on that basis alone? Interestingly enough, the introduction of Next Steps Agencies in UK central government was based on the Swedish model. However, Flynn and Strehl (1996) argue that both the Foreign Office in the UK and Sweden resisted the encroachment of agency status, which suggests a functional dimension as well as a state dimension. We might wonder at the extent to which the state itself is an appropriate unit of comparison. Rose (1991) argues, for example, that it is often easier to see similarities between the same policy areas in different countries than to find similarities between different policy areas in the same country.

A second major concern might be with how goals are achieved. This would involve some discussion of:

1 Different constitutional arrangements. In countries where power is firmly in the hands of central government, then any reforms become easier to implement. In the UK, for example, the Parliamentary strength and unity of successive Conservative governments made it easier to bring about change. In other countries such as the Netherlands, strong traditions of coalition governments may favour incremental change.
2 The relationship between central and regional or local government. Under federal systems power is located in lower tiers of government.
3 The role of politicians, particularly the power of local politicians and their place in the community.

Researchers tend either to compare countries or compare functions or to develop themes across countries. Examples of the former approach include the work of Pollitt (1993) and

Zifcak (1994) who compare public sector reforms in the UK with those of the USA and Australia respectively. Pollitt argues that since the late 1970s there have been remarkable similarities between disparate parts of the public sector in the UK and that many of the reforms that took place during this period could also be found in the USA. He argues that 'Some of the American terminology has been significantly different from that current in the UK, but much of the detailed practice has been surprisingly similar, given differences in political culture and institutions' (1993, p vii).

Managerialism is the uniting factor, which Pollitt considers to be the development of a generic model of management which minimised the differences between private sector and public sector business management. Pollitt sees managerialism as the 'acceptable' face of New Right thinking and he finds 'remarkable' similarities in terms of:

- regimes of tight cash limits and cash planning;
- staff cuts, particularly in civil service numbers;
- introduction of performance indicators;
- introduction of individual staff appraisal;
- merit pay schemes;
- devolved budgetary systems and activity costing;
- planning systems;
- the rhetoric of responsiveness to the customer.

Pollitt contends that the regimes of both former Prime Minister Margaret Thatcher and ex-President Ronald Reagan went for Neo-Taylorism, expressed as a concern with financial control through the use of targets, and cost cutting. In the UK context, Pollitt examines education, health and the role of the civil service in a fairly general way. It would have been instructive to examine areas that are not so tightly bound by statute such as those relating to economic development or environmental policies. Pollitt makes no real attempt at explanation or use of the comparative method. There is a description of developments in both countries. His findings are:

1 A broadly similar ideology coloured both, yet this is a limited claim. Even at the level of general ideas there are some prominent differences, as Pollitt recognises. For example, there is a strong moralising element in US social policy reflecting the strength of the fundamentalists and the neo-conservatives. There is also a less political and more technicist approach to local government in the USA.
2 Similarities did appear, in so far as there was an assumption of public service inefficiency, a recourse to private sector expertise, a belief in the usefulness of merit pay, a squeeze on public sector pay levels (although in the UK this tended to hit teachers and nurses rather than the police), the abandonment of national pay agreements.

Finding similarities is one thing but demonstrating convergence or comparison is another. Zifcak (1994) compared the public sector reforms in the UK with those in Australia. He found that the content of the programmes was almost identical; that both operated within Westminster systems of government; and yet the reforms were introduced by governments of different political persuasions. Zifcak argues that there was a similar environment for change in terms of economic downturn and a change in the intellectual climate. However, the two governments approached change differently – Prime Minister Hawke had a detailed plan and was collaborative and put a strong coalition in place to implement change. He paid more attention to the details. Zifcak argues that there were differences in terms of policy styles and in terms of commitment to implementation rather than because of differences in politics. In explaining administrative reform, Zifcak found that a very similar context led to the content of reform converging over time. Democratic and equity considerations were eclipsed by managerial efficiency and the use of private sector techniques. In both countries a concern with, for example, accountable management had been around for some time (for example, the Fulton Report (1968) on the UK civil service had argued that civil servants should be given greater responsibility). In both countries the reform agenda was not new. What was new was the impetus to bring about change, Thatcher for ideological reasons, and Hawke for more pragmatic reasons. In Australia, a comprehensive reform programme with the support of Canberra was implemented and increasingly staffed by people with economics and business administration backgrounds. Thatcher's approach was more combative, upsetting a generation of civil servants along the way. The reform processes were very different, with officials in Canberra very supportive. There were clear attitudinal differences between ministers and officials. There was senior administrative commitment in Canberra. Weaknesses in ministerial control and responsibility in Canberra meant that reforms to delegate authority were more easily accommodated than in Whitehall.

In comparing reforms in the UK and Australia, Zifcak identifies a number of areas for comparison: the context of change, the content of change, the processes through which change was to be implemented and the attitudes of key stakeholders.

Flynn and Strehl (1996) examine public sector management across Europe in Sweden, the UK, the Netherlands, France, Germany, Austria and Switzerland. They describe Sweden and the Netherlands as social democratic states, with traditions of relatively autonomous subnational governments, a liberal attitude to the state and relations between workers, employers and the public sector. Germany and Austria are described as federal systems, underpinned by strong constitutions. Switzerland is the most federal, with a tradition of subsidiarity, a low level of public expenditure, fewer problems of fiscal stress caused by unemployment. France has a strong tradition of a unified civil service, with competitive entry to the civil service, which is located at the heart of a centralised system of administration. They depict the UK as an adopter of market forces which claims to be a leader in field of privatisation. The reform agenda is examined from a number of different perspectives including political ideology, centre–local relations and the role of administration. The unifying theme is that all the countries are linked geographically.

The hypothesis that is subsequently investigated is that the biggest changes are sought in the countries with the highest proportion of public spending to GNP (the Netherlands, France and Sweden) and that there is less pressure for change where the proportion is comparatively lower (in Switzerland, Germany and the UK). They identify two exceptions:

- the Netherlands, with 55 per cent of GNP spent on the public sector, has not maintained reforms;
- the UK, with 40 per cent of GNP spent on reforms, has maintained the reforms.

One explanation for these discrepancies might be the strength and unity of the government in power in the UK, and the coalition governments that characterise government in the Netherlands – as we identified above. Flynn and Strehl are sceptical of claims of convergence, for the following reasons:

- the different constitutional arrangements of the countries investigated; centralised states find it easier to implement changes;
- the ideological commitments differ;
- the different cultural attitudes of the countries investigated to the role and nature of the state.

COMPARATIVE NEW PUBLIC MANAGEMENT?

A number of claims have been made in recent years concerning convergence, primarily involving assumptions concerning the nature of management as a generic activity. It is argued by those who support the belief in generic management that the manager's task is similar irrespective of organisational context. Critics argue that the macroenvironment of the public sector is sufficiently different to warrant treating managing in the public services as different from managing private sector organisations (*see* Chapter 4).

The OECD (1995) is keen to promote the virtues of NPM and identified its key characteristics:

- devolving authority, providing flexibility;
- ensuring performance, control and accountability;
- developing competition and choice;
- providing responsive service;
- improving the management of human resources;
- optimising information technology;
- improving the quality of regulation;
- strengthening steering functions at the centre.

However, our continuing concern in this chapter is with the evidence that such convergence has indeed taken place. Dunleavy (1994) argues for 'de-coupling' the delivery and investigation of public services from a single-country context. However, he argues that in NPM not all of the changes are present in all countries nor are they part of a coherent strategy and that there are varying levels of implementation across countries. He points to New Zealand where a backlash has occurred, to Germany where constitutional constraints have prevented its adoption, to Japan which has remained fairly immune and to Italy where it is not much in evidence. According to Dunleavy, there is little evidence that NPM supplies the benefits that it is supposed to do. He does however recognise and identify the pressures for globalisation:

1 *Bureau-shaping incentives*, which make it easier for corporations to move in and colonise production, since bureau shaping allows hiving-off and de-institutionalisation. The corporations have little stake in maximising budgets or building empires. Small central élite agencies will be encouraged.
2 *Radical outsourcing*, which encourages corporations to become more involved through producing standardised service packages across countries and which will adopt economies of scale. Intellectual and knowledge-based developments will dominate and the notion of 'Best in World' as an activity will be centred on a core competency.
3 *Government sector procurement rules*, for example defence procurement, particularly in the USA will favour the largest companies.
4 *Commodification processes*, which will cut back on face-to-face contacts though electronic media, with the result that the distinctiveness of state institutions will be diminished.

Dunleavy points to the growth of bodies such as the North American Free Trade Area (NAFTA) and the Asian Pacific Economic Council (APEC), and which come to compensate for the political loss of confidence in the nation-state. The argument is speculative but, given the propensity for French companies to acquire water utilities in the UK, it is perhaps not unreasonable.

In recent years, Christopher Hood has examined the nature of NPM in some detail. He argues (1995a) that it has important variations and identifies seven dimensions of change:

1 Shift towards disaggregation.
2 Shift towards greater competition.
3 Stress on private sector styles of management.
4 More stress on discipline and frugality in resource use.
5 More emphasis on visible hands-on-management.
6 Explicit formal measurable standards and measures of performance and success.
7 Greater emphasis on output controls.

Hood argues that there are hardly any comparative data of note and they are all very fragmentary. Even with limited data it is still possible to argue that not all countries have adopted NPM. Examples of those that have not include Japan, Germany and Switzerland. Thus, in Japan the decentralisation of personnel matters did not occur, quite the reverse in fact. Similarly, there has been no introduction of pay for performance in Germany. According to Hood, countries can be located on a continuum from those which have exhibited a high tendency to adopt NPM to those which exhibit a low tendency (*see* Table 17.2).

Table 17.2 New Public Management tendencies in OECD Countries

High NPM	Some tendencies	Low NPM
Sweden, Australia, Canada, UK	France, the Netherlands	Germany, Greece, Spain, Japan
New Zealand	Denmark, Norway, Ireland	Switzerland, Turkey

Pollitt (1993) implied that NPM was an Anglo-American phenomenon yet what are we to make of the different positions of South Africa, Hong Kong, Australia and New Zealand? English language could be a consideration, yet how does Sweden fit into this explanation? Hood investigated a further dimension, that of political ideology, which is set out in Table 17.3.

Table 17.3 Political views of government

NPM emphasis	Left	Centre	Right
High	Sweden	Australia, Canada, New Zealand	UK
Medium	France	Austria, Denmark, Finland, Italy, the Netherlands, Portugal, USA	
Low	Greece, Spain	Germany, Switzerland	Japan, Turkey

Source: Hood, 1995a, p 100.

Other variables might include the rise of a new management class which, in Australia, helped in the demise of the old public administration model. However, the argument that it is used to slim down big government does not hold up. Hood identifies a further set of variables linked to the emphasis on collectivism in service provision, and the unity of public service.

The comparative evidence presented in this article indicates that NPM is an international phenomenon inspired by a number of factors, including disaffection with bureaucracy and concerns about economic performance.

THE LOST GREY TRIBE

By John Plender

In May 1997 the French electorate passed a first verdict on two party leaders who had more in common with Tweedledum and Tweedledee than their hostile hustings rhetoric implied.

To the centre-right was Alain Juppe, the archetypal graduate of the Ecole Nationale d'Administration (ENA), the elite French school for public servants. To the left was another power-hungry enarque – the common designation for these bureaucrats beyond compare – in the cuddly shape of Lionel Jospin.

The election had been called by a president, Jacques Chirac, himself an alumnus of ENA, who had beaten fellow enarque, Edouard Balladur, for the Gaullist nomination in the 1995 presidential election, which he won after attacking the concentration of power in the hands of the ENArchie. So far, so incestuous.

The French are at least being offered a genuine political choice, albeit between timid reformism and 1960s dirigisme. But, in recent times, French politics have recalled the judgment of a departing British civil servant. Asked by the great bureaucrat Sir Edward Bridges what he had learned from his experience, he remarked, 'I have learned, Sir Edward, to distinguish between the various shades of grey.'

Disaffection with the habitués of bureaux is not confined to France. The government of Helmut Kohl was enraged this week when the Bundesbank, the residual legatee of the great Prussian bureaucratic tradition, delivered a devastating criticism of its feats of creative accounting – in this case, the reverse alchemy of turning gold into a single currency.

Meanwhile, Tony Blair's new government in Britain has sent disrespectful signals to the mandarins by making what are politely called 'political appointments', prompting a head-count caution from the watchdog responsible for protecting the integrity of the civil service.

The erosion of respect for super-bureaucrats is a worldwide phenomenon. The once lauded public servants of Brazil – the ones who literally put Brasilia on the map – now attract cynical jibes. Any remaining regard for the bureaucrats who run China owes more to fear than to a Confucian respect for the wisdom of the ruling class. Even the brilliant planners who helped engineer South Korea's economic miracle are under fire, if not under investigation.

So what has gone wrong in the bureaux? Will the end of ideology be accompanied by the banishing of the bureaucrat? Is there no longer room for what was a mandatory Manchu court? And, instead of enjoying a career, will these cadres simply be contract labourers?

Consider, first, the origins and nature of bureaucracy, which is one of the oldest forms of human organisation. There are two explanatory traditions. The first goes back to Confucius and Plato, and has been perpetuated in modern times by the sociologist Max Weber.

On this view, the ideal bureaucrat is hard working, clever, loyal and disinterested. It is a vision of rational administration, with a strong public service ethos. In the more elitist bureaucracies, the mystique is reinforced by schooling which imparts a sense of specialness to the future public servants.

This meritocratic tradition was invented in China, where records of written competitive examinations go back to 165BC. It was re-invented in late 18th century Europe by the Prussians and turned to good imperial use by Britain after the Northcote–Trevelyan report of 1854 on the civil service.

The training encourages a commitment to continuity and a consensual managerialism. Hence George VI's comment on Labour's landslide victory in Britain in 1945: 'Thank God for the civil service.'

Hence, too, the urgent need felt by such revolutionaries as Mao and Margaret Thatcher to undermine their powerful, independent civil servants. And Tony Blair? A special disingenuity trophy is being cast, in an alloy, for the Blair adviser who said this week that civil servants liked the inflow of political appointees because it spared them from carrying out political work.

In the former Communist countries, Lenin's theory of the vanguard constituted the most extreme version of rationalist elitism. The Russian leader called for a vanguard of revolutionaries drawn from the bourgeois intelligentsia to hold power in trust for the proletariat until the workers were ready to fill the post-revolutionary political vacuum.

What, then, of the alternative, and far less flattering, vision of bureaucracy? This is provided by novelists such as Dickens, Balzac and Kafka. It portrays obstruction, cupidity, laziness and arrogance.

Economists, too, have punctured the notion of the Platonic guardian. Later economists, led by James Buchanan, have asked pertinent questions, such as what do bureaucrats maximise? Not output or profits, comes the pat answer, but departmental budgets and personal utility.

If the second view of bureaucracy is now in the ascendant, it is, in part, because bureaucrats make excellent scapegoats when governments run into the inevitable bout of trouble. Certainly this is true of Britain, where the power of bureaucracy was famously caricatured in the 1970s by the late Lord Rothschild on taking up his position at Ted Heath's new Think Tank. 'Until this week,' he said, 'I never realised the country was run by two men I'd never heard of.'

These men, Sir William Armstrong and Sir Burke Trend, reflected the longstanding penchant of Britain's brightest and best to pursue a career in unelected politics. The same civil service had earlier been accused by Tory minister Rab Butler of running a Rolls-Royce machine. Oddly enough, its reputation was declining sharply in the early 1970s just when Rolls-Royce itself went bust.

A legitimate concern today for an incoming Labour government would be how far the civil service has been captured by Tory ideology and what obstacles this places in the path of a reform programme. In the past, its independence was not the question. The criticism was rather that British civil servants were generalist dilettantes.

Tommy Balogh, economic adviser to Labour prime minister Harold Wilson, declared that there was no room for classical scholars in the world of economic planning. Balogh's argument shows the superficiality of the criticism: planning today is more discredited than the British civil service. And the bureaucrats who were accused of precipitating Britain's decline often showed better judgment than their masters. In the Suez fiasco, top mandarin Sir Edward Bridges warned of the risk of a sterling crisis, especially if the Americans were not on side, months before Sir Anthony Eden embarked on the catastrophic adventure.

The modern bureaucrats who enjoy most domestic legitimacy are niche players such as the Bundesbank, with a clear and limited mandate, and the support of public opinion. How ironic that the least accountable of central banks should be providing a check on an elected government that wants to dump the D-mark against the will of the German people.

Source: Financial Times, 31 May 1997. Reprinted with permission.

Question to the case study

What are the different qualities of the civil servant recognised in different parts of the world, as discussed in the article?

Hood accepts that his discussion is relatively speculative but offers four conclusions (Hood, 1995a):

1 It is not clear that the classical model of accountability has collapsed everywhere.
2 Conventional explanations of change do not account for observed variations in the 1980s.
3 There is no simple relationship between macroeconomic performance and NPM.
4 There is no simple relationship between the political colours of the government and NPM.

In a further article, Hood (1995b) suggests that there might be a worldwide 'econo-management speak' but where different agendas may underpin the same slogans. There certainly has been the international promotion of reform ideas through the popularity of such books as Osborne and Gaebler (1992), the role of international consultancy firms and the role of the OECD in disseminating a reform agenda. However, Hood argues that the evidence for globalisation is not very convincing.

The importance of language and its role in the dissemination of assumptions concerning a reform agenda is also evident in a related field, that of health care reform. In their examination of health care reform in the Netherlands, Sweden and the UK, Ham and Brommels (1994, p 107) argue that: 'Notwithstanding the similarities, important and interesting differences of approach emerge on deeper analysis . . . although the vocabulary of reform may be international, terms such as "managed market", "budgetary incentives", "purchasers", and "providers" are interpreted differently in the three countries.'

In many ways the belief in NPM comprises a new paradigm in the understanding and exploration of public services management. This is certainly the view taken by the OECD (1995) – *see* Exhibit 17.1.

The concept of a paradigm was first used by Thomas Kuhn (1962) in his explanation of the nature of scientific revolution. He defined (1962, p x) paradigms as 'universally recognised scientific achievements that for a time provide model problems and solutions to a community of practitioners'. Paradigms share two characteristics. The first is an achievement sufficiently unprecedented to attract an enduring group of adherents away from competing models of scientific activity. Second, they are sufficiently open-ended to leave all sorts of problems for the redefined group of practitioners to resolve. Those whose research is based on shared paradigms are committed to the same rules and standards for scientific practice. Apparent consensus is generated and normal science is conceived as 'mop-up operations'. The only problems worth solving are those thrown up by the paradigm: the paradigm determines what is to count as a problem as well as offering solutions. If we reject one paradigm, it must be because we have something else with which to compare it. Anomalies occur, with the result that the paradigm does not appear to have the solutions to certain problems. Anomalies, in the first instance, can be ignored as aberrations but as they stubbornly refuse to go away a paradigm shift has to occur to

Exhibit 17.1

New Public Management

A new paradigm for public management has emerged, aimed at fostering a performance-oriented culture in a less centralised public sector. It is characterised by:

● a closer focus on results in terms of efficiency, effectiveness and quality of service;

● the replacement of highly centralised, hierarchical structures by decentralised management environments where decisions on resource allocation and service delivery are made closer to the point of delivery, and which provide scope for feedback from clients and other interest groups;

● the flexibility to explore alternatives to direct public provision and regulation that might yield more cost effective policy outcomes;

● a greater focus on efficiency in the services provided directly by the public sector, involving the establishment of productivity targets and the creation of competitive environments within and among public sector organisations; and,

● the strengthening of strategic capacities at the centre to guide the evolution of the state and allow it to respond to external changes and diverse interests automatically, flexibly, and at least cost.

Source: OECD, 1995, p 8.

---

accommodate the anomalies. Hence the nature of scientific revolution. You may recall the discussion in Chapter 13 which explored the concept of a paradigm within the context of public services.

PUBLIC ADMINISTRATION REFORM IN TRANSITIONAL STATES

Countries in many areas of the world including eastern Europe and Africa are undergoing transitions from centralised one-party regimes to pluralist democracies. In many cases, this change was accompanied by a transition from a centralised planned economy to a market economy. The pace and nature of these changes is uneven. For example, China has taken large steps towards a market economy but has made little transition towards democracy. States such as the Czech Republic and Hungary have made substantial market-led reforms and moved towards a pluralist democracy whereas Belarus and Slovakia remain relatively centralised both politically and economically. South Africa under apartheid had two parallel economies: one serving a relatively affluent white community and a second serving the black community. Political liberties are now extended to all groups whereas the system of apartheid is now principally economic.

This uneven pattern of transition reflects policy debates and political battles which have taken place within these countries since the collapse of the old regimes. Often battles have taken place between forces pressing for the implementation of free market solutions and those wishing to preserve the existing order. The costs of reform often fall on those least able to pay those costs. Galloping inflation eroded the value of savings and states were often unable to pay pensions to the elderly or ensure supplies of heat which was often generated on a collective basis at district level and supplied through a collapsing infrastructure.

Public administration reform is a prerequisite of both the transition to a market economy and the transition to democracy. Eastern European states typically had both production units and welfare provision concentrated in the hands of the state. Privatisation of state assets has taken place to varying degrees and with a variety of motives. International pressure exerted by supranational bodies such as the World Bank, the OECD and the European Union has encouraged states to dispose of their assets and often has made reform in this respect a condition of financial assistance and the focus of technical assistance. Within countries, motives for privatisation may have less to do with economic liberalisation than with the prosperity of élite groups.

The withdrawal of the state from spheres of production requires a redefinition of the role of the state. The creation of a new private sector in key areas of production requires the state to develop mechanisms for the regulation of the private sector in order that the interests of the state, the private sector and citizens can be balanced.

Hesse (1993, p i) argues that the former communist states share a number of characteristics. These are:

- a transition from one-party rule to a multiparty, pluralist system with democratic and accountable government;
- the deconcentration and decentralisation of political power;
- the creation of distinct spheres of economics and politics;
- economic liberalisation.

Central to the reforms that have taken place in these states is the reinvention of the state, with an accountable system of public administration. Two essential features of a new system of public administration are, first, the need for a deliberative policy formulation capacity which respects the distinctive roles of politicians and officials. Second, new systems require decentralised structures of service delivery which satisfy competing and complex requirements of efficiency, accountability and responsiveness. This development process takes place in parallel with the development of a polity, often with large numbers of small political parties, many with unclear identities or members familiar with old arrangements where the distinction between politics and administration was not an issue. In many cases the political process is underpinned by high levels of uncertainty and instability which, among others things, inhibit the process of administrative reform. Also, central to this reform process is the creation of a legal framework which clarifies the respective roles of the various actors in the process. Further, the process of economic reform is hampered by political instability and the absence of administrative structures and appropriate legal frameworks necessary for the creation of markets.

Those involved in assistance programmes need to take heed of not only the common factors that former communist states exhibit but also the different circumstances that individual countries face. Collins (1993, pp 323–4) argues that the circumstances of change are different in different countries for several reasons:

- the differing impetuses for change, both internal and external;
- the differing country characteristics: resources, market size, government and political system, the extent of private sector development, and the state of the infrastructure;
- the differing goals of change.

The shift to democracy from a system of one-party rule requires a redefinition of the administration. Often bureaucracies were little more than an adjunct of the Communist Party under communism. For example, in the Soviet Union decision making was centralised in Moscow, with administrative outposts such as Kiev acting as little more than postboxes. Under democratic systems, the administration was required to become a system of public administration prepared to serve changing groups of politicians. This necessitates capacity building, which has a number of elements. First, there may be the introduction of a constitution – for new countries such as Ukraine – or the reform of the constitution – for countries such as Poland. Additionally, all states in Eastern Europe have adopted a civil service law, often enshrining principles of conduct for public servants. Principles of public service neutrality are raised, though often implemented within existing structures. Local government, or local self-government as it is often termed in Eastern Europe, requires a reorientation towards local communities and democratic principles. None of this is easy. Often these states face the paradox that they are those which are in greatest need of reform but are those which are least able to reform. Their economies, which were built around the cold war and weapons production, have collapsed and gross domestic production has fallen to a fraction of what it was in the 1970s. Their revenue collection systems had little capacity to collect taxes from this declining base and the so-called shadow economy flourished. Shortages of public funds meant that very often public servants such as teachers were owed several months salary, with inevitable consequences for motivation. New schools of public administration designed to educate and train new élites of public servants often found that their best graduates found employment in the more lucrative private sector.

Public administration in the west takes place in the context of civil society. Institutions such as the churches, voluntary bodies and pressure groups relate closely to the state in that they exert pressure on policy makers and they provide welfare and support to communities. Transitional states rarely have this prerequisite of civil society. New systems of public administration have had to develop policy-making capacities. There was little existing expertise in formulating policy options and presenting them to decision makers. What Dror (1993) terms a meta-policy making capacity has had to be developed as a new competence. Added to this are the facts that new areas of substantive policy have had to be developed (e.g. environmental policy and consumer protection) and that in the newly independent states there was little expertise in international diplomatic relations or customs and excise.

CONCLUSIONS

In examining the nature of comparative public services management, we have raised a number of key issues;

- Are we comparing like with like?
- What is our unit of comparison?
- Is there 'one best way' for public services management?

We have also highlighted changes in the reform of public services management and have compared changes in the context, content and process of public services management. Thus, for example, Holmes and Shand (1995) distinguish between changes which are concerned with the role, boundaries and structure of governments and those more concerned with the internal management 'paradigm'. They argue that structures and boundaries are changing and a key concern is with what constitutes the core of public services. Structural reforms have taken place but, according to Holmes and Shand, changes in the internal management reflect greater convergence; managers now have the 'freedom to manage' but they also have to do more with less. Reforms take place at the level of the individual and at the system level concerning the structure of government and the procedures that support it.

However, there is no denying the impact of context, irrespective of whether management tools or organisational processes converge. For example, in some newly industrialised countries such as Korea, performance pay is linked to teamwork rather than to individuals, reflecting a set of values concerning the nature of individualism and the role of groups in society. In other less developed countries, reforms are seen as less relevant where a law-based, professional public service ethos is not well established and more basic reforms are needed. Increasingly, aid is tied up with the pressure to reform the public services. Different countries place different values on local government as a democratic institution. Thus, in the USA, local politics are not regarded as important and neither is local competence and local community.

In China it could be argued that NPM has in fact gone into reverse. Hubbard (1995, pp 341–2) has argued that:

> The devolution of greater responsibility, financial discretion and initiative to local government was the means chosen by [Deng Xiaoping] to stimulate production and commerce . . . .

Hubbard continues:

> ... the 'Contract Responsibility System' has allowed substantial scope for local variation between individual enterprises and their supervisory agencies, in the setting of output and quality targets ... In the late 1980s, the 'Contract Responsibility System' was also widely applied to state industrial enterprises, in a variety of forms. The purpose was not only to increase managers' autonomy over production and staffing, but also to motivate them by linking their pay to negotiated performance targets.

Hubbard argues that the role of entrepreneurial local government may be on the decline. Undeveloped markets and established local state trading networks favoured agencies of the local state in exploiting business opportunities. However, market development and the increasing autonomy of firms are now reducing the advantage of local government business agencies and they face a diminished and changed role. Hubbard concludes that a model of NPM is no longer appropriate, as far more private and less government ownership will occur.

In countries where communism has been, or is slowly being, eroded, such as China, which are very experienced in networking, now have to withdraw as the market takes over. The context of public services management is still crucial.

In conclusion, lessons can be learned from the comparative approach. For the academic, the use of such an approach not only is interesting but also allows for greater understanding of, and allows developments in, models of public service management. For the practitioner, it encourages an awareness of best practice and the recognition that 'the way we do things around here' may not be the best way. The comparative approach can satisfy the agendas of both the academic and the manager.

REFERENCES

Butler, Sir R (1995) 'The themes of public service reform in Britain and overseas', *Policy Studies*, 16(3), pp 4–25.

Castles, F G (ed.) (1992) *The Comparative History of Public Policy*. Cambridge: Polity Press and Oxford: Basil Blackwell.

Collins, P (1993) 'Civil service reform and retraining in transitional economies: Strategic issues and options', *Public Administration and Development*, Vol. 13, pp 323–44.

Dror, Y (1993) 'School for Rulers' in De Greene, K B (ed.) *A Systems-Based Approach to Policy Making*. Boston: Kluwer Academic Publishers.

Dunleavy, P (1994) 'The globalization of public services production: Can government be "Best in World"?', *Public Policy and Administration*, 9(2), pp 36–64.

Ferlie, E, Pettigrew, A, Ashburner, L and Fitzgerald, L (1996) *The New Public Management in Action*. Oxford: Oxford University Press.

Flynn, N and Strehl, F (eds) (1996) *Public Sector Management in Europe*. Hemel Hempstead: Prentice Hall.

Fulton, Lord (1968) *The Civil Service*, Vol. 1, Report of the Committee. London: HMSO. Cmnd 3638.

Ham, C and Brommels, M (1994) 'Health care reform in the Netherlands, Sweden and the United Kingdom', *Health Affairs*, 13(5), pp 106–19.

Hesse, J J (1993) 'Introduction' in special edition, 'Administrative Transformation in Central and Eastern Europe: Towards Public Sector Reform in Post-Communist Societies', *Public Administration*, 71, Spring/Summer, pp 1–12.

Holmes, M and Shand, D (1995) 'Management reform: Some practitioner perspectives on the past ten years', *Governance: An International Journal of Policy and Administration*, 8(4), pp 551–78.

Hood, C (1995a) 'The "New Public Management" in the 1980s: Variations on a Theme', *Accounting, Organizations and Society*, 20 (2/3), pp 93–109.

Hood, C (1995b) 'Emerging issues in public administration', *Public Administration*, Vol. 73, Spring, pp 165–83.

Hubbard, M (1995) 'Bureaucrats and markets in China: The rise and fall of entrepreneurial local government', *Governance: An International Journal of Policy and Administration*, 8(3), pp 335–53.

Kingdom, J E (ed.) (1990) *The Civil Service in Liberal Democracies; An Introductory Survey*. London and New York: Routledge.

Kuhn, TS (1962) *The Structure of Scientific Revolutions*. Chicago: University of Chicago Press.

OECD (1995) *Governance in Transition: Public Management Reforms in OECD Countries*. Paris: OECD.

Osborne, D and Gaebler, T (1992) *Re-Inventing Government*. Reading, MA: Addison-Wesley.

Pollitt, C (1993) *Managerialism and the Public Services* (2nd edn). Oxford: Blackwell.

Rose, R (1991) 'What is Lesson-Drawing?', *Journal of Public Policy*, 2(1), pp 3–30.

Schneider, S C and Barsoux, J.-L. (1997) *Managing Across Culture*. Hemel Hempstead: Prentice Hall.

Wanna, J, O'Faircheallaigh, C and Weller, P (1992) *Public Sector Management in Australia*. Melbourne: Macmillan.

Zifcak, S (1994) *New Managerialism: Administrative Reform in Whitehall and Canberra*. Buckingham: Open University Press.

QUESTIONS AND DISCUSSION TOPICS

1 What is to be gained by making comparisons of public services management across countries?

2 What are the key issues in comparative methodology?

18 Conclusions

Alan Lawton

AIMS

This chapter will:

- revisit themes introduced in earlier chapters;
- identify the emerging trends in public services management;
- evaluate existing ways of examining management of the public services;
- explore the character of management and the public services.

INTRODUCTION

Part 1 of this book examined the context for public services management. We explored the political, economic, social and technological factors and identified some of the complexities of that environment. That environment was identified as subject to change and we discussed the ways in which key themes such as accountability and organisational structures have changed in recent years. We also introduced the debate concerning the relationships between managing in the public services and private sector management. Part 2 identified some of the tools that can help make sense of the complex environment.

Chapter 1 tracked the changing political perceptions concerning the role of the state in providing public services. This normative base is concerned with key issues concerning the scale and scope of the public services. Public organisations are seen as political instruments to deliver a range of goals. However, as we saw in Chapter 13, there are difficulties with measuring outcomes. Not only that, but managers will need to be clear about whose goals they are meeting. They may have satisfied their clients but not the politicians! Public services managers may find it easier to deliver a range of services or to act in accordance with due process rather than with, as some commentators expect, democratic responsibility. The different character of public service organisations is captured by Antonsen and Jorgensen (1997) who argue that public service organisations take different forms and can be distinguished in terms of their degree of publicness. They distinguish between High Publicness (HP) and Low Publicness (LP). The former is characterised by complex tasks, a professional orientation, many external stakeholders, conflicting environmental demands, low managerial autonomy, tight ministerial control and formal and distant relations with the ministry. As a consequence these organisations are reluctant to adopt organisational change.

Organisations characterised by HP have a broad attachment to public sector values, which leads to bureaucratic controls and a low rate of change, termed 'public imprisonment'. In contrast those public service organisations which are characterised by LP have a low level of attachment to public service values, termed 'private freedom'. They have simple tasks, are dominated by autonomous managers and have few external stakeholders and loose controls from the ministry. Of course, different levels of publicness can be found in the same organisation. A local authority, for example, might find its freedom to manoeuvre much greater in, say, the provision of leisure services than in the provision of social services or child welfare. We might add to Antonsen and Jorgensen's set of criteria that of public interest which might be much greater in child care than in leisure activities.

Linking their analysis to change, Antonsen and Jorgensen argue that where publicness is externally defined and depends on the impact of the environment, any reform should address that environment as a whole. Where publicness is internally defined as a composite of tasks, professional norms and values, change at the individual organisation level is more appropriate. The implication is that organisations characterised by low publicness are more amenable to radical change than those characterised by high levels of publicness. However, the internal environment and the external environment will need to be in balance. The problems that can arise when one is ignored at the expense of another are demonstrated in the study of performance management carried out by McKevitt and Lawton (1996, p 51), who found that:

> The overwhelming evidence from the study is that performance measurement was implemented to satisfy the demands of the institutional environment of public service organisations . . . That is, if politicians and Treasury demand that public service organisations are required to show that they are visibly responding to the needs of external accountability, then the installation of performance measurement systems are largely a routine device to demonstrate compliance with external stakeholders. The unintended consequences of such a strategy are, however, considerable. Middle managers may find themselves uncomfortably 'close to the customers' to the extent that they now have to take responsibility for what they perceive to be inadequate levels of resources. This shifting of responsibility, from the political to the organisational, has given rise to significant pressure on middle level managers.

Chapter 7 examined the notion of strategic fit between the external environment and internal capabilities, between what the organisation wants to achieve and how it goes about it.

STUDYING PUBLIC SERVICES MANAGEMENT

The study and practice of public services management will reflect different agendas and the interests of different stakeholders. For example, the academic may be interested in developing theory, testing propositions or building models; the manager may be less concerned with the elegance of a theory than with its use. The manager may ask, 'Can I make use of this theory?' rather than, 'Has the theory been tested and proven?' The academic may be interested in drawing comparisons between different systems of public services management; the manager may be concerned with 'best practice', with what happens elsewhere as a short cut to making the best use of existing knowledge. Both need to recognise the concerns of the other, along with all the other stakeholders – including politicians, users, students and so on.

Those studying and practising public services management will recognise its complexity and will recognise that there is no monopoly of approach held by, say, economists or senior managers! Different researchers can find in the study of public services organisations plenty to absorb their attention. Historians, psychologists, economists, political scientists and organisational theorists will locate their agendas in the traditions of the civil service, the behaviour of managers, the motivations of officials, the power in organisations or the structures of organisations. The different approaches are all valid, and all limited. The researcher who examines policy outputs using quantitative tools should recognise the contributions of the researcher who studies culture using qualitative tools, and vice versa. Otherwise the researcher becomes a 'one-club golfer'. That is, researchers who use only quantitative tools are not giving themselves sufficient clubs to play the whole golf course. In much the same way there is a danger that only one approach to management may be recognised or considered legitimate. Managers in the public services have been exhorted to become more like their private sector counterparts. This is ironic at a time when commentators have long since recognised the limitations of the private sector model even for business organisations. As a sceptical Peters (1991, p 42) put it:

> All these paens of praise were being raised to the private sector despite evidence that the private sector was not performing particularly well in many of the industrialised countries. The same governments that were telling their own employees to emulate the private sector were bailing out banks, auto manufacturers, steel makers and a host of other financially failing enterprises.

The poverty of our concepts, and the complexity of managing in the public services needs to be recognised. Chapter 4 explored the debate concerning the uniqueness or otherwise of managing in the public services.

THE COMPLEXITY OF MANAGEMENT

Throughout the book we have explored the nature of New Public Management (NPM) and examined the skills of management which have been distinguished from, and encouraged at, the expense of administration. A shift from administration to management involves more than a change of name; more than a change in practice. It also involves a change in the way that researchers think about that practice and what their focus is. In the past, where it was considered that the administrator was merely the conduit for the implementation of political decisions, it was considered appropriate to examine how those decisions were made and what the outcomes were. Increasingly, it has been recognised that those charged with implementation will have an impact on the outcomes and that their beliefs and values will have an effect. In other words, research needs to focus on the policy implementers themselves, the managers, as well as policy makers and policy outcomes. However, a number of concepts are in use: management, managers and managerialism. Some researchers have been keen to attack managerialism as an ideology. Pollitt (1993, p 1) argues that 'Managerialism is a set of beliefs and practices, at the core of which burns the seldom tested assumption that better management will prove an effective solvent for a wide range of economic and social ills'.

Similarly du Gay *et al.* (1996) argue that the language of the private sector manager has come to dominate the language of public services management. Managers are now encouraged to be entrepreneurial, innovative, independent etc., and yet there is not a great deal of evidence that managers in private sector possess all of these qualities!

Metcalfe and Richards (1990) argued that the view of management held by government was an impoverished one and it assumed that:

1 Management is an executive function which presupposes the clear definition of objectives, policies and performance measures.
2 Management is an intraorganisational process in so far as it is concerned with what goes on in organisations, with routines and procedures.
3 Control is hierarchical, with clear lines of responsibility.
4 There are broad principles of management which apply, with only minor modifications, to any organisation.

Writing specifically about public management they argue (1990, p 17) that:

> These elements in combination impose severe restrictions on the scope of management. They limit the role of public managers to programmed implementation of predetermined policies. They disregard the problems of adapting policies and organizations to environmental change. If this is all that management means, giving more weight to it is likely to cause confusion and frustration rather than lead to long term improvements in performance.

From a generic perspective, Mintzberg (1996a) indicates that there are three assumptions that underlie the 'management' view of management:

1 Particular activities can be isolated, both from one another and from direct authority.
2 Performance can be fully and properly evaluated by objective measures.
3 Activities can be entrusted to autonomous professional managers who are held responsible for performance.

A number of writers refer to the myth of management and identify this with a western approach which sees management as a rational technical orientation which transcends any particular organisation. The myth of management is those core beliefs, values and meanings which form the culture of the organisation, are embedded in structures and are accorded legitimacy in wider society. According to Bowles (1997, p 784), 'The Myth of Management, is embodied and practised through the agency of individual managers who have internalised the myth from various management institutions, the role models presented by other managers, and the wider cultural symbol system of the business world'.

One myth is that of the manager as hero, the great corporate leader providing a vision and direction for change: a Richard Branson or an Anita Roddick. Another myth is that of the rational model of organisations which does not recognise organisational complexity in its obsession for control. The quest for control is like chasing fool's gold – it is very elusive and it is not quite what it seems when you have found it.

That control may be depicted as a myth reflects a belief in the complexity of organisations and their environments. Most managers are driven by short-term considerations, by firefighting rather than by planning, controlling, co-ordinating or organising. Chaos is the operating norm. Barry Quirk, Chief Executive of the London Borough of Lewisham, who argues that change is like a fire – unpredictable and uncontrollable – takes up this theme. Quirk (1997, p 576) argues that:

> In the past, organizations had clear boundaries, people knew their place within them and they knew their place within the organizational hierarchy. Now, managers are required to focus on the individual needs of their workers. They must be confident in tackling discrimination and disadvantage, comfortable in managing people of diverse attributes and needs. But it is not just the people who are more diverse, the nature of work is more diverse. Many more people are engaged on temporary contracts or are engaged for shorter times each week. These temporary and part-time staff sometimes have different work needs.

As we discussed in Chapter 2, the changing labour market may mean that individuals engage with organisations in ways that are different from those in which they engaged in the past.

THE COMPLEXITY OF CHANGE

Understanding the changes that have taken place requires an investigation of how change is perceived, not just by those who seek to bring about change but also by those who have to implement change and those who suffer the consequences of change. In an attempt to capture how managers think about some of the changes that they have undergone, a small-scale study involving students on the Open University Business School's MBA was carried out and some of the findings are reported in Exhibit 18.1.

The research summarised in Exhibit 18.1 involved 45 middle and senior managers drawn from across the public services who were studying for an MBA. It was carried out in 1997, prior to the General Election of that year. Admittedly it is a limited sample and it makes no claims to be representative. It is illustrative. Although the data are limited, a number of issues can be pinpointed.

1 There is now a greater use of formal contracts as a means of conducting the work of the public services managers but 46 per cent believe that this has led to a decline in trust.
2 Managers are output driven and 56 per cent believe that results are perceived to be more important than the processes taken.
3 Fifty-nine per cent argue that morale in the public services is lower than it was five years ago.
4 Forty-seven per cent believed that a new government would make a difference in its approach to public services.

In Table 18.2 the most striking finding appears to be in relation to career opportunities, security of employment and levels of commitment. The majority of those surveyed believed that the appointment of private sector people and private sector techniques will continue unabated. This is summarised in the White Paper:

> Change will continue to be a major factor for those managing the delivery of public services. A number of key areas have already been identified. For the NHS we have seen the publication of the White Paper 'The New NHS: Modern Dependable' (1997) whose key principles include a national service with local responsibility for delivery; partnerships with local authorities; efficiency; excellence; restore public confidence (1997, p 11).

Key features of the 'New NHS' include:

- the internal market will be replaced by 'integrated care' based upon partnerships;
- strategic considerations; work on the basis of three and five year funding agreements to replace short-term contracts;
- a change in Health Authority functions;
- the creation of Health Action Zones;
- the creation of Primary Care Groups;
- use of piloting as a policy tool;
- use of performance figures.

Exhibit 18.1

Survey of managers' view of change

Table 18.1 Managers' perceptions of changes in the public services (%).

		Strongly agree				Strongly disagree
		5	4	3	2	1
1	Managing in the public services is different than managing in a private sector organisation	15	52	13	10	0
2	Delivering public services is more concerned with costs than quality	10	28	14	43	5
3	Public services managers are accountable to their line managers rather than the public	5	49	5	36	5
4	Formal contracts have replaced informal relationships as the main way of doing business	15	39	28	15	3
5	This has meant a decline in trust	15	31	36	13	5
6	Reaching targets is more important than the processes taken	13	43	13	21	10
7	Managers in the public services now have more freedom to manage	3	43	23	21	10
8	Morale in the public services is lower than it was five years ago	39	20	21	15	5
9	Public services has become more business-like in its approach	25	60	10	5	0
10	A change of government will make no difference	5	20	28	40	7

Question on Table 18.1

What are the key issues that arise from the data in Table 18.1?

Answer

The issues addressed are the distinctiveness of managing in the public services; accountability; efficiency and effectiveness; morale; and the impact on managers of recent changes in the public services.

Management students were asked their views about possible changes, in the light of current trends, to various aspects of managing in the public services. Table 18.2 presents the results of this question.

Table 18.2 Perceptions of possible future changes (%)

	Increase	Stay the same	Decrease	Don't know
Career opportunities	13	26	61	0
Positive image of the public services amongst the public	18	38	38	6
Professionalisation	37	38	25	0
Political neutrality	4	40	50	6
Promotion on merit	30	36	30	4
Quality of services to public	38	13	49	0
Exposure to market forces	70	13	15	2
Accountability to the public	52	30	15	3
Security of employment	2	18	80	0

▶

Exhibit 18.1 *cont.*

Table 18.2 *cont.*

	Increase	Stay the same	Decrease	Don't know
Personal commitment	5	41	49	5
Commitment of colleagues	4	36	55	5
Public service as a life-long vocation	5	0	95	0
Job satisfaction	13	27	54	6
Recruitment of private sector people	57	27	11	5
Use of private sector techniques	76	19	5	0
Use of contracts	75	16	7	2
Staff morale	2	32	61	5

Question: What are the key issues that arise from the data in the Table 18.2?

However, the White Paper recognises the problems of too much change:

This White Paper marks a watershed for the NHS. It sets a clear direction for the NHS as a modern and dependable service. But it will not mean a wholesale structural upheaval, generating costs and disruption that get in the way of patient care. The NHS has had all too much of that. There is no appetite amongst patients or staff for such an upheaval. But there is an appetite for change that goes with the grain of the NHS and its traditional values (1997, p 76, para 10.1).

The NHS White Paper is illustrative of more general themes in the public services. There is a general change of emphasis towards relation-building rather than quasi-markets. This increases the importance of professional accountability (a new professionalism perhaps?). In other areas the Labour Government has sought to address issues of democracy, localness, underperformance:

1 The democratic deficit which we examined in Part 1 will be resolved through the creation of Scottish and Welsh Parliaments, the introduction of city mayors, the reintroduction of political representation into health (both in commissioning and in primary care authorities) and so on. However, at the time of writing, the Labour Government has accepted the spending plans of the previous Conservative administration, with GDP still at 40 per cent. Revenue from the windfall tax on the sale of the Utilities bodies and stronger economic growth provide financing for new programmes such as 'Welfare to Work' and so on.

2 Education Action Zones and task forces which will make use of the private sector are to be created and other task forces and a Social Exclusion Unit have been introduced to combat poverty, unemployment, welfare dependency and educational under-achievement.

3 As noted in Chapter 16, a 'Best Value' regime has been introduced.

The rhetoric of the Labour Government includes the concept of user and stakeholder involvement through, for example, focus groups. It also recognises responsibilities as well as rights, as, for example, in the new Patient's Charter. Performance remains a key issue.

CONCLUSIONS

We have tried to demonstrate the complexity of and to capture some of the ambiguities and tensions that are characteristic of the public services. We have discussed the tensions in terms of:

- structural tensions between centralisation and decentralisation;
- process tensions between control and the 'freedom to manage';
- stakeholder tensions between citizens, clients, customers, politicians, professionals and so on;
- human resource tensions between traditional notions of loyalty and security and the use of short-term contracts and part-time workers;
- political tensions in balancing the interests of the majority against those of minority, often underprivileged, groups.

Such tensions manifest themselves in different ways. Individuals can hold contradictory views, recognising that as citizens they may wish to limit the power of special interests, recognise claims of equity, control costs and keep taxation down. As users the same people may seek to maximise their use of a good or service, want more services and a wider range, want them now rather than later. In much the same way, managers and professionals will have to seek to reconcile competing claims on their resources.

We have indicated the form that change can take. We also need to recognise that a change in 'mindset' or a new paradigm may be required to enable us to see the organisation and management of public services in new ways. Chapter 3 on information technology makes a plea for a new understanding of public services. The interest in knowledge management and organisational learning reflects this and was discussed briefly in Chapter 16.

Organisations need to recognise that knowledge workers exist throughout an organisation. In terms of processes and practices it may be that clerical staff have most knowledge, for example. Those who are at the top of organisations may no longer control the knowledge in the organisation. Knowledge can exist at different levels and in different places. A key issue is to tap into organisational history and knowledge but also to seek new knowledge in an act of renewal and learning. There is no point in making staff redundant without assessing the consequent loss of organisational memory and knowledge. Traditions are important, as those who have tried, in vain, to change organisations overnight will recognise.

However, a different perspective on organisations is offered by Mintzberg (1996b) who suggests that we see organisations as circles. In the middle is central government which sees widely but not clearly because it is not close to the action. Those at the outer edge of the circle see with clarity, but only their segment. Middle managers are those who can see both widely and clearly. Mintzberg argues for a move away from hierarchies which get in the way of learning.

Although managing ambiguity and change is a key theme, as old certainties disappear, the case for change still has to be made. Thus, for example, the rhetoric adopted by successive Conservative governments concerning the need for change as a result of alleged inefficiency and ineffectiveness of public sector management may express a view that is not shared by all stakeholders. As Goodsell (1994) has argued in the context of public services in the USA, the users' experience of public sector bureaucracy may be very different from that expressed by politicians. In a survey carried out by Public Management Foundation (1997) involving 1000 individuals in four different locales, satisfaction levels with local performance in education, health and policing were high. Education scored 73 per cent 'high satisfaction' rates, health 72 per cent and policing 56 per cent. These services seem to be performing better than politicians would have us believe. The consistent message in all three services was that there should be much greater involvement of local people in setting performance indicators and that local managers should be given more power. Politicians, particularly those who operate at the central level, should be kept well away!

Finally, Mintzberg (1996b, p 65) asks, 'Why don't we just stop reengineering and delayering and restructuring and decentralizing and instead start thinking?' He offers the model of nursing as a model for management. This is an interesting reversal of the more usual suggestion, that the public sector adopt private sector models: 'Organizations need to be nurtured, looked after and cared for, steadily and consistently. They don't need to be violated by some dramatic new strategic plan or some gross new reorganization every time a new chief executive happens to parachute in' (1996b, p 66).

Managers will learn from experience, from models of best practice elsewhere, from colleagues in other organisations and their own and so on. At the same time they will recognise where the existing knowledge is located and draw upon that without fear or favour.

REFERENCES

Antonsen, M and Jorgensen, T B (1997) 'The "Publicness" of public organizations', *Public Administration*, 75 (Summer), pp 337–57.

Bowles, M (1997) 'The myth of management: Direction and failure in contemporary organizations', *Human Relations*, 50(7), pp 779–803.

Department of Health (1997) 'The New NHS: Modern, Dependable', Cm 3807. London: The Stationery Office.

du Gay, P, Salaman, G and Rees, B (1996) 'The conduct of management and the management of conduct: contemporary managerial discourse and the constitution of the "competent" manager', *Journal of Management Studies*, 33(3), pp 263–82.

Goodsell, C T (1994) *The Case for Bureaucracy: A Public Administration Polemic* (3rd edn). Chatham, NJ: Chatham House.

McKevitt, D and Lawton, A (1996) 'The manager, the citizen, the politician and performance measures', *Public Money & Management*, July–September, pp 49–54.

Metcalfe, L and Richards, S (1990) *Improving Public Management* (2nd edn). London: Sage.

Mintzberg, H (1996a) 'Managing government, governing management', *Harvard Business Review*, May–June, pp 75–83.

Mintzberg, H (1996b) 'Musings on management', *Harvard Business Review*, July–August, pp 61–7.

Peters, B G (1991) 'Morale in the public service: a comparative inquiry', *International Review of Administrative Sciences*, 57, pp 421–40.

Pollitt, C (1993) *Managerialism and the Public Services*. Oxford: Blackwell.

Public Management Foundation (1997) *Hitting Local Targets: The Public Value of Public Services*. London: Public Management Foundation.

Quirk, B (1997) 'Accountable to everyone: Postmodern pressures on public managers', *Public Administration*, 75, pp 569–86.

Index